Baptists in America

BAPTISTS IN AMERICA

A *History*

—◦◦◦◦—

THOMAS S. KIDD

BARRY HANKINS

OXFORD
UNIVERSITY PRESS

OXFORD
UNIVERSITY PRESS

Oxford University Press is a department of the University of
Oxford. It furthers the University's objective of excellence in research,
scholarship, and education by publishing worldwide.

Oxford   New York
Auckland   Cape Town   Dar es Salaam   Hong Kong   Karachi
Kuala Lumpur   Madrid   Melbourne   Mexico City   Nairobi
New Delhi   Shanghai   Taipei   Toronto

With offices in
Argentina   Austria   Brazil   Chile   Czech Republic   France   Greece
Guatemala   Hungary   Italy   Japan   Poland   Portugal   Singapore
South Korea   Switzerland   Thailand   Turkey   Ukraine   Vietnam

Oxford is a registered trademark of Oxford University Press
in the UK and certain other countries.

Published in the United States of America by
Oxford University Press
198 Madison Avenue, New York, NY 10016

© Thomas S. Kidd and Barry Hankins 2015

Cataloging-in-Publication Data is on file at the Library of Congress.
ISBN 978–0–19–997753–6

3 5 7 9 8 6 4 2
Printed in the United States of America
on acid-free paper

*The authors would like to dedicate this book
to our graduate students, past and present.
They have been and remain a source
of constant inspiration.*

Contents

Preface	ix
Acknowledgments	xiii
1. Colonial Outlaws	1
2. The Great Awakening	19
3. Baptists and the American Revolution	39
4. Baptists and Disestablishment	59
5. Baptists and the Great Revival	76
6. Baptists and Slavery	98
7. Slavery, Schism, and War	117
8. Black Baptists in Babylon	149
9. White Baptists and the American Mainstream	166
10. Baptist Schism in the Early Twentieth Century	183
11. Insiders and Outsiders at Mid-Twentieth Century	196
12. Baptists and the Civil Rights Movement	211
13. Schism in Zion: The Southern Baptist Controversy	228
14. Conclusion	247
Notes	253
Bibliography	289
Index	309

Preface

IN AMERICA, BAPTISTS were once the ultimate religious outsiders. The Puritans called them "the troublers of churches in all places" and banned them from the Massachusetts Bay Colony in 1645. Unwilling to submit to official state churches, or to baptize infants, Baptists found themselves reviled, fined, and sometimes brutalized by authorities in England and in the American colonies. Well might Roger Williams, the most famous colonial Baptist, have warned the Massachusetts governor that the voice of Jesus himself was crying out on the Baptists' behalf: "Why huntest thou me? Why imprisonest thou me? Why finest, who so bloodily whippest, why wouldest thou (did I not hold thy bloody hands) hang and burn me?"

Fast forward three and a half centuries, and a remarkable change has come over Baptists, who command tens of millions of American adherents, including the largest Protestant denomination in America (the Southern Baptist Convention) and the largest African American organization of any kind (the National Baptist Convention USA Inc.). Baptists such as Billy Graham have enjoyed access to the highest reaches of American political power. Baptist pastor Rick Warren seems (as much as anyone) to have taken on Graham's unofficial role as "America's pastor," even hosting a presidential forum at his Saddleback Community Church in 2008.

Baptists possess vast networks of cultural influence: publishing houses, missions organizations, disaster relief agencies, advocacy groups, phenomenally popular authors and speakers, and a good deal more. Although American religion has always been too diverse to allow one denomination to become dominant, Baptists have become the largest of a species of broadly evangelical American churches that have, at times, functioned like a de facto American establishment, especially in the South. In many ways, Baptists have become religious and cultural insiders.

Yet even during their times of greatest strength and access, Baptists have felt threatened by forces that appeared poised to overwhelm and marginalize them. These forces were as various as skeptics, secularists, pro- or antislavery advocates, Communists, civil rights activists, liberals, and/or fundamentalists. To understand Baptists, you must first realize that they are, to quote sociologist Christian Smith, "embattled and thriving." Baptists have fought to repel real and perceived threats, even when the raw numbers might suggest that they were doing quite well. Indeed, Baptists' enduring feeling of being under attack—a sense impressed deeply on them by English and colonial persecution—helps them to be vigilant and to flourish.

The majority of Baptists today, led numerically by the Southern Baptist Convention, are evangelicals, meaning that they are biblicist Christians who emphasize that salvation requires a personal conversion experience. (Some Baptists would, of course, quibble over evangelical tenets such as the divine inspiration of all Scripture, or the necessity of personal evangelism.) As Smith has argued, evangelicals in America thrive on "difference, engagement, tension, conflict and threat." There has been no shortage of these feelings among Baptists through the centuries. Sometimes Baptist vigilance has taken the form of political activism, sometimes intradenominational theological wars, sometimes tireless evangelism. Over time, Baptists have transformed numerically from a beleaguered minority into a Protestant behemoth. But that embattled mentality, the commitment to bearing witness to the gospel, the resistance to forces regarded as hostile to Christ, his Word, and his kingdom—those dispositions remain.[1]

In *Baptists in America*, we are seeking to tell the story of Baptist growth and battles through the centuries from the founding of England's colonies to contemporary America. Baptists, of course, now have a fully global history. We focus here on Baptists' part in the story of American religious and cultural history, using the great variety of Baptist experience to illuminate the tug of war between America's intense religiosity and its pioneering secularism. Baptists have been major players in both these trends, fighting to bring the gospel of salvation through Christ to all Americans, while also insisting, especially in the Founding era, that America should have no tax-supported, established church. They, perhaps more than most, embody this central tension of American religion.

IT MAY BE instructive to know that we, the authors, are both Baptists and evangelicals, both serve as members in (two different) Baptist churches in Waco, Texas, and both teach at Baylor University, one of the largest Baptist universities in the world. Neither of us has actively participated in Baptist denominational politics, and though we do not believe that any historian can claim to be pristinely objective, we do not feel like we have a theological or political ax to grind in this book. We hope that all types of Baptists whom we discuss here will feel that we represent their views fairly. We assume that some on all sides will not be entirely pleased with what we have emphasized, especially on the most controversial topics, such as race or biblical authority. Both authors have their own opinions about the range of issues that still divide Baptists, such as church-state relations, Calvinism, and inerrancy, and our views on those topics, so far as we have ever discussed them, are not identical. We both value the Baptist tradition a great deal, while acknowledging its many failings. We assume that such failings mark any religious tradition made up of fallen people.

Acknowledgments

Several individuals and institutions aided and encouraged this project. None is responsible for any errors of fact, judgment, or interpretation herein. Giles Anderson of the Anderson Literary Agency helped brainstorm and conceptualize the book and then guided meticulously the formulation of the original proposal. Keith Harper and Paul Harvey read the manuscript in its entirety and offered helpful suggestions, corrections, and additions. Gordon Melton rendered guidance and caution concerning religion statistics, Mark Noll answered various questions from his own research on Baptists, and Greg Wills responded to questions about specific facts and factoids related to his work on Southern Baptist Theological Seminary. At Oxford, our editor Theo Calderara was a constant source of guidance and encouragement. His editorial work rendered the manuscript more readable, as has the work of copy editor Susan Ecklund, who caught our myriad errors and whipped our notes and bibliography into shape. Production manager Peter Mavrikis did everything in his power to keep us on schedule, and almost succeeded. Gina Chung answered all our questions promptly, pointed us in the right direction whenever we were lost or confused, and secured the jacket blurbs to help promote the project.

The authors enjoy the comraderie and assistance of a cadre of Ph.D. students in the history department at Baylor. Adina Johnson, Elise Leal, Brendan Payne, Nick Pruitt, and Paul Putz all served as research assistants while the authors worked on the project, as did Tim Grundmeier, who also compiled the bibliography and index. The librarians and research staff at Moody and Jones Libraries at Baylor provided efficient and timely delivery of sources and tracked down everything the authors needed. Finally, the authors wish to acknowledge the support of Baylor University generally and the collegiality of the Baylor history department in particular. We can scarcely imagine a better, more supportive environment to do research on religious topics. It is nice to be in a place where our work is appreciated and valued.

Baptists in America

I

Colonial Outlaws

ON SEPTEMBER 5, 1651, a criminal named Obadiah Holmes was taken from his cell in Boston's prison to receive his punishment: thirty lashes with a three-corded whip. Holmes had been alone in prison for weeks, struggling to come to terms with the agony he would soon experience. But the day of his whipping, an unusual calm came over him. Although his captors tried to keep him from speaking, he would not be silent. "I am now come to be baptized in afflictions by your hands," he said, "that so I may have further fellowship with my Lord, and am not ashamed of his sufferings, for by his stripes am I healed." Holmes was tied to a post. The officer tasked with delivering the punishment spit on his hands, took up the whip, and began flailing Holmes with all his might. And yet Holmes felt the presence of God more strongly than at any other time in his life. The pain of the scourging floated away. When the captors untied him, Holmes stood up and smiled. "You have struck me as with roses," he admonished them.[1]

What had Homes done to provoke the wrath of colonial Massachusetts? He had preached the gospel of the Baptists. And that was against the law.

WHERE DID THE Baptist movement come from? Baptists would argue that their defining practice—the baptism of Christian believers by immersion—represents a recovery of ancient Christian tradition. In the gospel narratives of the New Testament, John the Baptist, the herald of Jesus as the Messiah, preached "the baptism of repentance for the remission of sins" (Luke 3:3).

The baptism of new believers was standard practice among Jesus's followers, seen especially in the book of Acts. For example, in Acts 8, an Ethiopian eunuch is convinced by the disciple Philip that Jesus is the prophesied Messiah. When they came to a pool of water, the eunuch asked Philip, "See, here is water; what doth hinder me to be baptized?" And Philip answered, "If thou believest with all thine heart, thou mayest." Philip took the eunuch into the water and baptized him. The Greek word for "baptize" here and elsewhere in the New Testament is *baptizo*, meaning to "dip" or "submerge." No indisputable examples of infant baptism (paedobaptism) occurred in the New Testament, as baptism normally followed repentance from sin and confession of faith in Christ. Children would, of course, have to reach a certain level of cognizance to do these things.[2]

The church father Tertullian of North Africa was the first writer to make a clear reference to infant baptism, in the late second century. He seemed to imply that this was a new practice, and in general he opposed infant baptism because very young children could not recognize their sin (if they had any) or their need for salvation.[3]

The practice of infant baptism appears to have begun as an emergency measure for small children at risk of dying. Christian parents did not want their children to die unbaptized because certain New Testament passages seemed to suggest that this would keep them out of heaven. From the second to the fourth centuries, infant baptism, especially in cases of dire illness, became more common for the children of Christian parents.[4]

It was in the early fifth century that Saint Augustine made the pivotal argument for the adoption of infant baptism. Augustine posited, unlike many early Christian writers, that infants were tainted with original sin and therefore were immediately in need of forgiveness. Infant baptism protected children from the power of evil, gave them pardon from original sin, and introduced them into the loving community of the church. The faith of the parents could be applied to the child in baptism, until he or she could place personal faith in Christ. Augustine's argument largely won the day, and by the sixth century infant baptism was pervasive.[5]

For about a millennium, infant baptism remained nearly universal among Christian churches. But then came the Reformation.

The Reformation had begun in 1517 when the German priest Martin Luther launched a crusade against the Roman Catholic Church. Luther argued that the church had become corrupt, particularly in its use of indulgences, or church donations, for the forgiveness of sins. He insisted that salvation only came as a free gift of God and could not be earned. Luther also began to teach that the Bible was the only authoritative source of divine knowledge, and he questioned the reliability of church tradition.

The church excommunicated Luther, who reluctantly became the leader of a new church bearing his name.

The Lutherans' challenge to church tradition spawned even more radical movements whose interpretations of Scripture did not always accord with Luther's. Among these were some who questioned the baptism of infants—approving only of adult baptism, or "believer's baptism"—along with a host of other church practices they regarded as unbiblical. These radicals were often tarred as "Anabaptists," or "rebaptizers," by their opponents. Dozens of Anabaptist sects emerged from the ferment of the Reformation.

Many of these groups faced persecution from Catholics and Protestants alike. Some tried to quietly negotiate the pressure to conform to state-sponsored religion, while others rose up against the state, believing that they might be able to usher in the kingdom of God. Some of these latter groups brought horrible notoriety to the name Anabaptist.

No sect reached greater heights of radicalism and terror than the Anabaptists of Münster. Led by the Dutch prophet Jan Bockelson (John of Leyden), the Anabaptists took over Münster in 1534 and created a theocracy. They reached incredible heights of mystical ecstasy, with people running through the streets, or writhing and seeing visions. Anabaptists from across the region flowed into Münster, while much of the remaining Lutheran population fled the city. Those who did not flee were expelled or forcibly rebaptized.

The leaders instituted a communal system in which residents could not possess private property, and deacons distributed goods based on need. One Anabaptist leader wrote that "everything which has served the purposes of self-seeking and private property, such as buying and selling, working for money, taking interest and practicing usury—even at the expense of unbelievers—or eating and drinking the sweat of the poor (that is, making one's own people and fellow creatures work so that one can grow fat) and indeed everything which offends against love—all such things are abolished amongst us by the power of love and community."

Jan Bockelson presided over the most extreme phase of the Münster experiment. Prior to setting himself up as the supreme ruler of Münster, Bockelson ran naked through the town and then fell into a three-day trance. Under his direction, the Anabaptists began to practice polygamy, and Bockelson himself soon collected fifteen wives. Some who resisted Bockelson's innovations were arrested and even executed. Finally, Bockelson appointed himself not merely ruler of Münster but messianic king of Jerusalem. He clothed himself in fine robes and jewelry and wore a gold medallion with the inscription "One king of righteousness over all."

Alarmed authorities in the region besieged Münster, and by the beginning of 1535 they had begun to starve out the Anabaptists. Bockelson maintained control through violence and intimidation, but finally in June the invading army attacked and captured the town. The Anabaptists' horrible experiment came to a miserable end, with most of the remaining residents massacred and their leaders captured. Bockelson was paraded about the region for months on a chain, and finally he was taken back to Münster and publicly tortured to death.[6]

The terroristic radicalism of Münster was hardly indicative of the Baptist movement to come, but the memory of Münster haunted Baptists for centuries thereafter. Many sects that practiced believer's baptism had to deflect association with the "Monsters of Münster."[7] Some rejected the name "Anabaptist" altogether because of its unfortunate connotations.

The followers of Menno Simons, known as Mennonites, practiced believer's baptism but rejected the extremes of Münster. Menno was a Catholic priest in Holland at the time of the Münster terror. He recalled that despite being a priest, he knew little about the Bible. He found himself questioning certain Catholic doctrines, such as transubstantiation (the idea that in communion the bread and wine become the literal body and blood of Christ) and infant baptism. He heard of the persecution of local Anabaptists, and "it sounded very strange to me to hear of a second baptism. I examined the Scriptures diligently and pondered them earnestly, but could find no report of infant baptism."[8] After an arduous search for illumination, Menno had a conversion experience and was baptized as a believer in 1536.

Even though Menno fought against the extremist tendencies of the Anabaptists in Holland, he still fell under persecution, and a bounty was placed on his head. Eventually he left for northern Germany, where in comparative peace and quiet he became Europe's foremost theological defender of the Anabaptist faith. He died of natural causes in 1561. Churches devoted to Menno's teachings would continue to thrive in Germany and Holland into the early seventeenth century, when they made contact with the earliest English Baptist churches.

HINTS OF A Baptist movement existed in sixteenth-century England, mostly among the English Separatists, members of a radical branch of

Puritanism. The Puritans believed that they should reform, or "purify," the Church of England from within, but the Separatists believed that the Church of England was corrupt beyond redemption. True believers should separate from it, they warned.

By the early seventeenth century, some radical Separatists concluded that complete purity in the church demanded a rejection of infant baptism. Infant baptism reflected an inclusive, geographic view of church membership that both Roman Catholics and Anglicans embraced, introducing the children of Christian families into the church as quasi-members. But what if those children never experienced conversion? The practice necessarily brought into the church people who, according to the Calvinist view of Puritans and Separatists, were not members of the elect, the chosen people of God. Baptists sought to clear up this confusion, and to foster a pure church membership, by baptizing only those who had actually experienced conversion.

Many of the Separatists adopted views similar to those of the Mennonites on issues such as the strong separation of church and state, as both experienced harsh persecution, fines, and imprisonment at the hands of political and church authorities. The Separatists and Mennonites undoubtedly influenced each other, as English and Continental radicals routinely crossed the North Sea in these decades, looking for economic opportunity and religious freedom.

Many of the early English Baptists also rejected the dominant Calvinist beliefs of the Separatists, including predestination and limited atonement (the idea that Christ died only for those predestined for salvation), in favor of the theology of a general atonement (the idea that Christ died for everyone). They probably picked up this new doctrine from Continental Anabaptists.[9] The "General" Baptists, as they came to be called, believed that all people could be saved, in contrast to the "Particular" Baptists, who believed that only the chosen elect of God could be saved.

The first English Baptist church in Holland was founded by Separatist pastor John Smyth. Educated at Cambridge, in 1600 Smyth began serving as a priest of the Church of England in Lincoln, in northeast England. Even though local officials knew of his Puritan leanings when they hired him, Smyth's preaching earned him powerful enemies. Two years later Smyth was removed from his pastorate for "undue teaching of matters of religion," and for attacks on elite residents of the town. Smyth became a minister of a Separatist congregation in nearby Gainsborough.[10]

Smyth's Gainsborough Separatists fled persecution by local authorities and arrived in the relatively free environs of Amsterdam by 1608. Liberty did not lead to peace within the congregation, however, as a faction led by John Robinson split off from Smyth's church and moved to Leyden. The rift may have been caused by Smyth's gravitation toward Baptist principles. Robinson's departure for Leyden represented the origins of the celebrated group of English Separatists—the "Pilgrims"—who came to Plymouth Colony in America on the *Mayflower* in 1620.[11]

In Amsterdam, Smyth became familiar with several Mennonite congregations. Smyth's church rented space (presumably for meetings and/or lodging) at a bakeshop owned by a local Mennonite. The Mennonites may have helped Smyth take the final step from Separatist to Baptist, and they likely also contributed to Smyth's developing belief in the general atonement. In his incendiary tract *The Character of the Beast* (1609), Smyth explained that infant baptism was one of the most pernicious practices of false communions like the Church of England, which he considered the daughter of the great harlot, the Roman Catholic Church. Only Christian believers could receive true baptism, and only authentic Christian churches could offer true baptism. Infants were obviously too young to understand the meaning of baptism or to repent of their sins. Baptizing infants was "the most unreasonable heresy of all Antichristianism: for considering what baptism is, an infant is no more capable of baptism than is any unreasonable or insensible creature: for baptism is not washing with water: but it is the baptism of the Spirit, the confession of the mouth, and the washing with water. . . . Infant baptism is folly and nothing."[12]

Smyth had accepted the idea of believer's baptism, but how would he actually be baptized? Taking his rejection of church tradition to the furthest extreme, Smyth decided to baptize himself, which he did by affusion (pouring water over his head). Then he baptized the rest of his congregation. Smyth shortly began to develop second thoughts about his self-baptism and approached local Mennonites about baptizing him. The Mennonites, surprisingly, refused to baptize Smyth and his followers, perhaps concerned about Smyth's mercurial views and conflicts within the English church. Although many of his followers would later join the Mennonite church, Smyth soon died of consumption (tuberculosis).

Smyth's doubts about his church's baptisms led to another split, with lawyer Thomas Helwys leading the dissenting faction. This small group bitterly parted ways with Smyth and returned to England in 1611 or 1612. They met at Spitalfields, in north London. Helwys quickly gained notoriety with the publication of his *Short Declaration of the Mystery of Iniquity* (1612). He personally inscribed a copy for King James I with a remarkable tirade against state authority in spiritual matters: "Hear O King, and despise not the counsel of the poor, and let their complaints come before thee. The King is a mortal man, and not God, therefore has no power over the immortal souls of his subjects, to make laws and ordinances for them, and to set spiritual lords over them. . . . O King, be not seduced by deceivers to sin so against God whom thou ought to obey."[13] Helwys's courageous but incautious statement helped land him in London's infamous Newgate Prison, where he died. Despite the untimely ends met by Smyth and Helwys, they had permanently established the Baptist movement in England.

IN AMERICA, THE beginnings of the Baptist movement followed a similar trajectory. Religious dissenters became radicalized by persecution, opening them to a wholesale reconsideration of their faith and rituals. Most of the early colonists in America were at least nominally Christian. Some, including the Puritans of New England, came largely for religious reasons. Others, including the Anglicans of the southern colonies, came more for economic opportunity. But almost all of them practiced infant baptism and saw the rejection of that ritual as a dangerous affront to the traditions of family, church, and society.

Radical Puritanism produced the first Baptists in America. And while many historians have identified liberty of conscience as these Baptists' chief concern, liberty of conscience served a higher purpose: the right to practice believer's baptism.

The Puritans who founded Massachusetts in 1630 did so for religious motives, but not for religious freedom. A group of Puritans in England, weary of persecution by the English church and state, decided to start a colony in the New World. Under the leadership of the talented lawyer John Winthrop, these Puritans secured a charter for the Massachusetts Bay Company that gave them an unusual degree of autonomy from England. They set out to establish their vision of a fully biblical order of church and state. This would require them to keep those with unorthodox religious opinions out of the colony. Religious toleration and permissive laws, to the Puritans, only invited the judgment of God.

One of the first pastors to run afoul of Massachusetts's strictures was Roger Williams, who became the most celebrated early Baptist leader in America. But Williams's status as a Baptist leader was fleeting; he remained a Baptist for only a few months. Williams arrived in Massachusetts in 1631 as a Puritan pastor well on his way toward Separatism. He took the Puritan concern for church purity to its logical extreme not only by repudiating the Anglican Church, but ultimately by renouncing infant baptism. The Boston church quickly offered to make Williams its pastor, but he determined that it was not sympathetic enough to Separatism. The church at Salem then offered Williams a position, but withdrew it under pressure from Boston. Williams and his family moved to Plymouth, where they lived among the Separatists for two years.

At Plymouth, Williams also ran into trouble with the church. Indeed, splits with churches over issues of purity were becoming second nature to him. He began airing controversial opinions, and the ruling elder of the Plymouth church feared that Williams "would run the same course of rigid separation and anabaptistry, which Mr. John Smith, the se-baptist [self-baptist] at Amsterdam had done." Requesting dismissal from the Plymouth church, Williams returned to Salem. This time Salem's church made Williams its teaching elder, giving him a platform for his unorthodox views.[14]

By late 1635, Williams had run afoul of Boston authorities for several of his controversial opinions. Williams had come out in favor of Native Americans' land rights, arguing that the English colonists were illegally taking their land. He also called on government authorities to stop policing people's religious beliefs, or the affairs of the church. He made a strict distinction between external actions and the internal matters of the soul. "The civil magistrate's power extends only to the bodies and goods and outward state of men," Williams taught.[15] For promulgating these views, Williams was banished from Massachusetts in 1636.

Williams fled to southern New England, where he helped establish the town of Providence and Rhode Island colony. Understandably, Williams pushed for the colony to respect liberty of conscience, and the colony's royal charter of 1663 stated that "no person . . . shall be any ways molested, punished, disquieted, or called in question for any differences in opinion, in matters of religion, and do not actually disturb the civil peace." Everyone would be permitted to believe as their consciences directed them, and the government would only act against violations of the civil law. Any government, led at least partly by unregenerate men, would necessarily corrupt the church. Although Williams believed that God had ordained civil governments, he did not believe that God had ever made any special covenant with any people since ancient Israel. That included Puritan Massachusetts.[16]

John Winthrop believed that Williams's severance of church from state would bear bitter fruit. The "devil was not idle" in the free environment of Rhode Island, Winthrop wrote, for many women, children, and slaves decided that they could attend whatever churches and meetings they liked, regardless of the preferences of the man of the house.[17] Many like Winthrop thought the radical Separatist and Baptist faith would result in chaos.

Rhode Island began filling with Separatists, some of whom were following the lead of their English brethren and becoming Baptists. The mercurial Williams went with this logical flow toward Baptist convictions and repudiated his original baptism as an infant. He was influenced in his decision by Catherine Scott, a sister of the controversial Anne Hutchinson, who had also been banished from Massachusetts for her "antinomian" views in 1638. ("Antinomians," to their critics, rejected God's moral law in a dangerous quest after the leadings of God's Holy Spirit.) That year, Williams joined with a small group of followers and established America's first Baptist church in Providence. Williams was baptized by Ezekiel Holliman, one of his followers from Salem, and then Williams baptized Holliman and the rest of the group.[18]

Like John Smyth, Williams quickly began to question his new baptism because he still believed that the validity of baptism depended on its performance by someone with the authority of the apostles. No one was available with such apostolic authority, and John Winthrop reported that Williams "bent himself that way, expecting (as was supposed) to become an apostle." From that point forward, Williams preached to anyone who would listen, but he refused to join a church. He remained sympathetic to the Baptist way, however, as he wrote to John Winthrop Jr., in 1649, "I believe their practice [believer's baptism by immersion] comes nearer the first practice of our great founder Christ Jesus, than other practices of religion do." Still, he hesitated to endorse or join the Baptists because of his continuing questions about apostolic authority.[19]

Shortly after the founding of Providence's Baptist church, another Baptist church was established at Newport, Rhode Island, by the physician and pastor John Clarke. Clarke came to Massachusetts in 1637 and immediately became involved in the antinomian controversy centering on Anne Hutchinson and her followers. The dispute revealed a rift between Puritans, who emphasized good works as a sign of grace, and those who emphasized salvation as an utterly free gift, and the witness of the Holy Spirit in one's heart as the best evidence for salvation. Hutchinson, following her pastor John Cotton, became the most notorious proponent of free grace. She exacerbated matters by declaring that she had received her contrarian views directly from the Holy Spirit. Clarke, a radical Puritan already on his way to becoming a Baptist, sympathized with Hutchinson and her camp. Clarke realized that siding with Hutchinson made Massachusetts a decidedly less friendly home for him, and he set out for Rhode Island. By 1638 he had begun serving as a minister in Portsmouth, Rhode Island, and then he relocated to Newport. There he started another congregation, which became Baptist by 1644. This was the only lasting church to emerge from the antinomian controversy.[20]

Clarke's Baptist church was no Spirit-filled free-for-all, but he remained faithful to his antinomian trajectory by putting a heavy emphasis on the ministry of the Holy Spirit in every believer. In true Christian worship, Clarke wrote, Jesus "speaks to the heart in the Spirit, and his words are as commands from the head to the members, which convey together spirit and life to obey them, by reason of which his commands are not grievous, for where the Spirit of this Lord is, there is liberty, and they by beholding the glory of the Lord, are transformed into the same image, from glory to glory, by the Spirit of the Lord." Although these sentiments merely echoed New Testament passages on the Holy Spirit, in the context of the antinomian controversy they raised the prospect of the Holy Spirit communicating to, and through, every believer. To the Puritans, this was dangerous business.[21]

Clarke believed that the Holy Spirit put all believers on the same footing in the church. Although Clarke appears to have received some theological education, there is no indication that he was ever ordained. He emphasized the right of all believers—or at least all male believers—to speak, or prophesy, in meetings. To Clarke, "prophesying" meant delivering brief exhortations on Bible passages for the edification of the church. "Quench not the Spirit," Clarke wrote, "is the exhortation to him that is thereby moved to speak; and despise not prophesyings, is the exhortation to them that are present to hear." Many early Puritans accepted prophesying, but the Cambridge Platform of 1648 stopped the practice in Massachusetts.[22]

By 1644, Massachusetts authorities had become alarmed about the presence of vocal Baptists in New England, even though their actual numbers remained quite small. John Winthrop wrote that "anabaptistry increased and spread in the country, which occasioned the magistrates at the last court to draw an order for banishing such as continued obstinate after due conviction." The 1645 law banning Baptists called them "the incendiaries of commonwealths and the infectors of persons in main matters of religion, and the troublers of churches in all places." The law banished anyone who questioned infant baptism, proclaimed Christian pacifism, or (like Roger Williams) denied the state's authority to police religious convictions.[23]

Massachusetts ministers also mobilized the printing presses against the Baptists in the 1640s. They published several anti-Baptist tracts, all in London. The first press in America had opened at Cambridge, Massachusetts, in 1638, but most American authors still published in England. Also, the key Baptist authors with whom the New England ministers were contending remained in England. No Baptist in America published a defense of their views until John Clarke's *Ill Newes from New-England* (1652), also published in London. These religious disputes, and the growth of the Baptist movement, were unfolding before a transatlantic audience. English Baptist treatises circulated in the colonies, too, and concerned parishioners were approaching their ministers with probing questions about infant baptism.

Thomas Shepard, the Puritan minister of Cambridge, Massachusetts, wrote an introduction to one of the anti-Baptist tracts and expressed concern that Baptist opinions would "gangrene far" if not met with a vigorous defense of infant baptism. Shepard declared that to deny baptism to infants was essentially to refuse God's covenant blessing on one's children. The Baptists, he wrote, condemned the finest Protestant churches as illegitimate and set up their own private assemblies, even if they had to use an uneducated man as a minister. They even indulged the "promiscuous prophecies" of Spirit-filled laypeople (as in Clarke's congregation) and argued that anyone who could preach could also baptize. To Shepard, this was sheer chaos. It represented the "abuse of liberty for every man to think what he pleaseth." A godly state and church should shut these heretics down.[24]

Persecution of the Baptists intensified in the 1640s. Provocative behavior by some Baptists was partially responsible. William Witter was brought before the court of Salem, Massachusetts, in 1643 for saying that infant baptism was "a badge of the whore." Although the judge sentenced him to repent before the church, he refused and was back in court in 1646 "for saying that they who stayed while a child is baptized, do worship the devil." Witter seems to have traveled to Newport, Rhode Island, to join John Clarke's church sometime in the late 1640s.[25]

In 1651, the stage was set for the whipping of Obadiah Holmes when William Witter asked the Newport church to send preachers to Lynn, Massachusetts, where he still lived. Holmes had received believer's baptism from Clarke and the newly arrived English Baptist Mark Lucar in 1649. Clarke and Lucar went on a missionary visit to nearby Seekonk, Massachusetts, where they heard a dissenting Baptist congregation had formed. Roger Williams wrote approvingly that "at Seekonk a great many have lately concurred with Mr. John Clarke and our Providence men about the point of a new baptism, and the manner of dipping: and Mr. John Clarke has been there lately (and Mr. Lucar) and has dipped them."[26]

Holmes saw his rebaptism as the culmination of his spiritual rebirth: "It pleased the Father of Light, after a long continuance of mine in death and darkness, to cause life and immortality to be brought to light in my soul." He realized that Christ wanted him to identify with his death, burial, and resurrection in baptism, and so he went into the water with Lucar and Clarke, and they immersed him. Holmes and other new Baptists ran into trouble with the Plymouth Court for holding illegal meetings. Soon Holmes left Seekonk for Newport, where he might practice his new faith in peace.[27]

Holmes might have remained undisturbed if only he would have stayed out of Massachusetts. Holmes, Clarke, and John Crandall went to Lynn, Massachusetts, to visit the cantankerous Witter and other Baptist sympathizers. As they held a service at Witter's home, two constables burst in and "with their clamorous tongues made an interruption." They arrested the Rhode Island Baptists and took them to the local alehouse, where they were detained. With no apparent humor intended, a constable told the Baptists, "If you be free I will carry you to the" local Puritan meetinghouse for services there. Clarke wittily replied, "Friend, had we been free thereunto we had prevented all this." The constable apparently wanted to force the Baptists to hear good gospel preaching, but Clarke warned him that if they went to the meeting, they would defend the Baptist way. The three evangelists removed their hats in greeting at the service, but then rudely put them back on: a major insult in a colonial church. Clarke tried briefly to explain the Baptists' actions, but an officer shut him up, and they were taken back to the alehouse.[28]

The three were taken to the County Court at Boston on charges that they had conducted an illegal religious meeting, had disturbed the regular Puritan meeting at Lynn, and were "seducing and drawing aside others after their erroneous judgments and practices, and for suspicion of having their hands in the rebaptizing of one, or more among us." At Boston they were tried and convicted for being Anabaptists. Clarke denied the name because he technically did not believe he was rebaptizing anyone: those baptized as infants had received no baptism at all. This argument only irritated the judge (Governor John Endicott), who told Clarke, "You affirmed that you did never re-baptize any, yet did acknowledge you did baptize such as were baptized before, and thereby did necessarily deny the baptism that was before to be baptism, the churches no churches, and also all other ordinances, and ministers, as if all were a nullity; and also did in the Court deny the lawfulness of baptizing of infants, and all this tends to the dishonor of God, the despising the ordinances of God among us, the peace of the churches, and seducing the subjects of this commonwealth from the truth of the gospel of Jesus Christ, and perverting the straight ways of the Lord."[29]

Clarke was fined twenty pounds, Crandall five, and Holmes thirty. Holmes received the harshest sentence because he had already been excommunicated at Seekonk, and because he had performed the baptisms. Clarke continued to ask for a public debate regarding the Baptists' views, and Endicott "somewhat transported broke forth, and told me I had deserved death, and said, he would not have such trash brought into their jurisdiction." The rulers in Massachusetts loathed the Baptists and were not used to having their authority so blatantly challenged.[30] Clarke was released from jail after friends paid his fine, and Crandall posted bail. But Holmes sought spiritual martyrdom. He refused offers to pay his fine and chose to be flogged instead. Holmes believed that the whipping only furthered the gospel, and he hoped the attention would lead more people to receive believer's baptism.

When Roger Williams learned of the Baptists' sentences, he wrote a scathing letter to Governor Endicott. He warned Endicott against persecuting people for spiritual reasons, for he might end up persecuting the religion of Christ himself: "It is a dreadful voice from the King of Kings, and Lord of Lords: Endicott, Endicott, why huntest thou me? Why imprisonest thou me? Why finest, who so bloodily whippest, why wouldest thou (did I not hold thy bloody hands) hang and burn me?" Williams insisted that true religion could not be maintained by the sword. But Endicott and the Massachusetts authorities were not moved, and the flogging of Holmes proceeded.[31]

The Baptists hardly got the worst of Massachusetts's persecuting ways, though. That distinction lay with the Quakers, who sought literal martyr-dom with a rashness well exceeding Holmes's. Some Quaker missionar-ies in the 1650s were banished and ordered not to return, but they did anyway. In 1658, two recalcitrant Quakers each had an ear cut off as a punishment, and then in 1659–1660 Governor Endicott made the ulti-mate example of three Quaker missionaries in executions by hanging. Unease over these punishments led to a slackening of the law, and after 1662 Quakers were whipped rather than executed.

The spread of Baptist principles continued in Massachusetts despite the threat of persecution, and in 1654 the Baptists nabbed their most prominent colonial convert: Harvard president Henry Dunster. The trou-ble started when Dunster refused to have his child baptized and publicly announced that he no longer believed in infant baptism. Massachusetts authorities were alarmed, but they had to handle the case delicately. Dunster could not be hastily tried or summarily whipped. A group of Puritan ministers met with Dunster to persuade him to return to the traditional view of baptism. But Dunster made compelling arguments for believer's baptism. "All instituted gospel worship hath some express word of Scripture," he said. "But paedobaptism hath none." He held his ground, and Harvard removed him from the presidency.[32]

Dunster did not become a celebrated Baptist dissenter on the level of Williams or Clarke because after his dismissal from Harvard he largely remained quiet about his Baptist convictions. Also, he never sought rebap-tism for himself. He left Cambridge for the relatively tolerant atmosphere of Plymouth in 1655. But Dunster presented a formidable challenge to the Massachusetts establishment, simply because he had once been a part of it. With Dunster's apostasy, it seemed that anyone could be led astray by the Baptists.[33]

It remained for the Baptists to establish an official presence in Massachusetts, and that process began in the mid-1650s when a farmer and wagon maker named Thomas Goold of Charlestown began to have doubts about infant baptism. Goold wrote that "God was pleased at last to make clear to me by the rule of the gospel, that children were not capable nor fit subjects for such an ordinance." When Goold and his wife had a daughter in 1655, he refused to present her for baptism. Goold may well have come under the influence of Henry Dunster, who had only recently become a Baptist. Goold referred to a "Master Dunstan," who advised him in his dealings with the church authorities. The church tried to convince him that he was mistaken about baptism, but to no avail. The county court admonished Goold repeatedly that he needed to have his child baptized, and the Charlestown church censured him, which meant that he could not participate in the Lord's Supper.[34]

Goold emerged as an advocate for believer's baptism at a time of theological turmoil in Massachusetts. Puritan churches maintained a demanding standard for full membership, requiring a convincing testimony of conversion. This meant that many New Englanders who received baptism as children never joined the church. But could these baptized nonmembers have their own children baptized? Traditionally, they could not, but in the 1650s pressure grew in some churches to open the privilege to all who lived a godly life, converted or not. A 1662 synod of Puritan ministers agreed to extend the right of baptism to baptized nonmembers. This agreement came to be called the Halfway Covenant. Under this system, baptized New Englanders could also have their children baptized, but they could not necessarily have access to the Lord's Supper. It took decades for the Halfway Covenant to be accepted widely in New England, but the debate raised major questions about the meaning of baptism. Many Puritan pastors and laypeople opposed the implementation of the Halfway Covenant, believing that it cheapened both baptism and church membership.

Goold's church at Charlestown embraced the Halfway Covenant in early 1663, which may have pushed Goold and others to begin holding private meetings at his home later that year. At least one member of Goold's group, John Thrumble, explained that until the 1662 synod, he had believed in infant baptism. When the synod extended the right of baptism to the children of the unconverted, it helped turn Thrumble into a Baptist. He and Goold did not wish to disrupt or dishonor the established churches, so they decided to meet privately instead.[35]

The dissenting group finalized their transformation in May 1665 when Goold and eight others were baptized as believers by immersion. They signed a church covenant declaring that "the church of Christ, commonly (though falsely) called Anabaptists were gathered together and entered into fellowship and communion each with each other, engaging to walk together in all the appointments of their Lord and Master the Lord Jesus Christ as far as he should be pleased to make known his mind and will unto them by his word and Spirit." Several people who had already received believer's baptism in Baptist churches in England joined the church.[36]

The Massachusetts authorities would normally have crushed Baptists like Goold and his new church. But now their reaction was muted, for a variety of reasons. One was the ongoing controversy related to the Halfway Covenant: clearly, baptism was an issue they needed to handle delicately. But the English government was also putting pressure on Massachusetts to temper its persecuting ways, especially in the wake of the recent Quaker hangings.

Nevertheless, the Charlestown church and colonial officials did take action against the Baptists. They excommunicated Goold and his wife along with Thomas Osborne, another key Baptist leader. Authorities hauled Goold into court in September 1665 so he could explain his actions. He presented the court with the church's statement of faith, which on several major issues—the Trinity, the Lordship of Christ, and the authority of the Bible—affirmed Puritan theology. But on the question of baptism, the document laid out the church's dissenting views. Citing the "Great Commission" (Matthew 28:19–20), the church contended that Christ had taught his disciples to make disciples and baptize. "Those that gladly received the word and are baptized are saints by calling and fit matter for a visible church," it declared. Obviously, infants could not "gladly receive the word," bringing the Puritans' baptisms and churches into question. The Baptists affirmed the right of all to prophesy in church meetings. They also acknowledged the worldly authority of the magistrate but expressed desire to "give unto God that which is God's and unto Caesar that which is Caesar's." To Baptists, matters of conscience did not belong to "Caesar."[37]

Goold's statement of faith did not convince the court, which convicted him and his church of "schismatically rending from the communion of the churches" and ordered them to stop their "pernicious practices." When they did not stop, the court disfranchised the men in the congregation who had been eligible to vote and warned them that they would be jailed if they kept meeting. In early 1666, Goold and two other members of the congregation were temporarily imprisoned. Soon the church began meeting on Noddles Island in Boston Harbor, which also served as a sanctuary where they could avoid arrest.[38]

The Baptists had friends among the Puritans, including residents of Noddles Island who protected them. Growing signs of support also appeared in March 1668 when Goold was tried yet again but was found not guilty. The court refused to accept the verdict, told the jury to reconsider, and got the result it wanted. Immediately following this debacle, the government of Massachusetts decided to take a different tack and challenged the Baptists to an unprecedented public debate. Officials said they had to protect New Englanders from the Baptists' poison but were "willing by all Christian candor to endeavor the reducing of the said persons from the error of their way, and their return to the Lord." The authorities were unwittingly playing right into the Baptists' hands, and Goold and his supporters eagerly agreed to the debate.[39]

The event was staged in April 1668 at First Church of Boston. On the whole, the debate was unfocused, primarily because twenty-two people in total took part. The central issue was whether the Baptists were really Separatists. The Baptists took a conciliatory tone, arguing that although they disagreed with the Puritans on an important issue, baptism, they still considered the Puritan churches legitimate. A few of the Baptists took a harsher view of the Puritan churches, though. By the end, it was clear that the Baptists would not countenance the baptizing of infants, and they believed that the Puritans should afford them liberty of conscience to practice believer's baptism. A recent Baptist immigrant from England, William Turner, summarized well their reasons for dissenting against the Puritan way: "1. Baptizing infants. 2. Denying prophecy to the brethren. 3. A spirit of persecution of those that differ from you." The Baptists were hardly "reduced" from their opinions, much to the disgust of the Massachusetts authorities and ministers. The Massachusetts General Court banished Goold and two others.[40]

The three Baptists tried to evade banishment and were reimprisoned. But support for the Baptists continued to emerge from outside their congregation. A group of sixty-six colonists, many of them relatively prominent citizens, petitioned for the Baptists' release. Some of the petitioners had also taken part in debates over the Halfway Covenant, and they reasoned that biblical evidence on the issue of baptism was not clear enough to warrant persecution. The General Court was neither impressed nor convinced by this argument, and it extracted apologies from a number of the petitioners. Two of the key organizers of the petition were fined.[41]

The long-standing dispute between Goold and Massachusetts entered an uneasy stalemate in 1669. Goold and his companions were released temporarily in March, but Goold absconded to Noddles Island. He apparently stayed there for several years, conducting Baptist services.

When the authorities failed to banish Goold, Baptists in Massachusetts sensed an opening, and in the early 1670s signs of Baptist activity began to appear all over eastern Massachusetts. In Woburn, north of Boston, Baptists started meeting openly. Although their leader, the prominent convert John Russell Sr., was fined and imprisoned several times, the Massachusetts officials did not stop the Baptists from meeting.[42]

Finally, in the summer of 1674, Goold and his followers slipped into Boston and began meeting at a private home. Goold led the congregation for one more year until his death on October 27, 1675. But the church carried on and grew, with about eighty people having been baptized into membership by 1680. They built a meetinghouse that opened in 1679. Officials tried repeatedly to stop their public meetings, on one occasion even nailing the door shut. But continuing pressure from London for religious toleration broke Boston's resistance, and in 1681 the General Court gave official approval for the Baptists to meet publicly.[43]

The first era of criminal actions against the Baptists had largely concluded. Over the next generation, Baptists in New England (and elsewhere in the colonies) grew slowly in numbers, but, more important, they grew in respect. The zealots for church purity and believer's baptism had established footholds, especially in Rhode Island but also in Massachusetts. Sixty years later, however, the cycle of Baptist radicalism would begin anew. Colonial churches—including the Baptists—would face their greatest challenge yet with the coming of the Great Awakening.

2

The Great Awakening

THE FASHIONABLE, HARVARD-TRAINED pastor Jeremiah Condy of Boston's Baptist church loathed the chaos of evangelical meetings. To him, preachers like the celebrated itinerant George Whitefield only encouraged frenzy among the laypeople, and Condy would not have that in his church. He wanted his Baptists to be respectable. But some of Condy's members were worried about their pastor's resistance to the mighty work of God happening all around them. They longed to have the Spirit descend on Boston First Baptist, too. When Condy dug in his heels, they began to consider drastic action. A group of the dissenters drew up a complaint against Condy's liberal theology, accusing him of teaching human-centered Arminianism, a theology that posited that anyone, not just the predestined elect, could accept Christ's offer of salvation. More critically, they thought he was confused about the meaning of conversion, or the "new birth," that Jesus had taught was necessary to see the kingdom of God. What did Condy's opposition to the revivals mean? "We cannot avoid questioning," the evangelical Baptists declared, "whether he ever experienced the saving operation of that most important doctrine in his own soul." Doubting whether their own pastor was heaven-bound, the dissenters formed a new Baptist church in Boston in 1743. Like most of the evangelical Baptist churches in New England, the Second Baptist Church flourished, while First Baptist entered a protracted decline.[1]

The Great Awakening of the eighteenth century had a most unusual effect on the Baptist movement in America. It virtually destroyed older Baptist churches, especially in New England. Newer Baptist churches associated with the Philadelphia Association of Baptists generally accommodated, but did not lead, the Great Awakening. From the radical fringe of the awakening's evangelicals, however, a new Baptist faction emerged. Like many radical evangelicals, these Separate Baptists experienced harsh persecution at the hands of the colonial governments. But the Baptists surging out of the Great Awakening would not back down. They took aim at America's established churches and eventually captured the hearts of millions of Americans.

BY THE EARLY eighteenth century, many Baptist churches had sprung up across America. In Kittery, Maine, a small church developed under the leadership of the merchant William Screven. He was baptized at Boston's Baptist church in 1681 and received a license to preach from the church the following year. Screven faced threats and fines from the Massachusetts government, which had owned the territory of Maine since 1679. It ordered him to stop holding Baptist meetings because of "his rash and inconsiderate words tending to blasphemy."[2] Hoping for relief from persecution, by 1696 Screven had relocated with a number of members of his church to Charleston, South Carolina, where they established the first Baptist congregation in that colony.

In Pennsylvania, Baptist churches struggled to establish themselves among the legions of churches and sects in the Quaker-founded colony, which afforded religious freedom to all. The most influential early Baptist church in Pennsylvania got off to an inauspicious start: its founding pastor was an impostor. The Pennepek (Lower Dublin) congregation was started by Elias Keach, who was known as the son of a famous Baptist minister in London. Upon landing in southeastern Pennsylvania, Keach dressed as a minister and fished for opportunities to preach. The problem was that the younger Keach was neither licensed, baptized, nor even converted. This was actually not an unusual scenario: many people in colonial America tried to pass themselves off as ordained ministers, often lying about their credentials from Britain, in pursuit of wealth and social status.

Local Baptist immigrants from England and Wales asked Keach to preach for them. But Keach's conscience got the better of him. During a sermon he began weeping and trembling, and admitted that he was a fraud. Keach counseled with a nearby Irish Baptist minister who led him through to conversion and then baptized him as a believer. The Pennepek Baptists still needed a minister, and so Keach the impostor became the real pastor of the church in 1688. He turned out to be an excellent, entrepreneurial preacher. He toured all over southeastern Pennsylvania and

New Jersey, establishing daughter churches in several New Jersey towns, and one in Philadelphia in 1698.[3]

Baptist congregations in Pennsylvania and New Jersey endured a scattered, uncertain existence. Churches feuded over a number of issues, including whether the "laying on of hands" should accompany baptism. This symbolic impartation of the Holy Spirit designated the recipient as set apart from the world in Christ. New churches also struggled to find adequately qualified ministers and to protect themselves from scoundrels. To alleviate these problems, the Philadelphia Association of Baptists was founded in 1707. Baptist churches would always maintain congregational autonomy, so the association could not dictate policy or theology to individual congregations. Instead, it helped regularize Baptist life in the Middle Colonies, solving congregational disputes, testing ministerial candidates, and sponsoring new churches and missionary journeys into unevangelized areas.[4]

The Philadelphia Association slowly established influence over the Baptist congregations of the region, but sometimes it was unable to steer churches away from trouble. In the late 1720s, the church at Piscataway, New Jersey, needed a minister to assist its aging pastor. Against the judgment of the association, the congregation ordained a man calling himself Henry Loveall. Soon Loveall was exposed as another impostor, but one much worse than Elias Keach. Loveall's real name was reportedly Desolate Baker, who was a runaway servant, a serial adulterer, a bigamist, and syphilitic, leading one wag to comment that his alias "Loveall" was precisely the right name for him.[5]

Nathaniel Jenkins, the pastor at Cohansey, New Jersey, wrote a letter to the Piscataway church in 1730 that expressed his disgust: "You neither minded my advice nor that of our Association, but as persons infatuated you have rushed on without rule or precedent. . . . Consider that reproach you brought on your profession hereby. I am ashamed of it. I could have told you." The wandering Loveall just relocated to Maryland and began working for a church there. In 1743, that church moved to Opeckon, Virginia, where Loveall's continuing improprieties were exposed, and he was removed from the church. Unfamiliar or recently immigrated ministers often helped address a lack of pastors in the colonies, but some were wolves in sheep's clothing.[6]

In general, Baptist churches between 1680 and 1740 received greater respect and less persecution than they had in the early colonial period. As a result of the Glorious Revolution of 1688–1689, the new English monarchs William and Mary championed the Act of Toleration (1689), which relieved persecution against dissenters like the Baptists. King James II had revoked Massachusetts's charter in the 1680s, but William and Mary granted a new one in 1692. It returned much of the colony's political autonomy but required it, in accordance with the Toleration Act, to give freedom to all Protestant Christians, including Baptists. The era of exclusive Puritanism had come to a close. Baptists could now worship in relative peace and quiet, but they still had to pay taxes to support the established state churches.[7]

At the same time that persecution was declining, Baptists also sought greater levels of respect in colonial American society. Whereas the original Baptist churches of the seventeenth century had depended on largely uneducated but militant leaders, in the eighteenth century highly educated pastors such as Jeremiah Condy were more common. In 1718, Elisha Callender became the first Harvard-educated pastor of Boston's First Baptist Church, and Congregationalist stalwarts Increase and Cotton Mather even participated in his ordination. In a few short years, Baptist pastors had achieved an unprecedented level of prestige.

Accepting believer's baptism was still a difficult choice, however, and the trend toward more moderate, fashionable Baptist churches was tempered by the established churches' ongoing commitment to infant baptism. The combination of growing sophistication and enduring distinctiveness was exemplified in the career of the talented pastor John Comer. At one point Comer considered becoming a Congregationalist pastor, and he joined the Congregationalist church at Cambridge, Massachusetts. One of his best friends became a Baptist, however, and after he investigated the question, Comer found "the churches not so fully in order in the point of baptism as they should be." For some time Comer remained in the Congregationalist church and did not seek rebaptism. The death of a close friend and personal brushes with death through sickness and the near wreck of a ship on which he was sailing, led Comer to obey his convictions and accept believer's baptism. Comer fearfully recalled Christ's words: "He that is ashamed of me and my ways, of him and his ways will I be ashamed before my Father and the holy angels." Elisha Callender of Boston First Baptist baptized Comer in January 1725.[8]

Even as he was leaning toward Baptist principles, Comer began studying for the ministry at Congregationalist-run Yale College. He did not finish his degree there, deciding to attend a school at Swansea, Massachusetts, which had a Baptist church nearby. His college studies, though incomplete, made him an attractive pastoral candidate. He received his first opportunity to preach at Swansea in 1725. Unlike the relatively democratic preaching practices of seventeenth-century Baptists, the office of teaching elder had become a distinct, revered position by 1725. Comer noted in his diary that "in the sincerity and uprightness of my soul . . ., and under deep humility considering my own unworthiness I entered into the work of the sacred ministry."[9]

Soon after he began preaching at Swansea, John Clarke's old church, the First Baptist Church of Newport, Rhode Island, invited Comer to become its pastor. The church had recently split over differences between Calvinist and Arminian members, a frequent point of controversy in the colonial churches. Comer personally leaned toward Calvinist (or Particular) Baptist theology, but Elisha Callender advised him never to bring up controversial points from the pulpit.

Comer still retained the old Baptist penchant for theological feuding, however. In 1728, apparently with little notice, Comer announced to his church that the laying on of hands would be required with baptism. The majority of the church members protested, but Comer bluntly wrote, "I refer the whole of this affair to God." He was dismissed as pastor shortly afterward. He preached for a time at the Second Baptist Church of Newport, but while that church accepted his ideas about the laying on of hands, it did not care for his Calvinism. So Comer moved to Rehoboth, Massachusetts, where he served successfully until his untimely death in 1734. He was just thirty years old.[10]

For all his sophistication, talent, and disputatiousness, we should remember that Comer (like his fellow colonists) lived in a harsh and uncertain world filled with perils such as shipwrecks, Native American attacks, and debilitating disease. Consumption, or tuberculosis, felled Comer in 1734, and as a teen he was desperately afraid of dying from smallpox, which ravaged Boston in 1721. Comer's diary is peppered with references to tragic deaths. His thoughts on the laying on of hands were interspersed with others on topics like a man dying when a well caved in on him, and a drunk falling off a chair and breaking his neck. He also noted that "a negro woman belonging to Thomas Wickom, was found dead in Dyre's Swamp. She ran away the day before."[11] Comer's early America was a period of deep inequality and the ever-present fear of death. Perhaps these bleak realities primed early Americans to think long and hard about their standing before God.

THE GREAT AWAKENING was a religious upheaval rooted in widespread dissatisfaction with the churches of the colonies, Britain, and Europe. This dissatisfaction left no denomination untouched, including the Baptists. In churches like First Baptist of Boston, the revivals caused lasting damage, usually when pastors failed to support the awakenings. Elsewhere, ministers of older Baptist churches offered tentative support to the revivals, which in turn caused other divisions.

Philadelphia's Baptist church offers an excellent example of the way that the Great Awakening divided Baptists. In 1740, the Anglican revivalist George Whitefield made a much-anticipated stop in Philadelphia. As was typical of him, he visited all supportive churches and pastors, including Baptist pastor Jenkin Jones, who impressed Whitefield. He heard Jones preach "the truth as it is in Jesus" and determined that Jones was "the only preacher that I know of in Philadelphia, who speaks feelingly and with authority. The poor people are much refreshed by him, and I trust the Lord will bless him more and more." This was quite an endorsement from the most influential evangelical minister in the Anglo-American world.[12]

Whitefield's preaching generated intense reactions and bouts of mystical elation wherever he went, including the Philadelphia Baptist church. Whitefield spoke with an African American woman who had been converted during Whitefield's first visit to Philadelphia in 1739. She had struggled to achieve assurance of salvation, but at a Baptist meeting led by the itinerating Abel Morgan Jr., of Middletown, New Jersey, she had a spiritual breakthrough. Even though he was ordained in 1734, Morgan himself had only recently experienced the new birth of salvation, partly as a result of hearing Whitefield preach in 1739.[13]

As Morgan preached, the woman was led to heights of spiritual ecstasy: "The word came with such power upon her heart, that at last she was obliged to cry out." Morgan, like many moderate supporters of the revivals, was not looking to whip up frenzy, so he stopped preaching and asked the woman to be quiet. But she could not remain silent: "The glory of the LORD shone so brightly round about her, that she could not help blessing and praising GOD, and telling how GOD was revealing himself to her soul." Eventually she was removed from the meetinghouse, but she fell to her knees, shouting and worshiping God in the street. Some at the meeting said she was crazy, but Whitefield thought otherwise. Her testimony was "rational and solid," he said, and he concluded that "when an extraordinary work is carrying on, GOD generally manifests himself to some souls in this extraordinary manner." Whitefield was no progressive on slavery (he would later own slaves himself), but he believed so strongly in the power of the Holy Spirit that he took this African American woman's religious experiences seriously.[14]

Although Abel Morgan tried to get this woman to be silent, he did support the revivals in spite of their mystical manifestations. But other Baptists rejected the Great Awakening precisely because of its "enthusiastic" characteristics. One of the Baptists who most vehemently opposed the revivals was Ebenezer Kinnersly, an assistant to Jenkin Jones at the Baptist church in Philadelphia. Kinnersly grew increasingly uncomfortable with the emotional extremes of the revivals, and a frenzied sermon preached at the Baptist church by Presbyterian revivalist John Rowland pushed Kinnersly over the edge.

The disgusted Kinnersly went public with his complaints in Ben Franklin's *Pennsylvania Gazette*. Franklin knew a good news story when he saw one, and he became the colonies' most influential publicist of the Great Awakening, giving a platform both to Whitefield and to his critics.

Kinnersly wrote that he did not mind ministers preaching about hell, provided it was "prudently managed." But John Rowland, the itinerant from New Jersey, went beyond all bounds of propriety and encouraged wild mystical experiences. Kinnersly deplored the way that converts were "filled brim-full of enthusiastical raptures and ecstasies, pretending to have large communications from God; to have seen ravishing visions; to have been encompassed, as it were, with flames of lightning, and there to have beheld our blessed Savior nailed to the cross, and bleeding before their eyes in particular for them! These and such like enthusiastic extravagancies some of our bigoted young zealots (who are not as yet distracted) have run into." Apparently the African American woman was not the only one seeing visions of light in the Baptist church.[15]

When Kinnersly next had a chance to preach after Rowland's sermon, he made his concerns known. It did not go over well. Some friends of the revival got so upset that they ran out of the meeting "in a most disorderly and tumultuous manner." Among the ringleaders of the walkout were a woman whom Kinnersly considered to be of ill repute, as well as several blacks and white indentured servants.

Kinnersly was disgusted by this display, but Jenkin Jones publicly censured him for opposing Rowland and the revival. Kinnersly blamed Jones's preference for Rowland on the fact that they were both Welsh. Moreover, Kinnersly contemptuously noted that women were allowed to participate in proceedings against him. They "seemed to pay not the least deference to the Apostle Paul, who says it is a shame for them to speak in the church," Kinnersly wrote. Kinnersly's censure caused a rift in his relationship with Jones and the church, and ultimately Kinnersly was excommunicated from the Philadelphia congregation. A committee established by the Pennepek and Philadelphia meetings (still technically branches of the same church) cleared Jenkin Jones of any wrongdoing in the matter, and in September 1740 the Philadelphia Association chose Jones to give the sermon at its next meeting. Although the association would never represent the vanguard of the revivalist movement, its vindication of Jones placed it within the moderate evangelical camp of the Great Awakening.[16]

IN THE 1740s and early 1750s, the Philadelphia Association was the key agency spreading Baptist influence across the colonies from New England to the Carolinas. New England and the Chesapeake actually outpaced the Middle Colonies in the number of Baptist churches, but the Philadelphia Association was critical in organizing Calvinist (also known as Particular, or Regular) Baptist congregations throughout the colonies.

Nowhere was this influence seen more clearly than in South Carolina, where Whitefield also brought revival and turmoil to the Baptists. Following the establishment of Charleston's First Baptist Church in the 1690s, Baptists had continued to spread through the Carolina low country. A pivotal congregation was formed on the Ashley River north of Charleston, where the English Baptist Isaac Chanler became minister in the 1730s. Along with the Congregationalist pastor Josiah Smith, Chanler became one of South Carolina's key advocates for George Whitefield in 1740.

In July 1740, Whitefield began preaching at the Ashley River church, describing Chanler as a "gracious Baptist minister." Whitefield had already encountered a hostile reaction from Anglican commissary Alexander Garden of Charleston. Even though Whitefield himself remained an Anglican priest, he found pastors like Chanler much more welcoming to his preaching than his fellow Anglicans were. To Whitefield, the gospel of the "new birth" mattered more than denominations, so pastors like Chanler were his friends, whatever their disagreement about baptism.

The top priority in evangelical preaching was convincing people that if they accepted Christ by faith, they could be forgiven for their sins and "born again." On July 9, Whitefield preached under a tree at Chanler's meetinghouse, as the crowd had become too big to meet inside the church. Chanler and other evangelical ministers in Charleston soon inaugurated a series of midweek sermons to continue the revivals in Whitefield's absence.[17]

Whitefield also preached at Charleston's Baptist church, although the minister there, Thomas Simmons, was not as supportive as Chanler. Simmons had seen the membership of the church decline to as few as three people by 1740, however, and Whitefield's arrival seems to have precipitated a number of conversions. Whitefield explained that he became so disgusted with the Anglicans of Charleston that he "went to the Baptist and Independent meetinghouses, where Jesus Christ was preached." He also privately served communion to groups of Anglicans, Presbyterians, and Baptists.[18]

The Philadelphia Association began a generation's worth of indirect and direct influence on South Carolina Baptists with the establishment in 1738 of the Welsh Neck Church, north of Charleston in the Pee Dee region of South Carolina. The founding members of this church came from the Welsh Tract Church of the Delaware Valley in Pennsylvania (later Delaware). Isaac Chanler and Thomas Simmons ordained Welsh Neck's first minister, Philip James, in 1743. James was born in Pennepek, Pennsylvania, and he first preached at the Welsh Tract Church before moving to South Carolina.

One rarely gets glimpses of the individual spirituality of these early American Baptists, but we do have an account of a remarkable experience by Philip James that may suggest that evangelical mysticism—including dreams, trances, and visions—was common among the Regular Baptists. Early Baptist historian Morgan Edwards noted that when one of James's children died in 1753, the despondent pastor fell into a kind of coma. When he awoke, he told his family that during the trance

> my soul quitted my body [and] the resemblance of a man in black made towards me, and (frowning and chiding for wishing to die) took me up towards the sun, which filled me with fear. As I was ascending, a bright figure interposed and my black conductor was pushed off. The bright man took me by the hand and said, "we go this way," pointing to the north. And as we ascended, I saw a company of angels and my

child among them, (clothed in white and in the full stature of a man) sing with them as the company passed by us, whereupon my bright conductor said, "I am one of that company and must join them." And as he quitted me I found myself sinking fast till I came to my body.

Edwards's admiring account of James's experience hints that this kind of spirit journey was acceptable among many early American Baptists, just as it was among American evangelicals more broadly.[19]

The most influential exemplar of the Pennsylvania-Carolina Baptist connection was Oliver Hart, a native of Pennsylvania who began his long tenure as the pastor of Charleston's Baptist church in 1749. Hart advocated Regular Baptist theology and evangelical piety. He was converted at the height of the Great Awakening under the influence of Whitefield and Abel Morgan. Hart had grown up in the Baptist church and received believer's baptism from Jenkin Jones in 1741. He was baptized, and later licensed to preach, in Southampton, Pennsylvania, at a branch of the Pennepek Baptist Church.[20]

When Charleston's pastor Thomas Simmons died, Jones recommended Hart as his replacement, a position that Hart accepted on a trial basis in 1749. Hart arrived at a particularly important moment: the day he disembarked in Charleston was the day of Isaac Chanler's funeral. In the vacuum left by Chanler's death, Hart would become the most prominent Baptist leader in colonial South Carolina. Not surprisingly, Baptists in the colony took Hart's timely arrival as a sign of special providence, and the Charleston church eagerly called him as its permanent pastor several months later.[21]

Hart worked not only to build up the Charleston congregation but also to strengthen the still-meager Baptist presence in South Carolina. The only way Hart knew to do that was on the Pennsylvania model. So in 1751, he led low-country Baptist churches, along with Welsh Neck, in forming the Charleston Baptist Association. It was modeled explicitly on the Philadelphia Association.

Hart contended with many of the typical tragedies and challenges of an American colonist. His one-year-old son, Seth, died less than a year after Hart's arrival in Charleston. Another child, Hannah, died at nine months old in 1753. The weather of the Atlantic seaboard also held frightening dangers, as Hart survived a hurricane in 1752 and a tornado in 1761. In the hurricane, Hart wrote, "my house was washed down, and all I had almost destroyed."[22]

Hart's resolve in the face of these troubles helped produce a major revival in Charleston in 1754. His longing for revival and conversions shaped Hart as a pastor. Like his mentor Whitefield, Hart took denominational boundaries lightly and focused primarily on promoting a vital relationship with God. It was not unusual to find Hart preaching about Jesus's teaching on the new birth from the Gospel of John, as he did on August 4, 1754, just before the revival began. "I felt my soul drawn out after the conversion of sinners," he wrote. "Oh, that they knew what the new birth means!" Hart promoted revival not only among Baptists but also among local evangelical pastors such as Savannah's Presbyterian minister John Zubly, with whom he spent a week in the summer of 1754.[23]

Upon his return from Savannah, Hart found that many of the young people in his church were eager for spiritual guidance. Hart described the experience of a servant woman, Margaret, who displayed the zeal of a new evangelical convert by trying to get friends to turn to Christ. " 'Oh Miss Betsey!' Said she, 'Jesus Christ is sweet, he is precious; had I known his sweetness,' said she, 'I would not have lived so long without him.' " She implored her friends to come to Christ. Many of the young people crowding Hart's home began weeping, crying out for God's mercy, and pleading, "Give me Christ! Give me Christ!" Hart saw many of these anxious youths convert in that season of revival. Under the leadership of Hart, Jenkin Jones, and others, the still-small Regular Baptist movement in South Carolina and the Middle Colonies grew steadily.[24]

LONG-ESTABLISHED BAPTIST CHURCHES of New England typically opposed the Great Awakening. Those affiliated with the Philadelphia Association supported it tentatively. But the new, radical Baptist movement emerging de novo from the Great Awakening transformed America's religious landscape. The spawning of the radical evangelical Baptists was reminiscent of the way that the English Puritan and Separatist movement had helped create the original English Baptists. In the 1740s and 1750s, radical Protestants stumbled again on the problems created by infant baptism, and the presence of so many who had received baptism as infants but never experienced conversion. Infant baptism was practiced by all Anglicans and Congregationalists, and to Baptists, it was the sign of an impure church. The heady environment of the Great Awakening presented a great opportunity for a return to biblical purity in all areas, including the practice of baptism. The Separate Baptists brought the radical edge back to the Baptist movement.

As one Baptist wrote in the *Boston Weekly Post-Boy* in 1743, "I am one of the many in this land, who in this time of general awakening and inquiry, are unable to reconcile the practice of infant baptism with the doctrine of the new birth, that has of late been preached up with such great power and remarkable success." Reformed Protestants had never clearly explained the purpose of infant baptism, the writer argued. It did not lead to regeneration, or forgiveness of sin, so what was the point? It left baptized children in the same lost spiritual state as unbaptized children. Believer's baptism would clear up the confusion. Converts would receive baptism as a testimony of their inner transformation by the Holy Spirit.[25]

Becoming a Baptist in New England during the Great Awakening usually entailed separation from one of the established Congregational churches. Hundreds of new Separate Congregationalist and Separate Baptist churches formed in the mid-eighteenth century. As with the creation of Boston's Second Baptist Church, the most common reason for the formation of a Separate congregation was that an existing church did not sufficiently support the revivals. But starting unauthorized churches was illegal. Separates often balked at paying taxes to support the established churches and ministers, as well, so they faced fines and legal harassment for failing to cooperate with the state-sponsored religious order.

In New England, the most influential Baptist convert of the eighteenth century was Isaac Backus, who came from a Congregationalist farming family in Norwich, Connecticut. When the Great Awakening reached Norwich, Backus was deeply familiar with Calvinist Christianity but had never experienced conversion. His mother had her faith renewed in the awakening, and she urged her son to seek the new birth. In mid-1741, Backus recalled, "God by his Spirit was pleased in infinite mercy to bring eternal things near to my soul and to show me the dreadful danger of delays." He worried that while thousands of others found release and forgiveness in Christ, he would be left out. Evangelical itinerants brought powerful revival meetings to Norwich. The leader of these radicals was the notorious James Davenport, who openly questioned the salvation of many hesitant pastors. Davenport, who was also a compelling orator, preached in Norwich in August. He did more than anyone to stir Backus's heart to conversion.[26]

Backus's breakthrough came in late August 1741.

> As I was mowing in the field alone I was thinking of my case; and all my past life seemed to be brought fresh to my view, and it appeared indeed nothing but a life of sin. I felt so that I left work and went and sat down under a shady tree. . . . the justice of God shined so clear before my eyes in condemning such a guilty rebel

that I could say no more, but fell at his feet. I saw that I was in his hands and he had a right to do with me just as he pleased. And I lay like a dead vile creature before him. I felt a calm in my mind— them tossings and tumults that I felt before seemed to be gone. And just in that critical moment God who caused the light to shine out of darkness, shined into my heart with such a discovery of that glorious righteousness which fully satisfies the law that I had broken. . . . Now my burden (that was so dreadful heavy before) was gone: that tormenting fear that I had was taken away and I felt a sweet peace and rejoicing in my soul.[27]

It was a classic evangelical conversion, the wrenching but joyous experience of thousands in the Great Awakening.

Conversion did not make everything right for Backus, however. He became increasingly dissatisfied with the Norwich church and its pastor, Benjamin Lord. Lord was supportive of the revivals, especially in their early phases, and a large number of new members—eighty-one, including Backus—joined the church between 1741 and 1744. Lord did not like the frenzied work of the evangelical itinerant preachers, however. When one of them, Nathaniel Lothrop, visited Norwich in early 1742, he dared his "opposers to say that I have not got the Spirit of God in me." Lothrop beat his chest and declared that he indeed spoke by the Spirit. He called out his opponents in the church by name, telling one woman that he would be delighted "to hear Christ give a commission to the devils to drag your soul down to hell, my dear sister Anne." Lord thought these antics were outrageous, and he banned radical preachers from the church. The church also refused to make a conversion testimony a requirement for full membership, instead requiring only the desire to live a godly life.[28]

By mid-1745, thirteen members of the church, including Backus, stopped attending and began holding private meetings by themselves. Lord insisted that the aggrieved members appear before him and explain themselves. Among their reasons for leaving were that the church did not make conversion a condition of membership, and that Lord was "not a friend to lowly preaching and preachers." One of the Separates simply stated that "the gospel is not preached here."[29]

Backus later explained his own views on what justified separations. He said that true Christians should separate from a church when the church knowingly admitted unconverted people to full membership, when the preacher taught corrupt doctrine, when the true gospel and its preachers were shut out of the church, and when a church's leaders exhibited a "form of godliness but deny the power thereof," citing 2 Timothy 3:5.[30]

Even though Backus had no college education or formal ministerial training, he joined the ranks of the itinerants and began preaching in Connecticut and Massachusetts. The twenty-three-year-old visited Titicut, Massachusetts, in December 1747, where he felt moved by the Holy Spirit to a ministerial calling. "My soul was constrained by divine light, love, and power to enter into their labors," he said, "and my heart was so drawn forth towards God, and in love to his people here, that I felt willing to impart not only the gospel to them, but my own soul." Backus knew none of the evangelicals there personally, but on the spot he committed to minister to them. That commitment lasted the rest of his life.[31]

When Backus and his new church drew up a covenant in 1748, it called the congregation to a life of fervent evangelical piety. It continued to endorse the practice of infant baptism but rejected the Halfway Covenant by which unconverted adults who had been baptized as infants could have their own children baptized. "True believers and their infant seed and none but such have a right to their ordinance of baptism," they wrote.[32]

But even this exclusive policy still did not settle Backus's troubled conscience about infant baptism. Baptizing infants necessarily muddled the issue of pure church membership, which had driven Backus and many others to separate in the first place. Still, deciding to become a Baptist was a more wrenching choice than separating from an established church. Backus and the Separates believed that when they separated they were simply taking the Congregationalist tradition back to its first principles. Becoming a Baptist would earn contempt from all observers, including many Separates. To most Reformed Protestants, denying baptism to babies seemed tantamount to child abuse. It cast children out of the protective spiritual canopy of the church and put their souls in danger of hell.

But the logical pressure to accept believer's baptism remained. In 1749, some members of Backus's church began to promote it as the only scriptural option. The ensuing controversy sent Backus into a depressive tailspin. He prayed and studied the Bible on the subject, until at last he began to believe that he had been misled all his life. He told his congregation in late August 1749 that "none had any right to baptism but believers, and that plunging seemed the only right mode." Backus whipsawed back to supporting infant baptism almost immediately, however. It was agonizing.[33]

Backus's mind churned over baptism for another two years. Once, when he returned from a preaching tour, Backus found that a local Separate Baptist had begun influencing the people of Backus's church, proselytizing for the Baptist way and immersing ten people. Soon Backus apologized to his congregation for speaking too rashly in favor of believer's baptism and, to emphasize the point, baptized an infant. But doubts continued to gnaw at him. "The changes about baptism, and my unsettled state now about it, wounds and weakens my soul," he confessed in his diary.[34]

Backus's breakthrough came in July 1751, when he set apart a day for fasting and prayer to consult every Bible verse relevant to baptism and definitively concluded that baptism was for believers, not infants. He announced this conclusion to his church, which led some who held the opposite view to discuss removing him as pastor. Backus persisted, however, and in August he took the final step of repudiating his own baptism as an infant and receiving believer's baptism. A Baptist pastor from Rhode Island had come to Titicut to preach, and in the afternoon he began to baptize those who chose to receive it. Backus could put it off no longer. He spoke to the assembled crowd about his conversion and hope in Christ and then entered the water, where the pastor immersed him.[35]

Receiving believer's baptism resolved the gravest crisis of Backus's life. But it only exacerbated the troubles in his church. Those who supported infant baptism were angry with Backus, and for a while Backus left the church, returning home to Norwich. He was called back with the understanding that the church would practice both infant and believer's baptism. But this arrangement did not work very well. The Separates and Baptists of New England, despite their common origins, were finding it difficult to coexist. At a synod in Stonington, Connecticut, in 1754, Separates decided to ban Baptists from their churches.[36]

Backus also became convinced that a mixed communion of Baptists and supporters of infant baptism was unsustainable. This determination drove him toward founding a new Baptist church in 1756. He wrote in January that "having a long trial on things, and after much searching of the Scriptures, and some freedom in crying to God for help and direction (particularly this morning about day) I am brought to this and now declared it, that I firmly believed that as none are the proper subjects of baptism but real saints: so that every such soul ought to be baptized by immersion before they come to the Lord's Supper." This was a declaration in favor of a pure Baptist fellowship. Backus concluded that although one could find many true Christians who believed in infant baptism, and that he loved them as brothers and sisters in Christ, they could not remain in church fellowship with one another. It was totally impractical because baptism represented, along with communion, one of the two primary rituals of the church. Their disagreement "has a natural tendency to offend and burden each other and to try to keep those who are so differently minded together is destroying the end to accomplish the means." It was tragic that the Separates and Baptists could not remain in the same churches, but baptism was far too important an issue to permit it.[37]

Some Baptist itinerants seized upon the opportunities presented by the Great Awakening to convert new evangelicals and Separates to Baptist principles. This was the case in Sturbridge, Massachusetts, where a Baptist preacher named Ebenezer Moulton convinced most of the Separate congregation to accept believer's baptism in mid-1749. When Moulton arrived and challenged the church's beliefs about baptism, their views "went away like the chaff of the summer threshing-floor," one of the converts wrote.[38]

Separates and Baptists still experienced severe persecution, usually for their refusal to pay taxes to support the established churches. Backus's own mother and brother were imprisoned in 1752 for this offense. Backus's mother relished her persecution for Christ's sake, writing that "though I was bound when I was cast into this furnace, yet I was loosed, and found Jesus in the midst of the furnace with me."[39]

Backus also documented the humiliating treatment the Baptists at Sturbridge received from authorities, who entered the dissenters' homes looking for valuables to confiscate: "They stripped the shelves of pewter, of such as had it; and of others that had not they took away skillets, kettles, pots and warming-pans. Others they deprived of the means they got their bread with, viz. workmen's tools, and spinning-wheels. They drove away geese and swine from the doors of some others; from some that had cows; from some that had but one they took that away. They took a yoke of oxen from one. Some they thrust into prison, where they had a long and tedious imprisonment."[40]

Other Baptists suffered physical violence. One provocative Baptist preacher in Connecticut, Joshua Morse, was converted to evangelical faith under George Whitefield but maintained the Baptist principles of his youth in Rhode Island. Morse faced repeated beatings and harassment from both government officials and angry mobs. On one occasion, he was dragged by the hair out of a revival service, down a flight of steps, and into the street. He was beaten severely and received a gash on his face that scarred him for life.[41]

This kind of official and unofficial persecution undoubtedly hindered Baptist growth in New England. But it also fired the zeal of committed Baptists, confirming that they should sacrifice everything for God's truth. Out of the renewed persecution of the Great Awakening, the Separate Baptist movement became one of the primary seedbeds for American ideas about the separation of church and state. Baptists saw firsthand the dreadful effect of state persecution of dissenting religion. The Separate Baptists also fueled an unprecedented missionary campaign into the South, which prior to the Great Awakening had only a minimal Baptist presence.

THERE WAS A time when Anglicans formally dominated the religious life of the South. In the 1750s, the evangelical zealots of the Great Awakening began to change that. A crabby Anglican itinerant minister named Charles Woodmason lamented the emerging religious chaos he saw in the southern backcountry. He thought nothing was so distasteful—even lurid—as the public baptism services of the wretched Baptists. Instead of reverent occasions supervised by learned priests, baptisms were becoming affairs "to which lascivious persons of both sexes resort, as to a public bath," Woodmason wrote. "I know not whether it would not be less offensive to modesty for them to strip wholly into buff at once, than to be dipped with those very thin linen drawers they are equipped in—which when wet, so closely adheres to the limbs, as exposes the nudities equally as if none at all."[42]

The Baptists tormented Woodmason, fueling his contempt for them. Scalawags set a pack of dogs to fighting outside one of Woodmason's services, and they rioted at weddings he conducted. They accused him of being a Jesuit priest in disguise (just about the worst accusation one could make in this era of bitter anti-Catholicism). In one episode, if Woodmason can be believed, an enemy stole his clerical gown while he was sleeping and then masqueraded as Woodmason as he tried to jump in bed with one of Woodmason's female parishioners. "This was a scheme laid by the Baptists," he declared. One way or the other, these kinds of evangelicals would break the Church of England's hold on the South.[43]

The key figure in exporting the Separate Baptist movement to the South was Shubal Stearns of Tolland, Connecticut. Stearns followed a familiar path to Separate Baptist convictions. He experienced conversion under George Whitefield's preaching, grew dissatisfied with the local Congregational church, and helped organize a Separate congregation. By the mid-1740s, Stearns had become an activist for religious freedom for the Separates, and he signed petitions to the Connecticut General Assembly asking for liberty of worship under the 1689 Toleration Act.[44]

In 1751 (shortly before Isaac Backus accepted believer's baptism about ninety miles away in Massachusetts), Stearns and most of his extended family were converted to Baptist principles under a visiting preacher, Wait Palmer. Palmer helped Stearns organize a Separate Baptist congregation in Tolland and ordained Stearns with the assistance of the provocative Joshua Morse. But Stearns did not stay long at the church, as he and his family left in 1754 to bring the Separate Baptist faith to the South.

Why did Stearns leave? Early Baptist historian Robert Baylor Semple chalked it up to the Separate Baptists' mystical piety: "Mr. Stearns and most of the Separates had strong faith in the immediate teachings of the Spirit. . . . Mr. Stearns, listening to some of these instructions from Heaven, conceived himself called upon by the Almighty to move far to the westward to execute a great and extensive work." Stearns had also likely learned that his brother-in-law Daniel Marshall and sister Martha, missionaries to Native Americans in Pennsylvania, had become Baptists and relocated to Virginia. The Stearns and Marshall families reunited in Winchester, Virginia, in 1754, but soon moved farther south, to Sandy Creek, North Carolina, in 1755. There, southeast of present-day Greensboro, they established a church that became the epicenter of Baptist revival in the South.[45]

The church at Sandy Creek grew like wildfire in its early years, multiplying quickly from fewer than twenty to more than six hundred members. It spawned sister churches, too: a total of forty-two congregations within seventeen years, not only in North Carolina but also in South Carolina and Virginia. In 1758, Stearns formed the Sandy Creek Association to help manage the exponential growth.[46]

The Baptist evangelicals of Sandy Creek tapped into longing for spiritual direction and comfort among backcountry people of the South. Stearns and his followers practiced an intense religion of signs, wonders, and devotion to the Bible. They preached in a deeply emotional style that generated heated reactions in the congregations, including crying, shaking, and visions. Stearns himself developed a quasi-mystical reputation, with many believing that he had mesmerizing power in his eyes. One convert, Tiden Lane, recalled that he first met Stearns at a meeting where Stearns was preaching under a peach tree. Stearns immediately locked eyes with the unnerved Lane. "I began to think he had an evil eye and ought to be shunned," Lane wrote. "But shunning him I could no more effect than a bird can shun the rattlesnake when it fixes his eyes upon it." Lane was so overcome with dread that he collapsed. Soon after the meeting he became a Baptist preacher.[47]

The Sandy Creek churches looked strictly to the Bible as their guide for church practice, implementing even obscure New Testament obligations. They practiced a total of nine rites. The first two of these were believer's baptism and the Lord's Supper, which they celebrated weekly. But the other seven were less common in colonial America: love feasts, laying on of hands at baptism, foot washing, anointing the sick with oil, the right hand of fellowship, the kiss of charity, and devoting infant children. Except for devoting children, each of these practices had clear, if limited, biblical sanction. Devoting children, in which the church would pray for the baby, and the child often also received its name, became a substitute for infant baptism among the Baptists. They never intended to refuse God's blessing to children; they only believed that baptism was not the proper means to convey that blessing.[48]

The Sandy Creek churches were normally governed by elders, and deacons took care of the needs of the congregation. Remarkably, women commonly served as both deaconesses and eldresses in the Separate Baptist churches of the South. Eldresses would primarily work with the women of the church, instructing and baptizing them, but it appears that they also occasionally taught before mixed audiences. The office of eldress, restricted as it might have been, represented the most far-reaching recognition of female authority to be found among eighteenth-century evangelicals. Indeed, one Baptist observed at the end of the eighteenth century that one of the first reasons for Baptists originally separating was because the established New England churches "did not allow women to exercise their gifts in public."[49]

Within ten years of settling at Sandy Creek, the Separate Baptists had established themselves as a formidable presence in the South. In a rare surviving letter, Stearns wrote from North Carolina in 1765 that "the Lord carries on his work gloriously in sundry places in this province, and in Virginia and South Carolina."[50] He continued preaching and baptizing until his death in 1771. The upstart Separate Baptists had not existed prior to the Great Awakening, yet they had substantially seized control of the future of the Baptist movement in America. To be sure, some Regular Baptists embraced the revivals of the Great Awakening, but the respectable Baptists who did not do so found themselves swamped by the rising evangelical tide. Because of the Great Awakening, the Baptist movement in America had been born again.

3

Baptists and the American Revolution

IN NOVEMBER 1776, Pastor James Manning of Providence, Rhode Island, wrote to English Baptist leader John Ryland. Trouble had come to the American colonies. Two winters before, Providence's Baptists had witnessed a prodigious revival; perhaps two hundred people had experienced conversion in just a few months. But the outbreak of war in 1775 brought an abrupt end to the revival: "The fatal 19th of April, the day of the Lexington battle, like an electric stroke put a stop to the progress of the work, as well as in other places as here. Oh horrid war! How contrary to the spirit of Jesus!"[1]

The Baptists saw a glimmer of hope, however, amid the travail of war. The Patriots' paeans to liberty, Baptists anticipated, might foster freedom of religion as well. Baptists felt that religious liberty had suffered for more than a millennium under oppressive state churches, beginning with the conversion of Constantine to Christianity in the fourth century C.E. Now, they speculated, God might use the cataclysm of war to bring about full freedom of conscience.[2]

Baptists were ambivalent about the American Revolution. Across America they lamented the tribulations of war, knowing that it smothered revival and paralyzed churches. And they recognized that the same Americans who clamored for liberty from Britain often denied religious freedom to dissenting churches. Could Patriot leaders be trusted? Over the course of the conflict, Baptists became more and more sanguine about its outcome. They were convinced that the American Revolution heralded liberty from Britain but, more important, liberty for the true gospel. As they embraced the war as a godly cause, they began to see the new American nation as a place uniquely favored by God.

AT THE OUTBREAK of the Revolution, rank-and-file Americans, including Baptists, carried on with their daily business, often oblivious to the great unfolding crisis with Britain. Average Americans often did not learn of major developments in the conflict until days or weeks later. For example, Baptist pastor Hezekiah Smith's solitary journal entry on the weekend the Declaration of Independence was signed in July 1776 read, "Something unwell, tho' kept about." Smith was struggling with an intestinal malady he called the "flux," for which he took a number of medicines, including "infusion of rhubarb" and niter drops, or saltpeter mixed with oil and water. World affairs seemed far from his mind.

But the war had changed Smith's life. Born in 1737 in Hempstead, Long Island, as a child Smith moved with his family to New Jersey. At nineteen he received believer's baptism and became a member of the Baptist congregation at Morristown. In 1762, he graduated from the evangelical College of New Jersey at Princeton. In 1765, he became the pastor at Haverhill Baptist Church in Massachusetts.

When the fighting in the Revolutionary War began in 1775 at the battles of Lexington and Concord, many men from Haverhill joined the Continental army, and Smith became one of first chaplains hired by the Continental Congress. Hundreds of chaplains served in the army; disproportionate numbers of them were evangelicals like Smith. He was stationed with George Washington in New York City, although some days the officers were so focused on training troops that he was not allowed to preach. Because of the growing threat of a British assault, Smith stayed with his regiment only occasionally. In August, the British army invaded New York, driving Washington and his troops from Manhattan. Smith missed it, having gone to New Jersey to stay with friends and relatives. His struggling health and rambling experiences reflect a larger point about the war's meaning: life went on for most Americans during the war, with only certain moments punctuated by excitement, fear, and violence.[3]

BAPTISTS, LIKE ALL American colonists, watched the growing turmoil between the colonies and Britain with trepidation. In 1765, colonists recoiled at a new tax program instituted by Parliament, the Stamp Act, which forced Americans to pay a duty on the most common printed goods used in the colonies. Even though such a tax was already in effect in England, Americans bristled at the notion that Parliament would levy new taxes without the blessing of colonial representatives. What the colonists really wanted was for their own legislatures, not Parliament, to be responsible for tax policy. British officials were shocked at the ferocity of resistance in the colonies, as people widely refused to pay the stamp tax and mercilessly harassed collection agents. In Boston, a mob hung, beheaded, and burned an effigy of stamp agent Andrew Oliver before wrecking his home. Oliver resigned the next day. Across the colonies, the act became unenforceable, and in early 1766 Parliament repealed it.

Samuel Stillman, pastor of Boston's First Baptist Church, rejoiced at this development. In the 1750s, Stillman had experienced conversion and baptism under Oliver Hart's ministry in Charleston, South Carolina. Stillman worked as a pastor in South Carolina and New Jersey before settling in Boston, where he became pastor of the First Baptist Church in 1765, just before word of the Stamp Act arrived. The town's unruly response to the act confirmed that Bostonians were "tenacious of [their] rights and liberties," as Stillman put it in a sermon celebrating the law's repeal. The Stamp Act might have signaled a growing threat against Americans' most basic liberties, Stillman believed, including religious freedom. But now, the pastor assured his congregation, the repeal heralded a "royal confirmation of your civil and religious liberties; these stand in immediate connection with each other." Colonists commonly argued that, were British aggression against political rights allowed to go unchecked, London might take away colonists' ability to worship God freely, too.

The decision to revoke the act, approved by King George III, indicated that all was right again in the empire, Stillman thought. The colonists had a deep-seated respect and love for the king that the Stamp Act could not shake. They assumed that he had their best interests at heart: "Our most gracious sovereign is the father of his people. . . . We, his most faithful subjects in America, have no small share in his royal affections." In England, some whispered that the Americans really meant to pursue independence from Britain, but Stillman would not hear of it—the outcome of this crisis confirmed that Americans would never have to separate from Britain, he said. If presented with the possibility of declaring independence, colonists would denounce it. The colonists remained "inviolably attached to his Majesty's most sacred person." The year was 1766, and with the happy news of the Stamp Act's demise, there seemed no reason to doubt that the American union with Britain would go on indefinitely.[4]

THE YEARS LEADING up to the American Revolution were a time of growth for Baptists. In New England, Baptists sought greater respectability, especially through the establishment of their first college, the College of Rhode Island (later Brown University). The key figures in the establishment of the College of Rhode Island were James Manning and Isaac Backus. The Separate Baptists, unlike those affiliated with the Philadelphia Association, were suspicious of educational requirements for pastors. Most of the early Separate Baptists, including Backus, did not have a college education, and they believed that the only essential qualification to preach was the indwelling presence of the Holy Spirit. Requiring a college degree for pastors seemed to denigrate the role of spiritual calling, for God would presumably call whomever he wanted, regardless of their worldly credentials. The Baptists looked to the example of Christ's apostles, some of whom were untutored fishermen.

Nevertheless, Baptist leaders in the 1760s came to believe that they needed a college to train pastors. None of the Baptists opposed education per se, and many accepted the idea that specialized education in theology could help develop better pastors. They worried that some aspiring pastors might go to Harvard, Yale, or Princeton and be tempted to become Congregationalists or Presbyterians. Already in 1756, Baptists had founded the precollegiate Hopewell Academy in New Jersey. One of its early graduates was James Manning, a New Jersey pastor affiliated with the Philadelphia Association. Baptists hoped that if they became a more respectable denomination with educated pastors, colonial religious authorities would have a harder time justifying their mistreatment.

In the early 1760s, Manning and Backus began to develop plans for the college, collaborating with some non-Baptists, including Congregationalist pastor Ezra Stiles of Newport, Rhode Island. Rhode Island had no college and was friendly to the Baptists because of its policy of religious freedom. So in 1764 the College of Rhode Island was opened in Warren.

Some Separate Baptists were appalled by the development, thinking that Backus, a college trustee, had sold them out in the name of respectability. One critic wrote, "I cannot see how he, acting faithfully, upon his own declared principles, can long keep his standing as a member of that body the chief of whose principles and views differing so widely from his." Backus countered that Baptists needed this kind of school to help train more effective pastors, but he admitted that there was danger in associating education with godliness. Baptists should "never imagine to confine Christ or his church, to that, or any other human school for ministers," he cautioned. Despite initial reservations, by the time the college moved to its permanent home in Providence, in 1770, the school had become widely accepted among both Separate Baptists and those of the Philadelphia Association.[5]

Brown remained the lone Baptist college in America for about half a century. Then other northern Baptist colleges appeared, including Maine's Colby College (1817), New York's Colgate University (1820), and Ohio's Denison University (1831). Baptist institutions of higher learning came more slowly to the South, but sixty years after the founding of the College of Rhode Island, Baptists founded a spate of new schools there, too, including Furman University in South Carolina (1826), Wake Forest in North Carolina (1834), Judson College (originally Judson Female Institute) in Alabama (1839), and Baylor, chartered by the Republic of Texas in 1845. Leading Baptists were also key players at state institutions; for example, Baptist pastor Basil Manly served from 1837 to 1855 as the University of Alabama's second president.

The founding of Brown illustrated the New England Separate Baptists' growing sophistication, and their increasing similarity to the more established Philadelphia Association. The founding of New England's Warren Association in 1767 further enhanced the move toward the mainstream. James Manning also spearheaded the founding of this association, which was modeled after Philadelphia's. As with the College of Rhode Island, some radical Separates viewed the association with suspicion, fearing that it could wield coercive authority over Baptist churches. But Manning insisted that the association would serve primarily as an advisory body and a coordinator of efforts on behalf of religious liberty. It would allow the Separates to become, as the association put it, "important in the eye of the civil powers." By founding the college and the Warren Association, the New England Baptists hoped to achieve the kind of serious reputation commanded by their brethren in the Middle Colonies. If they did, they believed, surely persecution would stop.[6]

EFFORTS TO CULTIVATE strong institutions came with social dividends, as illustrated by the 1764 funeral of Ellis Callender, a merchant and son of the late Elisha Callender, pastor of Boston's Baptist church. Callender's funeral garnered notice in the newspapers as the first one to eschew expensive imported mourning clothes. This was an act of protest against the recently passed Sugar Act of 1764, a British law that elicited the first rumblings of resistance from the colonists. The gentility of the affair was still evident, as Callender's sister wore (as reported in the newspaper) "a black bonnet, gloves, ribbons, and handkerchief." The funeral procession featured a "large procession of merchants and gentlemen of figure" who admired the family for their virtuous stand against the mourning-clothes tradition, "which had proved ruinous to many in this community." The funeral placed Callender's family in the first rank of Boston's elites.[7]

Not all Baptists garnered respect, however, nor was full religious liberty quick in arriving. In Ashfield, Massachusetts, in 1770, town authorities seized hundreds of acres of land from Baptists who had refused to pay to support the local Congregational church. In response to Baptist protests, Ashfield authorities asserted that the Baptists' claims to natural rights were "wholly superseded in this case by civil obligations and in matters of taxation individuals cannot with the least propriety plead them." Ashfield was unwittingly parroting the British reply to Americans' argument against taxation without representation. Ashfield's seizure of property, however, was so egregious that the Warren Association appealed directly to King George III for relief. The king annulled the law enabling the confiscation. This episode made many New England Baptists wonder whether their liberties were safer under the king of England than under colonial authorities. Ashfield's Baptist minister called the Sons of Liberty, who led the resistance against Britain, undeserving of their name: they only wanted "liberty from oppression that they might have liberty to oppress!"[8]

The most spectacular instances of persecution against the Baptists in the decade prior to the War for Independence occurred in Virginia. Aggressive evangelism and unwillingness to comply with regulations of the established church made the Virginia Baptists seem like revolutionaries. Numerous Baptists suffered beatings and imprisonment for illegal preaching. Samuel Harris, one of the early converts of Daniel Marshall of Sandy Creek, North Carolina, became known as the "Virginia Apostle" because of his heart-piercing preaching. But his meetings attracted unwanted attention, too. In one instance in Orange County, a man dragged Harris down from his pulpit "and hauled him about, sometimes by the hand, sometimes by the leg, and sometimes by the hair of his head," an early Baptist historian recalled. Harris's supporters clashed with his attackers, and friends brought Harris to a nearby house, where he took refuge in a hidden attic.[9]

In Culpeper, Virginia, itinerant James Ireland was also arrested and jailed for illegal preaching. Some of his followers came to hear him preach through the cell grate, but opponents drove them away. A number of his African American devotees were whipped for coming to see him. Ireland's enemies would not relent, and some burned brimstone and "Indian pepper" at the cell door, hoping to suffocate him. Some tormentors even urinated on him as he tried to preach. All told, about thirty-four Baptist preachers were jailed in Virginia in the 1760s and 1770s.[10]

Persecution hardly strangled Baptist growth. Individual seekers kept finding forgiveness and assurance among the Baptists. John Taylor, one penitent who attended James Ireland's meetings, wrestled terribly with whether God could ever forgive him for his sins. For a time, Taylor became convinced that he was damned, and that pleading for mercy would do no good. But then, in 1772, Taylor found himself meditating on the words of an Isaac Watts hymn, "I'm Not Ashamed to Own My Lord." Watts's poetic hymns had taken hold in evangelical churches during the Great Awakening; these songs often exercised enormous power over believers. One verse in particular, "Jesus, my God, I know his name," deeply affected Taylor:

> This verse kept repeating in my mind till I got out at the door, when it kindled into a heavenly flame. It seemed as if the name Jesus, never sounded so sweet before. . . . This scripture rose up in my mind, "Reach hither thy finger and behold my hands, and reach hither thy hand and thrust it into my side, and be not faithless but believing" [John 20:27]. I saw no man, nor heard any voice; but according to my sincere belief, the Lord Jesus spake the words, and to me, and was very near. A tide of heavenly joy flowed into my soul, and of the rapturous kind far exceeding any thing I had ever felt before. . . . I scarcely knew whether I was in the body or out of the body. I now believed I was born of God; that Christ was my Saviour.

Two weeks later, James Ireland baptized Taylor by immersion.[11]

Mary Read of Rehoboth, Massachusetts, had an even more dramatic experience than Taylor, according to a 1769 account by Isaac Backus. The ailing Read had been unable to walk for three years, but one day, while meditating on her Bible reading, these words (from Luke 8:48) "came to her like a voice audibly spoken, 'Daughter be of good cheer, thy sins are forgiven thee, arise and walk.'" She wondered whether this could truly be the voice of God speaking. But again, these words "came unto her, 'It is I, the Lord of Hosts, that speaketh unto thee, arise and walk, fear not.'" She heard the same message two more times. Then, as Backus told it:

> While the words were repeating, the use of her limbs were restored to her again; the cords and sinews on one side of her, which had been shrunk up six or seven inches, for so long a time, were then stretched out, and she became straight, and received strength, and immediately rose up from her bed and walked!

As if to confirm the healing, the "55th Hymn of Doctor Watts" then came to her mind. This was Watts's "Hezekiah's Song: Or, Sickness and Recovery," which includes the following lines:

> *Jehovah speaks the healing word,*
> *And no disease withstands:*
> *Fevers and plagues obey the Lord,*
> *And fly at his commands.*

In time, many Baptists would consider such experiences dubious and extreme. In the Revolutionary era, however, they were common.[12]

Baptist growth continued in the South, too, including among African Americans. Unlike many Anglicans, Separate Baptists evangelized slaves and sometimes gave blacks positions of leadership as exhorters, deacons, and even elders in mixed-race congregations. The Separate Baptists' message of God's love for slaves sometimes also translated into a critique of slavery, but such critiques were fitful and never gained much momentum.

One of the most influential early African American Baptist converts was David George. George was born into slavery in Virginia, and he suffered a childhood filled with fear and violence. He saw his mother, brothers, and sisters mercilessly whipped for minor offenses. George ran away from his master, but he was taken captive by Creek Indians and later purchased by another slave master in Silver Bluff, located near the Savannah River in western South Carolina. There he encountered the African American Baptist preacher George Liele and the white pastor Wait Palmer. David George became convinced that God would forgive him of his sins, and he was baptized by Palmer. Soon George also began preaching and was appointed an elder over a new Baptist congregation, the Silver Bluff Church, around 1773. The dislocations of the American Revolution led George to go to Nova Scotia in 1782 and, ultimately, across the Atlantic to Sierra Leone in 1792. But his Silver Bluff congregation was the first continuously operating African American church in the country, the first surge of what would become a deluge of African American Baptist converts.[13]

EVEN BEFORE THE American Revolution, Baptists had begun to turn their eyes to the western frontier, knowing that the Ohio River Valley held enormous potential for expansion and evangelism. Native Americans still inhabited these lands, and evangelicals saw them as potential converts. David Jones, the pastor of Crosswicks Baptist Church in Freehold, New Jersey, exemplified this fascination with the West and Native Americans. Jones took impromptu visits to Shawnee and Delaware villages along the Ohio River in 1772 and 1773, and while he had spiritual motivations, he also meant to survey possible places to settle in a future American colony on the Ohio, a scheme envisioned by several leading Pennsylvanians, including Benjamin Franklin.

Jones's preaching to the Indians ended in near-total disappointment, and he concluded that if he had known how resistant the natives were to Christianity, he might never have left home. He could speak with almost none of the Indians, for neither knew the other's language, and he struggled to keep good interpreters. Jones considered most of the Indians barbaric, and his trips did nothing to dispel that impression. One drunk Indian tried to stab him, and like many Anglo-Americans on the frontier, he recoiled at stories of certain Natives' terroristic methods. To torture white prisoners, he wrote, "a knife is run between the wrist bones, and drawing deer sinews through the wounds, they proceed to bind them naked to a post in the long house, and, instead of sympathizing, make all imaginable diversion of the helpless agonizing captive." The Indians would often make sport of the prisoner, until they finally killed him or her, and left the body in the open air for birds to eat.[14]

Jones concluded that the Indians knew nothing whatsoever about God but were lost in depravity. One day he watched a procession of mock devils who taunted him and asked for tobacco. Each wore a mask and a bearskin. Jones recorded that "The foremost had a red face, with a prodigious long nose, and big lips; the others had black faces with long chins resembling bears. All had cased tortoise shells, with artificial necks." They ended the procession with a dance mimicking a bear. Jones wrote "How absolutely needful to be born again! and how great that work of God's Spirit, to make such as these new creatures." Despite his pessimism, Jones hoped that a concerted effort could Christianize Native Americans. Maybe someday the Baptists would make such an effort, he hoped.[15]

BEFORE BAPTISTS AND other settlers could enter the West en masse, however, the Revolution intervened. Like all American colonists, Baptists had to react to the crisis that precipitated the war. One of the most influential Baptist voices of Patriot resistance was also one of the most unlikely. In 1772, the English Baptist pastor John Allen arrived in Boston, having fallen into debt and legal trouble in London, where he had lost his pastoral position. In 1769, Allen was charged with forging a promissory note, and though he was acquitted, he felt that he needed a fresh start in America. He preached for a time at Boston's Second Baptist Church. Some members doubted his qualifications, but church records show that "a number of gentlemen were desirous to hear him (Sons of Liberty)." The Sons of Liberty saw Allen as an advocate for America's God-given rights. But when the details of Allen's legal troubles became known, he lost his position at Second Baptist.[16]

Allen became one of the most popular advocates for American resistance against Britain when he published *An Oration upon the Beauties of Liberty*, originally delivered as a sermon at Second Baptist. Allen's *Oration* was printed in five editions across four cities, seizing upon the furor created by the burning of the British customs ship *Gaspee* in Rhode Island in 1772. Some Rhode Islanders proposed, preposterously, that Native Americans had perpetrated the attack, but everyone knew that Rhode Island merchants were behind the burning. The British government, becoming increasingly exasperated with the colonists, suggested that it might bring suspects to England for trial, assuming that no American jury would convict their peers. But colonists, led by Allen, protested that depriving the colonists of the right of a local jury trial violated their most basic liberties.

By 1773, most American writers blamed corrupt bureaucrats around King George III for causing the trouble in America. But Allen pointed at the king himself, arguing that when the king sanctioned the violation of the colonists' legal rights, he abrogated his authority to rule over them. Allen referenced the touchy subject of King Charles I's execution by Parliamentarians in 1649 and suggested that King George III might meet the same fate. "I reverence and love my king," Allen wrote, "but I revere the rights of an Englishman before the authority of any king upon the earth. I distinguish greatly between a king and a tyrant, a king is the guardian and trustee of the rights and laws of the people, but a tyrant destroys them." This was heady, seditious stuff. Three years ahead of time, Allen anticipated Thomas Paine's final rejection of King George III's authority in *Common Sense*.[17]

A majority of Baptists supported the Revolution, but they also wanted the campaign for American freedom to lead to disestablishment of the state churches. No one better exemplified this blend of support for both the Patriot cause and religious reform than Isaac Backus. Backus, the Baptists, and other evangelical dissenters pressured the New England governments for relief from supporting the established Congregationalist Church. Backus contended that the crisis with Britain represented a unique opportunity for disestablishment, because Americans' paeans to liberty would be hypocritical if they continued to deny other Americans their own freedom. (Others made the same argument, more pointedly, with regard to American slavery.) In *An Appeal to the Public for Religious Liberty* (1773), Backus asked how anyone could "reasonably expect that he who has the hearts of kings in his hand, will turn the heart of our earthly sovereign to hear the pleas for liberty, of those who will not hear the cries of their fellow-subjects, under their oppressions?"[18]

The First Continental Congress in Philadelphia presented a chance for Baptists to appeal directly to Patriot leaders for religious liberty. The Congress began meeting in September 1774 in reaction to the Coercive Acts, which shut down the Massachusetts government and blocked Boston Harbor's commercial ship traffic. Parliament passed these acts in response to the Boston Tea Party of 1773, in which loads of British East India Company tea were dumped into Boston Harbor. Backus and the Warren Association not only distributed copies of *An Appeal to the Public for Religious Liberty* to members of the Congress but also sent Backus and James Manning to Philadelphia to lobby for their cause.

In October 1774, Backus, Manning, and other Baptist pastors met with leaders of the Massachusetts delegation, including Samuel and John Adams (who were distant cousins). The Baptists presented their case for religious liberty and disestablishment. But the Adamses were unsympathetic and asserted that the burdens of the establishment were so light as to hardly matter. Backus threw the confiscation of Baptists' land in Ashfield in their faces to show just how oppressive the established church could be. Samuel Adams became indignant and "more than once insinuated that these complaints came from enthusiasts who made a merit of suffering persecution, and also that enemies to these colonies had a

hand therein." The Massachusetts delegates ended the meeting by promising to keep the Baptists' grievances in mind, but John Adams said to
Backus that "we might as well expect a change in the solar system, as to
expect they would give up their establishment." This was a disappointing
outcome that heralded years of failure for the Baptists of New England.
Although active persecution did stop, Massachusetts would keep a form
of religious establishment through 1833, when the state finally became
so pluralistic that the Congregationalists were willing to abandon their
status as the official church.[19]

With this kind of reaction coming from the likes of John and Samuel
Adams, it is not surprising that many Baptists balked at cooperating with
the Patriot rebellion against Britain. Congregationalist pastor and leading Patriot Ezra Stiles of Newport, Rhode Island, doubted the Baptists'
and pacifist Quakers' commitment to resistance against Britain. "Though
some few Baptists and Quakers are heartily with us, yet too many are so
much otherwise, that was all America of their temper or coolness in the
cause the Parliament would easily carry their points and triumph over
American liberty," Stiles wrote worriedly.[20]

Stiles was convinced that James Manning was "against his country in
heart," a Loyalist who was merely "affecting neutrality." Stiles believed
that Manning never prayed for the success of Washington's army until a
visit by George Washington to his church forced the duty upon him. Stiles
reported every rumor about Manning that he could gather. It was probably
true, as Stiles noted, that Manning wondered whether he and the Baptists
could trust Congregationalist and Anglican Patriots who had so routinely
persecuted them. Stiles had no patience for this kind of reluctance from
"bigoted Baptist politicians."[21]

Some Baptists, convinced of the righteousness of the American cause,
did promote the Revolution among their brethren. For example, the South
Carolina Patriot assembly sent Baptist pastor Oliver Hart of Charleston on
a recruiting campaign through the backcountry to convince reluctant settlers to embrace the Revolution. Hart traveled with Presbyterian minister
William Tennent III through the central part of the colony in the summer of 1775. Hart found that the message of American resistance was not
universally welcomed. One of Hart's hosts, Reverend Philip Mulkey of the
Fairforest Baptist Church, had sided with the British, yet he allowed Hart
to speak to his ambivalent congregation about the war. Some apparently
thought that Bostonians had recklessly stirred the conflict; one said he
did not care if "1000 Bostonians might be killed in battle." Overall, Hart

found the settlers to be "obstinate and irritated to an extreme," and suspicious of the Patriot leaders' motivations. But Hart and Tennent did convince a number of South Carolinians to pledge their loyalty to the South Carolina provincial government in the fight against Britain.[22]

Backcountry reluctance reflected widespread skepticism among pioneer settlers about the colonies' political leadership. Some Separate Baptists also adhered to a remarkable strain of pacifism. Certain Baptist ministers associated with the Sandy Creek churches in North Carolina warned their congregations that anyone fighting for either side of the Revolution would face excommunication. Pastor Erasmus Kelly of First Baptist Church in Newport, Rhode Island, also argued that it was not legitimate for Christians to take up arms for any reason, although he conceded that if any scenario demanded armed violence, it was the Patriots' cause. He also prayed publicly for the success of American forces.[23]

Other pacifist Baptists were not so accommodating toward the Patriots. James Miles of Cross Roads Meeting House near the Haw River in North Carolina went on a tirade against the Patriot leaders and recruiters. "Show him a great man with a half moon in his hat with liberty written upon it and his hat full of feathers," he said, "and he would show you a devil, and that poor men were bowing and scraping to them, and [the Patriots] leading them to hell as soon as they had come from the Congress." Miles averred that these charlatans "were blow'd up as big as a blather and that he did not value the Congress nor the Committee [of Correspondence] no more than as [a] parcel of raccoon dogs, for he got his [commands] from the King and the field officers got their [commands] from hell or the Devil." The Patriot leaders of North and South Carolina understandably worried that this kind of nonparticipating sentiment might capture the hearts of backcountry Baptists.[24]

Unlike James Miles, some backcountry Baptists enthusiastically supported the Revolution, most notably the young pastor Richard Furman of the High Hills of Santee Church, who would later replace Oliver Hart as pastor of Charleston's First Baptist congregation. Furman, reared as an Anglican, experienced conversion and received believer's baptism when he was sixteen and almost immediately began preaching at High Hills of Santee, in eastern South Carolina. When fighting commenced in South Carolina in late 1775, Furman penned a letter on behalf of the Patriot cause. He argued that Parliament had repeatedly acted against the colonists' rights by passing unfair taxes and asserting legal supremacy over America. He also excoriated Parliament for sanctioning the Quebec Act of 1774, which allowed the free practice of Catholicism in British Canada. Furman and many other commentators played on the American colonists' intense anti-Catholicism: "They have broken the principles of the [British] constitution, by taking away the power of our assemblies, and by establishing Popery, contrary to law, in one of the provinces, which gives us reason to suspect, they have a design to impose the same upon other provinces; at least they claim that power." According to Furman, Patriots had to resist, lest they lose both political and religious liberty. Patriot commander Richard Richardson of High Hills distributed Furman's letter among backcountry settlers during a December 1775 campaign to seize a key fort at Ninety Six, South Carolina, from Loyalist allies of Britain.[25]

Furman's advocacy for the Patriot cause made him a target for the British. He had to flee the state in 1780 as the war there turned against the Patriots. In May, Charleston fell to the British after a terrible siege, with the loss of five thousand American troops—their worst defeat of the war. In August, Patriot troops suffered another humiliating defeat at Camden, South Carolina, which was uncomfortably close to High Hills of Santee. Furman and his family sought refuge in north-central North Carolina, near the Virginia line. There he continued to preach widely, and in his travels Furman met and became friends with Patrick Henry, the great Patriot orator of Virginia, whose home was in south-central Virginia. Furman returned to the High Hills Church in 1782, then in 1787 he accepted a call to become pastor of Charleston's First Baptist Church.[26]

Although a number of Baptists refused to support the Patriot cause, most Baptists agreed with Furman that the Patriots' grievances against Britain were compelling. The Separate Baptists of Virginia declared in 1775 that although they had many religious differences with their fellow Americans, they shared the same political cause of liberty. They advised "military resistance against Great Britain in her unjust invasion, tyrannical oppression, and repeated hostilities." The Philadelphia Association took a more muted tone, worrying over the "awful impending calamities" of war and recommending that congregations hold days of fasting to pray for God's help and forgiveness for America's sins.[27]

The war did hold "awful impending calamities" for many Americans, including Baptists. Numerous churches were damaged, disrupted, and scattered by the conflict. Charleston's First Baptist Church essentially ceased to function for two years after the city fell to the British. Its popular pastor, Oliver Hart, fled for New Jersey and never returned to the South. The British reportedly used Charleston's Baptist meetinghouse for storage. Without securing the help of the talented Richard Furman, one wonders whether Charleston would have maintained its historic influence in Baptist circles after the war. Baptist churches elsewhere felt the heavy hand of the war, too. A Seventh-Day (Saturday Sabbath) Baptist congregation in Shrewsbury, New Jersey, for example, apparently stopped meeting for about two and a half years between 1778 and 1781.[28]

One of the most poignant scenes of the war transpired at the small Baptist church in Cambridge, New York. In 1777, the British sent a massive army to invade upstate New York. As the British approached Cambridge and nearby Bennington, Vermont, many church members at Cambridge doubted that the Continental army could withstand the fearsome foe. A number of them defected to the British side the night before the battle, and the British forced some of them to serve in their army. "During the bloody conflict," a Baptist historian recalled, "the heavens and earth witnessed the shocking spectacle of brethren, who, but a few days before had set together at the table of the Lord, arranged in direful hostility against each other, amidst the clangor of arms and the rage of battle. Brother fighting against brother! Such are the horrors and unnatural effects of war!" This wrenching experience ruined the church, and when the pastor returned in 1778, he could only find three members left with whom to hold meetings. Like many Baptist churches in the area, however, Cambridge's soon experienced revival again. By 1780, the membership stood at a robust 140.[29]

EVEN THE WORST depredations of war could not permanently douse awakenings, and New England saw a remarkable season of revival in the later stages of the Revolution that became known as the "New Light Stir." The New Light Stir was punctuated by New England's "Dark Day" of May 19, 1780, when much of the region fell under an eerie, smoky pall. The gloom was apparently quite stark, as birds returned to their roosts early, thinking it was night. Forest fires in Canada likely produced the darkness, but many in New England interpreted it as a sign from God and a possible harbinger of Christ's return.

The fright caused by the Dark Day kindled a new season of awakening among Baptists. One pastor reported from Connecticut that the "Sabbath after the late uncommon darkness I observed uncommon attention and solemnity among the people." A new sense of religious seriousness had begun at the Third Baptist Church of Middleborough, Massachusetts, in March 1780; by the end of May, Pastor Asa Hunt wrote that "God is doing wonders amongst us." At a meeting after regular worship, a group of converts retired to Hunt's house for singing and prayer, and the session reached heights of spiritual ecstasy Hunt had never seen. He likened it to the day of Pentecost, when the Holy Spirit had originally been poured out on believers. "Such rejoicing of saints and cries of sinners I never heard," he wrote. Between May and July, Hunt's tiny church baptized fifty-four new converts.[30]

Hunt's church also produced the most remarkable Baptist enlistee in the Continental army: Deborah Sampson, who posed as a man in order to serve. Sampson joined Third Baptist Middleborough as the revival was winding down. She was a schoolteacher in Middleborough and would have had to give a testimony of conversion in order to join the church. She did not tarry long with the Baptists, however, as she attempted to join the army under false pretenses in the spring of 1782 and ran afoul of the congregation for doing so.[31]

Minutes from a meeting held on September 3, 1782, recorded the church's consideration of the case: "Deborah Sampson, a member of the church who last Spring was accused of dressing in men's clothes and enlisting as a soldier in the army, and although she was not convicted, yet was strongly suspected of being guilty, and for sometime before behaved very loose and un-Christian like, and at last left our parts in a secret manner." The church withdrew fellowship from Sampson, who soon successfully joined the army as "Robert Shurtliff." She served for seventeen months, surviving grievous battle wounds in New York in 1782, and was honorably discharged in 1783.[32]

JUST AS THE revivals of the 1740s had spun off the Separate Baptists, the New Light Stir also fostered more radical, visionary sects. The Shakers, led by the messianic visionary Mother Ann Lee, traced their public ministry in America to the Dark Day of 1780. Among the Baptists, the most important offshoots of the New Light Stir were the Freewill Baptists, who combined the evangelical zeal of the Separate Baptists with a trenchant critique of Calvinist theology. The Freewill Baptists' leader was Benjamin Randel, a New Hampshire tailor who was one of the very last converts of the great revivalist George Whitefield. The unconverted Randel was skeptical about evangelical piety, but he grudgingly agreed to hear Whitefield preach in Portsmouth, New Hampshire, in 1770. Soon thereafter, the aging Whitefield died in Newburyport, Massachusetts, and the news of his demise tormented

Randel with thoughts of his own eternal destiny. Soon Randel experienced conversion, and he also became convinced that believer's baptism was the only proper mode. In 1776, he received baptism by immersion and began preaching.[33]

Up to this point, Randel had followed a fairly routine path to Baptist convictions: evangelical conversion, followed by doubts about infant baptism, culminating in believer's baptism and entry into a Baptist church. But Randel also struggled to accept the doctrine of predestination, commonly held among Baptists. He stopped preaching about God's sovereign choice in electing people to be saved. Striving to understand the Scriptures on this point, one day he retired to a cornfield by himself and sat down on a rock. In prayer, he surrendered himself completely to God. He professed that he

> had no feeling of any thing, but the great and awful, terrible and dreadful majesty of God, which sunk me, as it were, into nothing. When I was thus stripped, it appeared to me that I saw a white robe brought and put over me, which covered me all over. I looked down all over me, and I appeared as white as snow. A perfect calm, an awful reverence, and solemn fear of God, pervaded all my soul. A Bible was then presented before the eyes of my mind, and I heard a still small voice, saying look therein. . . . I saw that [the Scriptures] ran in perfect connection with the universal love of God to men—the universal atonement in the work of redemption, by Jesus Christ, who tasted death for every man.

From that day forward, Randel taught that God offered grace and salvation to everyone, not just to the elect. Within a year, Randel had opened fourteen Freewill Baptist churches in Maine and New Hampshire. The Freewill Baptist movement grew quickly in rural New England, to about three hundred congregations by 1827.[34]

Isaac Backus and his network of Calvinist Baptists did not look kindly on the Freewill Baptists, but there was plenty of evangelistic zeal to go around. Backus believed that the revival of 1779–1781 had produced dramatic results not only for the Baptists but for America generally. He considered it the most powerful spiritual event since the heyday of the Great Awakening and estimated that two thousand New Englanders had received believer's baptism in the year 1780 alone. Backus thought it came not a moment too soon for America, as the awakening "was undoubtedly a great means of saving this land from foreign invasion, and from ruin by internal corruption."[35]

Backus did not elaborate on this remarkable claim, but his assessment reflected a broader trend among Baptists: as the Revolutionary War progressed, many Baptists began to identify newly independent America as a nation specially blessed by God. Sometimes this belief was forged by Baptists' intense experiences during the war itself. For example, chaplain Hezekiah Smith traveled with General Horatio Gates's Continental troops as they faced the lumbering army of British General John Burgoyne in New York in fall 1777 (the campaign that wrecked the Baptist church at Cambridge, New York). Burgoyne brought an army of eight thousand men southward out of Canada into New York. A successful campaign would have isolated New England and probably ended the American rebellion.

Smith prayed with and ministered to American troops during the campaign, and he watched as a "very warm battle" took place on September 19, the Battle of Freeman's Farm. During this battle, Burgoyne tried to flank the American position at Bemis Heights, only to face fierce resistance by troops under the command of General Benedict Arnold, later the infamous traitor. On October 7, the Continentals counterattacked against Burgoyne's army and, as Smith put it, "drove the enemy into their works." Finally, Burgoyne's demoralized army surrendered to Gates at Saratoga on October 17. This was probably the most significant American victory during the war, as Britain's devastating loss soon helped to convince the French to come to the Patriots' aid. In his next Sabbath sermon, Smith captured the moment with a reflection on Exodus 15:2: "The Lord is my strength and song, and he is become my salvation." This text was from Moses and the Israelites' celebration after God drowned the pursuing Egyptian army in the Red Sea.[36]

Smith's exuberance at the victory only grew over time. On the two-year anniversary of the battle, Smith preached to his brigade and memorialized what he called, remarkably, "the grandest conquest ever gained since the creation of the world." He told the assembly that the victory at Saratoga should remind them of "another conquest, which so far exceeds the one now mentioned as scarcely to admit of comparison," Christ's victory over sin and death in his resurrection from the dead. Strange as it might seem for a pastor to say so, Smith concluded that it was proper for Christians to juxtapose Saratoga and the resurrection, "the one affording the happy prospect of earthly felicity, the other the most pleasing hope of celestial happiness." Smith's striking conflation was an early example of some

Baptists' tendency to blend American history with the Christian history of redemption.[37]

In the heat of war, Chaplain Smith joined other Baptists (and Christians from other denominations), such as Philadelphia's William Rogers, in making a tight connection between the success of American arms and the advancement of the kingdom of Christ. Rogers was the first student at the Baptists' College of Rhode Island, and in 1772 he became pastor at First Baptist Church in Philadelphia. Like Hezekiah Smith, Rogers left his pastorate and became a chaplain in the Continental army, working as brigade chaplain to Pennsylvania troops. In 1779, the brigade joined General John Sullivan's campaign against the Iroquois Indians of New York, who had allied with the British.

Like many Anglo-Americans, Rogers was disgusted with the British for allying with the Iroquois, whom he considered utterly barbaric. He wondered how any American could countenance loyalty to British officials who, as he saw it, commissioned Native Americans to torture and murder white colonists. (Rogers failed to note that frontier settlers had committed their share of outrages against Indians.) On Sunday, July 4, 1779, Rogers preached to the troops on Psalm 32:10: "He that trusteth in the Lord, mercy shall compass him about." In a rousing conclusion to the sermon, Rogers reminded the men, "Our fathers trusted and the Lord did deliver them; they cried unto Him and were delivered; they trusted in Him and were not confounded. Even so may it be with us, for the sake of Christ Jesus, who came to give freedom to the world." With these words ringing in their heads, the troops began a campaign in which they burned forty Iroquois towns, razing their crops and orchards.[38]

The growing Baptist enthusiasm for the new United States was perhaps best expressed by the Warren Association in 1784. The war had ended at Yorktown, Virginia, in 1781, when George Washington's army caught Lord Cornwallis, the British commander, in a pincer movement with French warships arriving in Chesapeake Bay. Then in 1783, American diplomats secured favorable terms for their nation in the Treaty of Paris. Patriots basked in the victory, which to most observers seemed guided by the hand of Providence. James Manning had received the news of the war's beginning with much trepidation, but now he and Isaac Backus heralded its conclusion as a sign from heaven. "The American Revolution, which has been accomplished by many astonishing interpositions of Providence, . . . stands closely connected with many others, which will take place in their order, and unite in one glorious end, even the advancement and completion of the Redeemer's kingdom," they exulted. "Nor is it at all improbable, that America is reserved in the mind of Jehovah, to be the grand theater on which the divine Redeemer will accomplish glorious things." They hoped that the American victory over tyranny would be followed quickly by its logical outcome: full religious liberty. Baptists had come a long way from their dissenting English roots and their days as colonial outlaws. The travails of the Revolution had helped them to become Americans.[39]

4

Baptists and Disestablishment

BAPTISTS HOPED THAT the American Revolution would bring about full religious freedom. Thomas Jefferson and James Madison became their key allies in fulfilling that ambition. Jefferson's collaboration with the Baptists was spiritually ironic. He remained relatively quiet about his religious skepticism during his political career, but in truth Jefferson did not believe in the resurrection of Christ, or that Jesus was the Son of God. Nevertheless, in 1802 President Jefferson appealed for religious liberty in a letter that has become known as the "wall of separation" letter.

"I contemplate with sovereign reverence that act of the whole American people which declared that their legislature should 'make no law respecting an establishment of religion, or prohibiting the free exercise thereof,' thus building a wall of separation between church and state," Jefferson wrote. Scholars and jurists have endlessly debated and dissected the meaning of Jefferson's wall of separation. In 1998, the Library of Congress even brought in FBI document analysts to reveal what Jefferson had written in an earlier draft. But the recipients of the letter are interesting as well: Jefferson, the deist, was writing to some of his staunchest supporters, the Baptists of Danbury, Connecticut. These evangelical dissenters still languished under an official state denomination, eleven years after the First Amendment's ban on "an establishment of religion" and guarantee of the "free exercise of religion." Jefferson's letter demonstrated the partnership between skeptical or liberal Christian politicians, and legions of Baptists in the cause of religious liberty. This alliance helped score the Baptists' most significant success of the Revolution, the widespread disestablishment of state churches.

The Danbury Baptist Association was founded in 1790 as an advisory council for Baptist churches in western Connecticut. From the start, it identified "full gospel liberty" as one of its core values. But it found gospel liberty difficult to achieve because of the state's continuing official support for the Congregationalist Church. Dissenters could file certificates to receive exemption from religious taxes, but in 1791 the state tightened the standards to qualify for such exemptions. Baptists thought that even filing the certificates was an obnoxious requirement and an intrusion of the state into the realm of the spirit.[1]

Baptists across America rejoiced when Thomas Jefferson was elected president because they saw Jefferson as the great champion of religious liberty, especially in light of his 1786 Bill for Establishing Religious Freedom in Virginia. The Danbury Baptists wrote to Jefferson in late 1801 and congratulated him on what they saw as a providential victory over John Adams: "We have reason to believe that America's God has raised you up to fill the chair of state out of that good will which he bears to the millions which you preside over." They knew that Jefferson could not alter state laws by fiat, but they hoped that his commitment to religious liberty would, "like the radiant beams of the sun, . . . shine and prevail through these states and all the world till hierarchy and tyranny be destroyed from the earth." To them, one of God's ultimate purposes for the War of Independence was to bring about gospel liberty, and Jefferson's election was the next milestone in that process.[2]

Jefferson was delighted to have such allies in predominantly Federalist New England, and he wanted his response to the letter to sow "useful truths and principles among the people" regarding religious liberty. During the 1800 campaign, Jefferson's opponents had attacked him as a heretic, and as president he was already coming under criticism for failing, unlike his predecessors, to declare public days of prayer and fasting. He wanted to clarify that, just like the Baptists, he really did support the interests of religion in America. To Jefferson, the best way to support religion was to grant all citizens religious liberty. This was the ingenious compromise of the First Amendment's religion clauses: the free exercise of religion required the absence of a national church.[3]

In the carefully drafted letter, Jefferson wrote that because he believed "that religion is a matter which lies solely between man and his God, that he owes account to none other for his faith or his worship, [and] that the legitimate powers of government reach actions only, and not opinions," he treasured the separation of church and state enshrined in the First Amendment. He looked forward to the "progress of those sentiments" at the state level, too. But he and the Baptists would have to wait until 1818 for Connecticut to disestablish the Congregationalist Church.[4]

Beginning with the Supreme Court's decision in *Everson v. Board of Education* (1947), jurists have used Jefferson's metaphor as a key gloss for interpreting the First Amendment's establishment clause. (They have also "incorporated" the establishment clause so that it applies to the states as well as the national government.) In *Everson*, Justice Hugo Black, an Alabaman and lapsed Baptist, cited Jefferson's letter and declared that the First Amendment's wall of separation must be "high and impregnable." But is a modern strict separationist view of church-state relations what the Danbury Baptists (or Jefferson) wanted? Did they wish for government to have no connection whatsoever with religion?

A clue to the answer came two days after Jefferson sent the "wall of separation" letter. That Sunday, an old ally of Jefferson's in the fight for religious liberty, Elder John Leland, preached before a joint session of Congress, with the president in attendance. Leland explicated the biblical text "Behold a greater [one] than Solomon is here." An incredulous Federalist congressman complained in his diary that "such a farrago, bawled with stunning voice, horrid tone, frightful grimaces, and extravagant gestures, . . . was never heard by any decent auditory before." Whatever else the wall metaphor meant in 1802, it permitted a Baptist pastor to preach before Congress. That remarkable moment, capping the dissenters' celebration of Jefferson's election, illuminated the alliance between evangelical Baptists and skeptics such as Jefferson that, in time, won disestablishment across the whole nation. That victory was the most important religious outcome of the American Revolution.[5]

AT THE BEGINNING of the American Revolution, most states had some kind of religious establishment, even if that only meant that officeholders were required to take a sacred oath. But most states also modified their establishments during the Revolution, moving toward greater religious liberty. In many cases, pressure from evangelical dissenters, especially Baptists, was the key factor that drove these changes. They did not push only in one direction: during the Second Great Awakening, many evangelicals would support voluntary and legal reforms, including Sabbath and blasphemy laws, to bolster the Christian character of public life.

Nevertheless, the Revolutionary period laid the legal foundation for religious liberty.[6]

In Virginia, where harsh persecution of Baptists continued through the early 1770s, Baptists began to realize that they could most effectively advocate for religious liberty by making their allegiance to the Patriot cause contingent upon the end of persecution. They explained that no one should expect them to serve in the military or otherwise support a government that continued to deny them the free exercise of religion. Already by 1770, the Virginia legislature had received a petition (a political device commonly employed by the Baptists) complaining that whereas Anglican parsons were exempt from military service, Baptist pastors were not. The legislature refused to grant the Baptists relief from this policy. But that was in 1770, and the grinding war with Britain had not yet begun. After 1776, Virginia authorities found it more difficult to refuse requests for fair treatment from dissenters.[7]

In 1774, the conscience of twenty-three-year-old James Madison was pricked as Virginia authorities continued to fine and imprison Baptists for illegal preaching. He wrote to a college friend deploring "that diabolical hell-conceived principle of persecution." He expected the legislature to continue ignoring the Baptists' petitions for equal treatment. The defenders of Anglican superiority fueled the dissenters' maltreatment by inventing "incredible and extravagant stories . . . of the monstrous effects of the enthusiasm [religious frenzy] prevalent among the sectaries." He anticipated that the establishmentarian Anglicans would "naturally employ all their art and interest to depress their rising adversaries." Madison, who remained an Anglican himself, resolved to do all he could to break the shackles of religious intolerance.[8]

In the meantime, Baptists did all they could to cajole the authorities into granting religious freedom. As the crisis with Britain reached the breaking point, Virginia began assembling its militia in March 1775, fortified by Patrick Henry's celebrated "Liberty or Death" speech. Baptists gave their members permission to join the militia, but they demanded that the legislature allow Baptist chaplains to minister to Baptist soldiers. In a petition, they acknowledged that the theological differences between them and the Anglicans were significant, but that "with respect to matters of a civil nature, [we are] embarked in the same common cause." The "shocking oppression which in a British cloud hangs over our American continent" compelled them to join their sometime oppressors in the Patriot movement. The Baptists assured the Virginia convention tasked with organizing resistance to Britain that many Baptists were willing to serve in the militia, but that they expected respect in exchange for that service. That respect would begin with permitting Baptist chaplains. The convention reluctantly agreed to this arrangement. It could not afford to do anything that might alienate potential allies against the British.[9]

As Virginia moved toward establishing a state government independent from Britain, Baptists continued to petition for full religious liberty. Again, they implied that refusing to afford liberty of conscience would encourage divisions among Virginians when unity was needed most. An appeal from Prince William County asserted that "the strictest unanimity among ourselves is very necessary in this most critical conjuncture of public affairs," so Baptists requested that they be granted the freedom to worship God their own way, without interference. They also asked that they be allowed to financially support only their own ministers, not the established ministers, and that their pastors be allowed to marry and bury people. "These things granted," they wrote in a veiled warning, "we will gladly unite with our brethren of other denominations" in the cause of American freedom.[10]

The tide of religious freedom was rising, bolstered by Baptist appeals and a sincere desire by Patriot leaders to match the rhetoric of liberty with the actual practice of it (for free men, at least). When Virginia adopted a constitution for its new state government, it included a Declaration of Rights. Fifty-year-old George Mason of Fairfax, Virginia, wanted this declaration to guarantee "fullest toleration" of dissenters, but James Madison argued for a broader assurance of "free exercise of religion." Madison won out, and so the Declaration of Rights affirmed "that religion, or the duty which we owe to our Creator, and the manner of discharging it, can be directed only by reason and conviction, not by force or violence; and therefore all men are equally entitled to the free exercise of religion, according to the dictates of conscience, and that it is the mutual duty of all to practice Christian forbearance, love, and charity towards each other." Madison also introduced language that would have set the stage for the disestablishment of the Anglican Church, but the convention rejected the proposal. The time had not yet come to decide whether the state would continue to have an official denomination.[11]

Baptists thought the time *was* right to abandon the established church. A relatively pleasant exchange of public letters between the Baptists of Louisa County and the new governor, Patrick Henry, hid latent tensions beneath Virginians' zeal for the war. The Baptists knew that Governor

Henry wanted to maintain state support for religion, but he also had a long track record of defending the rights of Virginia dissenters. So they simply commended Henry's "constant attachment to the glorious cause of liberty, and the rights of conscience." Henry was understandably pleased that the letter did not reopen the old wound of establishment, and he declared that in this season of war, "those religious distinctions which formerly produced some heats are now forgotten." But those "heats" were not forgotten for long.[12]

In mid-October 1776, Baptists and other dissenters delivered a prodigious "Ten Thousand Name" petition to Virginia legislators, which powerfully argued for disestablishment and full religious liberty. The Patriots complained of unfair British taxes, the dissenters scolded, yet Virginia placed even worse taxes on its own dissenters. Equal liberty was

> the birthright of every good member of the state [but] has been what your petitioners have been deprived of in that taxation [of] their property hath been wrested from them and given to those from whom they have received no equivalent. Your petitioners therefore having long groaned under the burden of an ecclesiastical establishment beg leave to move your honourable House that this as well as every other yoke may be broken and that the oppressed may go free.[13]

Jefferson and Madison both worked on a House committee in Richmond that handled the flood of petitions from dissenters. Jefferson later wrote that the barrage precipitated the "severest contests in which I have ever been engaged." And no wonder: the signatures on the Ten Thousand Name petition alone probably represented more than 10 percent of Virginia's white male population.[14]

Virginia legislators could not afford to ignore these kinds of popular grievances. They had a war to fight. So in December 1776, the assembly exempted Baptists and other non-Anglicans from paying required tithes to support the Anglican Church. Moreover, it suspended the establishment tax altogether, a policy Virginia maintained until the war's conclusion. Some of the Anglican Church's privileges remained, and the state would consider resuming tithes for a "general assessment" for religion in 1784, a modified establishment that would still mandate that Virginians pay a religious tax, but the taxpayer could choose which church would receive it. In the meantime, Virginia's dissenters had pressured the state into granting considerable relief, cleverly using their loyal service in the war to make progress toward liberty of conscience.[15]

THE BAPTISTS OF NEW ENGLAND, if anything, made a more vociferous case for religious liberty than their brethren to the south. But the established Congregationalist churches of New England—the successors to the Puritan churches of the colonial era—were a solid fixture of nearly every town in the region, and they proved difficult to dislodge.

Persecution plagued New England Baptists, too. An editorial written a month before the Declaration of Independence lamented how the state government continued to take people's money and property in order to support Congregationalist preachers they did not wish to hear. "I should have thought that the present exertions in the cause of civil liberty, would for a while have prevented such glaring instances of religious tyranny," the writer confessed. The hypocrisy was insufferable. The writer called on New Englanders to accept a better way, one that God might bless: "Let us therefore proclaim liberty to the enslaved, and let the oppressed go free, that the God of freedom may espouse our cause; and give success to our attempts to prevent the establishment of tyranny among us."[16]

But legal difficulties and harassment continued. One notorious incident transpired in Pepperell, Massachusetts, in 1778, where a group of the town's leading Congregationalists broke up the meeting of a visiting Baptist preacher and told the Baptists "upon your peril" never to come to Pepperell again. "We are united, and desire no Baptists in town. This is for your interest." The letter was signed on behalf of "all friends to freedom and unitedness."[17]

The Baptists refused to heed this warning, and a Congregationalist posse tried to disrupt a baptismal service shortly thereafter. They mocked the Baptists by dragging a dog into the river for baptism. When the Baptists cited their right to liberty of conscience, a captain from the local committee of safety told them, "Hold your tongue, or I will beat your teeth down your throat!" The Baptists tried to move their service to a more isolated place on the river, but the antagonists caught up with them, threatened them with whips, and told them to get out of town. The episode reminded Baptists that even in the middle of the American Revolution, open, violent persecution remained real. And the war was certainly continuing: as the Pepperell Congregationalists menaced the Baptists, George Washington's troops were massing for the ill-fated Battle of Monmouth Courthouse in New Jersey, which happened three days later.[18]

The question of religious liberty in Massachusetts came to a head in 1780, when the state moved to adopt a new constitution. The proposed constitution did guarantee that "no subject shall be hurt, molested, or restrained, in his person, liberty, or estate, for worshipping GOD in the manner and season most agreeable to the dictates of his own conscience." At the same time, it endorsed the legislature's right to continue providing support for churches and ministers.[19]

Baptists were crestfallen. Isaac Backus was particularly irked that in the debate over the religion clauses, John Adams and other supporters of establishment brought up Backus and James Manning's fruitless visit to the Continental Congress in 1774 to appeal for religious liberty. Adams evidently implied that the Baptists were disloyal to the Patriot movement. "If those gentlemen should persist in their accusations against us, without fairly supporting them, . . . the public will judge how far they will deserve regard for the future," Backus noted. Baptists once more hinted that denial of religious liberty could cost the Patriots the allegiance of religious dissenters.[20]

During the Massachusetts ratification process, towns with strong Baptist contingents rose up against Article Three, which endorsed the religious establishment. Indeed, Article Three was the most controversial part of the proposed constitution. The town of Granville spoke for many when it objected on these grounds: first, that "Christ himself is the only Lord of Conscience and King and Law Giver in his Church," and second, that "the interference of the magistrate in matters that belong only to the Christian Church is in our view an encroachment on the Kingly Office of Jesus Christ who stands in no need of the help of any civil legislature." Supporters of Article Three were forced to resort to some fancy counting—they likely did not achieve the required two-thirds of the vote—but the article and the whole constitution were ratified, taking effect in October 1780.[21]

WHEN THE WAR of Independence ended in 1781 at Yorktown, Virginia, the Baptists had already witnessed important progress on disestablishment and religious freedom. Yet they had operated for almost two centuries under a variety of legal disadvantages, and these had never prevented them from preaching the gospel or fostering revival. There were new places to reach, as Americans continued to spill into frontier regions, especially the

Ohio River Valley. The end of the war saw a new phase of expansion and revival for Baptists, newly comfortable with their identity as Americans, whatever legal restrictions and social animosities remained against them.

In Virginia, revival commenced in 1785, even as the controversy over public funding for religion proceeded. John Leland recalled five years later that this "Great Work" began during the summer months, in towns along the course of the James River. According to Leland, these revivals were not sober affairs but scenes of intense spiritual power. It was "nothing strange," he wrote, "to see a great part of the congregation fall prostrate upon the floor or ground; many of whom, entirely lose the use of their limbs for a season." Some cried out for mercy, while others broke out "in such rapturous expressions as these: 'Bless the Lord, O my soul! O, sweet Jesus, how I love thee!'" Some would "jump up, strike their hands together, and shout aloud . . . embrace one another, and fall to the floor." Men and women would find themselves indiscreetly rolling on the floor together. Such tumults lasted for several hours at a time, and various speakers across the meeting room would speak simultaneously. It was, to Leland, such a "heavenly confusion among the preachers, and such a celestial discord among the people," that while it did not edify the mind, it engaged the heart. He knew that some criticized such enthusiasm as raw frenzy, but he also knew that many repented and sincerely experienced conversion in these heated assemblies.[22]

Leland's colleague Henry Toler, pastor of the Nomini Baptist Church, likewise saw fervent, chaotic scenes throughout his travels in Virginia in 1786. At one meeting, a female penitent fell down immobile but kept pleading for sinners to come to Jesus. She remained in this state for an hour. He wondered about the necessity of her display: "Some may give way to their passions and get into form in this manner," but he thought it likely that she sincerely "felt and professed happiness" in the Lord. Women like this convert were allowed—even encouraged—to relate tales of their spiritual experiences publicly, as were African American converts, who regularly attended his preaching, and whom he often baptized. "The Lord is good and converts people of different colors and ranks," Toler noted gratefully.[23]

As with many Baptist preachers, Toler's successes attracted hecklers and persecutors. At one meeting, a "drunken servant of the devil" assaulted Toler, giving him "vast severe looks, hard sayings, and was coming towards me, and said that he would lose every drop of blood he had, but was immediately suppressed." On another occasion, antagonists planned to "duck" and perhaps drown Toler as he waited for a ferry. The surging popularity of the Baptists, and their loose enforcement of social distinctions between men and women, and whites and blacks, enraged some who preferred a more staid form of religion, or who found comfort in the hierarchical culture of Virginia.[24]

Toler's church at Nomini grew rapidly, despite the opposition. Formed in April 1786 with 17 members, by the end of the year, it had grown to 74. By 1795, the membership stood at 408 converted and baptized believers. These patterns of growth were replicated across wide swaths of the nation through the Civil War.[25]

Inspired by the opportunities in western settlements upon the end of the American Revolution, many Virginians began to relocate to Kentucky. Entire congregations moved there, along with many talented Baptist preachers, leading Robert B. Semple to call it "the vortex of Baptist preachers." In 1810, he estimated that perhaps half of all Baptist pastors raised in Virginia had moved west.[26]

The most remarkable migration transpired just a month before the Revolution's climactic battle at Yorktown, when the Upper Spotsylvania Baptist Church, led by Lewis Craig, relocated as a group to Kentucky, earning the moniker "the Traveling Church." In 1768, Craig garnered the distinction of becoming one of the first Baptists imprisoned for illegal preaching in Virginia. Craig had experienced conversion and received believer's baptism in 1767 and became the pastor at Upper Spotsylvania in 1770. "His sermons consisted in a plain pungent exhibition of the evil of sin, and its ruinous consequences, with the glad tidings of redeeming love, through a Savior," wrote an early Baptist historian. He reportedly preached the gospel "not in word only, but in power, in the Holy Ghost."[27]

Like many Virginians, Craig and his church members were attracted to the land prospects in Kentucky, but they knew that piecemeal migration could disturb the fellowship they enjoyed at the church. So in September 1781, the church, having acquired the necessary land grants, held a tearful farewell service to say goodbye to friends and family who would stay behind. Standing on a platform erected in front of the church, Craig extolled the bounties of the promised western lands: "The rich and illimitable acres of a western Canaan were offered to them," and they would go forward with faith in the same God who led the Israelites through the desert as a cloud by day, and a pillar of fire by night. Early the next morning, bugles awoke the caravan of five to six hundred people—men, women, and children—who set out for their six hundred–mile journey. It was the largest single migration ever of Virginians to Kentucky.[28]

The Spotsylvania Baptists brought slaves with them to perform many of the arduous tasks required during their journey over the mountains. The slaves included a preacher, Peter Durrett, also known, variously, as "Uncle Peter," "Brother Captain," or "Old Captain," who would go on to found the First African Baptist Church of Lexington, Kentucky, around 1790. (South Kentucky Association minutes of 1801 recorded concern about "Brother Captain, a black man, who is a member of our society, and is preaching and baptizing and is not ordained." The association urged him to join a church—presumably a white-led one—and have his baptized followers do likewise.) White Baptists generally remained conflicted about the morality of chattel slavery as of the end of the American Revolution. Some saw that Americans' arguments for political and religious liberty would ring hollow if they continued to enslave African Americans, depriving them of their abilities to earn a wage for their toil, and to work and live where they wanted.[29]

Among the Baptists, John Leland was one of the most ardent antislavery activists, helping to pass a 1789 resolution at the Virginia Baptists' general assembly that slavery was "a violent deprivation of the rights of nature, and inconsistent with a republican government, and therefore recommend it to our brethren, to make use of every legal measure to extirpate this horrid evil from the land." The assembly called upon the legislature to "proclaim the great Jubilee," presumably wishing that the state would enact a program of gradual emancipation, as most northern states had already done. Some resisted the resolution, however, and by 1793 the assembly voted to dismiss the topic of abolition. In the following decades, antislavery sentiments encountered insurmountable resistance in the form of white evangelical paternalism, or the notion that southern slavery offered Christians the best context in which to evangelize slaves. The paternalists embraced—in principle, if not in practice—the biblical injunction to take care of slaves as one would nurture children. Emancipation, slavery's defenders insisted, would likely leave slaves both unconverted and destitute.[30]

UPPER SPOTSYLVANIA'S LEWIS Craig went on to found two of Kentucky's earliest Baptist churches, at Gilbert's Creek in 1781—which was only the third Baptist church founded in Kentucky—and South Elkhorn, close to Lexington, in 1783. Four churches joined to form the Elkhorn Baptist

Association in 1785, and they agreed that the Calvinist 1742 Philadelphia Baptist confession would be "strictly adhered to" among the association's churches. The Philadelphia confession was nearly identical to the 1689 London Baptist confession of faith and affirmed that "by the decree of God, for the manifestation of his glory, some men and angels are pre-destinated, or fore-ordinated to eternal life, through Jesus Christ, to the praise of his glorious grace; others being left to act in their sin to their just condemnation, to the praise of his glorious justice." Of course the confession prescribed baptism to be performed by immersion of those "who do actually profess repentance towards God [and] faith in, and obedience to our Lord Jesus." This practice could not possibly include infants. Union between the Regular Baptists of Elkhorn and Kentucky's Separate Baptists remained difficult because of disagreements over strict adherence to the Philadelphia confession. They finally achieved reconciliation in 1801, however, when Elkhorn joined with the Separate South Kentucky association without requiring confessional adherence as a term of fellowship.[31]

The Elkhorn Association also confronted the status of slaves within member churches, stating that a slave "may be considered a proper gospel member" of a church. Ever since the Separates' stirring beginnings in the Great Awakening, white leaders had agreed to give slaves a place of spiritual equality, knowing that they stood on the same footing with whites before the cross of Christ. But whites struggled to deal with the social implications of the gospel for slaves. For example, the association took up the question of whether it was "lawful for a slave being an orderly member and compelled to leave his wife and move with his master about five hundred miles, then to take another wife?" This was not a theoretical matter, but undoubtedly referred to the case of an actual slave moved by his master from Virginia to Kentucky. The association could not decide what to do. It deferred the matter until the next meeting. That meeting's minutes recorded the question as "debated and withdrawn." A similar issue came up in 1789. A female slave was forced to leave behind her husband in Virginia, but in Kentucky she married a slave who had another wife twenty miles away. The association determined that the slave woman should be "debarred from membership."[32]

Many in the association wished to see Kentucky abolish slavery, and as the territory prepared to apply for statehood in 1791, the Elkhorn Association drew up a memorial recommending that abolition be part of the new state constitution. But the memorial apparently generated a backlash, as three months later the association noted that it now disapproved of the petition's advocacy of the "abolition of slavery."

Even as the association wrestled with the thorny implications of its faith in a slave society, however, its churches grew by leaps and bounds, through both migration and conversions. From 1788 to 1798, they increased from 11 to 32 congregations, and 559 to 2,376 members. In the next three years, they experienced even more explosive growth, to 4,853 members.[33]

The colorful memoirist and preacher John Taylor went to Kentucky in 1783 and carried the Baptist style of revival with him. Taylor experienced dreams, visions, and providential deliverances as part of his conversion and spiritual growth. At Clear Creek Church in 1788, a revival broke out, requiring Taylor to hold baptismal services twice a month, even through the cold winter. Echoing stories told by John Leland, Taylor recorded that he once baptized twenty-six converts in the frozen creek, where they had cut a hole in ice that was six inches deep. A crowd gathered on the "edge of the icy grave," he wrote, and when Taylor emerged from the water, his clothes froze and stuck to his body, yet he was not frostbitten. He knew some critics would be skeptical of this account and call it a product of "enthusiasm," but Taylor was undeterred: "I know not why enthusiasm may not be used in religion as any other laudable work." Taylor often received divine guidance from dreams and visions, and he encountered other Baptists who had similar experiences. When one of his neighbors related seeing a vision of "the Savior in his glorified state," Taylor affirmed the man's experience, noting that the prophet Joel had predicted that in the last days, young men would see visions and old men would dream dreams.[34]

THE MID-1780S WERE heady times for Baptists in Virginia and Kentucky, times of flowering revival and freedom. Even as the war ended and more Baptists moved west, those who remained in Virginia fought to secure religious liberty in the state. The end of the war led Virginians to revisit the issue of religious establishment. Patrick Henry, in particular, wished to resume public funding for religion. If, as most Americans assumed, virtue was essential to the health of the republic, and religion was the most obvious source of virtue, then how could the state stop supporting churches? Henry was aware, of course, of the growing strength of the dissenting denominations, including Baptists, so he proposed that the state not return to an exclusive Anglican (now Episcopalian) establishment but a "general assessment" in which taxpayers had to give tithes, but they could designate which church would receive the funds.

Baptists found even this plural version of establishment unacceptable. Memories of persecution were too fresh, even if this new plan might be financially beneficial to their churches. The Baptists' General Committee in Virginia formally opposed the idea. James Madison, the Baptists' key ally, outmaneuvered Patrick Henry when Henry agreed in late 1784 to become Virginia's governor for a fourth term. The Virginia governor's office had little legislative power; Madison considered the move "inauspicious to [Henry's] offspring," meaning the general assessment.[35]

Madison had the general assessment bill referred to Virginia voters for discussion, resulting in an avalanche of evangelical protests. The Baptist General Committee saw the general assessment as "repugnant to the spirit of the gospel," arguing that "every person ought to be left entirely free in respect to matters of religion" and that "the Holy Author of our religion needs no such compulsive measures for the promotion of his cause." The committee presented virtually the same arguments as Madison's more famous *Memorial and Remonstrance* against the bill. Madison, citing the principle of religious liberty already enshrined in the Virginia Declaration of Rights, wrote that "the Religion then of every man must be left to the conviction and conscience of every man; and it is the right of every man to exercise it as these may dictate. This right is in its nature an unalienable right." Evangelicals (primarily Baptists) produced approximately ninety petitions against the general assessment, while its defenders managed to summon only about ten. The legislature bowed to popular will and tabled the measure.[36]

The demise of Henry's general assessment opened the door for passage of Jefferson's Bill for Establishing Religious Freedom. He had originally proposed this statute in 1779 but did not have enough support to pass it until 1786. (Madison engineered passage of the bill because Jefferson was away in Paris.) The expansive bill put Virginia firmly on the side of religious freedom, concluding that "no man shall be compelled to frequent or support any relig[i]ous Worship place or Ministry whatsoever, nor shall be enforced, restrained, molested, or burthened in his body or goods, nor shall otherwise suffer on account of his religious opinions or belief, but that all men shall be free to profess, and by argument to maintain their opinions in matters of religion." Baptists were delighted. They had waited years for this bill to, as they put it, place "religious freedom on its proper basis."[37]

The bill's passage set the stage for a religious liberty amendment to the new US Constitution. Madison, justly called the "father" of the Constitution, did not originally believe that the Constitution needed a Bill of Rights or a statement regarding religious liberty because he believed that the Constitution only granted the national government the powers articulated within the document. Nothing in the Constitution granted the government the ability to infringe upon religious liberty, so the operative assumption should be that the government could not do that. Anti-Federalists, including many Baptists, were not convinced. Many Baptists in Virginia opposed the unamended Constitution because of the absence of a religious liberty clause. A correspondent wrote to Madison in February 1788 warning him in rough dialect that among "the Baptus's, the Prechers of that Society are much alarm'd fearing Relegious liberty is not Sufficiently secur'd." The correspondent thought that "thay pretend to other objections but that I think is the principle objection."[38]

John Leland typified Baptist resistance to the Constitution. He had many concerns about potential abuses by the new national government, but the "clearest of all" was the Constitution's threat to religious liberty. "If Oppression does not ensue, it will be owing to the Mildness of Administration and not to any Constitutional defence," Leland wrote. Madison, Washington, and other defenders of the Constitution had argued that popular unrest in the states, such as Shays's Rebellion in Massachusetts, dictated the need for a stronger national government. But Leland thought that "if the Manners of People are so far Corrupted, that they cannot live by Republican principles, it is Very Dangerous leaving Religious Liberty at their Mercy." The Baptist General Committee agreed, saying in March 1788 that the Constitution did not make "sufficient provision for the secure enjoyment of religious liberty."[39]

Other Baptists took a different view of the Constitution. Many agreed with Madison that an explicit endorsement of religious liberty was not necessary. And many, like the Philadelphia Association, believed that the country was indeed at real risk of the "national dishonor, injustice, anarchy, confusion and bloodshed, which have already resulted from the weakness and inefficiency of the present form" of government. They published a circular letter endorsing ratification. Likewise, Isaac Backus supported the Constitution at the Massachusetts ratifying convention, even though he estimated that two-thirds of the twenty Baptist delegates at the convention were Anti-Federalists. Backus was particularly comforted by the Constitution's refusal to impose any religious test or oath for officeholders, seeing that provision alone as a great practical step in favor of religious liberty.[40]

The ratification decision in Virginia, as in Massachusetts, was going to be close. Madison realized that he needed to return to the state to defend the Constitution at the ratifying convention and to convince some open-minded Anti-Federalists to support it. A Baptist friend encouraged Madison to visit Leland, to "call on him & Spend a few Howers in his Company" to discuss the absence of the religious liberty clauses. Madison probably did visit Leland in late March 1788, and although we do not know exactly what transpired at that meeting, we do know that Leland, and most Virginia Baptists, eventually decided to support the Constitution. Madison assured them that, in spite of his initial reservations, he intended to craft an amendment in favor of religious freedom in the first Congress.[41]

When Madison ran as a candidate for Congress in 1789, he actively courted Baptist support. He wrote to Baptist minister George Eve that he planned to pass amendments including "satisfactory provisions for all essential rights, particularly the rights of Conscience in the fullest latitude." Like Leland, Eve was convinced—perhaps a little awed—by Madison's personal appeal, and soon Eve was openly campaigning for Madison's election. After the narrow ratification of the Constitution, Madison followed through on his promise in Congress, where he doggedly pursued the framing and ratification of the Bill of Rights. The First Amendment guaranteed the "free exercise of religion" and banned Congress from making laws "respecting an establishment of religion."[42]

The religion clauses of the First Amendment, then, were a triumph of the Baptists' and Madison's shared view of religious liberty. The Baptists' perspective was crafted out of the bitter experience of persecution in the colonial era. At every step, especially in Virginia, Madison utterly depended upon their support to bring about freedom of conscience. In the Constitution, Baptist pressure pushed Madison further than he originally sought to go.

The Baptist vision for religious liberty had won out on the national level; it would be confirmed by Jefferson's election in 1800 and the "wall of separation" letter, which made explicit his alliance with the Baptists. In Virginia, and in most of the states outside of New England, momentum was growing for robust endorsements of religious liberty, especially through disestablishment of state churches. When Kentucky, the new home of so many Baptists, became the fifteenth state in the union in 1792, its constitution echoed Virginia's commitment to religious liberty.

"All men have a natural and indefeasible right to worship Almighty God according to the dictates of their own consciences," it said, and "no man can of right be compelled to attend, erect, or support any place of worship, or to maintain any ministry against his consent." The state also affirmed that "no preference shall ever be given by law to any religious societies or modes of worship." The Baptist view of religious liberty was becoming America's, too. Soon the Baptists' gospel would enter a similar era of ascendancy, in the lonely reaches of the American backcountry.[43]

5

Baptists and the Great Revival

JACOB BOWER WAS born into a devout German Baptist family in Lancaster County, Pennsylvania, in 1786, and when he was nineteen he moved to the Kentucky frontier. In spite of his upbringing, he dabbled in Universalist thought, until fear of judgment and conviction of sin turned him back to his parents' faith. He began to see his heart as a "cage of every unclean and hateful thing." Indeed, in a complete reversal from the Universalist conviction that everyone would be saved, he began to wonder if God would even save him.[1]

In December 1811, Bower and his wife were awakened by the terrible shaking of an earthquake. He thought to himself, "We shall all be sunk and lost, and I am not prepared." He expected "immediate destruction, had no hope of seeing the dawn of another day. Eternity, oh eternity was just at hand, and all of us unprepared." The dawn did come, accompanied by a horrifying aftershock. Panicked neighborhood families huddled in prayer, fearing that the Judgment Day had come. Occasional aftershocks reportedly continued for almost two years. In the aftermath of the first quake, many distraught people dropped their worldly duties and sought salvation. "Deists and universalists in those days were scarce," Bower noted.[2]

Yet for three months, Bower could not break through. He rambled in the woods and tried to pray but could not find solace. He despaired, thinking he was destined for hell. As he sat by himself one night musing, his thoughts suddenly turned to Christ's sufferings on the cross: the sorrow, the sweat, and the blood. "It was for sinners that he thus suffered that they might be saved," Bower told himself. He knew these things in his head, of course, but it felt like he was realizing them for the first time. "If it was done for sinners," he thought, "it was done for me. I believed it."

Peace flooded into his soul, and he wandered outside in a placid reverie. "The trees (I thought) lifted their hands up towards Heaven as if they were praising God." The stars were twinkling the Creator's glory. "What is the matter with me," he thought. "I never felt so strange before, strange wonderful—wonderful indeed. A little while ago I felt as if I were hanging by a slender thread over the pit of ruin." Now he was at peace.[3]

Bower was converted, but what church should he join? The decision hinged on his view of baptism. In the evenings he searched his Bible by firelight for guidance. The Dunkards of his background used immersion, but they dipped a convert three times. Bower, however, came to believe that baptism was a representation of a believer's death, burial, and resurrection in Christ. That spiritual experience only happened once; thus, he concluded, baptism should be by immersion, and the convert should be dipped only once. And so he was dipped, at Hazle Creek Baptist Church, along with fifteen others. (Two others who came for baptism were rejected, perhaps because they did not have a clear testimony of conversion.) He was one of seventy-six who joined the Hazle Creek congregation during this earthquake revival.[4]

Bower's experience was unusual—especially the earthquake part— yet he was just one of multitudes of converts in these decades. Critics in Kentucky mocked the Baptists, saying that they were all really "shakers, [and] that when the earth is done shaking, they will all turn back." But nothing could have been further from the truth. Well before and well after the earthquake episode, Baptists and other evangelicals saw massive awakenings from New England to the Ohio River Valley to the frontier Southwest. In 1776, there were roughly ten thousand Baptists in America. By 1800, there were one hundred thousand, and by 1848, there were approximately eight hundred thousand. Baptist growth was not limited to America: the number of English Baptist congregations also more than doubled during that period. Nor was revival unique to their denomination; indeed, the growth of Methodism was even more spectacular. But by the eve of the Civil War, older denominations such as Congregationalists and Episcopalians lagged far behind, and Baptists and other new denominations, fueled by the Second Great Awakening, had become evangelical juggernauts.[5]

IT IS DIFFICULT to assign specific dates to the Second Great Awakening because revivals—and hopes and prayers for revivals—had become such staples of evangelical life. The "New Light Stir" of the 1780s was followed by significant regional awakenings, and then Kentucky saw a phenomenal outburst in the early 1800s, highlighted by the Cane Ridge revival of 1801. For Baptists and other evangelicals, the First Great Awakening bled into the Second.

The 1790s saw remarkable Baptist growth in northern New England and upstate New York. As settlements spread west and north, Baptists kept pace by planting new churches and sending out itinerant preachers and missionaries to frontier regions. The desire for awakening was ever-present. The member churches of the Shaftsbury Baptist Association (organized in 1780 with churches from Vermont, Massachusetts, and New York) held a day of prayer and fasting in late summer 1790, imploring God to "pour down his Holy Spirit in the land, and revive pure and undefiled religion among us." They might well have believed that God answered those prayers, as the association grew at breakneck speed over the next decade, from twenty-six churches and seventeen hundred members in 1791, to forty-six churches and forty-one hundred members in 1800. Baptist associations frequently noted participation in "concerts of prayer" for revival, based on a model originally proposed by the Congregationalist pastor-theologian Jonathan Edwards. Yet Baptists saw the mid-1790s as a time of theological testing from deists and other antagonists, or as "a day neither clear nor dark," with no decisive evidence of massive revival or of debilitating decline.[6]

Nevertheless, countless reports of Baptist growth came from the New England frontier and elsewhere in the 1790s. The overwhelming majority of Baptist churches in this decade remained Calvinist—one estimate counted 956 out of 1,024 white-led Baptist churches as "Particular" in theology, meaning those who believed that Christ died only for the elect. But new Freewill Baptist churches were growing, too, from eighteen congregations to fifty-one over the course of the decade.[7]

One striking report of revival came from Job Seamans, a Calvinist Baptist pastor of New London, a central New Hampshire village about a hundred miles from Boston. Although he was born in Massachusetts, Seamans grew up much farther to the northeast, in Sackville, New Brunswick. (The connections between American and Canadian evangelicals, including Baptists, remained quite active in the era of the American Revolution.) In 1767, after a service where he watched some friends get baptized, Seamans had a vivid and terrifying vision, believing that he saw "with his bodily eyes, the Savior, in the act of being crucified for his redemption." He never forgot the sight of Christ's bruised and pierced body; ultimately he came to believe that God would forgive his sins, and he experienced conversion. Although people rarely claimed to see visions with their "bodily eyes," Seamans's experience was otherwise not unusual among Baptists. In 1785, Esther Peak of Claremont, New Hampshire, was riding along a bank of the Connecticut River when a dramatic crimson sunset gave the smooth surface of the river "an appearance not altogether dissimilar to a vast body of blood." This vista gave her new depths of insight into the "fountain of the Savior's blood" and the gravity of her sin. Soon she too put her faith in Christ and received believer's baptism. Her husband (a Baptist minister) recalled that, as a Calvinist, Peak still believed that even "if God should elect and save all others, she deserved nothing short of eternal condemnation," making her all the more thankful for grace.[8]

Like Peak, Job Seamans communicated his salvation ordeal to his local Baptist church, and it baptized him. By the early 1770s, he had returned to Massachusetts determined to become a pastor and itinerant preacher. Isaac Backus and James Manning participated in his ordination. Seamans and his wife moved to New London in 1788, where they and ten others formed a Baptist church. He initially preached in a dirt-floor meeting-house. Strangely, given the Baptists' general hostility to church establishments, Seamans received tax support from residents as the first settled minister in town. A major revival broke out at the church starting in 1792. "Some things in this work have exceeded anything I ever saw before," Seamans wrote. Congregants warmly received his Calvinist preaching on "the justice and sovereignty of God," and he thought they "have desires beyond what I have ever before known, for the universal outpouring of the Holy Spirit." When the awakening began, the church had eighteen baptized members; by the end of 1794, it had 115—in a frontier town of about fifty households.[9]

Stories like Seamans's proliferated in the 1790s, and the Baptists' growth bred a desire to expand the churches' missionary reach and to connect regionally and nationally with other Baptists. Some of this expansion happened organically: Baptist growth followed new Anglo-American settlement on the frontier following the American Revolution. For instance, in 1788 a group of twenty-eight pioneers from New Jersey settled on the Ohio River near the future site of Cincinnati. Some of these migrants were Baptists, and in 1790, with the help of the visiting Baptist pastor Stephen Gano, they organized the Columbia Baptist Church, which claims to have been the first Protestant church in the Northwest Territory. (Ohio would become a state in 1803.) In their declaration of faith, these Baptists affirmed that "before the world began God did elect a certain number of souls unto everlasting salvation whom he did predestinate to the adoption of children by Jesus Christ from his own free grace."[10]

A group of Baptists from South Carolina similarly journeyed to Mississippi in the 1780s in search of fertile farmland. They suffered an attack by Cherokee Indians as they traversed the Tennessee River near the present-day site of Chattanooga, but they eventually made it to a settlement near the Mississippi River north of Natchez and began worshiping in private homes. They formally organized a church in 1791, with seven charter members who committed to the doctrines of baptism "according to the apostolic mode" and "particular redemption." Following the American Revolution, the British had ceded West Florida, including lower Mississippi, to the Spanish, who made Catholicism the official religion of the territory. As the Baptists began to spread in the 1790s, Spanish authorities ordered Baptist minister Richard Curtis and his followers to "desist from their heretical psalm-singing, praying and preaching," or they would send them to the silver mines of Mexico. They did not desist, and Curtis was arrested and hauled before the Spanish territorial governor. He was released when he promised to obey the laws of the province, but the threat of a second detention caused him to flee back to South Carolina. When the United States assumed control of the Mississippi Territory in 1798, Curtis returned and established the Salem Church.[11]

One of Curtis's pastoral colleagues was Joseph Willis, who had been born a slave—the child of a Cherokee/African slave woman and her white master—but was emancipated in 1787. He moved to South Carolina and became involved with the Baptist church that sent Curtis to Mississippi. Willis ultimately received a license to preach. He went west with Curtis in 1798, but by the early 1800s he had crossed into Louisiana and likely delivered the first Baptist (perhaps even the first Protestant) sermons west of the Mississippi River. At Bayou Chicot, south of Alexandria, he founded the Calvary Baptist Church in 1812, shortly after Louisiana (acquired from France in 1803) became a state. Reportedly, "his color, and being a Baptist, rendered him obnoxious to the very few Protestants" in the area. "He was exposed to strong prejudice, and threatened with violence." Nevertheless, he helped establish a number of Baptist congregations and became the first moderator of the Louisiana Baptist Association. Perhaps befitting Louisiana's strong Catholic background, he became affectionately known as "Father Willis."[12]

Baptist pioneers like these did a great deal to spread the faith, but there were also many denomination-led efforts to foster growth. Baptists from New England to the Carolinas had long maintained national connections through correspondence networks and by sending pastors to unevangelized areas. But the 1790s and early 1800s saw the expansion of these webs of communication. Sometimes the work was as simple as Baptist associations sending "messengers" to other association meetings. In 1791, the Stonington Association appointed messengers to visit several Baptist meetings elsewhere, and it commissioned pastor Valentine Rathbun to travel to assemblies in Philadelphia and Virginia. The Shaftsbury Association likewise sent Stephen Gano, who was then pastor of a church in Hillsdale, New York, as a messenger to Philadelphia in 1791; the Charleston Association appointed Richard Furman to correspond with the United Association of Virginia (formed out of a union of Separate and Regular Baptists in 1787), and another pastor to write to Philadelphia.[13]

Regional Baptist associations also multiplied during this period, helping to foster communication and standardize practices among member churches. The associations often displayed an interest in stabilizing Baptist church life, which had emerged from the Great Awakening in a state of godly chaos. The fledgling Neuse Association of southeastern North Carolina, organized at Bear Marsh meetinghouse in 1794 out of the older Kehukee Association, adopted "Rules of Decorum" for its meetings, emphasizing order and discipline. No one was allowed to laugh or whisper while someone was speaking, and all attendees were to refer to one another as "brother."[14]

Given the rise of groups including the Shakers, Freemasons, Universalists, and Arminians, the dominant Calvinist Baptists perceived the 1790s as a time of especially pressing theological trials. "The adversary [Satan] never worked more powerfully in any age," reckoned the Groton (Conn.) Union Conference in 1800. Association minutes reflected regular questions about how to handle members or member churches who dabbled in heterodox theology. The new Rensselaerville (N.Y.) Conference received a query in 1798 from a church about what to do with a member who believed that "the punishment of the wicked will not be eternal; and likewise believes it is not agreeable to the justice of God, to save one part of mankind, and punish the other." The conference recommended that the offending member be treated in accordance with Titus 3:10: "A man that is an heretick after the first and second admonition reject."[15]

Even though most Baptist churches in the early national period were Calvinist, there were still controversies over the nuances of Calvinist theology, beliefs about election, and the effects of Christ's atonement for sin. So much friction emerged from what the Danbury Association called the "erroneous extremes" of Arminianism and hyper-Calvinism that it feared the "most serious and alarming consequences." Those consequences played out in disciplinary procedures against erring congregations and individual members. The Neuse Association ejected Swift Creek Church in 1797 because it held "armenian [sic] principles, and every means made use of to reclaim them, proves ineffectual."[16]

Most Baptist churches espoused moderate Calvinist beliefs. They generally held to the doctrinal views of English Baptist minister Andrew Fuller, who advocated a modified Calvinist view of the atonement. Fuller argued that Christ's death on the cross was "sufficient" to forgive the sins of all, but "efficient" only for the elect. In 1795, the Danbury Association entertained a query from a member church: "Are the non-elect in any sense bought by the blood of Christ?" It answered, "If by being bought, you mean to ask, whether the atonement is sufficient for the whole world; we answer in the affirmative: but if you mean to ask, whether the atonement of Christ has bought any of the fallen race, so as to release them from the curse of the divine law until they are regenerated, we answer in the negative." Some thought that this position was quasi-Arminian, suggesting that Christ had somehow died for all humankind. Staunch Calvinists saw the atonement as sufficient for only those predestined to salvation. At the Powelton Baptist Church in Georgia, four members separated in 1791 because the church endorsed Fuller's theology of the atonement. Pastor Silas Mercer polled the congregation, asking whether it should "excommunicate a member, for holding what is called a general provision." A majority voted in the negative, and they decided to expel the four hyper-Calvinist schismatics instead.[17]

The strongest Arminian Baptist sentiments in the early republic were found among the Freewill Baptists, centered in New England. That denomination's founder, Benjamin Randel, objected to "the whole doctrine of John Calvin, with respect to eternal, particular, personal, unconditional election and reprobation."[18]

As seen in the controversies over Calvinism and Arminianism, Baptist church records are filled with the exclusions of ostensibly immoral and heretical members, with southerners excommunicating at higher rates than northerners. Baptists in the antebellum South expelled almost

2 percent of their members per year. Church discipline presents an intriguing resource for understanding the dynamics of power between blacks and whites, and men and women, in Baptist churches. Compared with the broader society, Baptist churches practiced a striking spiritual egalitarianism in discipline. Beginning in the eighteenth century, civil courts became more professionalized and less friendly to women and nonwhites overall. Yet in Baptist church proceedings, women and even slaves could still get a hearing and often could vote on whether to expel members for immorality or heterodoxy. Overall, Baptists tended to accuse white men most often, even though white men held the most power in the churches, politics, and society. Although white women represented the largest bloc of church members, the percentage of accusations against white men was typically higher than their percentage as members in congregations.[19]

The types of accusations leveled in Baptist disciplinary cases tended to change depending on the race and gender of the accused, however, and evidence would suggest that blacks and women often received harsher penalties than white men. Charges often followed fears about the accused's social roles, from the rowdy white man and the licentious white woman, to the disobedient black man and the saucy black woman. Men often ran afoul of the church body for sins of the public sphere such as drunkenness, fighting, and abusive or profane language. Women tended to be accused of sins of a sexual or flirtatious nature, including adultery and dancing. Black males, especially slaves, routinely faced charges of theft, running away, and drunkenness, while black women were often charged with adultery and lying.[20]

The presence of slaves as members in Baptist churches caused consternation and sometimes puzzlement among whites. As we have seen, white Baptists struggled to regulate slaves' marriages, which were commonly broken up when one partner was sold or moved away with his or her master. This put pious slaves in a bind: Could they legally remarry if they had no reasonable hope of seeing their current spouse again? The Bethel Association of South Carolina wrestled with the contradictions between slavery and Christian practice at its 1794 conference. "What shall be done," one query asked, "with negro [Christian] professors that have been married (in their way) and separated by compulsion: May they marry while their husbands or wives are yet alive?" The association answered by not answering: "We find such difficulties attending to this question, arising from the nature and existence of slavery, that we judge it best to leave it to the discretion of every church to decide on." It did, however, recommend that masters try to prevent such breakups from happening.[21]

As if that question was not vexing enough, the association confronted another topic raised by slavery: "Where a master and negro servant are both members in a gospel church, is the master justifiable in correcting the servant with stripes [beatings] for disobedience?" It answered that "both masters and parents (while the children are in their non-age) have a right to govern their household, and to use the rod, if need be." However, the association reminded the churches that Baptist slave masters remained under the church's discipline in instances of "cruelty and oppression." Indeed, masters did occasionally face punishment for cruelty. In 1772, the Meherrin Church in Virginia unanimously decided that it was not lawful to punish slaves by "burning" them. The question was prompted by the actions of Brother Charles Cook, whom the congregation immediately suspended. The next month, Cook was reinstated after apologizing to the church body, both blacks and whites.[22]

IN 1793, SOUTH Carolina Baptist minister Richard Furman wrote to his mother about a fast proclaimed by the Charleston Baptist Association. He expected good to come from it, writing: "May God of his great mercy hear the prayers of his people, and not only avert national calamities, but revive a work of grace in his churches." The Baptists of early national America, along with other evangelicals, had come to expect cycles of decline and awakening. Although they could not control the timing of revival, they believed it incumbent upon them to pray, preach, and prepare for new waves of commitment to Jesus. So in the 1790s, Presbyterians, Methodists, and Baptists across America were fasting and praying for new revivals, and at the turn of the century, they came.[23]

We must not be too eager to call this event the "Second Great Awakening," which is more a convenient label than an accurate description of what was happening. Participants at the time certainly did not speak of the "Second Great Awakening," a term that did not come into common use until the late nineteenth century. (As late as the 1870s, some called the First Great Awakening the "second" Great Awakening, following the Reformation, which was the first major revival in Protestant history. Others said, variously, that the "second" Great Awakening began in the early 1820s or 1830s.) Leonard Woolsey Bacon's *History of American Christianity* (1897) was probably the work that established the "Second Awakening" as beginning with the Kentucky camp meetings, especially the massive revival at Cane Ridge in 1801. Earlier historians spoke of events from 1800 to 1803 as the "great revival," a term that Theodore Roosevelt still used in his popular book *The Winning of the West* (1896).[24]

Instead of breaking up the First and Second Great Awakenings into discrete events, we might see the century from the 1740s (the emergence of the Separate Baptists) to the 1840s (the sectional division of the Baptists) as a unified whole, because there were significant revivals happening among the Baptists and other evangelicals throughout this period. Baptists certainly saw massive stirs in the early 1800s, but those events did not necessarily exceed the ferment of awakenings that happened in the 1780s, 1820s, or 1830s.[25]

During the period from the end of the American Revolution to the onset of America's sectional crisis in the 1840s, Baptists (along with Methodists, Presbyterians, and the Churches of Christ) proved zealous and flexible enough to keep pace with the booming settlement in the trans-Appalachian West. From upstate New York to the territories of the new Southwest (Alabama to Texas), Baptist associations monitored settlement patterns of Anglo pioneers (many of whom brought slaves along) and commissioned preachers and missionaries "to travel into new places where the Gospel was likely to flourish," as Baptist historian Robert Baylor Semple noted. In an era of dramatic population shifts, "the spoils would go to those who were prepared to be mobile, and who had a powerful religious message to trade," as one writer put it. Some Baptists, as in the case of the early Ohio and Mississippi settlers, were among the first Anglo pioneers and opened churches wherever they went. Because Baptist elders and pastors were not required to have college educations at the time, there was a ready supply of pastoral candidates whose primary qualification was zeal for the gospel. Churches in established areas saw revivals, too, but what is most striking is the way that Baptists' passion for evangelism helped build entrepreneurial church organizations that moved west with the frontier. They also won the allegiance of growing numbers of African Americans as slavery spread into new regions of the South. From the Revolution to the Civil War, Methodists and Baptists achieved the greatest organizational success in American religious history.[26]

For Baptists in New England, the turn-of-the-century revivals were marked by intense fervor and the repudiation of deism, which had been on the rise since the advent of the French Revolution and the publication of Thomas Paine's skeptical *Age of Reason* (1794). Pastor Caleb Blood of

Shaftsbury, Vermont, keyed the opening of his church's awakening to the testimony of a young woman in July 1798. Her powerful conversion catalyzed spiritual interest in other youths, and people began receiving baptism and joining the church in droves. In nine months, the church's membership more than doubled, to 346. Blood particularly wrote that "some of our most noted deists have bowed the knee to King Jesus; and a number of Universalists have forsaken their delusions, and embraced the truth." Similarly, the itinerant and champion of religious liberty John Leland saw a massive awakening in his home town of Cheshire, Massachusetts, in 1799 and 1800. Leland testified that prior to the revival, "a heavenly visitant came to my house—my heart, with the salutation of 'Peace to you—peace on earth and good will to man.'" Repeatedly he had the words *The Lord will work* impressed upon his heart. Soon the revival broke out, and in March 1800 he held a service where he baptized more than two hundred converts—more than doubling the church's membership, to a total of 394 (out of Cheshire's total population of thirteen hundred).[27]

Even more remarkable news came from the west and south, however. Stephen Gano reported to the Groton Conference in 1801 that he had received reports from Kentucky of a "marvelous work of God in that state, where 1400 persons had been added to 7 or 8 churches in a few months." As the Kentucky revivals began in earnest, Baptists worked alongside Methodists and Presbyterians at massive outdoor assemblies, or "camp meetings," although the Baptists remained somewhat peripheral to events such as the great Presbyterian communion gathering at Cane Ridge. (Baptists would preach but not "commune," noted one observer.) Evangelicals fed on one another's energy, in spite of divisions over Calvinism and the proper mode of baptism; Baptists in Kentucky grew alongside Methodists and Presbyterians.[28]

Baptists and other evangelicals had seen many revivals since the 1740s, but the titanic excitement in Kentucky was awe-inspiring; observers employed metaphors of flood and fire to describe the scenes. One Baptist wrote from Lexington that "it appears like a fire that has been long confined—bursting all its barriers, and spreading with a rapidity that is indescribable." One of the earliest stirs occurred at Port William (Carrollton), Kentucky, at the confluence of the Ohio and Kentucky Rivers. The itinerating Baptist preacher John Taylor visited Port William and found a "mixture of Methodists and Baptists together" noisily worshiping late into the night. Soon he returned to Bullittsburg Church, where he was emboldened to speak out against a group of youths who regularly danced together, despite the evangelicals' warnings against it. The woman who taught them to dance told her "disciples" before they went to hear Taylor preach that they would "hear enough of our dancing today, but let us not mind that Mr. Taylor says." But Taylor wept bitterly as he compared his disobedient neighbors to the wandering, stubborn Israelites of the Old Testament. His emotional sermon cracked the teacher's resolve, and she also began crying uncontrollably. Three months later she received baptism, so that "what the Lord did at this meeting entirely broke up all the dancing in the settlement."[29]

At the 1800 meeting of the "Elkhorn Association of Babtists" (delightfully misspelled, and instructively, as we can hear their Appalachian accent), tales from Bullittsburg offered the only hint of the stunning growth coming in Kentucky. By August 1800, the Bullittsburg church reported 22 new baptisms, bringing its total membership to 82. By August 1801, the revival flood had truly broken loose in Elkhorn's congregations: South Elkhorn Church reported 309 new baptisms, Clear Creek Church 326, Bryan's Church 367, and Great Crossings Church 376. The Rolling Fork Church baptized 71 new converts in 1801–1802, accounting for almost its entire membership of 77. In 1800, the total membership of the Elkhorn Association's churches stood at 1,642. In 1801, it nearly tripled to 4,853 (and that does not include the almost 400 who died, moved, or were excluded in that year). One estimate suggested that about 2,464 people received believer's baptism in the Kentucky churches between August and December 1801. (This represented more than 1 percent of the state's entire population and does not account for those baptized before and after this five-month stretch, or the thousands who joined other evangelical churches during the period.) That pace did not continue, of course: in 1804 the Elkhorn Association's twenty-six member churches baptized a total of only thirteen people, far fewer than their number of deaths and exclusions.[30]

One observer participated in the creation of a new Kentucky Baptist congregation, where the baptism of seven converts brought the total membership to seventeen. The correspondent wrote to Baptist leader John Rippon of London, saying that the people of the little church were "greatly agitated," continuing "all night, exhorting, praying, and singing; sometimes the professors of religion appear in raptures, as if they were ready to take their flight to glory, and distressed souls, lying on the floor, crying out for mercy, in such distress, as if they saw the yawning pit of destruction ready to receive them." The writer knew of at least one other Baptist congregation where "those extraordinary bodily agitations are prevalent," but he thought that in most other Baptist churches "great solemnity" prevailed.[31]

With this phenomenal growth among frontier Baptists, distinctively Calvinist theology began to wane. Often this was just a matter of things no longer said. In 1785, the Elkhorn Baptist Association had adopted the robustly Calvinist Philadelphia Confession of 1742. But when it united with two other Kentucky associations in 1802, they agreed that "the preaching Christ tasted death for every man [general atonement], shall be no bar to communion." Some Baptists may have felt that they had more fundamental theological challenges with which to contend than the division between Calvinists and Arminians. In 1804, the Elkhorn Association took action against two member churches in which significant portions of the congregation, and probably at least one pastor, had begun denying the doctrine of the Trinity and contending that "Jesus Christ is not truly God." The nearby Bracken Association was also troubled by this news and reminded its member churches that "the Christian religion stands or falls with the doctrine of the Trinity."[32]

As Baptists battled these threats, rigorous Calvinism became less of a priority. The doctrine of limited atonement seems to have become particularly muted after 1800. We should not overstate the rapidity of Calvinism's decline, however, as Calvinist doctrines such as total depravity and the chosen elect remained standard Baptist fare through the nineteenth century. Moreover, many Baptists still defended a limited atonement. In 1808, for instance, the Bowdoinham Association, meeting in central Maine, affirmed again the Fullerite view of the atonement: "In some sense all mankind are benefitted by it," they conceded, but Christ died only for his sheep. It was inconceivable, they argued, contrary to what "many have asserted, that Jesus died as much for one as for another, as much for Judas as for Paul."[33]

WORD SPREAD BACK east of the remarkable work going on in the West, and the news helped precipitate more revivals. Lemuel Burkitt of North Carolina's Bertie Baptist Church traveled to Tennessee and Kentucky, witnessing the scenes there and reporting them to the Kehukee Baptist Association. The association meeting itself became awakened, and then the participants "carried the sacred fire home to their churches." Burkitt and his fellow pastor Jesse Read observed several key characteristics of these revivals. One was congregational singing. Burkitt had published pamphlets with hymns he had brought back from his western tour, distributing about six thousand copies. Meetings opened and closed with singing, and at the end of services ministers would often make their way through the still-singing audience, shaking hands. As simple as it might seem, Burkitt and Read noted that some converts registered this tender moment as the beginning of their journey to salvation.[34]

During the great revival, Baptists also prayed at the front of the church for those under conviction of sin. (Some churches would later formalize this practice with the placement of an "anxious seat" near the pulpit.) Burkitt and Read said that at large meetings, as many as two or three hundred might come forward at once, pressing in to get close to the pastor. Similarly, great spectacles of baptism drew many toward conversion: sometimes, "while the [baptismal] candidates were relating their experience, the audience would be in floods of tears, and some almost convulsed." Often groups of fifteen or twenty would be baptized in one service at a river or pond. Those receiving baptism would march into the water, singing a song like the oft-anthologized "Come, all ye mourning souls, who seek rest in Jesus' love."[35]

Burkitt and Read emphasized the ecstatic experiences commonly seen in these revivals, with some participants enduring uncontrollable tremors, and others swooning and falling helpless to the ground. (Sometimes these fits would seize people not at the revival meetings but when they were at home or in their fields.) Baptists also engaged the long-running debate about whether these reactions were signs of the Holy Spirit or instead represented ungodly "enthusiasm." The Charleston Association declared that in the recent revivals, "Pentecostal seasons have been experienced yet so strangely have both the minds and bodies of many been affected since this revival has commenced, particularly at some extraordinary meetings," that many had begun asking whether the Holy Spirit or fleshly enthusiasm was behind the furor. It acknowledged that the Spirit played an indispensable role in convicting sinners and leading them to a saving knowledge of Christ. But it also warned that even "persons of piety" could fall into emotional excesses, prompted by "loud and earnest speaking, extravagant gestures, the particular tone of voice used by a public speaker; a dream, an unexpected occurrence of a scripture text, an appearance in the heavens, or some event of Providence arbitrarily interpreted." Believers should watch out for these experiences, lest they be tempted to "transgress all the rules of decency and order, not only as established by right reason, but even by the Word of God." More firmly, they cautioned that no one could rightly claim apostolic inspiration of the

Holy Spirit, "including prophecy, infallible direction, and power of working miracles." Such gifts had ceased after the age of the apostles.[36]

Nevertheless, at the leading edge of many Baptist revivals, signs of
spiritual ecstasy did often appear. There were massive revivals along the
North Carolina/South Carolina border in 1802 and 1803, with meetings
in the "Kentucky Stile," as Richard Furman put it. Furman witnessed
one of these at Waxhaw, North Carolina, where thousands camped at
the meeting area, and Methodist, Baptist, and Presbyterian pastors took
turns preaching. Furman was impressed by the spiritual seriousness of
the assembly, but he was also concerned about the "bodily affections" he
observed. Furman was ambivalent, knowing from decades of experience
that physical manifestations often came with real revival. He did think
some of the penitents were simply enthusiasts—or worse, were faking
the displays. Some people of an "enthusiastick disposition" preyed on
opportunities offered by the fluid setting at the camp meeting to spread
their delusions. But in some of the affected, Furman perceived "strong
evidence of supernatural power and gracious influence."[37]

The "great revival," then, was centered in Kentucky. It also influenced some Baptist churches to the east, and lasted from about 1800 to
1803. The longer-term revivals of what is often called the "Second Great
Awakening," lasted from the 1780s to the 1840s. It would be difficult, even
if one restricted them to Baptists, to trace all the local and regional revivals that transpired during this period. A historian of the Second Great
Awakening in Connecticut, for example, notes that at least one church
in Connecticut experienced revival every year from 1797 and 1831, with
particular upsurges in 1798–1801, 1808–1809, 1812–1814, 1816, 1818–1819,
1820–1821, and 1824–1825. These kinds of dizzying statistics could be
multiplied across the East Coast and the expanding frontier.[38]

WITH THE GREAT revival, Baptists had successfully entered the
trans-Appalachian region and northern New England, and they would
continue to flourish as the frontier moved farther west and north. (For
example, Baptist churches appeared in Illinois in 1796, Indiana in 1798,
Alabama in 1808, and Michigan in 1822.) Although many Baptist leaders
professed that their brand of revivalism was sober and "rational," ecstatic
manifestations of revival did not vanish with this movement into frontier regions. Many sought to balance the ecstatic and the rational in their
accounts of revival: one Baptist observer from Isleboro, on an island off
the coast of Maine, reported a work similar to that "in Kentucky." There a

number of converts were "struck down motionless, as if dead." But when they came to, they would "appear very rational" and give a satisfying testimony of God's work in their souls, the correspondent noted.[39]

In an account from 1810, one Baptist convert described being struck down at a meeting. The young man had long wrestled with his fear of divine judgment, and during the previous night's prayer meeting, a Baptist elder (pastor) had called his name publicly and asked whether he wished for the church to pray for his conversion. He agreed, and the next night, the congregation began to sing an Isaac Watts hymn, "Show pity, Lord, O Lord forgive." The man prayed along with those words, and suddenly, "in the full enjoyment of my senses," he wrote, "such a feeling came upon me, as cannot possibly be described." He dismissed all alternative explanations for this strange sensation: he was not numb from cold; it was not a "palsy" or a cramp. Instead, he concluded that it was "an effect of the immediate power of God." He insisted that the experience was not "fiction or the mere impulse of passion." Soon he came into the peace and confidence of forgiveness.[40]

The *Massachusetts Baptist Missionary Magazine* also included a remarkable account of a visionary convert in 1805. Although the editors cautiously noted that they could not "vouch for its accuracy," they received the account from a "respectable authority." The convert, Patty Long, contracted measles not long after her baptism, and as she approached death, she recounted a number of extraordinary spiritual experiences. One night she asked those keeping vigil with her if they thought angels ever physically visited people. She asked, she said, because "I verily see one in the room now." Later that week she reported having a spectacular vision of the Last Judgment, and the new heaven and earth. She saw "the world sinking in a flood of fire, above the flood of fire there seemed to be an ark prepared, and all that were in the ark were saved; and those that were not were swept away in the flood of fire." After the earth dissolved in the conflagration, she witnessed the coming of the new earth, which needed no sun because the light was seven times brighter there than the current sun. She also testified to having seen Christ suffering for sinners. Soon thereafter she passed away. (Baptists seemed more ready to accept such accounts if they came as deathbed visions.)[41]

Baptists routinely reported other sorts of mysterious supernatural displays accompanying revival, even as they described the awakenings as free from fleshly chaos. In 1815, Elder Minor Thomas wrote from Ovid, in the Finger Lakes region of western New York, about an awakening during which he baptized several hundred converts. He insisted that the work was "remarkably free from enthusiasm or religious frenzy," but then went on to report that before it started, he heard unexplained singing that seemed to come out of thin air. "The most melodious singing" he ever heard woke him up in the night, but the only phrase he could make out was "bring the ransomed rebels home." From that moment his "mind was impressed with the idea that there would be a display of divine power in bringing sinners home to God." The editors of the Baptist periodical *The Vehicle, or New York Northwestern Christian Magazine*, said that while they agreed to publish this account, they "cautiously avoid expressing any opinions of our own" about it. A subsequent book on that period's revivals repeated Thomas's testimony and explained that "whole regions were filled with hosts of angels singing, *Bring the ransomed rebels home.*"[42]

WHATEVER FLUID BOUNDARIES Baptist leaders permitted regarding the practice of revival, the era of the great revival heightened Baptists' commitment to evangelism, church planting, and missions. Although Baptists had long engaged in itinerant and migratory evangelism, formal "missions" and missionary agencies were new concepts at the turn of the nineteenth century. These initiatives received a major boost from the excitement of the great revival. At the beginning of these awakenings, Baptist evangelists—whether ordained or not—often preached among people without easy access to churches, either by itinerant preaching or by permanent relocation to frontier settlements. But by the 1810s, Baptists began commissioning domestic and international missionaries to undertake more systematic outreach to the unchurched. White Baptists (along with other evangelicals) often came to view "missionaries" as those who went out to evangelize nonwhites, either in America or around the world.

The publication of English Baptist William Carey's *Enquiry into the Obligations of Christians, to Use Means for the Conversion of the Heathens* (1792) and his role in founding the English Baptist Missionary Society were turning points not only in Baptist missions but in the history of Christian missions generally. Carey was hardly the first to call for foreign missions—Christianity was a missionary religion from its beginnings—and many Baptists had wittingly and unwittingly been working as missionaries for centuries. (Think of the Separate Baptists' movement into the South in the 1750s, for example, or former slave David George's ventures in Nova Scotia and Sierra Leone after the American Revolution.) Nevertheless, Carey's work, and his voyage to India in 1793, signaled a new seriousness about missions among Baptists and other evangelicals.[43]

Baptists' descent on America's frontier areas did as much as anything to scatter seeds of their gospel, but in the 1790s American evangelicals began to follow their English brethren's lead by commissioning missionaries and founding missionary societies. Among the first was the Baptist- and Presbyterian-led New York Missionary Society, which was committed to "sending the gospel to the frontier settlements, and among the Indian tribes in the United States." It appointed Elkanah Holmes, a Baptist pastor, as a missionary to the Indians of western New York. Holmes initially worked among the Christian Indians of Brothertown and New Stockbridge but then expanded his travels to western New York, eventually establishing a mission station on the Niagara River. Tribal chiefs welcomed Holmes; the Tuscaroras wrote in diplomatically submissive (and liberally translated) language that they would be delighted to have "our father Holmes live among us." "We are in darkness; we are very ignorant—we poor . . . you have much light; you are wise and rich. Not but two in our nation can read in the good book, the Bible," they confessed. We should be skeptical about just how eager to convert these Indians actually were, but these responses were music to the missionary society's ears. When Holmes arrived among the Senecas to speak (through an interpreter) about the gospel, he found that some of the young men there caused a ruckus by laughing and rolling on the ground. "One made a very undecent report," Holmes wrote. "I endeavored to keep from being discomposed." Ultimately, he did address them successfully. He was doubtful about the Senecas, though, for they were "great pagans. They sacrifice white dogs to the Great Spirit." However, the New York Baptist Association wrote that Holmes's labors had "raised our expectations that God is about more extensively to fulfill his glorious prophecies . . . where he has said, 'I will even make a way in the wilderness, and rivers in the desert. [Isaiah 43:19–20]' "[44]

Some of the Baptists who were crucial to the early missions movement came out of a Calvinist Congregationalist background. One of these was Mary Webb, the founder in 1800 of Boston's Congregationalist- and Baptist-led Female Society for Missionary Purposes. Webb, a paraplegic from age five, grew up in a Congregationalist family, but she accepted Baptist principles and received believer's baptism in 1798. In 1800, she read a sermon on missions by Nathanael Emmons, a key "New Divinity" pastor who preached that a true understanding of the Calvinist theology of Jonathan Edwards should lead to an activist faith and support for missions. Webb and thirteen other Boston women started the Female Society later that year, committed to the distribution of Bibles and other religious publications "by missionaries in destitute places."[45]

Adoniram Judson, an early Congregationalist missionary and convert to Baptist convictions, was also deeply influenced by New Divinity theology. His father, a Congregationalist pastor, was also a follower of Nathanael Emmons, and Judson himself confirmed his New Divinity principles while attending Brown University and Andover Theological Seminary. Ann Hasseltine, Judson's first wife, was likewise influenced by Emmons and other New Divinity theologians such as Jonathan Edwards's protégé Joseph Bellamy.[46]

Judson experienced conversion during his first term at Andover and quickly became a major player in the emerging American missionary movement. In 1810, he helped to create the American Board of Commissioners for Foreign Missions, the first organization in the United States committed to sending missionaries around the world. Judson was one of the board's first missionaries, too. In two remarkable weeks in February 1812, Judson wed Ann Hasseltine, received ordination, and, with Ann, departed for India. Judson had plenty of time for reflection on the long shipboard journey, and he began to study the doctrine of baptism. He knew that he would interact with William Carey and the other English Baptist missionaries in India, and he wanted to have clear answers prepared if they questioned his commitment to infant baptism. But as he studied the New Testament, he became convinced that the English text transliterated, but did not actually translate, the word *baptismos*, which obviously meant "immersion" or "dipping." Even luminaries who supported infant baptism, such as Luther and Calvin, admitted as much.[47]

Ann was initially alarmed at Adoniram's investigation, and she warned him that if he became a Baptist, she would not follow. They continued probing the topic, however, and both decided that the New Testament nowhere contemplates the baptism of anyone but believers. Ann Judson told a friend that "we are confirmed Baptists, not because we wished to be, but because truth compelled us to be." When they arrived in Calcutta, the Judsons arranged for one of William Carey's associates to baptize them at the Lal Bazar Baptist Chapel.[48]

The Judsons established a Burmese mission in 1813. Their colleague Luther Rice, who also converted to Baptist tenets, returned to America to help raise funds for the Judsons, who had resigned from the American Board of Commissioners. Rice became a key advocate for a national Baptist missionary organization, which became a reality in 1814 with the founding of the Philadelphia-based (and wordily named) General Missionary Convention of the Baptist Denomination in the United States of America, for Foreign Missions—later known as the Triennial Convention, because its assemblies met every three years. It was committed to "sending the glad tidings of salvation to the heathen, and to nations destitute of pure Gospel-light." The respected Richard Furman was elected its first president, and in his inaugural sermon he reminded attendees that "millions are perishing in ignorance and sin, held in the chains of idolatry and gross superstition, under the power of Satan." Hinting at the ongoing War of 1812 and Napoleonic Wars in Europe, Furman declared that the nations were "convulsed; and great events with respect to the Kingdom of Christ appear to be drawing near." It was time for the people of God to mobilize for the global advancement of the gospel.[49]

One of the Triennial Convention's first missionaries was John M. Peck, who began serving in Missouri in 1818. Baptist immigrants from the southeast and Kentucky had started arriving in the Missouri Territory in the 1790s, and Missouri's first enduring Baptist congregation (1806) was the Bethel Church in present-day Jackson, across the Mississippi River from Illinois. (It was one of the first Protestant meetinghouses, if not the very first, erected west of the river.) Peck helped establish the first Baptist congregation in St. Louis, too, and performed baptisms in the Mississippi River, "waters that never, since the creation, probably, were employed for such a purpose." When the Triennial Convention withdrew support from Peck due to financial struggles, Peck founded the Illinois-based United Society for the Spread of the Gospel.[50]

By the late 1810s, Baptist missionary agencies had popped up across the country. Among these was African American pastor Lott Cary's Richmond (Va.) African Baptist Missionary Society. Cary had purchased freedom for himself and his family in 1813 and had received a preaching license from First Baptist Church, Richmond. Then he became pastor of Richmond's African Baptist Church. In 1815, Cary organized the African Missionary Society, but a white Baptist, William

Crane, had to serve as president because of fears of slave assemblies and insurrection in Virginia. The Triennial Convention was delighted with the society's founding, saying that it might signal God's providential design to have permitted "unoffending Africans to be brought slaves to our shores" so that they could experience salvation and return to the "land of Ham" (Africa) with the gospel. Cary went to Liberia as a missionary in 1821.[51]

The creation of these missionary organizations presented the first opportunity for major Baptist schism of the antebellum period. Not long after the Triennial Convention started sending out missionaries, signs of disaffection began to appear among Baptist churches, especially in the South and West, regarding missionary societies' legitimacy. In 1819, the Elkhorn Association in Kentucky endorsed the missionary and Bible agencies (the American Bible Society was founded in 1816) as embracing the "most important concerns which can engage the attention of mortals." However, it admitted that the "missionary cause has opposers even in the Western country. This we believe is in a great measure owing to misrepresentations which have originated from a distance, designed to vilify and slander the characters of those who are more immediately employed in the management of it." But opposition to the missionary cause continued to fester. The Hephzibah Association of south Georgia in 1819 refused to support, or even to correspond with, the Triennial Convention. Similarly, the Wood River Church in present-day Upper Alton, Illinois, noted in its minutes for 1820 that it was "not willing for any of her members to have any thing to do with the bord [sic] of Western missions." The surge of formal missionary societies, and their efforts to raise money, generated a backlash. "When the mission spirit waxed hot," one critic recalled, "the anti-mission began to wax warm also." As we shall see, the controversy would eventually cause massive defections from the "missionary" Baptist ranks.[52]

In 1820, those troubles lay largely in the future. During the era of the great revival and the expansion of missions, Baptists had proved themselves capable of matching the growth on the American frontier, from Mississippi to Michigan. They surged into northern New England, the Ohio River Valley, and the Lower Mississippi Region, sometimes going self-consciously as missionaries, and sometimes simply as immigrants. As they moved, they saw periodic revivals, and a broader pattern of itinerant preaching and new church starts, all leading to a vast ingathering of Americans. The experiences of converts such as Jacob Bower, physically and spiritually awakened by a Kentucky earthquake, were immeasurably valuable to each man and woman who went through them. They also fit into a template replicated in the lives of hundreds of thousands of Baptists during this period. A dynamic, nationwide Baptist movement had emerged.

6

Baptists and Slavery

RECORDS OF DISCIPLINARY cases from the Forks of Elkhorn Church in Kentucky evoke everyday troubles on the Baptists' antebellum frontier. Brother James Robertson was excluded for horse racing, Brother William Ware for stealing fowl. The church rebuked parents who let their children attend "Barbecues, Balls," and similar events.[1]

A steady drumbeat of cases also spoke to the Baptists' struggles with slavery. "Mr. Coles' Nancy" was charged for falsely "saying Brother Stephens said he would give her a hundred stripes and every six stripes dip the cow hide in salt and water—and saying while she was in irons she suffered every day for fire, victuals, and water." The church convicted and excluded her for lying. At the same meeting, the church considered whether "Baptist preachers are authorized from the Word of God to preach emancipation." They deferred the issue to the next month, when they decided Baptists should not publicly oppose slavery. Concurring with their association, these Kentucky Baptists concluded that it was improper for ministers or churches to "meddle with emancipation."[2]

Whether white Baptists meddled with the issue or not, slaves and free blacks rued the injustices of slavery in the Baptists' courts. Perhaps the most remarkable indictment came in 1807 when Winney, a slave at Forks of Elkhorn owned by Sister Esther Boulware, ran afoul of the church for saying that she once thought it right to obey her owners, "but since the Lord had converted her, she had never believed that any [real] Christians kept Negroes or slaves." More provocatively, she said she believed there were "thousands of white people wallowing in Hell for their treatment to Negroes—and she did not care if there was as many more." The church expelled her for saying so.[3]

As Baptists spread throughout the American South in the early nineteenth century, so did slavery. Some white Baptists in the Revolutionary era had condemned Christian slave owning, but over time most white Baptists in the South made peace with the institution, whether they owned slaves or not. This trend accelerated as Baptists helped fashion a new kind of cultural and religious establishment, especially in the southern states of the Atlantic seaboard, and many Baptist elites came to own slaves. Yet the issue of human bondage festered as the small but boisterous antislavery movement won over some white northern evangelicals. Everyday pressure against slavery came most directly from black Baptists themselves, including slaves like Nancy and Winney.[4]

BAPTISTS OF THE early republic believed in liberty, especially religious liberty and the spiritual "liberty wherewith Christ hath made us free," as Paul's letter to the Galatians put it. Baptists routinely commemorated the Fourth of July with patriotic sermons (although the Elkhorn Association drew the line at attending "barbecues on the 4th of July," enjoining its church members to avoid such festivities). On July 4, 1795, young Jonathan Maxcy, who had succeeded James Manning as president of the College of Rhode Island, declared that the anniversary signified the "resurrection of liberty, the emancipation of mankind, [and] the regeneration of the world. . . . we love liberty, we glory in the rights of men, we glory in independence." The American victory in the Revolution was positively millennial: "The Angel of Liberty descending, dropped on Washington's brow the wreath of victory, and stamped on American freedom the seal of omnipotence. . . . We tread a new earth, in which dwelleth righteousness; and view a new heaven." Maxcy was conspicuously silent about how these changes comported with the enslavement of Africans. Rhode Island was a hub of the Atlantic slave trade. The Brown family, key benefactors of the college that would soon bear their name, were involved in the slave transport business. Maxcy's circumspection partly explains why he was chosen as the inaugural president of South Carolina College in Columbia in 1804, a position in which he served for sixteen years. That college would purchase a slave named Jack during Maxcy's tenure.[5]

Maxcy was typical: most white Baptists spoke reverentially of the Revolution's significance for universal liberty, but they avoided the Revolution's (or the gospel's) implications for slavery. The Salem Kentucky Association received a query in 1789 about whether Christians could properly own slaves, and responded that it regarded it "improper to enter in to so important and critical matter at present." A member church of South Carolina's Bethel Association submitted a similar question in 1799 and got no response. (About 40 percent of Baptist preachers in late eighteenth-century South Carolina owned slaves; the vast majority of those slave owners possessed eleven or fewer slaves.) In the 1790s, it became common for Virginia's Baptist associations to assert that debate over emancipation belonged more properly in a "legislative body" than an ecclesiastical one. This position ironically resulted from disestablishment: Baptists could now spiritualize the business of the church and insist that divisive moral issues like slavery were not their concern.[6]

Some Baptists continued to speak forthrightly about slavery. The Shaftsbury (N.Y.) Association in 1792 registered its "detestation of the SLAVE TRADE" and looked forward to the day "when the Ethiopian, with all the human race, shall enjoy all that liberty due to every good citizen of the commonwealth." (New York would enact a program of gradual emancipation in 1799.) It was easier to sustain this position in Shaftsbury's upstate New York and Vermont, however, where slavery played little role in the economy.[7]

Even in the South, however, fleeting signs of white antislavery sentiment would appear through the 1820s. In 1794, the Georgia Baptist Association approved a petition to the legislature calling for a ban on the importation of slaves. And in 1796, the Ketocton (Va.) Association received this query from the Happy Creek Church: "Can the present practice of holding Negroes in slavery be supported by Scripture and the true principles of a republican government?" The association declined to take up the question, saying that it was not religious but a "proper subject of legislation." The next year, however, the association adopted a bold position against "hereditary slavery" as "a transgression of the Divine Law." It further recommended that the state consider a program of gradual emancipation. But when member churches expressed dismay at the proposal, Ketocton's messengers withdrew it and returned to their earlier notion that policy on emancipation was best left to the legislature. They brought up the issue again in 1801 but only to note that their decision to withdraw the emancipation plan from consideration did not bar future discussion of the topic.[8]

By 1810, however, Ketocton's tone had changed, as the association received an indignant query from Alexandria Baptist Church: "Is there not a fault among the Baptist churches in general in suffering so many of the people of color to assume to themselves the privilege of public speaking?"

Alexandria's whites justified their concern by contending that "there is no hope the Lord has committed a dispensation of the gospel unto [blacks]." It is unclear whether they meant to say that white Baptists tolerated too many blacks who clearly were not fit for the gospel ministry, or whether there was "no hope" that God would call *any* African Americans as preachers. In any case, the church at Alexandria had already "experienced some evil," it noted, from the preaching of blacks. In 1806, African Americans had formed a "conjoined" church with Alexandria's white congregation, obtaining a rented meeting place in 1818. Apparently this black Baptist meeting was chafing certain white members by 1810.[9]

The Ketocton Association agreed with the white Alexandria church's complaint, affirming that Baptist churches had been "too indulgent in suffering the people of color in public preaching." It warned that no blacks should preach unless they had all the requirements that would be expected of white candidates, and that slaves should only preach with the express permission of their masters. But in 1811, the association declined to consider a query from the Buck Marsh Church, which asked whether the "people of colour among us, who are retained in slavery, [can] become members of a Baptist church, consistent with the constitution of said church." Buck Marsh had a long history of questioning the legitimacy of black membership and bringing charges against its black members.[10]

The most remarkable outburst of white Baptist antislavery activism in the early national period was undertaken by Kentucky's David Barrow, who had helped organize the Black Creek Baptist Church in Southampton County, Virginia, in 1774. In 1784, Barrow freed his own slaves, having become convinced that owning slaves was sinful and inconsistent "with a republican form of government." In 1786, he persuaded the church— located in a strong slaveholding region—to declare slavery "unrighteous," even though more than a third of church members owned slaves. In 1798, the forty-five-year-old Barrow decided to move to Kentucky, but not before publishing his antislavery *Circular Letter*, in which he explained his hope that Kentucky would offer profitable farming where small farmers would not have to compete against slave masters and their unpaid black workers. Barrow also registered a summary of his "creed, in a religious and political point of view," in which he affirmed eternal election, limited atonement, and that liberty was "the unalienable privilege of all complexions, shapes, and sizes of men." He looked forward to the time when all slaves would be "delivered from the iron talons of their task-masters."[11]

Barrow found no peace regarding slavery in Kentucky, however. Strife between pro- and antislavery advocates split several Baptist associations there between 1805 and 1807. Barrow faced repeated charges of "preaching the doctrine of emancipation," and in 1806 the North District Association expelled him for refusing to be silent on the issue. William Hickman, who had pastored the Forks of Elkhorn Church for nineteen years, likewise withdrew from the church and the Elkhorn Association in 1807 for its toleration of slavery. (He returned in 1809.) In 1807, Barrow and messengers from nine churches organized the Baptized Licking-Locust Association, Friends of Humanity. Their first circular letter proclaimed that they were "now distinguished from our former brethren, by reason of our professed abhorrence to unmerited, hereditary, perpetual, absolute unconditional slavery." To answer critics, they cited Baptist missionaries such as Adoniram Judson, and the former slave David George (by then ministering in Sierra Leone), as opposing slavery. The Friends of Humanity association struggled to maintain support, however, and ceased to exist shortly after Barrow's death in 1819.[12]

These pockets of protest notwithstanding, the overall trend among white Baptists in the South was toward affirming slavery. A dual flood of cotton and evangelical faith into the interior South meant that Christian whites faced growing pressure to sanctify slave ownership. Eli Whitney's invention of the cotton gin in 1793 revolutionized the processing of short-fiber cotton, leading to a massive boom and the expansion of settlement into the new Southwest. South Carolina alone went from producing less than 80,000 pounds of cotton in 1793 to more than 8 million pounds in 1801. Ambitious farmers filled the lower Mississippi Valley; by 1803, cotton plantations lined both banks of the Mississippi from Natchez to Baton Rouge. As we have seen, many of these pioneers were Baptists and other types of evangelicals.[13]

Pressure from revolutionary ideology ("all men are created equal") and the egalitarian message of the revivalists required evangelical defenders of slavery to acknowledge that slaves were human, loved by God, and deserving of benevolent treatment. Baptists and others put new emphasis on the household relations of slavery, as Paul's New Testament letters had repeatedly done. Slaves, in this "paternalistic" view, should receive treatment akin to that of children: fatherly care had to complement judicious discipline in the Christian master's home. Good masters provided for basic needs, even into a slave's old age, and offered elementary education for the purposes of spiritual devotion and Bible reading. Christian slaves, likewise, were expected to work hard and obey their masters. This nurturing vision of slavery was needed more after Congress closed America's international slave trade in 1808, limiting the slave population to those already in the country and their offspring: now slavery had become a fully self-replicating institution on America's farms. In contrast to colonial slaves, many of whom came directly from Africa speaking no English and often knowing nothing of Christianity, the antebellum slaves were typically born in America, spoke English, and were exposed to Christian evangelism. The extent to which Christian slave masters actually manifested the paternal ideal of slaveholding varied widely. Certainly the topic of slaveholders' Christian obligations received regular attention from southern pulpits, especially as antislavery criticism from the North became more biting.[14]

Some southern whites remained skeptical about black literacy and religious autonomy. Frequent rumors (if only occasional incidents) of slave revolt stoked their fears. Critics routinely blamed evangelicals for inspiring slave revolts. This sentiment peaked in Charleston in 1822 when blacks affiliated with the city's African Methodist Episcopal Church, led by the free carpenter Denmark Vesey, were accused of plotting a major insurrection. Vesey and thirty-four alleged co-conspirators were executed. In recent years, some historians have argued that the plot was virtually invented by whites, while others have maintained that there actually was a conspiracy, if a smaller one than what whites imagined. In any case, the furor over Vesey generated debate over the Christianization of slaves, with some openly calling for restrictions on slave education and a ban on independent African worship services. But the respected Richard Furman, who knew Vesey personally, defended the practices of Christian slaveholding in an address commissioned by the newly formed South Carolina Baptist Convention (the first statewide Baptist convention).[15]

Furman thanked God for foiling the Vesey plot, which providentially warned disgruntled slaves that they had no hope of successfully revolting anywhere in America. Contrary to antislavery Christians, Furman insisted that "the right of holding slaves is clearly established in the Holy Scriptures." Making what would become the standard proslavery argument, Furman noted that the Bible generally assumes slavery's existence and nowhere condemns it. Critics employed the "golden rule" against slavery, but Furman countered that the requirements of mutual love hardly erased all social or familial distinctions. Mass emancipation would be disastrous for the slaves and their owners; therefore, masters should treat slaves generously and fairly, just as the master would want to be treated *if he were a slave*. If slaves achieved enough learning and self-sufficiency to be fit for freedom, masters would consider emancipation. In the meantime, they should treat their slaves as fully human dependents and as "accountable creatures, having immortal souls." Christian slaves would respect and obey their masters, so evangelizing them was "one of the best securities to the public, for the internal and domestic peace of the state." He denied that the Vesey conspirators were attached to "regular" (meaning white-led) churches. Instead, they were "members of an irregular body, which called itself the African Church." Christian slaves under the watchful, nurturing care of Christian masters: this was Furman's formula for a stable slave regime.[16]

WE MIGHT IMAGINE that Furman's brand of paternalism would drive away slaves, and untold thousands of blacks surely accepted evangelical faith more enthusiastically than they embraced white pastors' strictures. But we must also remember that to white and black Baptists (as well as the small numbers of Native American Baptists), salvation and a right standing before God were their primary religious concerns. Worldly considerations were secondary.

Consider the testimony of Letty, a slave owned by Kentucky Baptist minister John Taylor. Letty's brother Asa had experienced conversion, received baptism, and become an exhorter, and his influence led Letty to her own conversion in 1800. Although her master and overseer were both Christians, she worried that she could not trust them, and for some reason her brother also questioned the legitimacy of her spiritual concerns. She lived near the south bank of the Ohio River, and one day she began to contemplate drowning herself. She flung herself onto the bank, with her head pointing down toward the water, figuring that she was "immediately to go to Hell." Suddenly, however, the verse Matthew 25:34—"Come, ye blessed of my Father, inherit the kingdom prepared for you from the foundation of the world"—surged into her mind. She realized that these words were for her, and she rose up from the muddy ground, repeating to herself, "Jesus Christ is my Savior, and God is my friend." God had released her from the fear of judgment, and when she related her experience in front of Taylor's church, it affirmed it and admitted her to baptism.[17]

There was an irreducibly spiritual quality to Letty's conversion, and the conversions of thousands of other slaves and free blacks during the antebellum period. Their cumulative experiences led to a surge in black membership in white-led churches, as well as the advent of many African American–led Baptist churches across the North and South. Black Baptist congregations not only provided settings in which both free and enslaved members could worship God in (relative) freedom but also served as mediating institutions between the black individual and the white-led American state. In the African American church, blacks could help one another address the various social and political problems confronting them. We have already seen examples in David George's Silver Bluff Church, Lott Cary's congregation in Richmond, and the African Baptist church of Alexandria, Virginia. One of the black congregations of the most enduring significance was Savannah's, led by Andrew Bryan. Like David George, Bryan was a former slave who came to Baptist convictions through the ministry of George Liele. Liele, who had also been a slave, helped to start an African American congregation in Savannah in 1775 and then sailed to Kingston, Jamaica, in 1782, where he also planted that city's first Baptist church.[18]

Bryan began exhorting blacks and a few whites at a "rough wooden building" outside Savannah, but nervous whites soon "artfully dispossessed" them of the meetinghouse. Bryan refused to stop preaching, and irate white antagonists jailed and whipped him. Bryan's master was Jonathan Bryan, who had converted under the great itinerant George Whitefield's ministry decades earlier. Jonathan intervened on Andrew's behalf, providing his congregation with a barn for meetings. In 1788, they formally organized a Baptist church; by 1792, the congregation had grown to 235 members, and 350 other attendees, some of whom could not obtain permission from their masters to be baptized. In the early 1800s, the church planted two new African American congregations, and by 1812, the parent church stood at 1,500 members. After the early persecution, Bryan happily reported that they enjoyed the "rights of conscience" and freedom of worship. They celebrated the Lord's Supper quarterly and held baptismal services at the wide Savannah River. Bryan, who purchased his freedom when Jonathan died, went on to amass a sizable estate prior to his own death in 1812. Remarkably, Bryan seems to have imbibed some of the spirit of paternalism, too, as he came to own eight slaves, "for whose education and happiness" he was able to provide, he wrote in 1800.[19]

African American Baptists also founded churches in major northern cities in the early nineteenth century. With the encouragement of white Baptists, blacks established Boston's African Baptist congregation in 1805 and called Thomas Paul as their pastor in 1806. Paul was born in 1773 in Exeter, New Hampshire, to "respectable colored parents," a white Baptist historian noted. He received baptism at age sixteen and was ordained at twenty-eight. Paul did not initially receive a warm welcome in Boston, however, as the venerable pastor of First Baptist, Boston, Samuel Stillman, told him that "it was Boston, and that they did not mix colors." In other words, Paul was not welcome to preach in the city's white-led churches. Thomas Baldwin, pastor of Second Baptist, said that some in his congregation would undoubtedly leave the meeting if Paul were asked to speak. "We are too proud to have him preach," Baldwin said, "and as long as there are other white men to preach, I do not think it best for him to preach here." Undeterred, Paul not only built the African Baptist church but began an extensive itinerant ministry. He helped to found New York's Abyssinian Baptist Church in 1809, and in the 1820s he ministered in Haiti with the backing of the Massachusetts Baptist Missionary Society. As American and Baptist settlement proceeded west, so did African Baptist churches: to Lexington, Kentucky, a congregation pastored by "Old Captain" Peter Durrett, and onward to St. Louis (1822), Detroit (1837), and Indianapolis (1846). By 1830, there were about twelve officially constituted black Baptist churches in northern states, and thirty-five in the South.[20]

AS BAPTISTS MOVED into the West, they also increased their efforts to bring the gospel to Native Americans. As a boy, the Baptist missionary Isaac McCoy had relocated with his family to frontier Kentucky, and he converted and received believer's baptism there in 1801. Having moved to the Indiana Territory and heard news about the Baptists' missionary work, McCoy reflected that "it would not be foreign, from the general missionary cause, for these western regions to turn their attention in part, to the destitute more immediately under their notice." In 1817, the Triennial Convention's Board of Foreign Missions sent him to minister to white settlers in Indiana and Illinois, and to reach local Indians "as far as practicable." But McCoy developed a primary interest in the region's Indians, establishing several missions stations in Indiana and Michigan, including one among Ottawa Indians in 1826 on the Grand River, at the future site of Grand Rapids.[21]

Obstacles confronted McCoy at every turn. He had to depend on interpreters to communicate with prospective converts. Travel, especially during Great Lakes winters, was forbidding. The Indians did not trust white Americans' motives—starting in the 1790s, the new American nation had forced them into one dubious land agreement after another. During the War of 1812's conflict between the United States and Britain over territorial claims in the Great Lakes, most of the region's Indians had sided with the British. Although they had officially ceded their hold of the region in the 1760s, the Catholic French maintained an economic and missionary presence. In McCoy's view, the French never wasted an opportunity to undermine the Indians' estimation of the Americans.[22]

McCoy knew that Ottawas and other Indians had their own religious beliefs, which he regarded with puzzlement and pity. As he traveled in Michigan in 1827, he passed by a lake that Ottawas considered an "abode of spirits." The water emitted noises like gunshots and held an ancient tree that seemed never to rot. Any canoe that got too close to the tree, they said, risked being "capsized by an invisible hand." Another tree on the shore had caught fire and reportedly kept burning all winter. A shooting star appeared in the heavens, and an Indian asked McCoy what it portended. "Did the good book give any information on the subject?" he wondered.[23]

McCoy's greatest concern was the effect of white traders among Indians, especially the introduction of alcohol, which wreaked havoc among Native American men. Accordingly, McCoy became one of America's staunchest advocates of Indian colonization west of the Mississippi. He saw westward migration as an unfortunate outcome for Native Americans, but the best option for all involved. Colonization in the West, he wrote, would place them in a secure country that whites (ostensibly) could not take from them, and where they could receive education and Christian instruction "before they would be pressed by people of clashing interests, or be dragged into the vortex of ruin by whiskey sellers." We know that Indian relocation would only turn into a fatal farce for Native Americans, but McCoy was convinced that colonization was their most promising path to survival. Indian resettlement proceeded in Kansas and Oklahoma in the 1830s and 1840s. In 1842, McCoy was appointed to direct the new American Indian Mission Association based in Louisville, Kentucky.[24]

During his ministry, McCoy saw occasional conversions among the Indians, especially among pupils at his mission stations, and among interpreters whom he employed. An awakening that began in late 1824 led to the baptism of several Indian youths, as well as several white workers at the station. McCoy relished the experience of "sitting down to the communion table with Indian youths whom we had gathered from among the ruins of savage life." In more than six hundred pages of his *History of*

Baptist Indian Missions, however, this was the only "revival" McCoy noted. He focused more on the logistics of educating and colonizing Indians than on proselytizing them.[25]

He did occasionally come across Native American pastors and missionaries, such as the Creek pastor John Davis, who had experienced conversion in Alabama and came to the Arkansas and Indian Territories in the late 1820s. In 1832, McCoy helped Davis establish Muscogee Baptist Church (north of present-day Muskogee, Oklahoma) among Creek Indians who had relocated to the area as a result of the Indian Removal Act of 1830. It was the first Baptist congregation founded in the Indian Territory, a region that had been set aside for Native American colonization. A number of Creeks owned African slaves, who became the core of the Muscogee fellowship, which in 1836 was reported at 80 members—58 blacks, 18 Creeks, and 4 whites. Attendance at Sunday services ran to several hundred. The church held an early baptism in the Verdigris River, with McCoy preaching and Davis interpreting. The missionaries and baptismal candidates descended into the river, singing the oft-reprinted eighteenth-century hymn "Jesus and shall it ever be." (William Carey also reported using this hymn in translation at his Serampore mission in 1800.) In spite of such experiences, McCoy thought that Davis (as well as some white missionaries) was lax in his church admission practices: he urged Davis to bar from membership anyone who "could not give satisfactory evidence of their conversion."[26]

In all, the number of Native American converts among Baptists remained small. One history estimates that perhaps two thousand Native Americans received believer's baptism from the beginning of McCoy's work through the Civil War. Probably three-quarters of those converts were Cherokees.[27]

The key white Baptist missionary to the Cherokees was Evan Jones. He began working among western North Carolina's Cherokees in 1821, directing a school funded partly by the Board of Foreign Missions and partly by the federal government's Indian Fund. Jones was dismayed by the Cherokees' physical and spiritual conditions, seeing them as "buried in wretchedness and misery, literally without hope and without God in the world." Many Christians, he knew, had given up on the Indians as "irrecoverable slaves and the hopeless, helpless prey of the prince of darkness." Trying to encourage donors, one missionary wrote bluntly about the potential of the students: "Though their skin is red, or dark, I assure you, their mental powers are white."[28]

The key to the Baptists' evangelistic breakthrough among the Cherokees was the leadership of native converts and preachers, whom the white missionaries rechristened with Anglicized names. These included Tastheghetehee (Jesse Bushyhead), Kaneeda (John Wickliffe), and Dsulawee (Andrew Fuller). Bushyhead was the most effective. He had been converted at a mission school run by the American Board of Commissioners for Foreign Missions, but he accepted Baptist principles in the late 1820s. Jones arranged for Bushyhead's ordination and his employment by the Baptist missions board in 1833. Bushyhead would become the first native Christian to pastor a Cherokee church and a major opponent of the Cherokee nation's removal.[29]

Signs of evangelistic gains among the Cherokees began to appear in 1830. Jones immersed thirty-eight Cherokee converts that year, by far the highest total in his missions work thus far. In 1831, the conversions continued, with emotional scenes at baptismal and communion services. Jones and Kaneeda took turns preaching and used special benches for those seeking prayer and conversion. At one meeting, according to Jones, "A great number came to the anxious seats, manifesting the bitterness of their souls by sobs, and tears, and groanings which could not be uttered." By summer 1831, Jones's church had grown to seventy-eight members, including sixty-eight Cherokees. These numbers lagged behind Congregationalist and Methodist adherents among the Cherokees, but Bushyhead and Kaneeda's success among the non-Anglicized Cherokees was striking. Among these Cherokee Baptists, only four could speak English. The Baptist mission board regarded Jones's station as the most "encouraging" work among Native Americans.[30]

The Cherokee conversions proceeded amid what Jones called the "political excitement" of the removal controversy. In 1830, Congress passed the Indian Removal Act, and in 1832, President Andrew Jackson mocked John Marshall's decision in *Worcester v. Georgia*, which required Georgia to observe Cherokee territorial sovereignty. In stark contrast to McCoy, Evan Jones defended the Cherokees against removal, even when other evangelical missionaries accepted Jackson's policy as a fait accompli. Jones was appalled when the American army rounded up sixteen thousand Cherokees for forced deportation in 1838. He frantically kept track of converts, and he and Bushyhead preached the gospel even as soldiers herded the Cherokees into detention camps along the Tennessee River. A Baptist magazine reported that at one summer service, "as a result of a sudden outpouring of the Spirit," Bushyhead and Jones baptized fifty-five converts. Jones, Bushyhead, and the native preachers traveled among the Cherokee legions during their thousand-mile march west on the infamous Trail of Tears. At the end of 1838, Jones wrote from Missouri that he feared "an immense amount of suffering and loss of life attending the removal. Great numbers of the old, the young, and the infirm will inevitably be sacrificed." Indeed, the Trail of Tears eventually resulted in the deaths of about four thousand Cherokees.[31]

BAPTISTS AND OTHER frontier settlers often found themselves in conflict with local Native Americans, too, sometimes with tragic results. No episode was more poignant than the killings at Fort Parker, Texas, in 1836. There the Parker clan, led by Baptist elder John Parker, had emigrated from Illinois, after a wandering series of settlements through Virginia, Georgia, and Tennessee. Parker and his extended family had formed the Pilgrim Church of Predestinarian Regular Baptists in 1833 and promptly relocated to central Texas, choosing an idyllic spot along the Navasota River. In the midst of their abundant farmland, the Parkers erected a stout fort and compound, necessary because the family's acreage stood at the outermost limits of white settlement in the Republic of Texas, which had won its independence from Mexico in April 1836. Their property lay in the southeastern part of the Comancheria, the interior empire of grassland and horses controlled by the powerful Comanches. On May 19, 1836, a group of about a hundred Comanches came to the fort, which the settlers had inexplicably left open and undefended. The Comanches attacked, slaughtering the seventy-seven-year-old John and four others. The Comanches took several captives, most famously the nine-year-old Cynthia Ann Parker, who lived with them into adulthood, forgetting English and marrying a Comanche. Her son, Quanah Parker, would become one of the most influential chiefs in Comanche history.[32]

Although John was the patriarch of the Parker clan, his son Daniel left a deeper imprint on Baptist history. By the time that Daniel joined his family in Texas—he had settled farther east, thereby avoiding the Fort Parker attack—he had already become one of the leading Baptist voices against missionary societies. As we have seen, grumbling against the missions agencies began to appear among Baptists in the 1810s, as some argued that such extracongregational societies did not appear in Scripture, and that their representatives seemed awfully concerned with raising money. Historians have also attributed the rise of these antimission "Primitive" Baptists to the antielitist mood of the Jacksonian era and the strength of populist opinion in the wiregrass South (south Alabama and south Georgia, as well as the Florida Panhandle). In these and other impoverished areas of the southern states, the Primitives flourished.[33]

Parker had been converted and received baptism at Nail's Creek Baptist Church in northeast Georgia in 1802, and by the mid-1810s his sojourning had taken him to Wabash County, in southeastern Illinois. There he encountered the missions advocacy of Isaac McCoy, but also antimission sentiment. In 1818, Parker submitted a query to the Wabash Baptist Association, asking, "Is there any use for the United Society for the Spread of the Gospel? If so, wherein does its usefulness consist?" The association subsequently withdrew support from the national Baptist mission board.[34]

Parker stoked the growing antimissionary crusade with *A Public Address to the Baptist Society, and Friends of Religion in General, On the Principle and Practice of the Baptist Board of Foreign Missions* (1820). Although other prominent Baptists, such as Massachusetts's John Leland, had registered concern about them earlier, this was the "first systematic attack on the new Baptist institutions" on the basis of Scripture and Baptist tradition. In the *Public Address*, Parker confessed that his formal learning was limited, but he felt this was no barrier to his credibility. The worst theological errors appeared "amongst the wise and learned," those who leaned on the "wisdom of the world" instead of the authority of the Word of God. Indeed, much of Parker's critique was reminiscent of the older Separate Baptist distrust of associations and college-educated pastors. The call to preach came from Jesus alone, and when Christ sent out preachers during his earthly ministry, he did so "whether they had learning or not, and gives no account that a seminary of learning was essential to the ministry." Nor should extrachurchly agencies take it upon themselves to train or assign the ministry of Baptist pastors, he said. For Parker, this was no mere policy dispute. The agencies' representatives were in sin, having "rebelled against the King of Zion" and departed from "the gospel plan and the common, constant, and constitutional faith and practice of the Baptist church."[35]

Parker also made an antislavery argument that confirmed his hostility toward elite Baptists. He excoriated slave masters who supported missions off of money made for them by slave laborers. The masters "do not labor one day in a year, and yet possess great wealth and throw in liberally to the support of missions." Meanwhile, these hypocrites let their slaves languish in gross ignorance of Christianity and squalid living conditions. "Is not the soul of a negro as precious in America as in Africa?" Parker wondered. Parker's words remind us that, even as late as 1820, not all white southern-born Baptists sympathized with the slaveholding class.[36]

Parker's writings signaled the beginning of massive antimissionary unrest that raged across the frontier South and West in the 1820s. At the Hephzibah (Ga.) Baptist Association in 1822, a delegate's proposals that the member churches affiliate with the Georgia state missions organization met with violent rejection: "A motion was made to lay the [proposals] on the table, this was amended to a motion to throw them under the table, this by another to kick the bearer out of the house." The pro-missionary minister was finally escorted to the door and warned to never mention the word "missions" at the association again.[37]

The key organizational break that led to the creation of the Primitive Baptist movement came in 1827 with the Kehukee Association's "Declaration of the Reformed Baptist Churches in the State of North Carolina," written by Joshua Lawrence. For years Lawrence had wrestled with the fear of judgment for his sins, until he experienced spectacular visions around 1800. As he lingered alone in a field, "thinking how I should bear the pains of hell, and live in fire that none could quench, it appeared in a moment and unexpected that I saw the Lord Jesus Christ, about thirty feet from the earth in the air, as plain as if it had been with my natural eyes." Until that moment, Lawrence wrote, he had no more knowledge of Jesus than did a horse. Then God gave him a terrifying apparition: "Hell opened to the eyes of my mind, in twenty steps of the place where I stood in the similitude of a large pit and pillars of flooding fire and smoke." He knew that he deserved to be cast into that furnace "to drink liquid sulfurous flames forever." He pled with Christ for pardon, and his dread lifted. He believed that God had rescued him.[38]

After his conversion and baptism, Lawrence became pastor of the Falls of the Tar River Baptist Church. Questions about the validity of missions began to stir the Kehukee Association by 1812, but not until 1825 did Lawrence produce his tirade against the missionaries and their societies, titled *The American Telescope, by a Clodhopper, of North Carolina*. Lawrence did not hide his contempt for these "northern beggars" and their affected finery: "hearty, hale men, and young men in the prime and vigour of life, clothed in the finest black and blue broad cloth, with fur hats, boots, spurs, silk jackets, silver tipped bridles and stirrups, watches, &c. &c. turned beggars." Like many antimissionary Baptists, Lawrence played on fears of crypto-Catholicism and a loss of religious liberty. He forecast that if the churches kept creating money-grubbing missionaries and extrabiblical associations, they "will soon be no better than the church of Rome, and the High Church of England; for money and titles have always been the object of Popes and Popish priests."[39]

In 1826, Lawrence crafted the Kehukee Association's declaration, which one historian regards as the "beginnings of antimission schism and the Primitive Baptists." The *New York Telescope*, a chief outlet for antimission writing, prefaced the declaration with a Bible passage describing the Beast of Revelation, with a pointed implication about the missionary societies. The Kehukee Association not only deplored the work of the missionary agencies but also declared "NON-FELLOWSHIP with all such societies and proceedings, and with all churches who hold members" of them. The association banned any member of a missionary society from joining its churches and prohibited any "missionary preacher or beggar" from addressing its congregations. The same went for members of tract and Bible societies. The association also denounced "theological seminaries" as unbiblical, calling their representatives "agents of Anti-Christ." Echoing Daniel Parker's critique, it exhorted slave owners to "first learn their own negroes to read the Bible, who have sweated and toiled for the very money perhaps they are giving to others."[40]

Banning fellowship with missionary adherents took this schism to a ferocious level. The Kehukee Declaration was widely reprinted in cities such as New York, Philadelphia, and Providence, Rhode Island. The declaration also generated a backlash: one editorial titled "The Dark Ages Returning" expressed disgust that a church body "in a country so enlightened as our own United States, should not only entertain opinions so derogatory to revelation, but actually avow an intention to withhold fellowship from men, to whom the world is indebted for their labors of love in endeavoring to reform and convert the heathen."[41]

The antimission schism went fully national in 1832, with a convention of twenty-two elders and laymen held at Black Rock, Maryland. In an address directed to "the Particular Baptist Churches of the 'Old School,'" delegates regretted that their former brethren, sucked in by missionary charlatans, now charged them with "antinomianism, inertness, stupidity, &c., for refusing to go beyond the word of God." They denounced not only the usual societies but also "sectarian colleges," including Baptist schools, because such institutions imply that "our distinct views of church government of gospel doctrine and gospel ordinances, are connected with human sciences." This was "a principle which we cannot admit." They further opposed institutionalized revival or camp meetings and extrabiblical inventions like the anxious seat (a pew at the front of churches where revivalists would pray for those in the travail of conversion). They could not countenance assemblies where "all the borrowed machinery from Methodist campmeetings is introduced," nor did they wish to see if "a four days' meeting will not induce the Holy Ghost to produce a revival among us commensurate with the strange fire enkindled by others." The Holy Spirit was not "somehow so the creature of human feelings that he is led to regenerate persons by our getting their animal feelings excited." They welcomed all like-minded Baptists to attend future national assemblies.[42]

The antimission Baptists went by many names: "Black Rock Baptists," "Old School," "Old Fashioned," "Predestination," "Particular," and, more dismissively, "Square-Toed," "Hard Rined," "Broad-Brimmed," "Ironsides," and "Hard-Shell." Most commonly, they called themselves "Primitive Baptists," which to them meant biblical Baptists. One estimate suggests that by 1844 more than sixteen hundred antimission churches and sixty-eight thousand members had broken with the missionary Baptists. Most of this devastating exodus transpired in the South and Midwest.[43]

The antimission controversy was the largest of a host of theological fracases among Baptists in the antebellum era. Baptists also suffered defections by the followers of Alexander Campbell, founder of the Disciples of Christ, or Churches of Christ, who rejected the Baptists' requirement of a conversion testimony prior to baptism. Campbell asked only for a profession of faith in Jesus and implied that baptism secured forgiveness of sins and regeneration of the believer. Campbell also adopted strong antimission views. Entire churches and some Baptist associations went over to the Campbellites, with severe losses in Kentucky, Tennessee, and Indiana. Pro-missionary Baptists perceived the Campbellites and the antimission movement as a conjoined threat, with one Indiana association recalling the "destruction of the two antagonisms—baptismal regeneration . . . on one hand, and antinomian antimissionism on the other. The adverse winds . . . swept over the western churches like the simoon or sirocco, splitting, dividing and rending all before them."[44]

BUFFETED BY CROSSCUTTING theological winds generated by Freewill Baptists, Campbellites, antimission movements, and others, many Baptist churches embraced the new statement of faith published by the New Hampshire Baptist Association in 1833. This statement moderated the Calvinism of older statements such as the Philadelphia Confession of 1742, but just how moderate it was stood open to debate. The statement remained elusive on the thorniest questions of limited atonement and God's immutable decree of election, allowing a range of Baptists to interpret those matters as they wished. Some strong Calvinists did see the New Hampshire Confession as too moderate, or possibly even free-will Arminian. In the 1840s, for example, the Florida Association of Baptists, having once accepted the New Hampshire confession, on second thought rejected it in favor of articles affirming "the doctrine of eternal and particular election."[45]

The New Hampshire confession also declined to use the term "elders" when describing biblical church officers but only mentioned the synonymous terms "bishops or pastors." (The term "elders" reappeared in the 1925 Baptist Faith and Message, which dropped the word "pastors.") Over time the term "pastor" became more conventional in pro-missionary Baptist congregations, while Primitive churches continued using the term "elder." Baptists also debated whether a single "elder" (or pastor) was the proper biblical system, or whether a "plurality" of elders was the norm. Evidence suggests that early churches of the Separate Baptist tradition, especially in Virginia and the Carolinas, often used a system of plural elders. Early churches of the Philadelphia Association did so as well.[46]

The New Hampshire Confession remained popular for the better part of a century, but no statement of faith could forestall theological controversy among Baptists. In the 1850s, the Landmark controversy arose over issues similar to those in the antimission controversy, especially the nature of the New Testament church. James Robinson Graves, the most articulate Landmarkist, recalled with disgust how, in the early 1830s, he attended baptisms and saw a mishmash of sloppy, unbiblical practices, including "the immersion of my mother and sister by a Pedobaptist minister, and the plunging of another subject face forward as he knelt in the water, and the pouring water upon another while kneeling in the water, the sprinkling upon several others while standing on the banks of the stream, and yet others out of a pitcher in the meeting-house."[47]

Graves, a Baptist pastor in Nashville, was convinced that these casual deviations did not please God. True Christians should insist on New Testament practices and condemn all others. Graves and other Landmarkists assaulted the notion that "evangelicals" could make common cause in missions and revivals, because non-Baptist churches were illegitimate. "Baptist churches are the churches of Christ," he wrote, and "they *alone* hold, and have alone ever held, and preserved the doctrine of the gospel in all ages." Presbyterians, Methodists, and the other churches that had worked with Baptists in revivals and evangelical societies were not true churches, and Baptists should cut off fellowship with them. Many Landmarkists further argued that there was an unbroken succession, however scattered and small, of local Baptist churches that had existed since the time of Christ, and that these congregations alone constituted the apostolic work of God's kingdom on earth. A failed Landmarkist attempt to have the Southern Baptist Convention (SBC) turn away from denominational (as opposed to local church-based) missions agencies in the late 1850s led some to abandon the SBC, but Landmarkist themes continued to color Southern Baptist theology after the Civil War.[48]

From missions to Indian removal, then, a host of theological, political, and social debates embroiled antebellum Baptist churches. As it turned out, the greatest and most dangerous of those debates concerned slavery. Resentments harbored by slaves such as Winney at the Forks of Elkhorn, growing antislavery northern sentiment, and a hardening proslavery ideology in the white South made for a volatile combination. Mere theological debate, Baptists and all Americans would discover, could not contain this festering crisis.

7

Slavery, Schism, and War

IN 1825, THE slave and lay Baptist preacher Nat Turner had a vision. He saw "white spirits and black spirits engaged in battle, and the sun was darkened—the thunder rolled in the Heavens, and blood flowed in streams." The troubling apparition made Turner long for holiness and true spiritual knowledge before the advent of Judgment Day. Then, in a Virginia field where he was toiling, he saw blood on the corn. He told both white and black neighbors about these miraculous portents of the Day of the Lord. Wandering in the woods, "hieroglyphic characters, and numbers, with the forms of men in different attitudes, portrayed in blood" appeared to him on the leaves of trees. One white man, Etheldred Brantley, was impressed by Turner's prophecies. When white Baptists would not allow Turner to baptize Brantley, he and Turner took to the waters themselves. There they "were baptized by the Spirit."[1]

Turner's transcendent encounters grew more intense. On May 12, 1828, he "heard a loud noise in the heavens, and the Spirit instantly appeared," telling him that the "Serpent was loosened, and Christ had laid down the yoke he had borne for the sins of men, and that I should take it on and fight against the Serpent, for the time was fast approaching when the first should be last and the last should be first." The signal to make war against the Serpent came in the form of a February 1831 eclipse. Turner initially planned the "work of death" for the Fourth of July, but he fell ill. So he waited. "The sign appeared again" in another eclipse—this time a total solar eclipse—on August 7, 1831. He decided to act. Turner gathered some seventy slaves and free blacks, who used axes and clubs to murder sixty white men, women, and children, mostly members of slave-owning families. In the massive backlash that followed, state officials and white vigilantes executed and killed hundreds of blacks, most of whom had nothing to do with Turner's insurrection. Turner himself was captured, and then hanged, skinned, decapitated, and quartered in Jerusalem, Virginia.[2]

Other Baptists saw Turner's eclipse, too. In upstate South Carolina the phenomenon precipitated the Sun Spot Revival, an awakening "which, for extent and duration, has hardly a parallel in the history of revivals." According to reports, the sun dimmed dramatically, the landscape took on a rosy hue, and "men who were not alarmed felt humbled as under the finger of God." Baptist preachers, "eager to lay hold of every means adapted to the awakening and humbling of sinners, made happy and forcible allusions to the surrounding scene." The awakening, which began at a meeting of the Saluda Baptist Association, touched both the upstate and the low country of South Carolina. It lasted the better part of three years.[3]

Not coincidentally, the revival transpired during the nullification controversy, which saw South Carolina officials face down the federal government over tariff policy. The standoff anticipated the secession crisis of thirty years later. Revival reports from across the state recorded "scenes, bursting upon us so suddenly, so unexpectedly, so extraordinarily, so powerfully, the whole seems like some bright vision delightfully passing before our wondering eyes." This nullification revival—and similar revivals elsewhere—helped to sanctify the slaveholding ethic of the plantation South. It also stamped Baptist churches as uniquely comprehensive southern institutions, encompassing large numbers of both blacks and whites, planters and yeoman farmers.[4]

The Saluda Association and Nat Turner experienced two kinds of Baptist visions: one of spiritual power for awakening, the other of spiritual power for racial justice. The two visions both grew out of a common conviction that God ministered directly to individuals, regardless of class, ethnicity, or gender. But these visions also evoked a grinding tension over slavery. That tension would permanently rend Baptist community in 1845 and ultimately would divide the nation itself.

OF COURSE, MOST Baptists who opposed slavery did not go to Turner's bloody lengths to stop it. The tension over slavery among Baptists and other evangelicals is easier to discern in hindsight than it was for Americans living through the antebellum era. Baptist churches continued to grow—sometimes furiously—in the North, South, and West, and among blacks, Native Americans, and whites. They prospered even as the slavery and secession crises loomed. In addition to the South Carolina awakenings and those among the Cherokees, the early 1830s saw reports of revival from all corners of the country, among Baptists and other denominations. (The great Presbyterian revivalist Charles Finney saw an enormous response in Rochester, New York, beginning in the fall of 1830, for example.)

The controversy over missions did not inhibit revival among member churches of the Kehukee Association (N.C.). W. B. Worrell estimated that some 280 people received baptism in Kehukee member churches over a five-month period in 1830 and 1831. "I have never before seen such a reformation among white and black, rich and poor," he wrote. Worrell also noted that, unlike some of his antimission associates, he was friendly toward the Bible and temperance societies.[5]

The antialcohol crusade became an integral part of some revival campaigns in these years, as evangelists called on people to commit themselves to Christ and to give up the bottle. William Henry Brisbane, a South Carolina Baptist and slave owner who would later move to Ohio and emancipate his slaves, reported that during a visit to Pennsylvania in 1832 he attended a protracted meeting at a Baptist congregation outside Philadelphia. There, "along with the usual exercises of devotion," he wrote, "we introduced the subject of temperance." Before the meeting was over, some seventy attendees pledged total abstinence. The next day five people testified about their conversion, and they soon received baptism; over the ten days of the assembly, forty-eight people were baptized. Brisbane also noted that temperance was making gains in the Carolina low country. "Now barbecues, musters and political meetings are conducted without the use of any ardent spirits or even wine. On the 4th of July last, about 800 persons sat down to a dinner in this village, and the toasts were all drunk in cold water." Brisbane's former church, Pipe Creek, banned from membership anyone who refused to "abstain wholly from the use of ardent spirits." While drunkenness had always been a concern among Anglo-American evangelicals, many now made total abstention a test of fellowship. Baptists (aside from Primitives, who distrusted the antialcohol associations) were often the "most forward" among evangelicals on temperance, and they had established scores of temperance societies across the country by the early 1830s.[6]

Baptist growth continued to accompany new settlement in the West, as well. A remarkable Baptist revival transpired in 1841 in the frontier settlement of Washington-on-the-Brazos, Republic of Texas, 140 miles northwest of the Gulf of Mexico. Agents of the American Baptist Home Mission Society, including James Huckins and William Tryon, were integral to Baptist efforts in the region. Tryon re-gathered a defunct Baptist church in Washington in early 1841, and in July, Robert Emmett Bledsoe Baylor accompanied Tryon to his monthly meeting there. Baylor had served in the US House of Representatives and the state legislatures of Kentucky and Alabama prior to coming to Texas, where he worked as a Baptist minister and judge. As historian David Bebbington has vividly recounted, at a Sunday morning baptismal service at the river, Tryon immersed a slave girl who had recently experienced conversion. Baylor then preached "with power." As a result of the subsequent revival, which absorbed virtually the whole town, thirty-two new members joined the tiny church, bringing total membership to fifty.[7]

Pro-missionary Baptists had been under attack from the "rough culture" of drinking and gambling, the antimission sentiment of Primitive Baptists, and local freethinkers. The revival helped turn the tide. Huckins, who regarded Washington as the "high ground of Satan," contended that the awakening brought about moral reform and converted some of the most irreligious men in the county. In spite of its relatively isolated location, Washington had several notorious deists and antievangelical critics, some of whom experienced conversion during the revival. Finally, antimission settlers had a strong presence among Texas Baptists, going back to the coming of the Parker clan in the 1830s. But when representatives of missions agencies helped bring about revival, it represented a victory for the pro-missionary view. Following the revival, its key leaders endorsed proposals for a Texas Home Mission Society, as well as the Texas Baptist Education Society, the latter combining a missionary ethos with an emphasis on a learned ministry. The society, led by Baylor, Huckins, and Tryon, went on to establish Baylor University, chartered in 1845 by the Republic of Texas. The school was initially located down the road from Washington, at Independence, Texas. (In 1886, Baylor merged with Waco University and relocated to Waco.) The new university represented the "spirit of the Washington awakening."[8]

This was the Baptists' "frontier age," as historian Robert Johnson notes, and settlement in the Far West brought Baptists to the Pacific coast in the 1840s. Oregon received its first Baptist congregation in 1844. The nearest Baptist church to it might well have been at Washington-on-the-Brazos, some seventeen hundred miles to the southeast. But by 1848 there were four Baptist churches in Oregon, and one in Oregon City built a meetinghouse—the first Baptist church structure west of the Rockies. Following a familiar pattern, these pro-missionary Baptists created an educational society in 1849 and founded McMinnville (later Linfield) College in 1858. The Baptist Home Mission Society likewise sent workers to San Francisco in 1849. The first Southern California Baptist congregation was organized at El Monte, east of Los Angeles, in 1853. Having reached the Pacific, Baptists filled in the states and territories from the Mississippi River to the Rocky Mountains and also proceeded northwest up the Pacific coast, coming to Alaska in the mid-1890s.[9]

Some Baptist missionaries sought to reach Asian immigrants, including Chinese settlers in San Francisco and Portland, and Japanese immigrants in Seattle. As with the Cherokees, ministry to Asians was most successful when undertaken by fellow Asian converts. Chinese Baptist preacher Fung Seung Nam preached to crowds numbering in the thousands in early 1870s San Francisco, while Japanese minister Fukumatsu Okazaki became a Baptist in Denver in the 1880s, and in 1899 he became the original pastor of Seattle's Japanese Baptist Church.[10]

Baptists also began some tentative outreaches to Hispanic Americans around this time, especially in New Mexico. The northern Baptist missions board intended to send missionary Hiram Read and his wife to California, but when she became ill in 1849 in Santa Fe, the Reads decided to stay, with the encouragement of the territory's military commander. They were likely the first Protestant missionaries in New Mexico, where Catholic friars had arrived two centuries earlier. Read resolved to learn Spanish and even began calling himself a "bishop," to accord with the region's typical Catholic terminology. Baptists sent more missionaries into the area and saw successes in the 1850s, partly through the efforts of Hispanic exhorters. The missionaries recorded more than a hundred baptisms, but no lasting Hispanic Baptist congregation emerged. The work faltered with the coming of the Civil War. More permanent institutions emerged in Texas in the 1880s, with San Antonio's Primera Iglesia Bautista Mexicana, founded in 1887, becoming the first lasting Hispanic Baptist congregation in the state.[11]

European immigrants continued to fuel Baptist growth, too, as illustrated by the founding of America's first Swedish Baptist church in 1852 in Illinois. A Swedish immigrant named Gustaf Palmquist came to Baptist convictions during a revival at the Galesburg (Ill.) Baptist Church in 1852, receiving believer's baptism along with 106 others, twenty-one of whom were Swedes. A month later, the church ordained Palmquist (who had originally experienced evangelical conversion in Stockholm in 1844) and commissioned him to preach among the region's Swedish immigrants. Six weeks later, he organized a church, which performed its baptisms in the Mississippi River at Rock Island, Illinois. In 1853, the Baptist Home Mission Society put Palmquist on its payroll. By 1856, there was sufficient Swedish Baptist strength in the Midwest for them to hold a conference in Rock Island. This was the beginning of the Swedish Baptist General Conference, which in 1945 became known simply as the Baptist General Conference. The denomination has slowly moved away from its exclusively Swedish origins, and although it remains doctrinally evangelical and Baptist, it has also retreated from Baptist particularity. Thus, in 2008 the denomination renamed itself Converge Worldwide. John Piper, pastor of Bethlehem Baptist Church in Minneapolis, and founder of Desiring God Ministries, became the most recognized leader of the Baptist General Conference by the beginning of the twenty-first century. In 2012, Converge reported 1,182 member churches in the United States and total attendance of roughly 260,000.[12]

BY THE LATE 1840s, Baptists had achieved phenomenal growth, sweeping from coast to coast and numbering perhaps eight hundred thousand adherents. Although Episcopalians, Congregationalists, and Presbyterians still claimed more influence over elite culture, Baptists now possessed substantial institutional sway. The most influential Baptist intellectual of the antebellum period was Brown University's Francis Wayland, who wrote the era's most popular textbooks, *The Elements of Moral Science* (1835) and *The Elements of Political Economy* (1840). These were used at a range of denominational colleges, across both North and South. Reflecting broader trends in American evangelical thought, Wayland cast ethics as "the Science of Moral Law." But reason alone could not fully apprehend moral truth; we also need the Holy Spirit to illuminate Scripture in order to understand God's laws, Wayland argued. In Wayland's system, reason and revelation served as "completely harmonious principles," as historian George Marsden has put it. Although Wayland was certainly an evangelical, his belief in the complementary quality of reason and revelation was a notable way station in the secularization of American education. If reason comported perfectly with revelation, then future educators could justify leaving revelation aside, or quietly taking it for granted.[13]

Wayland served as president of Brown from 1827 to 1855, shaping legions of students through his books and teaching. Among his pupils were Baylor founder James Huckins and James Angell, a Congregationalist who would become the University of Michigan's longest-serving president, from 1871 to 1909. Other instances of elite Baptist intellectual influence before the Civil War included Jonathan Maxcy's presidency at South Carolina College, and Baptist pastor Basil Manly's presidency at the University of Alabama from 1837 to 1855. But one should not overstate their overall status: Baptists remained somewhat marginal in the halls of educational, cultural, and political power. Not until Abraham Lincoln did a person of Baptist background become president, and not until the (scandal-ridden) presidency of Warren Harding did a Baptist occupy the White House.

Average Baptists lived their faith not in the halls of power but in the daily affairs of piety and congregation. The Baptist church of tiny Cades Cove in east Tennessee was representative of how evangelical congregations could "dominate the social and cultural mores of the community and, in a very real sense . . . determine the fabric of the developing community," says a historian of that village. The monthly records of Cades Cove Baptist Church, established in 1827, reflect the litany of disciplinary cases common to nineteenth-century congregations. The controversy over missionary agencies was the church's most bitter dispute prior to the Civil War. In 1839, an investigative committee of the Tennessee Baptist Association found that a majority of members would not fellowship with any who had "joined any of the benevolent institutions of the day." Ultimately, the pro-missionary minority was excluded and created a separate Missionary Baptist church in the hamlet. The remaining majority took on the name "Primitive Baptist" for their congregation in 1841. That church stopped meeting during the Civil War, from 1862 to 1865, because "of the rebellion and we was union people and the rebels was too strong here," the church records noted. There were almost no slaves in Cades Cove, and the church book made no references to disputes over slave owning. Yet the conflict was impossible to avoid; it forced the Primitive Baptists to make grave decisions about their wartime affiliation.[14]

IN 1813, BAPTIST historian David Benedict wrote, "The Baptists are by no means uniform in their opinions of slavery. Many let it alone altogether; some remonstrate against it in gentle terms; others oppose it vehemently," while those who held slaves "justify themselves the best way they can." (We can assume that most black Baptists took a dim view of the institution.) Periodically, northern churches faced unrest about fellowshipping

with slaveholders. We have already seen Kentucky's church and association splits over slavery. Those "Emancipating Baptists" also spread in
small numbers across Illinois and Missouri in the early national period.
Similarly, the New York Baptist Association in 1809 stopped short of recommending a ban on slave owners from membership, but it did aver that
"the practice of slave-holding ought to be discountenanced as much as
possible" among church members. The Scioto (Ohio) Baptist Association
went further in 1816, saying that it would not associate even with slave
masters who treat their slaves equitably, and that it would have no fellowship with any churches or associations "that do in principle or practice
hold to involuntary slavery."[15]

Generally, though, white Baptists agreed to leave slave owning as a
matter of individual conscience and politics. Because it was a political issue, it was best left to legislators to decide. For Baptists and other
Americans, 1831 was a critical turning point, as Nat Turner's Rebellion
demanded a response. Many whites felt that they should recommit to a
Christianized, benevolent, and (hopefully) less volatile version of slavery.
Others—mostly nonslaveholders—agitated for emancipation, seeking to
eliminate the threat of future Nat Turners. Legislator Thomas Jefferson
Randolph, grandson of his famous namesake, introduced a plan for
gradual emancipation in early 1832, but it was soundly defeated by slaveholding interests. Virginia Baptists were particularly defensive about the
Turner episode, as critics argued that the radical evangelicals had deluded
blacks with "a ranting cant about equality." Some antagonists even proposed banning missionary and educational work among blacks. White
Baptists insisted that missionary efforts should continue, but educators
and evangelists should discourage any forms of black independence.
Turner and his minions were not real Baptists, white Virginia Baptists
said. They were deluded, depraved fanatics.[16]

Virginia churches dealt with visceral resentments between whites and
blacks for years after the insurrection. God only knew, the Portsmouth
Association mused, "whether in those churches a union can ever be
restored between our white and coloured members." Both state and
church officials took measures to prohibit blacks from preaching and
holding separate meetings (measures that they enforced only selectively
once the furor over Turner subsided). In Williamsburg, whites forced the
closure of the city's independent black Baptist church, which had existed
for almost four decades. Richmond's First Baptist revoked the licenses
of twelve African American exhorters and preachers. A segregationist

mindset within the white-led churches replaced the tenuous biracial ethos of earlier southern Baptist congregations. One church even recommended that the Portsmouth Association amend its constitution so "that where ever the words male members are inserted the word white should precede, so that it should read white male members."[17]

THE PASSAGE OF Britain's Slavery Abolition Act in 1833 put direct pressure on American slaveholders to follow suit. English Baptists wrote their American counterparts a pointed letter, pleading with them to work for slavery's "speedy and entire destruction. . . . The evil is so monstrous, its opposition to the rights of humanity and to the spirit of the gospel is so palpable," that the English brethren assumed that all right-minded American Baptists would follow their lead.[18]

They were wrong, of course. The letter elicited a nervous response from the Triennial Board of Foreign Missions. Slavery, the board noted, was a "peculiar difficulty" that required handling with "great caution." Mass emancipation was fraught with danger and impassable legal barriers. Trying to effect abolition would disrupt unity among the "multiplying thousands of Baptists throughout the land." The board members knew that criticizing the abominations of slavery implicitly condemned their slaveholding brethren, whom they defended as "sincere followers of Jesus Christ." Southern whites were "liberal and zealous in the promotion of every holy enterprise for the extension of the gospel." (For twenty-one of the first thirty years of the Triennial Convention, a slaveholder had served as convention president.) White southern Baptists did not necessarily think slavery was right, but they could see no way to safely abolish it. Baptist officials saw no reason to disrupt their national fellowship in the name of abolition. In light of the antimission controversy and breakaways, the need for unity among pro-missionary Baptists seemed even more pressing.[19]

The mission board's tepid response was not good enough for some northern Baptists, a group of whom sent a letter with 180 signatories commending the English Baptists for their admonition. "SLAVEHOLDING," they thundered, "is now the most heinous sin with which America is chargeable." Southerners responded in kind, with the Charleston Association deploring the work of "deluded and mischievous fanatics . . . to interfere with the domestic institutions of the Southern and Slave-holding States." Such efforts to convince southerners of slavery's immorality would fail, they proclaimed, as long as southerners had "the

Bible in their hands." The association regarded outside interference on the issue "not only as officious and unfriendly but incendiary and murderous." It could fatally damage the union of American states, the Charlestonians averred—fifteen years before their state would actually secede. The association also reaffirmed its commitment to the evangelization of slaves and cautioned against restricting the religious liberty of blacks except in cases of compelling urgency.[20]

But abolitionism had begun to take hold among many northern evangelicals, especially in New England. For them, slaveholding was no longer a matter for individual Christians to decide, nor should churches remain silent about it. The Hancock (Maine) Baptist Association resolved in 1837 to have no more fellowship with slave owners (which could only mean their southern brethren, since slavery had been illegal in Maine for more than fifty years). The Washington (Maine) Association concurred, vowing to have no connection with those who practice this "abomination and thus defile the church of God." The Shaftsbury (N.Y.) Association resolved to send "letters of admonition to their Southern brethren" advising them to repent of their sin. African American Baptists weighed in, as well. By 1834, the African Baptist Church of Albany, New York, had begun holding special prayer meetings on behalf of the "Southern brethren." Other black Baptists, both northern and southern, presumably joined in those prayers.[21]

Tensions between northern and southern Baptists became acute in 1840, with the formation of the American Baptist Anti-Slavery Convention. The convention elected as president New York pastor Elon Galusha, who also served as vice president of the Triennial Board of Foreign Missions. Adopting a different tone than the national board, Galusha and four hundred antislavery Baptist ministers published a scathing letter reproaching Baptist defenders of slavery. Human bondage was "a perversion of the first principles of justice," they contended, and "a positive transgression of the revealed will of God." They declared that they would no longer acknowledge slave-owning Baptists as "consistent brethren in Christ." Neither would they warmly clasp a hand that also "plies the scourge on woman's naked flesh, which thrusts a gag into the mouth of man, which rivets fetters on the innocent, and which shuts up the Bible from human eyes."[22]

Because they were evangelicals, the Baptists' antislavery argument had to hinge upon Scripture. But antislavery activists had difficulty with a literal reading of the Bible, which seemed to tacitly accept the existence of slavery—at least in the forms that existed in ancient Israel and the Roman Empire of Jesus's time. Slavery's defenders often noted that the Bible never explicitly condemned slavery. Jesus was silent on the matter. Galusha explained this reticence by suggesting that the disciples were "too busy" with other pressing matters to address every conceivable sin. The Savior, likewise, had never "witnessed a scene of slavery . . . the chained coffle,- the naked gang of the cotton field,- the exposed female reeking under the lash,- the child torn forever from its mother's breaking heart,—these, and worse acts of slavery's tragedy, were not performed, so far as history, before the face of Jesus." Human bondage was a modern crime to which Scripture did not speak directly, but one could intuit from Christ's teachings and character that he would have deplored American slavery. Although Galusha and the antislavery evangelicals were as eager as proslavery Christians to cite Scripture, they indirectly acknowledged that the letter of Scripture alone did not supply a definitive word on slavery "in the abstract."[23]

The home and foreign mission boards tried to contain the damage wreaked by Galusha's antislavery declaration, but white southerners were appalled. Some called for Galusha's removal from the Board of Foreign Missions, making their "future connection with the Board" contingent upon his expulsion. The 1841 Triennial Convention voted Galusha out, replacing him with Richard Fuller, a slave-owning pastor from South Carolina.[24]

Neither side was placated, however. At the 1844 Home Mission Society meeting, a delegate introduced a resolution to the effect that owning slaves would not preclude appointment as a home missionary. In response, South Carolina's Fuller offered a substitute resolution affirming that no one should inject slavery or antislavery activism into the society's work. Fuller's resolution won. It read, in part, "that to introduce the subjects of slavery or antislavery into this body, is in direct contravention of the whole letter and purpose of the said Constitution, and is, moreover, a most unnecessary agitation of the topics with which this Society has no concern."[25]

Baptists in Georgia decided to test the Home Missions Society's actual stance by nominating a slaveholder as a missionary. As was customary, they raised money to support him and then offered him for the society's approval. They admitted that they wanted to see if the society was really neutral on the issue of slavery, saying at one point they wished to "stop the mouths of the gainsayers." Home Mission Society officials believed that to act on such a nomination would violate neutrality on slavery, so they did nothing, which effectively denied the appointment.[26]

Alabama Baptists pressed the same issue in international missions. They submitted an inquiry to the Triennial Convention asking bluntly whether slaveholders could be appointed as foreign missionaries. Furthermore, they questioned whether the Triennial Convention had sole power to appoint missionaries, or whether this power was shared with the churches. Triennial Convention board members disagreed among themselves about how to respond. Essentially, they believed they were left with a choice of either alienating southerners with a statement against slavery or satisfying the South by agreeing to appoint slaveholding missionaries, thereby provoking some northern Baptists to leave the Triennial Convention. After intense debate, the board affirmed that the Triennial Convention retained sole appointive power. But the statement also insisted, "One thing is certain; we can never be a party to any arrangement which would imply approbation of slavery." Alabama Baptists responded by charging that the Triennial Convention had violated neutrality resolutions of 1841 and 1844.[27]

In reaction to these test cases, the Virginia Baptist Missionary Society called a meeting to discuss a southern response to the Triennial Convention. On May 8, 1845, slightly fewer than three hundred southerners—and a few northerners from the American Baptist Publication Society—met in Augusta, Georgia. Some wanted to immediately withdraw from the Triennial Convention, while others counseled patience. In the midst of the debate, William B. Johnson of South Carolina offered an outline for a new convention. Johnson had helped form the constitutions of the Triennial Convention in 1814 and the Baptist State Convention of South Carolina in 1821. Johnson carried in his coat pocket a speech that amounted to a plan for a southern constitution. With only minor changes, Johnson's draft became the framework for the new Southern Baptist Convention (SBC). As the assembly finished its business, delegates joined hands and sang "Blest Be the Tie That Binds." Observers then and historians since have noted that the Baptist schism, as well as similar divides among Methodists and Presbyterians, boded ill for the future of the nation itself.[28]

The original SBC consolidated home and foreign mission boards under one umbrella, and the constitution stipulated that other boards would be developed as representatives to convention meetings saw fit. The new body issued a statement acknowledging that "a painful division has taken place." The release also stated that the SBC was not formed to defend slavery. Its purposes were the "extension of the Messiah's kingdom, and the glory of our God." The SBC wished to move beyond the needless controversy precipitated by the "ultra Northern brethren" and focus again on the gospel. In 1995, upon the convention's 150th anniversary, the SBC—by then the nation's largest Protestant denomination—would apologize for the "role that slavery played in the formation of the Southern Baptist Convention." This formally repudiated the notion that slavery was not at the heart of the schism.[29]

ALTHOUGH THE STAGE was set for the secession crisis, we should not imagine that Baptists just sat around from 1845 to 1860 waiting for the Civil War to begin. First of all, they grew numerically and geographically during the period. The SBC's talk of extending the Messiah's kingdom was not merely a facade, nor did northern Baptists give up the missionary enterprise. In 1846 alone there were reports of revivals in Baptist churches throughout New England, including North Stonington, Connecticut; Nantucket, Massachusetts; and Valley Falls, Rhode Island. At tiny Springvale, Maine, about thirty miles north of Portsmouth, New Hampshire, Baptist pastor John Peacock held joint revival meetings with the Freewill Baptist pastor in town. The Calvinist Baptist congregation had just twenty-five members. At the combined meetings, however, "manifest tokens of the presence and power of God" appeared. After a month of sustained revival, Peacock and his Freewill colleague baptized fifty individuals.[30]

Steady Baptist gains also continued in the South, among both whites and blacks. The forty-one churches of the Broad River (N.C.) Association, for example, averaged about 140 baptisms total per year in the era following the establishment of the SBC, with spikes to 291 and 226 baptisms in 1848 and 1850, respectively. A "great revival" transpired in those years in churches in and around Boiling Springs, on the North Carolina line between Charlotte and Spartanburg, South Carolina.[31]

Perhaps more surprising was the vigorous Baptist growth among southern African Americans. One estimate holds that from 1845 to 1860, black Baptist membership doubled from two hundred thousand to four hundred thousand. Many white Baptists, feeling the sting of the abolitionist controversy, and remembering the tumult over Baptist outreach to blacks in Nat Turner's wake, redoubled their efforts to evangelize blacks in the fifteen years following the creation of the SBC. In Virginia, the influential Dover Association, in Richmond, saw the percentage of black members go up consistently in the years after 1844. That year, black membership stood at just over eight thousand; in 1860, it had reached just under fourteen thousand. Many African American Virginians belonged to "quasi-independent" churches, often technically pastored by a white minister but in reality allowed to operate with relative autonomy. In 1843, whites reopened the Williamsburg African Baptist Church, which they had anxiously closed after Turner's revolt.[32]

Baptists were so successful at reaching southern blacks that it generated contempt among northern observers. One figured that "negroes" preferred believer's baptism because "it makes more of an event of the baptismal ceremony, thus gratifying their passionate fondness for excitement." This skeptical observer had visited Carolina rice plantations and noted the blacks' separate "prayer houses" there. In their services, a slave would preach, the congregation would sing, and eventually they would "work themselves up to a great pitch of excitement, in which they yell and cry aloud, and finally shriek and leap up, clapping their hands and dancing," tearing their clothes and falling into "cataleptic trances." Some masters banned such displays, regarding them as faux-spiritual nonsense, at best. How many—and how often—black (or white) Baptists worshiped in such a demonstrative manner is not clear, but clearly some found it compelling.[33]

BAPTIST OPINION ON slavery remained fluid through 1845, hardening into clearer positions only after the withdrawal of southerners from the national agencies. Many Baptists had certainly become convinced that slavery in any form was sinful. Black Baptist leaders rarely went on record on the topic, but some, like runaway slave and pastor Israel Campbell, did. In an address in Ohio, Campbell assured his audience, "Truth and mercy, righteousness and justness are on our side. Then let us never yield to the will of tyrants. No compromise with men-stealers and people-robbers and heart-breakers, but contend for right until the last slave's chain is broken."[34]

In spite of white southerners' departure from the Triennial Convention, abolitionist Baptists were still frustrated with moderate northern Baptists' unwillingness to cut ties with slaveholders. Northern Baptists created a new American Baptist Missionary Union in 1846 but rebuffed efforts to bar slave owners from becoming members or holding office in the agency. Like SBC officials, Francis Wayland wished for the new missionary union to be "equally free from slavery and antislavery," and committed to evangelism alone. Abolitionists formed the American Baptist Free Mission Society in order to free themselves from supporters of slavery.[35]

In the mid-1840s, Baptist opinion on slavery ran along a continuum from abolitionist activists to those who considered slavery a God-ordained good. Many of the most influential white Baptists, in both the North and the South, stood in between these poles. Some whites argued that while slavery was ethically problematic, it should not break fellowship between believers. Others readily conceded that slavery as practiced in America was rife with problems, but that Christians could redeem the institution. The intense but civil debate between Wayland and Richard Fuller in *Domestic Slavery Considered as a Scriptural Institution* (1846) illustrates just how much weight both northerners and southerners gave to moderate opinion regarding slavery. This extended "exchange was one of the United States' last serious one-on-one debates where advocates for and against slavery engaged each other directly, with reasonable restraint," according to historian Mark Noll. Fuller agreed that there were "gross crimes" often associated with slavery. "The crime" in such cases, however, "is not slaveholding, but cruelty." Fuller crisply stated the proslavery biblical argument: "The Bible did authorize some sort of slavery; if now the abuses admitted and deplored by me be essentials of all slavery, then the Bible did allow those abuses." The only logical options were to reject the Bible for endorsing the immorality inherent in slavery, or to concede that slavery's abuses were only incidental to the system, Fuller contended.[36]

Wayland counted many southern Baptist pastors, including Richard Fuller, among his friends. This personal history helps account for the irenic tone of his antislavery writings and his "kind and fraternal" response to Fuller. Wayland rebuked zealous abolitionist Baptists just as much as slaveholders, blaming abolitionists for harsh condemnations that broke fellowship between sincere Christians. When the SBC withdrew from the Triennial Convention, Wayland told Richmond Baptist pastor Jeremiah Jeter that he understood: "You will separate of course. I could not ask otherwise. Your rights have been infringed." Nevertheless, Wayland held that the system of slavery was wrong because it violated the God-ordained equality of all people. The moral wrong of slavery and the guilt of slave owning were different issues, however. Some slave masters abused their slaves and worked to stop any plans for gradual emancipation; others treated their slaves with Christian benevolence and would free them if the law and circumstances would allow it. Both participated in an immoral social system, but the abusive slave master was also personally guilty of sin, Wayland opined. The charitable master was not.[37]

Proslavery advocates exploited this logic to focus not on the practices of southern slavery but on slavery in the abstract. To them—and to their abolitionist foes—there could be no middle ground. The question was whether slave masters committed sin, or did not commit sin, by owning slaves. Clearly, they argued, the Bible accepted the existence of some kinds of slavery, and even Wayland had admitted that some slave masters did not sin in owning slaves. Therefore, slavery was not by definition sinful, and abolitionists had no grounds for demanding the precipitous destruction of the South's economic and social order. As debates focused on slavery in the abstract, it became more difficult to ameliorate or slowly abolish slavery. Kentucky Baptist pastor and gradual emancipationist James Pendleton was exasperated by this overtheorizing. "Pro-slavery men," he said in 1849, "most ridiculously transfer their idea of the innocence of slavery in the abstract to slavery in the concrete. Because they can conceive of circumstances in which a master may hold a slave without doing wrong, they infer that there is nothing wrong in the system of slavery in Kentucky." The abuses, proslavery advocates argued, were peripheral to a God-permitted social arrangement.[38]

Proslavery thought began to stabilize in the South as these debates proceeded, and as the defenders of slavery felt beleaguered and patronized by abolitionists. Jeremiah Jeter recalled his own transformation—and white Virginia's—on the subject. He grew up hoping never to own a slave, but his wife brought slaves into their marriage. The laws of the state effectively barred manumission, and Jeter did not think most of his slaves would fare well if he simply set them free in the world. Nor did he think most of them were interested in schemes to colonize West Africa, which many Christian abolitionists had proposed. In the 1820s, many white southerners regarded slavery as a necessary evil, but after the debates precipitated by Turner's insurrection, public opinion began to change. Few whites now questioned the institution. Some vociferously defended it, and some even began to praise southern slave society as "eminently adapted to secure the highest intellectual and social development." Slavery, they insisted, was a safe and simple solution to the age-old question of relations between "capital and labor."[39]

Jeter's own view was powerfully shaped by reading fellow Virginia Baptist Thornton Stringfellow. Stringfellow convinced Jeter that "the

Scriptures were more favorable to slavery than I had been." Jeter became convinced that slavery was, at a minimum, permitted by Scripture, and that under some circumstances, it could "belong to the best order of society that human, or even divine, wisdom can devise." Stringfellow's oft-reprinted *Brief Examination of Scripture Testimony on the Institution of Slavery* advanced the standard proslavery biblical argument and gratefully noted how millions of blacks had received salvation via the institution of slavery. But he feared that "an officious meddling with the institution, from feelings and sentiments unknown to the Bible, may lead to the extermination of the slave race." Like Thomas Jefferson before him, Stringfellow warned that precipitous mass emancipation could lead to a genocidal race war between whites and blacks.[40]

IVESON BROOKES, BAPTIST minister and planter of Hamburg, South Carolina, had a recurring nightmare in 1836. "I suppose you will think it a plausible dream," he wrote his wife. "The substance is that in some twenty or thirty years a division of the Northern & Southern States will be produced by the Abolitionists and then a war will ensue between the Yankees & slaveholders." Split the difference, and the date of Brookes's nightmarish estimate was spot on: twenty-five years later, the war came.[41]

As the crisis escalated, the calcified views of both abolitionists and proslavery forces made reconciliation increasingly difficult. When northerners elected Abraham Lincoln as president in the divided election of November 6, 1860, all hope of avoiding secession and bloodshed seemed to vanish. A week after Lincoln's election, the Alabama Baptist Convention resolved that though it wished to steer clear of politics, it could no longer ignore the fact that the American Union had failed. Under a Republican administration, the convention could "no longer hope for justice, protection, or safety." Secessionist whites did not believe Lincoln's repeated assurances that he would not interfere with slavery. "We hold ourselves subject," the Alabama Baptists proclaimed, "to the call of proper authority in defense of the sovereignty and independence of the State of Alabama, and of her right as a sovereignty to withdraw from this Union." The Lower South did secede, led by South Carolina. Alabama's Basil Manly, serving in Montgomery as chaplain to the Provisional Congress of the Confederate States, prayed at the inauguration of Jefferson Davis as the Confederacy's president in February 1861. The Upper South joined the

Confederacy later, in the spring of 1861, following the southern bombardment of Charleston's Fort Sumter and Lincoln's preparations for a full-scale military conflict.[42]

The Southern Baptist Convention affirmed Alabama's sentiments at its May 1861 assembly. About half of the delegates there were from heavily proslavery Georgia. Chaired by Richard Fuller, who had relocated to a Baptist congregation in Baltimore, the convention charged that the "fanatical spirit of the North has long been seeking to deprive us of rights and franchises guaranteed by the Constitution; and, after years of persistent aggression, they have, at last, accomplished their purpose." The convention insisted that radical abolitionists had forced secession upon the South and it chastised the northern churches for "breathing out slaughter, and clamoring for sanguinary hostilities with a fierceness which we would have supposed impossible among the disciples of the Prince of Peace." Setting aside the first two days of June for "humiliation, fasting, and prayer," it called on Baptists to ask God to forgive their sins and to show them mercy and favor.[43]

Northern Baptist opinion was often just as certain of the rectitude of the Union cause and the evil of secession. The Hudson River (N.Y.) Baptist Association resolved to "uphold our Federal Government in the deadly contest that has been ruthlessly forced upon it, until it shall have reestablished its supreme authority . . . and shall have caused our desecrated banner to wave again over every spot of earth whence the hand of treason may have displaced it." The association denounced the Confederacy's doctrines as "essentially Anti-Christian, Pagan, barbarous, and inhuman." Of course, it preferred peace, it said, but submitting to the Confederates was worse than war. The conflict matched "the absolute supremacy of a despotic earthly power on the one hand, against the rightful dominion of our Lord Jesus Christ, whose kingdom guarantees the inalienable and universal rights of our redeemed humanity, on the other."[44]

Even northern moderates such as Francis Wayland resigned themselves to war. Wayland had deplored the pointlessness of civil war in his textbooks, but beginning with the move to extend slavery into the West in the Kansas-Nebraska Act (1854), Wayland turned against his southern friends and denounced what northerners called the "Slave Power." Southern colleges subsequently stopped using his textbooks. Once secession occurred, Wayland saw war as inevitable and tragic, yet providential. "God is about to bring slavery to an end," he told his son. "He has taken it into his own hands, and allowed the south to have their own way." Months before Fort Sumter, Wayland wrote to one of his former students, Senator Lafayette Foster of Connecticut, and asked whether there was any doubt "on which side God will declare himself? Can we doubt that, if we look to him in faith, he will bring forth judgment unto victory?"[45]

Not all southern Baptists favored secession. Perhaps the most fascinating case of white Baptist reluctance on secession was that of James P. Boyce. Boyce was a student of Wayland's and the first president of Southern Baptist Theological Seminary, originally located in Greenville, South Carolina. He opposed secession not because he was against slavery but because he thought (presciently, as it turned out) that launching a precipitous war was as likely to destroy slavery as to save it. Boyce joked that he had "always been old fogy enough to love the past, with all its glorious associations. Moreover, I believe I see in all this the end of slavery. I believe we are cutting its throat, curtailing its dominion. And I have been, and am, an ultra pro-slavery man." He was so proslavery, then, that he opposed secession. Boyce ran as a candidate for the state secession convention against James C. Furman, the pro-secession president of Furman University. Boyce lost. Once secession and war became a reality, Boyce committed himself to South Carolina's defense, serving for a time as a chaplain to a Confederate regiment. Many Baptist pastors did likewise. About half of Alabama's Baptist pastors were serving the Confederate military in various capacities by the spring of 1862.[46]

Some of those chaplains saw combat. Pastor I. T. Tichenor of Montgomery's First Baptist Church experienced a bloody encounter at the Battle of Shiloh. Tichenor, future president of what would become Auburn University, was chaplain to the Seventeenth Alabama Regiment, which came under unrelenting Union fire on April 6, 1862. The clash killed or wounded a third of the Seventeenth Alabama's men. Tichenor himself was wounded but exhorted his men to fight back. It was a Sabbath morning, and the chaplain shouted that at that very moment, their families and friends at First Montgomery were supporting them in prayer. "I called upon them to stand there and die, if need be, for their country." The effect was electric, and the soldiers "piled that ground with Yankees slain," Tichenor recalled. The chaplain himself shouldered a gun and shot down at least six Union men on the churning battleground.[47]

Clergy served on the other side as well. Baptist pastor Winfield Scott (not to be confused with the Union commander of the same name), of Syracuse, New York, enlisted in the Union army in 1862. Scott rose to the rank of colonel and received at least five battlefield wounds during the war, including one at Spotsylvania Courthouse that (legend has it) might have killed him except for a New Testament in his shirt pocket that broke the force of the bullet. Going west after the war, Scott organized several churches around Leavenworth, Kansas, and pastored in Denver, Los Angeles, and San Francisco, before founding the town of Scottsdale, Arizona, in 1888.[48]

Baptists' Civil War experiences were as varied as all Americans'. Few were as spectacular or celebrated as Tichenor's or Scott's. Sometimes the war distracted Baptists from spiritual concerns. At other times both the armies and the home front saw surging revival, born out of desperate times and ubiquitous mortality. The war ravaged congregations, depriving them of many men who might have served as church leaders into the next generation. It debilitated Baptist missions and schools. Churches in both North and South faced pressure to vocally and financially support the war effort. Some congregations responded warmly to these overtures, while others maintained cool silence.

In areas where sentiment was mixed about the war—especially in the Border States—political squabbles disrupted congregational harmony. One Baptist historian has noted that virtually every Baptist church in Kentucky was divided over the conflict. Similarly, in late summer of 1863, the Pleasant Run Baptist Church in Indiana became embroiled in a furor over pro-Union resolutions that a Republican partisan introduced and wanted the congregation to endorse. Among them was a statement that failure to pray for Union authorities was tantamount to treason. The vote resulted in a tie, but the pastor, a Democrat, was so disgusted that he left the church. Pleasant Run's neighbors noticed the controversy: no one sought membership in the congregation during the war. Another Indiana Baptist association declared that Confederate sympathizers were "enemies to their Country, and to their God."[49]

Death touched all but a few Baptist families and churches during the conflict, especially in the South. The Stone Creek Baptist Church in Twiggs County, Georgia, saw a high proportion of its membership serve the Confederacy. The church had 307 members at the start of the war, evenly split between blacks and whites. The majority of the white men labored as soldiers, and at least a few of the black members found themselves pressed into Confederate noncombat duties. At least eighteen soldiers from Stone Creek church died during the war, killed by disease or in battles, including Cold Harbor, Chickamauga, and Atlanta. Four Stone Creek soldiers were present for Lee's surrender at Appomattox Court House in 1865.[50]

The instability of war offered new opportunities for African American Baptists, even before emancipation dawned. As Union forces occupied parts of the South, blacks seized chances to establish fully independent churches. African American Baptist congregations proliferated in Alexandria, Virginia, following Union takeover of the city in 1861. Ex-slave Clement Robinson became the pastor of Beulah Baptist Church in 1863 and taught hundreds of pupils at the First Select Colored School, which operated out of the church basement. By 1864, the city had at least four autonomous black churches. Alexandria's preexisting African Baptist Church obtained its first black pastor, Samuel Madden, in 1863.[51]

A different kind of opportunity—both vocational and spiritual—presented itself to Kentucky slave Allen Allensworth, who was nineteen and still unconverted when the war broke out. After several failed attempts, Allensworth ran away at the war's outset and volunteered for the Forty-Fourth Illinois Infantry. Later he served in the Union navy, attaining the rank of petty officer. When he returned to Louisville, Kentucky, following the war, he experienced conversion at the Fifth Street Baptist Church (the city's first African Baptist congregation, founded in 1829). He went on to pastor Cincinnati's oldest black congregation, the Union Baptist Church, before becoming a chaplain to the Twenty-Fourth US Colored Infantry Regiment in 1886. The Twenty-Fourth was part of the famous "Buffalo Soldiers," all-black infantry units stationed in western states and territories after the war. These glimmerings of African American Baptist independence hinted at massive black Baptist increases to come in the decades following the war.[52]

Women generally stayed away from the battlefront, but they managed new challenges associated with the war's deprivations. The devout Baptist Maria Baker Taylor of Marion County, Florida, a granddaughter of South Carolina's Richard Furman, wrote in her diary in January 1861 as she waited for news of her state's secession convention. "Be thou with this state Oh thou Arbiter of Nations," she prayed, "and may we make Thee our trust and not be put to confusion. Direct our course. Establish us in righteousness, and let not man oppress us." On the Tuesday after she received word that Florida had seceded, Taylor went on with business: putting buttons on a vest, making a pie, sewing loops on towels, and scraping limes to make preserves. She became worried, however, following news of Union blockades in Florida. Her husband sold sugar to the Confederate army; she assisted with the Ladies Military Aid Society, a support agency for southern soldiers. By the end of her Civil War diary, in July 1864, Taylor was not so sure about the conflict's outcome. The state was drained of most of its military-age white sons. Confederate General Robert E. Lee was suffering through the longest summer of the war, with the Union laying siege to Petersburg, Virginia. "A dark hour seems to have come, and in God only is our trust," Taylor wrote. Georgia Baptists were similarly left to wonder whether God had forsaken them and "left us to wail, to weep, and to mourn." Such questions grew only more pressing after Appomattox.[53]

With Lee's surrender and Lincoln's assassination shortly thereafter, the shell-shocked nation turned to God to understand what had happened. Members of the Rappahannock (Va.) Baptist Association assured themselves that all the trials through which they had passed and "the darkness which now overshadows us are a part of the workings of Providence." The chastisements they suffered were "ordained of God, as instruments to work for us a far more exceeding and eternal glory." Many northern and Midwestern Baptists rejoiced at the war's outcome: the Flat Rock Association of southern Indiana rejoiced at the "return of peace to our bleeding country," thanking God that he preserved the United States and destroyed human bondage. The Indianapolis Association heralded the advent of liberty for all Americans "irrespective of race and color." Many pro-Union Baptists also lamented the president's death. A Hartford, Connecticut, Baptist bluntly declared that Lincoln's assassination was "the aftertype of the tragedy which was accomplished on the first Good Friday, more than eighteen centuries ago. . . . Jesus Christ died for the world," but "Abraham Lincoln died for his country."[54]

THE WAR'S DENOUEMENT had begun as William Sherman's army set out from a shattered Atlanta in November 1864, carving a path of destruction on the infamous "March to the Sea." On December 20, Union forces entered Savannah. Sherman cabled President Lincoln: "I beg to present you as a Christmas gift the City of Savannah." Soon thereafter, one of Sherman's officers, George Whitfield Pepper, observed a meeting of black Baptists at the city's Second African Church. The standing-room-only crowd had gathered to celebrate their liberation. "The meeting was opened by one of the brethren in a prayer of great pathos and rare power," Pepper wrote. "In a strain of rude but hearty eloquence, he thanked God that the black people were free, and forever free. The whole congregation here gave vent to their joyous emotions, in bursts of: *Glory to God! Hallelujah! Praise his name!"* Then they first read, and then sang, the hymn:

> *Blow ye the trumpet, blow,*
> *The gladly solemn sound,*
> *Let all the nations know*
> *The year of jubilee has come.*

As he read these words, the presiding elder broke down and wept.[55]

On January 10, 1865, five hundred African American children met in the sanctuary of Savannah's First African Baptist Church—Andrew Bryan's old congregation—and then paraded into the city streets. They wound their way to the former Bryan Slave Mart, which had now become a freedmen's school. The slave auctioneer's desk had become the teacher's. Savannah's African American community naturally gravitated to the Baptist churches when it came time to celebrate the advent of freedom. One particularly bold black girl reportedly taunted her mistress, chanting, "All de rebel gone to hell; Now Par Sherman come."[56]

Emancipation had arrived for America's black Baptists, and for enslaved people generally. It had not come the way that Nat Turner envisioned. Though freedom certainly required violence, it was violence wrought by the hands of soldiers, many of whom were former slaves themselves. With freedom came massive growth in newly independent African American Baptist churches. White southern Baptists also grew in numbers, even as they licked their wounds. Unfortunately, many problems remained in the aftermath of slavery's destruction.

First Baptist Church, Providence, Rhode Island. Founded in 1638 as the first Baptist church in America. Courtesy of Daniel Case.

py of a portrait by C. B. King of the Rev Jesse
bhyhead Cherokee minister; courtesy of his

Cherokee Baptist preacher Tastheghetehee, rechristened Rev. Jesse Bushyhead (1804–1844). The first American Indian to pastor a Cherokee church. Courtesy of Research Division of the Oklahoma Historical Society.

Baptist preacher, runaway slave, and abolitionist, Israel Campbell, circa 1861.
Courtesy of the Charles Deering McCormick Library of Special Collections,
Northwestern University Library.

First African Baptist Church, Richmond (1865). Courtesy of the Library of Congress, LC-DIG-cwpb-02905.

Nannie Helen Burroughs (1878–1961). Home missionary and promoter of women's causes in the National Baptist Convention. Courtesy of the Library of Congress, LC-USZ62-79903.

Black baptismal service at Buffalo Bayou near Houston, Texas, circa 1900.
Courtesy of Special Collections, University of Houston Libraries.

Southern Baptist statesman George Truett of First Baptist, Dallas, preaches on the steps of the US Capitol Building (1920). Courtesy of the Southern Baptist Historical Library and Archives, Nashville, Tennessee.

The world's most famous Baptist, Billy Graham (1966). Courtesy of the Library of Congress, LC-DIG-ppmsc-03261.

Newly elected conservative president Charles Stanley (right) shares a laugh with his moderate opponent Winfred Moore at the 1985 Southern Baptist Convention. Courtesy of the Southern Baptist Historical Library and Archives, Nashville, Tennessee.

8

Black Baptists in Babylon

LIKE MANY BLACK Baptist churches before the Civil War, First African Baptist in Richmond, Virginia, had a white proslavery preacher, Robert Ryland. After the city fell into Union hands in April 1865, he admonished his black parishioners to remain with their masters and to resist the temptation to join the Union forces. Black Union officers wanted to arrest Ryland for his remarks, but the members of his church intervened on behalf of their pastor. Still, the soldiers attempted to keep Ryland out of the pulpit. A member of the Christian Commission of the Union Army, Alva Hovey, was sent to resolve the dispute. Hovey knew that Baptist churches were governed by their congregations, so he suggested that the question of Ryland's legitimacy as pastor of First African Baptist be put to a vote. The members voted to retain him, but Ryland knew that with the Confederacy about to fall, and emancipation of slaves imminent, his time as the white pastor of a black church had come to an end. Within a few weeks he submitted his resignation. When James R. Holmes became the first black pastor of First African Baptist that summer, Ryland assisted in the installation service. He then volunteered his services at the black seminary in Richmond that would later become part of Virginia Union University.[1]

After the Civil War, black Baptists in the South began to grapple with their newfound freedom. As we have seen, the history of black Baptists can be traced from the eighteenth century. First Baptist Church in Richmond, Virginia, from which First African Baptist emerged, was founded in 1780. Slave members were prominent from the beginning and soon came to outnumber whites significantly. By 1836, the church had roughly twenty-four hundred members, two thousand of them black. This was five years after Nat Turner's uprising, which resulted in heightened restrictions on slave activities throughout the South. In response, slave members at First Baptist, Richmond protested their treatment and called for a separate meeting place. In 1841, First African Baptist Church was founded to accommodate them. White leaders of First Baptist justified the black church by arguing, "Our hearts are greatly set on furnishing separate religious instruction for our colored people. Their number calls for a larger place of meeting and their peculiar habits, views, and prejudices demand peculiar instruction."[2] The wording seems apt, since slavery was already being referred to as the South's "peculiar institution." But what whites found "peculiar" in this case were black Baptist worship practices. In the years following the Civil War, African American Christianity would become an almost completely separate institution.

THE STORY OF Richmond's First African Baptist is something of a microcosm of the history of Baptists after the Civil War in that it foreshadowed the near-complete racial separation of black and white Baptists. Moreover, the religious segregation among Baptists mirrored that of the larger culture, especially in the South. The Reconstruction era (1865–1877) brought hopes that blacks could be truly free and full participants in society. During the era when the South was under the often heavy-handed control of Radical Republican state governments installed by the North, there were efforts to ensure that freed slaves became full citizens. But the promise of Reconstruction never materialized. Racial justice fell victim to southern resistance, missteps on the part of northern politicians, military occupation of the South, and eventually loss of interest on the part of northern whites. After the contested election of 1876, President Rutherford B. Hayes withdrew the last military presence from southern soil, leaving blacks to fend for themselves.

Reconstruction was no golden era of race relations, but there is strong evidence that legal segregation in the South developed only slowly until the 1890s, when southern white politicians began in earnest to strip blacks of the vote and relegate them to second-class citizenship. Blacks responded by building their own institutions. These institutions were pervasively religious, and the black Baptist denominations that resulted were by far the largest and most influential. Civil rights scholar-activist W. E. B. Du Bois called the black church "the first distinctively Negro American social institution . . . the gift of black folk to the New World." Moreover, black churches were, in Du Bois's words, "curiously composite institutions, which combine the work of churches, theaters, newspapers, homes, schools, and lodges."[3] The largest black Baptist body, the National Baptist Convention USA Inc., remains to this day the largest black organization of any kind in America, secular or religious. Like other black Protestant denominations, the National Baptist Convention was the product of twin forces—the desire for racial self-determination among blacks and discrimination on the part of white Baptist institutions.[4]

AFTER THE CIVIL WAR, Northern Baptist missionaries rushed to the South to help freed slaves build churches. At first these struggling black congregations relied almost entirely on the support they received from Christians above the Mason-Dixon Line.[5] Congregationalists provided support for education, but black Christians were not fond of the Congregationalists' worship style. Instead, African Americans attended Congregationalist schools during the week and then flocked to Baptist churches on Sunday. According to some estimates, when the Southern Baptist Convention was organized in 1845, black Baptists outnumbered white Baptists in the South. It was not uncommon in antebellum Baptist churches for black membership to dwarf that of whites, as at First Baptist, Richmond. First Baptist, Natchez, Mississippi, for example, had 442 members, 380 of whom were black, while in Columbus, Mississippi, 80 percent of Baptists were black. At the end of the Civil War, First Baptist Church of Montgomery, Alabama, had 600 black members out of a total membership of roughly 900. Thirty-five to 40 percent of Baptists in Georgia were black; by the early twentieth century they had become a majority.[6]

Across the South, blacks experienced unequal treatment in the region's Baptist churches. After the Turner rebellion, they held few leadership positions, especially over whites, and often sat in back pews and balconies.[7] African American preference for separate churches, plus hostility from whites, led to the nearly complete racial separation of Baptist churches in the South. Blacks wanted to form their own congregations in order to exert leadership and control, and whites were happy to help them. In Montgomery in 1867, virtually all of the more than six hundred black Baptists left First Baptist to form their own congregation. When they did, the three hundred or so whites of First Baptist helped erect the church building that would house the black worshipers.[8] Still, the lion's share of credit goes to black Baptist preachers whose spirit of independence and entrepreneurship resulted first in black churches within white associations and conventions, then in the development of black denominations.

As one black preacher put it, "We act toward them as brethren, but never again shall we let them rule us as masters."[9]

Many whites aided independent black Baptist churches, often out of a spirit of racial paternalism. But other whites saw independent black churches as a threat to the southern power structure and the racial caste system of the South. The Ku Klux Klan was particularly forceful in suppressing black power. Black Baptist history in the postbellum period is riddled with stories of harassment and attacks on anything that smacked of black independence and success. As one Arkansas woman described the situation, when black preachers led independent black services, "Here come the Ku Klux and run em clear out. If they hear least thing nigger preacher say they whoop him. They whooped several."[10] Much of the resistance to black churches stemmed from the fact that many preachers were politicians and their churches served as a rallying place for the black community. As one observer wrote of the black churches in Virginia, "There was not an evening or afternoon that had not its meetings, its literary or social gatherings, its picnic or fair for the benefit of the church, its Dorcas society, or some occasion of religious sociability."[11] Black churches quickly became the "training forum for black leaders to emerge and actively participate in the reconstruction of the union." Indeed, the black churches of the era have been called "schools in political activity."[12]

As black Baptist congregations proliferated, individual churches came together to form associations and eventually state conventions. The first black Baptist association formed in Ohio in 1834, and black Baptists in Illinois formed an association four years later. Black Baptists in former slave states began organizing state conventions immediately after the war. The first black state convention in a former Confederate state was formed in North Carolina in 1866, followed by Virginia and Alabama in 1868. Mississippi followed the next year and actually had two rival black Baptist state conventions until they merged in 1890.

The first attempt to form a national convention of black Baptists began in 1866 when three regional conventions combined to form the Consolidated American Baptist Convention (CABC), which met every three years until its demise in 1878. Regional and sectional differences were largely responsible for the failure of the CABC.[13] As the CABC declined, W. W. Colley led in the formation of the second black Baptist organization. He served as the first black missionary appointed by the Southern Baptist Convention. While in Nigeria with fellow missionary

William J. David, who was white, Colley became convinced that African Americans had a duty to start missionary work in Africa. "I hope the colored brethren will begin their work in Africa this year. This is their field of labor," he said in 1876. "I ask when will they obey their savior's commission."[14] The answer came four years later when Colley joined 150 black Baptist leaders at the First Baptist Church in Montgomery. Together they formed the Baptist Foreign Mission Convention, which sent Colley back to Africa as one of its first missionaries.

Over time tension developed within the Baptist Foreign Mission Convention over the extent to which black Baptists should cooperate with whites. A strong separatist impulse grew among some black Baptist leaders. The separatist spirit transcended religion, but it began in the black churches and was a response to the hardening of racial segregation and black disfranchisement in the final two decades of the century. Stripped of the right to vote, blacks created their own body politic within their churches.[15] Those who wanted stronger cooperation with white Baptists than the Baptist Foreign Mission Convention allowed formed the American National Baptist Convention in 1886. While disagreeing over separatism, the two conventions cooperated with each other, and the Baptist Foreign Mission Convention carried out mission work on behalf of the American National Baptist Convention.

In 1893, a third significant black Baptist organization formed called the National Baptist Educational Convention. As the name suggests, this group promoted schooling among black preachers. Black Baptists were widely criticized for their lack of education. In 1890, for example, Booker T. Washington told the Fisk University graduation assembly that the vast majority of black Baptist ministers were uneducated and unfit to be leaders.[16] The National Baptist Educational Commission brought all black Baptist schools under one umbrella. The leaders of all these organizations envisioned unity among black Baptists across the nation. This vision came to fruition in 1895 when representatives from the three groups met at the Friendship Baptist Church of Atlanta, Georgia. There they united to form the National Baptist Convention of the United States of America.[17] As is always the case with Baptists, black or white, some associations, regional conventions, and congregations remained aloof from the new denomination. Moreover, the twentieth century would see splits within, and splinters from, the national denomination. Nevertheless, by 1906 there were more than 2.2 million members in National Baptist Convention churches.[18]

Baptist churches played a major role in black separatism in areas beyond religion. In 1889, for example, the American National Baptist Convention adopted a resolution to "ask the President of the United States to recommend to the United States Congress an appropriation of $100,000,000 to aid colored people in leaving the South." The resolution suggested that black Baptists should head west and establish all-black communities.[19] No consensus existed on the issue of separation from whites, however. Indeed, this era of black Baptist history saw continuing tension between separatists and cooperationists. Cooperationists believed it was an affront to white Baptists to start black Baptist institutions that were wholly separate from white denominations. After all, many of those white churches and associations had aided and funded the development of black churches in the first place. Elias Camp Morris, the president of the National Baptist Convention, would have none of this argument.

Morris was born a slave in 1855 in the north Georgia hill country near the town of Springplace. When he was nine years old, his family was moved to Stevenson, Alabama. Both of his parents died when Morris was fourteen, and he was apprenticed to a cousin who worked as a shoemaker and preacher. Morris learned both trades. In 1879, he accepted a call to the Centennial Baptist Church of Helena, Arkansas. A gifted organizer, he formed Arkansas Baptist College in 1884 and served for many years as chairman of its board. He also served as president of the Arkansas State National Baptist Convention for more than thirty years, founded a newspaper called the *Baptist Vanguard*, participated in state politics, and traveled to the Belgian Congo as a diplomat appointed by President Theodore Roosevelt. With the founding of the National Baptist Convention in 1895, he became the natural choice to lead the new denomination. He served as NBC president for twenty-seven years.[20] Morris believed that the only way blacks would ever get a fair shake was to establish their own denominational structures.

Like Morris, Richard Henry Boyd (1843–1922) played a major role in creating a black Baptist identity. Given the slave name Richard Gray by his masters, Dick, as he was called growing up, moved with the Gray family from Mississippi to Texas prior to the Civil War. After the war, he changed his surname to Boyd after discovering that it had been his father's family name. As a free man, he was ordained in the Hopewell Baptist Church of Navasota in 1869 and thereafter emerged as a primary leader in the Texas Negro Baptist Convention. For the next twenty years, he traveled about the state preaching unity among black Baptists. This was during the era of the so-called Christian Reconstruction, when the white American Baptist Home Mission Society (ABHMS) was active among black Baptists. By the 1890s, Boyd grew critical of the ABHMS, whose white leaders seemed all too ready to take black contributions but not to publish sermons and articles written by black ministers for ABHMS publications. In 1896, Boyd teamed with a small group of black Baptist leaders in the newly formed National Baptist Convention and founded the National Baptist Publishing Board (NBPB) in Nashville. This proved highly controversial. Some in the NBC wanted to continue cooperating with the white ABHMS, using Sunday school literature published by the white Baptists. Others opposed Boyd's idea that the new publishing board be affiliated with the NBC yet legally independent. Boyd prevailed on both counts.[21]

Initially pouring his own finances into the NBPB, Boyd traveled the South urging other black Baptist preachers to abandon the ABHMS and support the cause of separate black Baptist institutions. He joined Morris in promoting black Baptist independence. Boyd also served as founder and president of a Nashville bank from 1904 to 1922 and as the first president of the company that published the *Nashville Globe*, a black newspaper. With Boyd as the lead investor and president and his son Henry as editor, the *Globe* became one of the leading black newspapers in the country, surviving until 1960. Success in these business ventures earned Boyd a prominent place in Booker T. Washington's National Negro Business League.

Boyd promoted Washington's self-help and accommodation strategy. Washington outlined this approach in a famous speech in Atlanta in 1895, where he said, "In all things that are purely social we can be as separate as the fingers, yet one as the hand in all things essential to mutual progress." Essentially, Washington accepted a benign form of segregation as long as black people had opportunities for economic advancement. By contrast, black scholar and activist W. E. B. Du Bois wanted full equality for blacks in every sphere, social as well as economic. Moreover, Du Bois hoped that black people would become broadly educated in the arts and letters and not just trained for jobs. He believed Washington's approach amounted to a sellout, or at least sold black people short. Du Bois called Washington's famous speech the "Atlanta Compromise."

As an ardent black Baptist separatist, Boyd found Washington's approach conducive to building separate black economic institutions. The Baptist separatist impulse meshed quite well with Washington's vision of economic opportunity over equality and integration. In keeping with his focus on separatism and economic development, Boyd's newspaper urged blacks to patronize black-owned businesses, and Boyd engaged in several black entrepreneurial enterprises, including the National Negro Doll Company. The development of black dolls is usually associated with the more secular black separatist Marcus Garvey and his United Negro Improvement Association, but Boyd was probably more important for marketing the dolls nationally. While shopping for Christmas gifts for his children, he noticed the way toy dolls projected a negative stereo-type of black people. One of Boyd's advertisements said in part that the black dolls would not be "made of that disgraceful and humiliating type that we have been accustomed to seeing black dolls made of. They rep-resent the intelligent and refined Negro of today, rather than that type of toy that is usually given to the children, and as a rule used as a scare-crow."[22] Such ads ran in Boyd's *Nashville Globe*, other black newspapers, and in the Sunday school literature published by the NBPB. The dolls became an important symbol of black pride, so much so that in 1908 the National Baptist Convention resolved that black Baptists should remove "the flaxen-haired, blue eyed Caucasian dolls from the homes of every self-respecting Negro."[23]

While Boyd worked in service of Washington's racial accommodation, he also resisted the most discriminatory aspects of Jim Crow. In 1904, with fellow Nashville pastors J. A. Jones and Edward W. D. Isaac, Boyd helped organize a black boycott of streetcars because segregation therein was separate but in no way equal (foreshadowing Martin Luther King Jr.'s leadership of the Montgomery bus boycott of 1955). Boyd demonstrated his resistance to racial paternalism again in 1917. After an editor for the *Christian Index*, the white Georgia Baptist newspaper, wrote that blacks had been "well managed" in the South, Boyd responded with an editorial saying, "We do not like the idea of being 'managed.' "[24]

As was the case with many black Baptist leaders, the self-help, accom-modationist emphasis of Washington and the civil rights emphasis of the more radical W. E. B. Du Bois coexisted quite naturally for Boyd. Moreover, while Boyd remained a separatist, he also cooperated com-fortably with white Baptists in both the American and Southern Baptist Conventions, as long as such cooperation met his standard of equality. As historian Paul Harvey has observed, "Boyd combined separatism as an ideology with cooperation as a practice."[25] In other words, he promoted independent Baptist organizations run by blacks, but once such institu-tions developed, he proved open to working in cooperation with white institutions. Boyd is remembered as both a "Black Baptist Entrepreneur" and a civil rights activist.[26]

IN TERMS OF lasting cultural influence, the most significant project of Boyd's NBPB may have been the publication of William H. Sherwood's hymnbook. Sherwood ran an orphanage for black children in Petersburg, Virginia, led local choirs and bands, and composed music. In 1893, he set out to publish the *Harp of Zion* hymnbook, which contained original tunes as well as songs by other composers. The style of music Sherwood wrote and promoted served as a bridge between the traditional Negro spiritual and gospel music that emerged thirty years later. Spirituals tended toward the otherworldly, while many of Sherwood's songs focused on the daily struggles of faith. Boyd heard about the *Harp of Zion* and seized the opportunity to publish it as the *Baptist Young People's Union National Harp of Zion.*[27]

Publication of the hymnbook served merely as the launching point for the National Baptist Convention's promotion of black gospel music. In 1915, the denomination named Lucie Campbell (also spelled Lucy) music director for its brand new Baptist Young People's Union Congress. Born in 1885, Campbell grew up in Memphis and first learned to play piano by eavesdropping on her older sister's lessons. She eventually taught English and history at Booker T. Washington High School in Memphis, but her musical efforts secured her place in history. In her duties as director of the Young People's Union, she trained huge youth choirs to sing at annual convention meetings. She also composed several of her own hymns, wrote musical pageants, and served on the denomination's music committee. As part of a team of coeditors headed by church music professor Willa A. Townsend, Campbell helped produce a series of hymnbooks, the most important of which was *Gospel Pearls*. *GP*, as it became known, contained mostly hymns by famous white composers such as Isaac Watts, Charles Wesley, Fanny Crosby, and others. But *GP* also included roughly twenty songs that incorporated the ecstatic and emotional music flourishing in black holiness and Pentecostal churches. The book became the first black music publication to include the word "gospel" in the title. By the 1930s, the type of music Campbell wrote, taught, performed, and promoted was commonly called "black gospel."[28]

When *GP* debuted at the 1921 National Baptist Convention meeting, one of the book's coeditors, W. M. Nix, preached the convention's Sunday sermon. Hoping to demonstrate the soul-winning power of the new hymnbook, Nix performed E. O. Excell's "I Do, Don't You?" In the congregation that day sat a twenty-two-year-old blues and jazz musician, Thomas Andrew Dorsey. Born in Georgia in 1899, Dorsey grew up in the home of an evangelist father and musician mother. Dorsey also had an uncle who became a blues guitarist. After dropping out of school at age eleven, Dorsey studied piano and in his teen years began playing in brothels and clubs, becoming one of Atlanta's best-known performers. He moved to Chicago in 1916 and performed in clubs for nearly five years. By 1920, he was in the midst of a spiritual crisis and suffering from depression. He returned briefly to Atlanta, then headed back to the music scene on the South Side of Chicago, where the 1921 National Baptist Convention annual meeting convened in September. An uncle who worked as a druggist in Chicago persuaded Dorsey to attend. Nix's singing set in motion forces that would transform Dorsey and American music. As he said later of the 1921 meeting, "My heart was inspired to become a great singer and worker in the Kingdom of the Lord—and impress people just as this great singer [Nix] did that Sunday morning." When the second edition of *GP* appeared, the hymnbook included Dorsey's first gospel tune, "If I Don't Get There."[29]

Dorsey became the most significant force in the development of black gospel music. But he continued performing for years in blues and jazz clubs, largely to make a living. He played for a time in the same band that launched the career of eventual jazz legend Lionel Hampton, and he knew the blues pioneer W. C. Handy. In 1924, he became band leader for Ma Rainey, the so-called Mother of the Blues, and her band the Jazz Wild Cats. He then formed his own band called the Hokum Boys with guitarist Tampa Red Whittaker. Joined sometimes by another blues legend, Big Bill Broonzy, the Hokum Boys recorded more than sixty Dorsey originals. As Dorsey toured with secular bands while composing both secular and gospel music, his life in the 1920s became a metaphor for the black religious experience that combined African influences with the religion slaves learned from their masters. But well-established urban black Baptist churches in Chicago and elsewhere in the North resisted Dorsey's music and shunned black styles of worship. They sought to avoid association with black holiness and Pentecostal churches, as well as anything that seemed rural and southern. Instead, they preferred classical hymns and the staid worship style of white Protestantism.

That changed at the 1930 National Baptist Convention meeting, which convened once again in Chicago. One of the morning sessions included a performance of Dorsey's tune "If You See My Savior." The song became a huge success. Lucie Campbell invited Dorsey to set up a booth where he sold sheet music, and within a few weeks the song had spread to churches across the nation. The next year the Reverend J. H. L. Smith of Chicago's Ebenezer Baptist Church invited Dorsey and singing evangelist Theodore Frye to organize a gospel choir. A Birmingham, Alabama, transplant, Smith believed gospel music could be a vehicle for reaching southern blacks who poured into Chicago in the Great Migration. Dorsey and Frye's choir performed in February 1932 at Pilgrim Baptist, one of the largest black Baptist churches in Chicago. After the service, Pilgrim's pastor, Junius C. Austin, invited Dorsey to organize a gospel choir for his church. Dorsey's Pilgrim Baptist choir began performing at churches across Chicago, and gospel music gained wide acceptance. He never returned to secular music.

In bringing the blues to the gospel, Dorsey reintroduced northern and urban black Baptist churches to the soulful and emotional form of worship that characterized the African American experience in the South. His songs and those of other black gospel singers helped recapture the longings of the Negro spiritual and the rhythms of Africa. As Dorsey's principal biographer puts it, the music Nix inspired Dorsey to develop allowed black Baptists to "rejoin that part of themselves they had sacrificed for another religion."[30]

In 1929, Dorsey invited a seventeen-year-old female singer to perform his tunes on street corners in order to promote the sale of his sheet music. Her name was Mahalia Jackson, and she had moved to Chicago just two years earlier. She grew up in the Plymouth Rock Baptist Church of New Orleans, but she lived next door to a black holiness church and was strongly influenced by the music she heard there. In Chicago she began singing at the Greater Salem Baptist Church and joined the pastor's three sons in a gospel quartet called the Johnson Singers, considered the first organized gospel group in the city. The group met the same kind of resistance to black gospel that Dorsey had experienced. In their first performance, the Baptist pastor told Jackson and the Johnson Singers to "get that twisting and that jazz" out of this church.[31] They all but quit the established Baptist churches and performed instead in storefront Baptist, holiness, and Pentecostal churches, where congregations often used a worn copy of *Gospel Pearls*.

Before long Jackson was traveling from Detroit to St. Louis performing in such churches, first with the Johnson Singers, then with Dorsey, as the larger black Baptist churches dropped their resistance to gospel music. For a time she associated with the Reverend C. L. Franklin and his wife, Barbara. Gospel music shaped their daughter Aretha, who went on to stardom as a soul singer and pop diva. By the 1950s, Jackson's music had crossed over into secular venues. She performed with Duke Ellington's big band and at the renowned Newport Jazz Festival. Like Billy Graham and Martin Luther King Jr. a few years later, she became a world-renowned religious figure whose stardom transcended her Baptist identity. Columbia Records signed her to a lucrative contract and pushed her toward white audiences, giving her wider exposure but in some ways compromising her black Baptist roots in the process. By the 1960s, she stood at the top of gospel music and was rivaled only by the best secular singers in the world. She sang "The Star Spangled Banner" at an inaugural gala for President John F. Kennedy in 1961, then stood with jazz giant Ella Fitzgerald and signed autographs.[32] Two years later she performed at the March on Washington. Appearing just prior to King's delivery of his "I Have a Dream" speech, she sang "Precious Lord, Take My Hand," Dorsey's most famous composition. By that time she had become the unparalleled singing voice of the civil rights movement. When she died in 1972, President Richard Nixon declared a time of mourning, and forty thousand people paid their respects as her body lay in state at the Greater Salem Baptist Church. At Jackson's funeral in Chicago's Arie Crown Theater, Coretta Scott King quoted her late husband: "A voice like this comes not once in a century, but once in a millennium."[33]

TO RECKON WITH any Protestant denomination's historical development, one must come to grips with the role of women, for in almost all denominations they were the majority. Within black Baptist denominations women served as teachers, wives, students, missionary workers, and financial contributors. But even more, they carried into their work the late nineteenth-century spirit of racial consciousness. Like their black Baptist brothers, they too struggled for independence.[34] Moreover, black Baptist women experienced a double consciousness. They struggled alongside black male leaders in the drive for black self-determination but against these same black Baptist leaders for gender self-determination. Amelia Johnson, for example, affiliated with the white American Baptist Publication Society but nevertheless, like Boyd and Morris, condemned the racial paternalism of white Baptists.

As a novelist and wife of separatist pastor Harvey Johnson of Baltimore, Amelia Johnson wrote journal articles advocating racial equality. In one instance, she mimicked the paternalistic view of whites, paraphrasing the typical white attitude: "We cannot allow this host of people [blacks] to roam the country untaught and unchecked. . . . It is our [white people's] fault that they [blacks] are ignorant and untrained, and it is but just that we do what we can to remedy the evil we have wrought." She followed this hypothetical quote with her own response: "A strange phase of the matter is, that, while all along, the understanding has been that the colored people were, as soon as prepared, to help in educating, uplifting and upbuilding of their own people, . . . the white portion of the nation is inclined to refuse them the right to do this, and only allows them to work under protest." On another occasion she urged black people to look to their own leaders for inspiration and guidance and stop "trying to prove to the world that we were born into it for the sole purpose of admiring white people." "If our white brethren close their avenues to us because of this determination, we must create avenues for ourselves," Johnson concluded.[35] While advocating separatism in her nonfiction, Johnson used her novels in part to probe gender issues in the Christian home.

In several mostly southern states, black Baptist women formed various agencies and conventions and fought vigorously for independence and control of these women's organizations. The men insisted that there be male oversight, but women raised their own funds, initiated educational programs, and engaged in mission work on their own. A leading light in such efforts was Tennessee Baptist Virginia Broughton. While teaching in the public schools of Memphis in the early 1880s, she met white American Baptist missionary Joanna Moore. Moore invited Broughton to a missions meeting exclusively for women. Inspired by what she saw, Broughton soon founded a group called Bible Band, which served as a Bible training program for black women. The Bible Band affiliated with the Women's Baptist Home Mission Society, an auxiliary of the white American Baptist Home Mission Society. Beginning in 1887, Broughton taught school during the week and on weekends rode horseback throughout rural districts preaching the gospel. She traveled as far as Cooter, Missouri, which by her own estimation was "a place where few Negro men dared to go to preach, and a woman missionary of no race had ever gone."[36] By the 1890s, there were more than fifty Bible Bands in Tennessee, and black Baptist women had started holding their own conventions to foster mission work and raise funds for black Baptist educational institutions. Recognizing her stellar work, the Women's Baptist Home Mission Society appointed Broughton as a missionary.

The black Baptist women's movement in Tennessee and elsewhere did not lobby for female ordination, but the women vigorously resisted male dominance in theological interpretation. They insisted on the right of theologically trained women to join with men in judging the fitness of ministerial candidates. Such efforts met male resistance in many quarters. Some churches barred Bible Bands or shut them down entirely. While portraits of Broughton hung in the homes of many women deeply influenced by her, her opponents dubbed her "a mannish woman."[37]

Just as Broughton's work met resistance from many black Baptist ministers, so the work of black Baptist separatists clashed with those who wanted to continue working under the auspices of the northern white American Baptist denomination. While William Camp Morris, Richard Henry Boyd, and Amelia Johnson led the separatists, the nonseparatists put such a premium on winning souls that they viewed publications and business ventures aimed at black uplift as distractions from evangelism. As one nonseparatist editorial put it, "If some of our brethren must have an Afro-American Publishing House and nothing else do them, then let them have it." The editor then advocated continued cooperation with the white American Baptist Publication Society, adding caustically, "Afro-American Baptists cannot afford to divide upon so small a matter as the starting of a useless and needless publishing house, which has never been established and which is not destined to be."[38]

In 1897, a group of nonseparatists formed the Lott Carey Foreign Mission Convention, named for the former slave and evangelist who in 1821 had gone to Liberia, a nation founded by freed American slaves. Black congregations that aligned with the Lott Carey mission efforts tended to maintain their ties with the American Baptist Publication Society instead of joining Boyd's NBPB. Morris, Boyd, and others continued to advocate for separate black institutions.[39] But many black Baptist women saw no contradiction between working both in favor of black separatism and in conjunction with white Baptists to advance female Baptist enterprises.[40]

Within the National Baptist Convention, Nannie Helen Burroughs emerged as the key advocate of this dual approach. Like Virginia Broughton and Amelia Johnson, Burroughs worked vigorously to extend the work of women within the new denomination. In 1900, she attended the annual National Baptist Convention meeting in Richmond, Virginia, and gave a rousing address titled "How the Sisters Are Hindered from Helping." She proclaimed what she called a "righteous discontent" among black Baptist women who made up the majority of the denomination but faced resistance in their efforts to spread the gospel and promote Baptist causes. By the end of the meeting, Burroughs and other women had formed the Woman's Convention Auxiliary to the National Baptist Convention. Women had attempted to form such a convention in 1895, at the outset of the NBC's existence, and even elected as officers Alice Bowie of Alabama, Broughton of Tennessee, and Mrs. C. J. Robinson of Arkansas. But as Broughton put it, "By the Counsel of the brethren, the women's auxiliary national convention was disbanded and women were placed on the various boards of the NBC."[41] This time the women succeeded, meeting secretly at the Third Street African Methodist Episcopal Church to organize. Broughton was chosen as one of four representatives to lobby the male preachers of the NBC for official sanction. Ministerial support came largely from the NBC's Foreign Mission Board in the persons of Lewis G. Jordan and Charles H. Parrish, the former offering the official recommendation that the Woman's Convention be formed, the latter seconding the motion.

Almost immediately the Woman's Convention became the largest organization of black women in America. Not surprisingly, its first action was to support the Foreign Mission Board's sending of Spelman College graduate Emma Delaney as a missionary to Africa. The Woman's Convention built a house for Delaney in what is now Malawi and engaged in continued support over the next several years while also raising money for other missionaries. Heeding their motto—"The world for Christ. Women arise. He calleth for thee"—the Woman's Convention developed state and local missionary societies across the nation.[42] As they engaged in fundraising for missions, the local groups followed Burroughs's handbook *What to Do and How to Do It*. Burroughs proved to be an effective missions entrepreneur, developing leaflets, buttons, photos, guides, letters, and postcards that local chapters of the Woman's Convention used to raise awareness and support for missionary enterprises. The organization also distributed tracts and other pieces of literature in cities and towns across the nation, concentrating especially in areas with large black populations.

The Woman's Convention worked in conjunction with secular organizations to advance the cause of civil rights and gender equality—groups such as the National Association for the Advancement of Colored People and the National Association of Colored Women.[43] Operating as a semiautonomous body within the National Baptist Convention, the Woman's Convention enhanced the autonomy of black Baptist women. Burroughs secured Booker T. Washington as a keynote speaker for the 1902 annual meeting, and he addressed the Baptist women every year thereafter until his death in 1915. As Evelyn Brooks Higginbotham, the leading historian of black Baptist women, has written, "The convention accentuated the [black Baptist women's] presence within the denomination and, equally important, thrust issues of race and gender into the broad discursive arena of American social reform."[44] The convention was the culmination of efforts started decades earlier by Broughton, Johnson, and others.

Joanna Moore's recruitment of Broughton marked the beginning of Baptist women's solidarity across racial lines. In her autobiography, Broughton cited Moore as one "who has given her life to the development of the women and children of our race." Broughton called Moore "this mother of Israel," and wrote, "I believe she has been given to us [black women], as an apostle, as truly as Paul was given to the Gentiles. Praise the Lord for her."[45] When the Woman's Convention formed, it exhibited this spirit of gender solidarity by forming, almost immediately, a cooperative relationship with the Woman's Missionary Union (WMU) of the Southern Baptist Convention. WMU corresponding secretary Annie Armstrong attended the Woman's Convention meeting in 1901 and helped work out an agreement whereby the WMU offered financial assistance to the Woman's Convention.[46]

IN HIS 1899 presidential address to the National Baptist Convention, Elias Camp Morris contrasted the national unity of black Baptists to the continued North-South separation of white Baptists, a separation caused by slavery. He cited as a prime objective of the NBC to "have one grand national society which would know no North, no South, no East, no West. . . . From Maine to California we are one."[47] But his dream of one denomination for all black Baptists foundered in the second decade of the twentieth century as the National Baptist Convention experienced a major split. The schism stemmed largely from a decade-long dispute over the relationship of the NBC to Richard Henry Boyd's NBPB.

Under Morris's leadership, the NBC incorporated, becoming the National Baptist Convention, USA, Inc. This enabled the denomination to create boards to govern various agencies. Boyd's NBPB was one of those, or so Morris and his supporters believed. The denomination demanded that Boyd transfer to the NBC all copyrights held in his name. Having largely built up the publishing company himself, investing his and his family's money, Boyd believed his company was separate and merely affiliated with the NBC. He refused to transfer copyrights or ownership of the publishing board, which led to a struggle for control. The controversy pitted Morris and Boyd against one another and dragged on for a decade. After years of legal wrangling, the matter came to a head at the convention of 1915. Boyd attempted to disrupt the meeting and swing things his way. Unsuccessful, he convened his faction at a nearby church and formed the National Baptist Convention of America, Unincorporated, later to be called simply the National Baptist Convention of America, then the National Baptist Convention of America, Inc., as it is known today.[48]

Over the next several decades, efforts to bring the two National Baptist denominations back together failed. Meanwhile, the Lott Carey Foreign Mission Convention functioned as yet a third black Baptist denomination, often working cooperatively with Boyd's National Baptist Convention of America on joint mission efforts.[49] In 1988, the National Baptist Convention of America endured yet another split over the NBPB. Several black state conventions aligned with a new body that took the name National Missionary Baptist Convention of America. By 2012, this new group was the third-largest black Baptist denomination in America.

THE MAJOR BLACK Baptist denominations formed for sociological rather than theological reasons. The slave experience often overshadowed theological differences over Calvinism that white Baptists inherited from the Protestant Reformation in Europe. Black Baptist cooperation emerged instead out of the struggle for freedom, a struggle often chronicled in black gospel music.[50] Another way of putting this is that black Baptists were outsiders to the dominant white/European way of doing church. Instead, they forged a history of their own, and even their own distinct form of sacred music. In so doing, they turned their churches into institutions of African American identity within a society dominated by whites. Long after white Baptists became insider elites, especially in the South, black Baptists were still marked by the outsider/dissenter posture of early Baptist history.

9

White Baptists and the American Mainstream

ON THE HEELS of the Civil War, white Baptists in the South, like all southerners, were chastened yet resilient. As the editor of the Georgia Baptist newspaper the *Christian Index* wrote, "[God] has done what he thought best. . . . He may have laid his hand heavily upon us; certainly we are deeply smitten, but in the midst of it all, we rely on his goodness, and would not, if we could, interfere with his workings of his Providence."[1] The Georgia editor articulated what would later be called the "myth of the lost cause." Essentially, southerners believed that while the political reality of the Confederacy died during the war, the culture of the South would endure, and indeed the region could become a religious kingdom. As one historian has argued, white southerners used the myth of lost cause to construct "an identity as a chosen people."[2] And Southern Baptists led the way.

At its formation the Southern Baptist Convention (SBC) consisted of 4,126 churches with 351,951 total members. But despite its size, the SBC appeared merely to add one more Baptist entity to a landscape littered with societies, state and local conventions, independent churches, and the like. But the split of 1845 is recognized today as one of the most crucial events in Baptist history.[3] Unlike their Methodist and Presbyterian counterparts, northern and southern Baptists never reunited. Moreover, the schism gave birth to what is now America's largest Protestant denomination, called, in jest, the "Catholic Church of the South."[4] Indeed, by the early twentieth century, Southern Baptists were "at ease in Zion," as historian Rufus Spain put it, having grown comfortable as the dominant cultural institution of the region.[5]

WHILE THE SBC'S growth and centralization proved significant, even more important was the cultural evolution it fostered. In the years following the Civil War, white Southern Baptists became consummate cultural insiders. As they built a southern Zion, they identified closely with American ideas of democracy and freedom. Conflating the kingdom and the American nation was not entirely new—Revolutionary-era Baptists had done much the same thing. But as Southern Baptists renewed the identification of Christ's kingdom with America, they both molded and reflected a transformed South. White southerners believed their cause had been just, and they insisted that the Confederacy, not the Union, was the truly Christian society. Southern Baptists explained the South's defeat as the result of judgment for personal sins (not for slavery) and God's greater plan for their culture. This belief that the South was a separate culture or kingdom may have been enough to keep Baptists divided between North and South. Add the military occupation, Republican imposition, and political corruption of Reconstruction governments, and the Baptists' split of 1845 proved more permanent than the political division over slavery that brought on the Civil War. Discussion of closer cooperation with northern Baptists occurred at Southern Baptist Convention annual meetings from 1867 to 1869 and in 1879. After that, reunion was a dead issue. The Southern and Northern Conventions continued fraternal exchanges of delegates but never again entertained the idea of a merger in any serious way.

Following the Civil War, and especially after Reconstruction, the South instituted legal segregation—Jim Crow—and white Southern Baptists led the way. As black Baptists grew eager to form their own independent congregations, white Southern Baptists encouraged the formation of black churches and black denominations. As one state Baptist newspaper put it, "We prefer most decidedly that they shall take the initiative in this movement. Then we shall be innocent of any evil consequences that may arise from it."[6] State Baptist conventions moved to bar blacks from convention meetings, while white Baptist leaders urged that blacks not be allowed to vote even in congregations. The leading white argument for separation of churches was that equality in the churches would lead to equality in society, which would lead to the "mongrelization of our noble Anglo-Saxon race." Other factors may have played a role as well, including the belief that, by separating, each race could evangelize its own kind more effectively. But race was decisive. As a leading Baptist editor put the case in 1869, God had placed between the races "an instinctive repugnance . . . which no training and no philosophy can eradicate, and which divine grace does not."[7]

HAVING SETTLED ON segregation as the answer to the race question, Southern Baptists faced one of their most intense theological controversies, this time over Landmarkism—the belief that only Baptist congregations are true churches and that there exists an unbroken succession of Baptists since apostolic times. The controversy centered on Southern Baptist Theological Seminary and its president, William H. Whitsitt.

Whitsitt grew up as a member of Landmark leader James R. Graves's church. His experience in the Civil War put him in contact with non-Landmark Baptists whom he came to view as authentic Christians. After the war he attended Southern Seminary. His studies there convinced him more fully of the errors of Landmarkism, and he debated those still in its throes. After seminary, Whitsitt studied at the University of Virginia, then the University of Berlin, where he adopted what was called "scientific history," essentially the quest to document with evidence what actually happened in the past. In 1872, he returned to Southern Seminary as a faculty member.

Whitsitt began a quest to pinpoint when Baptists actually started baptizing by immersion, concluding that it was not until 1641. This meant that the earliest English Baptists had baptized adult believers by affusion (pouring) or even sprinkling for an entire generation before adopting immersion. Such a view rejected the unbroken line of Baptist churches that Landmarkers insist existed from the time of the apostles forward. Landmarkism dominated the western half of the SBC, so Whitsitt published his views anonymously in 1881 to avoid the wrath of powerful Landmark leaders. As he grew more secure in his position on Southern Seminary's faculty, he began to oppose Landmark views publicly, sometimes in less than gracious ways. In 1895, he ascended to the presidency of the seminary, a move that threatened to divide the denomination. The following year he published A Question of Baptist History, a thorough demolition of Landmarkism that drove the controversy to new heights.[8]

Several state conventions and local associations passed resolutions calling for Whitsitt's dismissal as president of Southern, the SBC's only theological seminary. In 1897, he and his supporters barely headed off a movement to have the SBC's annual meeting in Wilmington, North Carolina, consider a motion condemning Whitsitt and perhaps even removing him from office. Whitsitt had many supporters, probably the vast majority of the faculty at the seminary and most of the preachers in the eastern half of the denomination. But he mishandled the situation, especially when his enemies learned that he had authored the anonymous articles in the 1880s. It appeared to many that he had concealed his views in order to maintain his position at Southern. Whitsitt made things even worse when he apologized for those articles and added that they had been written "from a pedobaptist standpoint." Taken at face value, this would have meant that nearly a decade into his tenure at Southern Baptist Seminary he had written as a pedobaptist. Given Whitsitt's penchant for alienating people, by 1898 many of his supporters concluded that he would have to resign in order to save the seminary and avoid denominational schism. That strategy prevailed.[9]

Even as Landmarkers forced Whitsitt's resignation, they lost the battle to capture the SBC. Landmark congregations and fledgling associations continued to exist, usually forming around various preachers and Baptist newspaper editors. Ben M. Bogard was the most notable of these. As a young man in Kentucky in the 1880s, Bogard began to read Landmark founder James R. Graves's *Tennessee Baptist* newspaper. He subsequently heard Graves lecture extensively, met him, read all of his books, and became an enthusiastic promoter of Landmarkism. Bogard published his first two books in the early 1890s. Although he played no role in the Whitsitt Controversy, the affair drew Bogard into fellowship with other Landmarkers. In the late 1890s, he began debating non-Landmark Baptists, attracting attention as a forceful voice for Landmark views. In 1899, the Baptist congregation in Searcy, Arkansas, called Bogard as its pastor, and two years later he became co-owner and coeditor of the *Arkansas Baptist* newspaper.

These positions put Bogard in the middle of several controversies between Landmark and non-Landmark Arkansas Baptists. When in 1902 the state convention voted to defund Bogard's newspaper as a result of one of these controversies, he led Landmarkers out of the state convention. They formed the General Association of Baptist Churches in Arkansas (GABCA). Within months, half the Baptist associations in the state affiliated with the new GABCA. The Bogard Schism, as it came to be called, led eventually to the formation of the American Baptist Association (ABA) in 1924. That year the Bogard group, by then called the General Association of Baptist Churches of the United States of America (GABCUSA), met in Texarkana with a Texas Landmark group called the Baptist Missionary Alliance (BMA). The BMA was associated with the views of Samuel

A. Hayden, who had been at odds with the Baptist General Convention of Texas since 1879. In the 1880s, Hayden had held anticonvention beliefs derived from both Landmarkism and the nineteenth-century antimission movement of Daniel Parker. But by 1900 the Haydenites, as they were sometimes called, had dropped the antimission stance. The Texarkana meeting resulted in the merger of Bogard's GABCUSA and the BMA. While national in aspirations, the ABA remains concentrated in Arkansas, Texas, and Oklahoma, with a significant presence in Louisiana and Florida. Today, the ABA has roughly sixteen hundred churches with a total of one hundred thousand members.[10]

WHILE SOUTHERN BAPTISTS dominated the segregated South, Northern Baptists remained one of several mainline Protestant denominations in their region. But massive theological controversy loomed on the horizon. The early twentieth century was an era of Protestant ecumenical efforts, as Baptists, Presbyterians, Methodists, and others sought to put aside their denominational differences and engage in massive reform. This was the heyday of progressivism, the optimistic belief that by combining Christian goodwill with modern techniques, the world could be transformed for the better. Perhaps the most significant religious movement in this vein was the Social Gospel, and the leading Social Gospel theologian was the Baptist Walter Rauschenbusch.

Rauschenbusch was born in 1861 in Rochester, New York, the son of a German Baptist pastor. He converted in 1879 and graduated from Rochester Seminary in 1886. After doing graduate work for a time at the University of Berlin, he returned to the United States and took a pastorate in the notoriously poor area of New York City known as Hell's Kitchen. Here he befriended sociologist Jacob Riis, who would later document the grinding poverty of America's inner cities with photographs that he collected into a book entitled *How the Other Half Lives*. Shepherding his Baptist flock in Hell's Kitchen, Rauschenbusch decided he should do more than preach individual conversion. Some in his congregation were hungry or could not afford shoes for their children. What might the gospel have to say to them beyond the fact that they needed redemption? Pastors from other denominations came to similar conclusions, perhaps the most important being Washington Gladden, a Congregationalist in Columbus, Ohio. Collectively, Rauschenbusch, Gladden, and a cadre of preachers and Christian social scientists began to articulate a Social Gospel or social Christianity.

In 1897, Rauschenbusch joined the faculty of Rochester Seminary and began to write theology. *Christianity and the Social Crisis* appeared in 1907; his last and most important book, *A Theology for the Social Gospel*, appeared in 1917. In his writing, Rauschenbusch articulated the key themes of the movement. Sin resided not merely in individuals but also in corporations, governments, and other social institutions. But the kingdom of God was breaking into history and salvation could come to society itself and not just individuals. Appropriating key themes from liberal Protestantism, Rauschenbusch and the other Social Gospelers believed human beings could be perfected if their institutions were reformed. This sense of the latent perfectibility of humans stood in tension with traditional Reformed notions of the depravity of humankind, making the Social Gospel controversial among Baptists.

Long before Rauschenbusch wrote *A Theology for the Social Gospel*, many inner-city churches from a variety of denominations embodied Social Gospel principles. Known as "institutional churches," they sought to alleviate the suffering of the poor and working-class residents of the cities. As had Rauschenbusch's church in Hell's Kitchen and Gladden's in Columbus, these churches provided a variety of social services—soup kitchens, clothing banks, medical facilities, child care, kindergartens, recreation programs, employment agencies, and even banks. The leading institutional churches among Baptists were the Baptist Temple in Philadelphia and the Ninth Street Baptist Church in Cincinnati.

Social Gospel impulses spread to some parts of the South as well, especially the more industrialized region of north Alabama, where steel mills abounded. There, preacher, professor, and editor L. L. Gwaltney appropriated the teachings of Rauschenbusch for his Southern Baptist context. While never abandoning the primacy of individual conversion, Gwaltney said it was "worse than stupid" for Christians not to "bring their Christian influence to bear on all social ills of this age."[11] In his pastoral theology courses at Howard College (now Samford University), Gwaltney taught his students to study anthropology, sociology, and labor management so they would be equipped to deal with the problems of millworkers. He became an advocate for the rights of labor unions, believing that the right to collectively bargain with one's employer was an economic extension of the Baptist ideal of religious liberty. The Social Gospel impulse among Alabama Baptists also led to the development of the Good Samaritan Hospital for blacks, the Alabama Baptist Hospital for whites, and the Birmingham Baptist Health System.

The WMU also engaged in Social Gospel efforts. Following a wave of post–World War I Italian immigration, Mary Strange, a graduate of the Women's Missionary Union training school, worked with two Italian Baptist pastors to develop social services for children of immigrants in Pratt City. WMU women developed Good Will Centers that provided English training, sewing classes, medical services, and a variety of other programs for immigrants in various Alabama towns.

As an interdenominational movement the Social Gospel embodied the spirit of its times. A significant part of that spirit was the belief that if Protestant denominations would set aside their differences and work together, they could change the world. In 1908, Protestant leaders, some of them Northern Baptists, founded the most significant ecumenical institution, the Federal Council of Churches (FCC). The Social Gospel was central to the FCC. Such ecumenical efforts created controversy among Baptists, often dividing conservatives from moderate and liberal Baptists in the North. The Interchurch World Movement (IWM) became the most controversial of these ecumenical efforts among Baptists.

On December 17, 1918, a group of 135 Protestant mission leaders met in New York to discuss a unified effort to evangelize the world. The meeting opened with a devotional led by renowned Presbyterian missions advocate Robert Speer, which was followed by the keynote address of James I. Vance, moderator of the southern Presbyterian Church US. "The church has come to the greatest hour in its history," the venerable Vance remarked. "Will it measure up or fall down?"[12] Coming on the heels of World War I, which had ended the previous month, attendees were flush with optimism at the prospects for postwar Protestant reform. The meeting launched the Interchurch World Movement. The IWM's goal, in the words of one participant, was "nothing less than a complete evangelization of all of life," and the movement's unofficial motto became "The giving of the whole gospel to the whole world by the whole church."[13]

In January 1920, eighteen hundred leaders from forty-two denominations attended the IWM's annual meeting. Northern Baptists had the largest delegation, with 363 representatives. Northern Baptist Curtis Lee Laws summed up his views of the meeting, writing, "As a thorough-going Baptist I heard not one word in the conference to which I take exception— no jibes at narrowness, no jokes about obscurantism, no pleas for compromise. . . . It was the most dignified, serious, thoughtful, able convention that I have ever had the privilege of attending."[14] Within six months, Laws completely reversed himself.

Originally from Virginia, Laws was one of the most prominent Northern Baptists. After graduating from Crozer Theological Seminary in 1893, he pastored churches in Baltimore and Brooklyn before becoming editor of the *Watchman Examiner*, the most widely circulated Baptist periodical in the North. In his editorial on the 1920 IWM meeting, Laws attempted to assure his fellow conservatives in the Northern Baptist Convention that the IWM was not a conspiracy among the liberals in Protestant denominations to foist progressive theology onto others. Between 1890 and 1920, the three largest northern Protestant denominations—the Baptists, the Presbyterians, and the Methodists—had divided into two factions. On one side were those who came to be called fundamentalists. Those in the competing camp were called modernists, also known as liberals. As their name suggested, the modernists sought to harmonize Protestant theology with modern ways of thinking, particularly evolutionary science and "higher criticism" of Scripture. Higher criticism applied modern scientific and literary techniques to ancient texts. Going beyond the long-standing attempts to date various books of the Bible, higher critics tried to determine to what extent biblical stories were historically factual. And higher critics entertained, often enthusiastically, the possibility that the Bible contained many ancient myths. In so doing, many modernists rejected as unscientific fundamental doctrines of the Christian faith, including the virgin birth of Christ and his bodily resurrection. Moreover, modernists applied the progressive interpretation of history to Christianity. The Christian faith, they argued, had evolved from its rudimentary beginnings recorded in the New Testament to a glorious, modern, twentieth-century faith. Modernists came to view religious experience, not the Bible, as the centerpiece of Christian authority, and their form of Protestantism emphasized a natural as opposed to supernatural religion.

In response, conservatives rose to defend the fundamental doctrines of the faith, insisting that the Bible stood as the sole source of authority. For the most part they rejected higher criticism of Scripture. By 1920, the conservatives had for two decades defended what they called the "fundamentals of the faith." That year Laws coined the term "fundamentalist" to describe those prepared to "do battle royal for the Fundamentals."[15]

Fundamentalists in the Northern Baptist Convention were initially divided over the value of the IWM. In March 1920, New York fundamentalist John Roach Straton weighed in against Laws, his usual compatriot.

Originally from Indiana, Straton was a product of Southern Baptist institutions, Mercer University and the Southern Baptist Theological Seminary. He spent the last twelve years of his life and career (1918–1929) at Calvary Baptist Church in New York City, where he became a fierce defender of orthodoxy and a prominent city fixture. Among his other activities, when Catholic Al Smith ran for president in 1928, Straton dogged the Democrat in editorials, challenged the candidate to a debate, then shadowed Smith's campaign through the South, denouncing him at every stop.

In answer to Laws's initial enthusiasm, Straton said it would be denominational suicide for Baptists to join the IWM. He made this claim to 150 fellow Baptist ministers gathered in New York as part of a conference that included more than one thousand representatives from more than thirty Protestant denominations. Straton's efforts notwithstanding, the Baptist ministers endorsed the IWM. Oddly, Straton agreed to distribute IWM literature to the members of Calvary Baptist, and he said he would contribute to the financial drive as well. Still, he warned that the extent of Calvary's ongoing participation would depend on the will of his congregation.[16]

Meanwhile, I. M. Haldeman of First Baptist, New York City, went further than Straton, calling the IWM "the slickest scheme the devil ever brought about." Haldeman pastored First Baptist for nearly half a century before his death in 1933. No less militant than Straton, he was also a brilliant orator and often preached to standing-room-only crowds. He said the IWM represented modernist theology in disguise and that leaders of the movement believed in a moral but not literal resurrection of Christ. The modernist leaders of the IWM deceived people, he claimed, by telling them they are already the sons of God instead of telling them they are sinners in need of salvation. He also warned that the movement would result in "ecclesiastical autocracy and church sovietism." Haldeman's church voted to abstain from participation in the IWM.[17]

Northern Baptist leader John Y. Aitchison possessed a more moderate temperament than either Straton or Haldeman. Director of the Baptist General Board of Promotion and a cabinet member of the IWM, he called Haldeman's remarks "deplorable."[18] Undaunted, a week later Haldeman lashed out again, saying the IWM resulted from Protestant fear of the consolidation and power of the Catholic Church. He also claimed that his life had been threatened for his previous criticism. Someone, he alleged, had warned him to be careful what he said, "if he did not want to go home in a shutter."[19] The substance of his attack, however, was his charge that the

IWM sought to solve the world's problems through a naive application of the Golden Rule. Given the human propensity for self-interest that leads to competition, he argued, "You've got to have a basis for the Golden Rule, and that basis is the Son of God, not a religion based on ethics alone. You can't get that nature by evolution."[20] Haldeman's critique took aim at both the Social Gospel and the liberal attempt to harmonize Christianity and modern science.

By June, when the Northern Baptist Convention annual meeting took place, Laws had changed his view of the IWM. While still holding that the effort was noble and led by men of goodwill, Laws now sided with Straton and Haldeman on the theological issues. They and others had convinced Laws that the IWM was a liberal effort that would damage the drive to maintain orthodox theology in the Protestant denominations. The IWM pursued unity at the expense of theological rigor, Laws argued. "The Interchurch Movement has emasculated Christianity by eliminating all doctrinal emphasis from its pronouncements and appeals," Laws editorialized. "It has no doctrinal basis, and yet it seeks to explain to the world the meaning of Christianity." As a result, the IWM "stands before the world to-day as a discredited organization."[21]

Complicating the IWM controversy, the Northern Baptists attempted to raise $100 million for their own denominational missions drive called the New World Movement. Headed by Atchison, this effort mirrored the Southern Baptist $75 Million Campaign, underway at the same time. The name similarity between the New World Movement and Interchurch World Movement confused rank-and-file Northern Baptists, with many churches refusing to donate to their own denominational effort for fear their contributions would fund the liberal IWM. When Laws and the *Watchman Examiner* turned against the IWM, he cited both theological and financial issues, writing, "The failure of our own $100,000,000 was due largely to the division among us arising from the principles and practices of the Interchurch World Movement. We have no doubt that this has been more or less true in all the co-operating denominations." He then urged the 1920 convention to withdraw from the IWM.[22]

At the 1920 Northern Baptist Convention meeting, debate extended for three hours in a packed Broadway Baptist Church in Buffalo, eventually resulting in a decision to leave the IWM. The Northern Baptist move came one month after northern Presbyterians had taken the same action. Mitigating the withdrawal somewhat, Northern Baptist delegates voted to make good on a portion of their previous $2.5 million pledge to the IWM.[23]

Pulling out of the IWM did nothing to stem the tide of controversy in the NBC. Concerned about liberal encroachment, the Social Gospel, and the IWM, fundamentalists persuaded delegates to appoint a committee to investigate Baptist seminaries, colleges, and secondary schools in an effort "so far as is possible to cleanse them of all infidel teaching." The impetus for the formation of the investigative committee was a report written by J. C. Massee for the "Fundamentals of the Christian Faith" conference organized by Minnesota fundamentalist William Bell Riley, Laws, and others. Riley's move into the center of the controversy proved natural. Like Straton, he was born in Indiana, and like Haldeman, he was educated at Southern Baptist Theological Seminary. By the twenties, Riley had built a Midwestern religious empire at First Baptist, Minneapolis, and may have been the most prominent fundamentalist in the country. At the NBC meeting, Massee's resolution was softened somewhat, prompting Straton to call the final wording "a weak substitute."[24] When the dust settled following the 1920 NBC annual meeting, fundamentalists had won two victories, the IWM and the investigative committee. But they were not satisfied, and neither were the defeated liberals. The denomination clearly contained two irreconcilable theological parties, and the battle had just begun.

As if controversy between fundamentalists and liberals were not enough, the convention was also marred by the collapse of a set of bleachers seating three hundred attendees. Forty people were injured, including an eighty-three-year-old woman, fourteen severely enough to require medical attention at a local hospital.[25] In almost every way, the Northern Baptist Convention meeting of 1920 was a portent of things to come, and those things were not good.

With both northern Presbyterians and Northern Baptists pulling out and scaling back their financial support, the IWM collapsed. Riley gloated, "Let not the liberals forget that the greatest single endeavor ever attempted by them went down to signal if not disgraceful defeat."[26] The collapse of the IWM left denominations holding the debt for bills already incurred by the IWM. The *Watchman Examiner* likened the situation to "paying for a dead horse which was not worth much even when it was alive."[27]

SOUTHERN BAPTISTS HAD nothing to do with the IWM, the Federal Council of Churches, or any other ecumenical effort. But they were as flush with postwar optimism as their northern counterparts, and they were poised to lead. In many ways World War I reintegrated southerners into national life. While neither the myth of the lost cause nor its sense of southern distinctiveness and chosenness disappeared completely, the great crusade against Germany and its allies nationalized southerners. Southern Baptists sensed this and prepared to lead the nation. M. E. Dodd of First Baptist, Shreveport thundered in his 1919 Southern Baptist Convention sermon in Atlanta, "We have arrived at that moment in our history for which our forefathers toiled and sacrificed and prayed; for which they suffered and bled and died. The Baptist hour of all the centuries has sounded."[28] The following year another Baptist leader made the case even stronger: "As goes America, so goes the world. Largely as goes the South, so goes America. And in the South is the Baptist center of gravity in the world."[29]

What were Baptists to do now that their hour had arrived? The answer came at that 1919 convention meeting, and it was very much like the efforts of northern Protestants involved in the IWM. Following Dodd's sermon, SBC president James B. Gambrell challenged the forty-two hundred messengers to launch a massive missions campaign to take the gospel around the world. Convention leaders formed a committee that proposed a campaign to raise $75 million in five years primarily for mass evangelism and missions. The SBC adopted the committee's report and set up a commission chaired by Dallas pastor George Truett that named Southwestern Baptist Seminary president Lee R. Scarborough director of the campaign. Scarborough took a one-year leave of absence from the seminary and called the commission to order a mere two weeks later. The commission began a media blitz that lasted from July through November and featured denominational literature buttressed by sermons from preachers across the South. The plan culminated in a "Victory Week" in late November and early December during which churches made five-year pledges. The cash was to be in denominational coffers by the end of 1924.

Victory Week was the easy part. Churches pledged a total of $92 million. In anticipation of enlarged revenue streams, SBC agencies began borrowing money to expand their operations. But a postwar recession hit the South the next year, and the campaign began to falter. By its end, only $58 million had been raised. Still, the sum represented a significant increase in per capita giving over previous years. Moreover, Southern Baptists launched their $75 Million Campaign the same year, 1919, that Northern Baptists started their New World Movement, the goal of which was $100 million. The Disciples of Christ, Methodists, and Presbyterians had likewise launched campaign drives between 1913 and 1918, the largest of which was the Methodist Centenary Fund at $115 million. Southern Baptists raised a higher percentage of their targeted goal than most other Protestant denominations, and the campaign set a course of increased giving that continued throughout the 1920s. Baptisms also increased steadily, as did the number of students in Southern Baptist colleges.[30] The $75 Million Campaign may have missed its target, but in shooting for the stars, Southern Baptists at least hit the moon.

By the 1920s, white southerners were not just reintegrated within the larger nation; they were becoming its most prominent exponents of American exceptionalism. And Baptists were at the forefront of this movement. Nowhere can this be seen better than in the two leading Southern Baptist statesmen of the first half of the twentieth century, George W. Truett and E. Y. Mullins, both of whom came to identify American democracy with Baptist democracy.

In 1920, Truett was well on his way to becoming one of the most influential and revered Baptists of the twentieth century. He had become pastor of First Baptist, Dallas in 1897. In June 1911, he preached the closing sermon at the Baptist World Alliance (BWA) meeting in Philadelphia. The BWA was formed in London in 1905 and meets roughly every five years to promote missions, religious liberty, and other Baptist ideals. Southern Baptists participated enthusiastically in the BWA, in large part because it was not ecumenical. At the 1911 meeting, Baptist representatives from around the world got a taste of Southern Baptist triumphalism that would mark the rest of the century. Truett remarked, "The currents are now in this country beginning to run our way even more and more." He then tied Baptist success to the forward march of democracy, saying, "This is democracy's hour . . . when Demos is in the saddle . . . when the average man has been given and is being given his dignity . . . when Mr. Nobody is rapidly becoming the family of Mr. Somebody." Making the tie between Baptists and democracy explicit, Truett exulted, "The triumph of democracy, thank God, means the triumph of Baptists everywhere."[31]

Several minutes later, Truett asked, "What is the task of America?" His answer: "The task of America is that she herself become thoroughly and truly Christian. Brethren, this mighty America can command the conversion of the world on one condition only, and that is that she be Christian through and through, and that is the pre-eminent call of this hour to America."[32] On another occasion, Truett said that democracy "is the goal for this world of ours—both the political goal and the religious goal."[33] With World War I billed by President Woodrow Wilson as "a war to make the world safe for democracy," little wonder that Truett joined the president's handpicked brigade of preachers that traveled to Europe. When the war ended, Truett was in France and wrote in his journal, "Today is probably the most notable day in all history, next to the day when Jesus died on Calvary."[34]

Little more than a year and a half later, in May 1920, Truett preached the most famous sermon in Southern Baptist history. While attending the annual meeting in Washington, DC, SBC messengers convened on the steps of the Capitol to hear their revered preacher. The Baptists were joined by US congressmen, members of the Supreme Court, and representatives from President Wilson's cabinet. Truett's topic that day was "Baptists and Religious Liberty."[35] The official introduction to a published version of the sermon attests to the document's stature among Southern Baptists. The foreword reads, in part, "Since Paul spoke before Nero, no Baptist speaker ever pleaded the cause of truth in surroundings so dignified, impressive and inspiring."[36]

The sermon became the classic articulation of the Baptist principles of religious liberty, separation of church and state, individualism, democratic polity, and freedom of conscience. Truett also covered the centrality of the Bible, as well as the lordship of Christ. The central thrust of the sermon, however, was a triumphal one: Baptists and Baptists alone, he claimed, championed the principles of religious liberty. Truett quoted a spurious passage attributed to John Locke: "The Baptists were the first propounders of absolute liberty, just and true liberty, equal and impartial liberty." Locke almost certainly never wrote these words, but the quote circulated widely among Baptists from the 1840s on, and Truett was hardly alone in using it.[37] Like many a Baptist orator, Truett used the Locke quote to pit Baptists against the Catholic Church, which they saw as the chief obstacle to religious liberty. Rife with anti-Catholicism, the sermon reads in part, "The Baptist message and the Roman Catholic message are the very antipodes of each other. The Roman Catholic message is sacerdotal, sacramentarian, and ecclesiastical. . . . The Baptist message is non-sacerdotal, non-sacramentarian, and non-ecclesiastical." Truett gave a rundown of Catholic authoritarianism in both religion and politics and cited for good measure Lutheran persecution of Anabaptists, Calvin's support for the infamous burning of the heretic Michael Servetus in Geneva, and Zwingli's taking up the sword of battle for Zurich in 1531. While these and other Protestant denominations came eventually to accept religious liberty, it was a Baptist achievement first and foremost, Truett maintained. He even grouped "our Baptist fathers" with America's Founding Fathers—Washington, Madison, and Jefferson—as together responsible for the success of the American experiment.

Truett's sermon became the clearest evidence that white Baptists were now American insiders. As he said oddly of Baptists, who had once had been dissenters against the colonial governments that persecuted them, "Happily, the record of our Baptist people toward civil government has been a record of unfading honor. Their love and loyalty to country have not been put to shame in any land." He then boasted erroneously that not a single Baptist could be found among the loyalist Tories during the American Revolution.[38]

E. Y. Mullins was no less an advocate of the convergence of American democracy and Baptist ways. Generally recognized as the most influential theologian in Southern Baptist history, Mullins succeeded William Whitsitt as president of the denomination's flagship Southern Baptist Seminary and served there from 1899 until his death in 1928. He also served four years as president of the SBC (1921–1924) and as president of the Baptist World Alliance. He is generally credited with steering the SBC safely away from the fundamentalist-modernist controversy that wracked Northern Baptists, holding at bay both liberal theology and the fundamentalists who battled against it.

Mullins promoted a middle way that accounted for the modern world without gutting the faith of its unique and supernatural elements. He defended the orthodox tenets of Christianity against modernism, writing, "Modernism soft pedals or denies the resurrection. . . . You cannot leave out the supernatural and keep the Christian religion."[39] At the same time, he based Christian theology first and foremost on "the fact of religious experience," as he put it in his systematic theology *The Christian Religion in Its Doctrinal Expression* (1917).[40] Here he clearly borrowed heavily from the older liberal theology of German theologian Friedrich Schleiermacher, as well as early twentieth-century theology known as Boston Personalism. Essentially, Mullins agreed with Protestant liberals that experience was the foundation of the Christian faith. But he also agreed with conservatives on essential doctrines such as the deity of Christ, the incarnation, and the resurrection. And he insisted that experience alone could not suffice, warning, "It is not implied . . . that the data of experience are sufficient apart from the New Testament."[41]

In defending a moderate, experiential, yet supernatural faith, Mullins had an advantage over his Northern Baptist counterparts, who were at that very moment gearing up for a full-blown denominational war. In the South, the basic tenets of orthodox Protestantism could still be taken for granted. The challenge of Protestant liberalism existed only on the margins of southern culture, so basing Christianity on experience seemed less threatening to doctrinal orthodoxy.

Northern Baptist Augustus H. Strong tried to maintain a similar moderate position and ended up a man without a country. Strong served as professor and president of Rochester Theological Seminary from 1872 to 1912. Walter Rauschenbusch was one of his star pupils, and Mullins a close friend. Strong lamented late in life that he failed to get Mullins appointed as his successor at Rochester. As the liberal party grew in the seminary and the Northern Baptist denomination, Strong maintained a moderate stance. Like Mullins, he accepted the use of the higher critical method of biblical scholarship. The problem with liberals was not that they used higher criticism, Strong argued, but that they used nothing else.[42] Strong believed that if one started with the orthodox tenets of the faith as a basic worldview, the use of modern scientific tools could aid in understanding the Bible. He straddled the growing divide among Northern Baptists for two decades, arguing as vigorously for orthodox doctrine as for modern methods. But when the denomination plunged into the fundamentalist-modernist controversy of the 1920s, he was fit for neither side. He died just as the controversy peaked.

By contrast, the southern consensus on fundamental doctrines left Mullins free to emphasize experience. And his denomination remained intact. Unlike Strong, Mullins wrote theology in the context of a religiously saturated culture. Still, even as he drew sharp distinctions between his evangelical faith and the modernism of Northern Baptist liberals, he, no less than they, believed in a progressive march of democracy that paralleled the spread of Protestant religion. As he wrote succinctly in 1911, "In the social and political sphere throughout the earth, Baptist principles are making rapid strides forward. . . . [T]he Baptist type of religion is most fundamentally in accord with the ongoing of the world toward democracy."[43] In his most popular book, *The Axioms of Religion*, Mullins turned instinctively to the American principle of church-state separation. He labeled his fifth axiom "The religio-civic axiom," which was none other than the First Amendment. "The American principle of the relations between the Church and State," he wrote, "is so well understood and is accepted by the people of the United States so generally and so heartily that it is unnecessary to spend time in pointing out at length what the axiom implies."[44] This axiom rested on Baptist history, practicality, and Americanism, rather than natural law, the doctrines of creation and fall, the sinfulness of humanity, the Bible, or even Christian experience. In his final chapter, Mullins expressed his belief that through reform "Christianity in America will become the religion of the State, although not a State religion."[45] "We may regard American civilization as a Baptist empire," he wrote, "for at the basis of this government lies a great group of Baptist ideals."[46] Mullins and Truett assumed that Baptist principles and American democracy were virtually synonymous and that the one had led directly to the other.

TRUETT'S AND MULLINS'S views dominated Southern Baptist life in the early twentieth century. While Southern Baptists extolled the virtues of institutional separation of church and state, and revered their history of dissent, they at the same time saw church and state as allies in the promotion of freedom and democracy. As Baptist scholar, preacher, and critic Christopher Canipe has argued, the cherished wall of separation had come to function like a mirror. When Baptists looked at American democracy, they saw themselves.[47] This was true not just of Southern Baptists. Northern Baptist liberals routinely trumpeted the ways in which a progressive Social Gospel worked hand in hand with the march of civilization and democracy. A major thrust of Rauschenbusch's theology included transforming the conception of God from "despotic" to "democratic." As he concluded his classic book, A Theology for the Social Gospel, "The era of prophetic and democratic Christianity has just begun."[48] Nothing could have signaled any more clearly that many white Baptists had gone from outsiders to insiders and joined the American mainstream.

Baptist Schism in the Early Twentieth Century

IN MAY 1922, Harry Emerson Fosdick preached a famous sermon entitled, "Shall the Fundamentalists Win?" Fundamentalists and modernists
had been at odds for years, but after Fosdick's sermon, tensions escalated into open warfare, and the fundamentalist-modernist controversy
became a national event. Fosdick was the best-known Baptist in America
and a staunch liberal. He was also, oddly, pastor of the First Presbyterian
Church in New York City. Fosdick's liberal views combined with his
being a Baptist in a Presbyterian pulpit made him a central figure in the
Presbyterian fundamentalist-modernist controversy, and his sermon put
fundamentalists in all denominations on alert.

Having grown up an orthodox Baptist, Fosdick came to liberal views
largely under the tutelage of theologian William Newton Clarke, who
taught at Hamilton Seminary, which was connected to Colgate College,
where Fosdick received his undergraduate education. After Colgate,
Fosdick took his seminary degrees from Union Theological Seminary
in New York. He pastored in New Jersey before going back to join the
Union faculty, then on to First Presbyterian, or Old First, as the church
was affectionately known. From Clarke, Fosdick came to embrace the
typical liberal belief: "We must distinguish between abiding experiences
and changing categories."[1] Like E. Y. Mullins in the Southern Baptist
Convention, Fosdick emphasized religious experience. But Fosdick jet-
tisoned old categories much more enthusiastically than Mullins. For
liberals, the old categories included the ancient biblical way of speaking
about faith. Such ancient ways no longer applied to a modern, scientific
age, so the task of the theologian or preacher was to rearticulate the faith,

making it plausible for modern people. The centerpiece of the Christian faith became personal experience, which supplanted Scripture and doctrine as the source of religious authority.

For liberals like Fosdick, Scripture continued to serve as a valuable guide. But it could not be taken literally anymore because the categories for understanding an experience with God had changed so dramatically. The modern era of the Enlightenment created a distinction between objective facts and subjective experience that had not existed when the Bible was written. Much of what was recorded in Scripture could not possibly be true in an objective, scientific sense. Fosdick, therefore, dismissed much that was miraculous or supernatural, saying, for instance, that the virgin birth of Christ was "a biological miracle our modern minds cannot use." Likewise, Christ's second coming was "an old phrasing of expectancy" that should be replaced by a modern, progressive view he summed up this way: "[God's] will and principles will be worked out by God's grace in human life and institutions," not through a supernatural intervention at the end of time as premillennialist fundamentalists believed.[2]

Few liberals understood fundamentalists better than Fosdick. Fundamentalists were not merely conservatives, in his view, but conservatives with a particularly intolerant agenda. He declared that the fundamentalists intended "to drive out of the evangelical churches men and women of liberal opinions."[3] This was true of some fundamentalists, not so for others. There were moderate fundamentalists in both the northern Presbyterian Church USA and Northern Baptist Convention who believed liberals and conservatives could coexist in the same denomination. Today these moderates would be known as evangelicals, but in the 1920s anyone who adhered to conservative doctrine was usually labeled a fundamentalist. Fosdick concerned himself only with the more militant conservatives and answered his sermon's titular question, "Shall the Fundamentalists Win?," with: "Well, they are not going to do it; certainly not in this vicinity."[4]

Among Presbyterian fundamentalists, Clarence Macartney of Philadelphia answered Fosdick's sermon with one of his own entitled, "Shall Unbelief Win?," while the Baptist John Roach Straton responded with "Shall the Funnymonkeyists Win?," a reference to the brewing controversy over evolution. The more tempered Curtis Lee Laws countered Fosdick's charge of fundamentalist intolerance with an editorial titled "Intolerant Liberalism." Laws acknowledged Fosdick's general goodwill, saying he was one of those preachers who, although nonevangelical in his views, "at the same time manifest forth to a remarkable extent the spirit of their master." But Fosdick had destroyed that reputation of tolerance with his sermon, Laws believed. Laws argued that one could hardly expect clear thinking from "a Baptist preacher who is at once the pastor of a Presbyterian church and a professor in a theological seminary disowned by the Presbyterian denomination." Laws then characterized Fosdick's sermon as "a bitter arraignment of good and true men; a gross and unpardonable ignorance of facts; a remarkable illustration of the intolerance of liberalism."[5] Fosdick responded to these sorts of critiques by characterizing his sermon as a "frank, kindly, irenic plea for tolerance, not likely to be misunderstood except by people who persist in misunderstanding it."[6]

As a moderate fundamentalist, Laws bristled when Fosdick classed all fundamentalists as premillennialists and antievolutionists. Laws had coined the term "fundamentalism" in a July 1920 article in which he protested that "premillennialist" was too restrictive a term for the movement because fundamentalism consisted of "premillennialists, postmillennialists, pro-millennialists and no-millennialists." In his response to Fosdick, Laws also refuted the charge that fundamentalists wanted to set up a tribunal to exclude liberals from the denomination. Laws did want the Northern Baptist Convention to adopt a confession outlining the orthodox views held by most Baptists, but he said consistently that he opposed using such a creed to drive liberals out of the denomination. How the NBC could have a creed and tolerate those who rejected it was not altogether clear.

However much Laws believed Fosdick had misrepresented fundamentalism, many Baptists recognized themselves in Fosdick's definition. They were proudly intolerant of liberalism because liberalism taught "revolutionary and destructive heresies," as Straton put it. Less than two weeks after Fosdick's sermon, J. C. Massee, the newly appointed pastor of Boston's Tremont Temple Baptist Church, announced that the fundamentalists intended to "elect to every board and committee [of the Northern Baptist Convention] a clear majority of pronouncedly conservative men and women." "Modernism and modernists must go," Massee explained. "It is my hope that we shall there serve notice on the denomination that we are no longer tolerant of the drift from the ancient moorings."[7]

Fundamentalists in the NBC chose the 1922 convention as the time to take their stand against liberalism, and Fosdick's sermon increased their determination to fight. Only two years earlier they had succeeded in steering the NBC out of the Interchurch World Movement (IWM) precisely because it was a liberal enterprise. Now they wanted to ensure that the NBC remained orthodox and conservative. Fundamentalist Baptists of both the moderate and militant varieties within the NBC rallied under the banner of the Fundamentalist Fellowship. Joining Massee on the executive board were John Roach Straton, Laws, and other high-profile fundamentalists. Kicking off their new drive to purify the denomination, Massee sent a letter to fundamentalist pastors across the country identifying their "inalienable right" to protest the departure from the historic tenets of the faith. "We deplore the drift away from a sound doctrine. We reject the leadership of men of liberal theological views. We repudiate the over-emphasis of a social gospel," he told his fundamentalist brethren.[8]

For Massee, the central problem of the Social Gospel was its focus on the "application of the ethics of Jesus to unregenerate human lives" at the expense of the proclamation of Christ's saving grace for sinners.[9] On the eve of the convention, Laws stated explicitly that fundamentalists had organized in order to stop the modernist "warfare against supernaturalism," which was undermining the foundation of historic Christianity.[10] Fundamentalists rebuked all tendencies toward a naturalistic gospel. As Massee put it, "In my judgment every man of modernistic theological tendencies, though he may at heart hold the faith of Christ, should be discontinued from any office in the Northern Baptist Convention for the simple reason that his tendency is wrong. . . . Every officer of the convention this year should be distinctly and pronouncedly a conservative man."[11] Laws may have resisted the urge to drive liberals out of the denomination, but Massee and other fundamentalists made this their primary objective. And it was this that Fosdick had in mind when he preached his famous sermon.

A FEW DAYS before the opening of the 1922 convention, the fundamentalists gathered in Indianapolis to hold their third annual preconvention Fundamentals Conference, which was a pep rally of sorts. They brought in the Presbyterian William Jennings Bryan, who delivered his standard anti-evolution message, while Laws gave an extensive address on the definition and nature of fundamentalism. Liberals referred to fundamentalists as "literalists, dogmatists, separatists, medievalists, cranks, and ignoramuses," Laws charged, but in reality "we are simply good old-fashioned Baptists." It was the modernists' attacks on traditional faith that forced them to adopt the label "fundamentalist." "Fundamentalism, then, is a protest against that rationalistic interpretation of Christianity which seeks to discredit supernaturalism," he thundered. Modernism "scorns the miracles of the Old Testament, sets aside the virgin birth of our Lord . . . laughs at the credulity of those who accept many of the New Testament miracles, reduces the resurrection of our Lord to the fact that death did not end his existence, and sweeps away the promises of his second coming as an idle dream of men under the influence of Jewish apocalypticism."[12]

The convention itself opened on June 14. A banner in the convention hall read, "Agreed to Differ, Resolved to Love." It defied the spirit of this convention.

Northern Baptist president Helen Barrett Montgomery opposed the fundamentalists. A layperson and the first woman president of the convention, Montgomery was a longtime progressive reformer, missions advocate, and fundraiser. An excellent scholar of Greek, in 1924 she would become the first woman to translate the New Testament. Over the previous two years, fundamentalists had used their investigative committee to oust liberal professors at Baptist colleges and seminaries. Montgomery believed the preservation of the Christian character of Baptist colleges was essential, but she also decried scaring people into withholding their contributions. Just the week before the convention, trustees at Crozer Seminary in Chester, Pennsylvania, had rejected a fundamentalist petition to have church historian Henry Clay Vedder thrown off the faculty for his views. Seminary president Milton G. Evans responded with the standard retort of many liberal Baptists: "There can be no such thing as a heresy trial in the Baptist denomination." This, he said, was because Baptists "have no authorized or standard confession of faith."[13] He went on to reference the "creed" the fundamentalists had fashioned for themselves at their conference the previous year. Evans drew a distinction between the reputedly noncreedal Baptists and the Presbyterians, who adhered to the Westminster Confession of Faith. While Baptist fundamentalists pressed for a creed in the NBC, Presbyterian fundamentalists attempted to persuade their denomination to enforce the creed they already had.

Montgomery also drew attention to creedalism in her opening address. She acknowledged that the issue of a standardized, denomination-wide confession of faith was violently opposed by some while ardently supported by others. Like Evans, she pointed out that there existed no denomination-wide body capable of enforcing a creed on the independent congregations of the NBC; nor did state conventions have such authority. Montgomery said that if a committee were appointed for the purpose of drawing up such a confession, the committee should never be allowed to report back to the convention. "We should allow the committee sufficient funds to give publicity to the statement and leave it in the hands of the local church to modify or abridge or adopt bodily as it sees fit," Montgomery said. For her and many other Baptists, the autonomy of the local church was a core principle of the Baptist faith. "For us Baptists to have an official confession of faith," she continued, "would come perilously near to abandoning one of our fundamental principles. . . . We Baptists are the recognized democrats of the Protestant world."[14]

Much of the rest of Montgomery's opening address outlined the need for Baptist unity, which she viewed as a prerequisite for spreading the gospel to a lost world. Like the fundamentalists, liberals began to caucus together, planning strategy for how to stop fundamentalism. Cornelius Woelfkin of Park Avenue Baptist in New York emerged as the leader on the liberal side. Popularly known as John D. Rockefeller's church, Park Avenue would soon invite Fosdick to succeed Woelfkin upon his retirement.

For two years, Laws had answered the anticreedal drumbeat. The week before the 1921 convention meeting, he had editorialized on the need to maintain doctrinal rigor and orthodoxy and urged the adoption of a confession of faith. Characterizing his opponents' arguments, he wrote, "But are not all such confessions in some sense a violation of the principles of soul-liberty—a principle dear to the hearts of all Baptists? We desire here to declare that this matter of soul-liberty is being tremendously overworked by many who reject the very principles of those who died to make soul-liberty the heritage of the present-day Christian world."[15]

Laws acknowledged that soul liberty meant no one had the right to dictate to another what he or she had to believe. But he vigorously rejected the idea that people could believe anything they wanted and still be Baptist. "Our Baptist fathers had a very clearly defined system of truth," he argued, "and this was put into many noble confessions of faith. They knew no soul-liberty that guaranteed to men the right to believe what they pleased while still claiming to be Baptists." He believed that using the idea of soul liberty to reject the very beliefs Baptists had been touting in their confessions for three hundred years was to "pervert the doctrine and to make it a menace to the church of Christ."[16]

The fight over a Baptist creed began on the very first day of the convention when Frank Goodchild of New York offered a resolution to form a committee that would write a "declaration of faith." Such a committee would seek the cooperation of Canadian and Southern Baptists in an effort to bring forward a statement that the major Baptist denominations in North America could agree on. The long resolution included the standard fundamentalist litany of charges, including "notorious instances of false and subversive teaching in certain of our schools and seminaries."[17] Talk of a creed in conjunction with Southern Baptists prompted *The New York Times* to editorialize the next day, "Freedom of conscience had certainly been one of the 'fundamentals' of Baptist doctrine, and it is now seriously threatened." The editorial then called Southern Baptists "almost all Fundamentalists."[18]

Over the next two days, the convention grew raucous, with Montgomery on one occasion hammering her gavel and shouting to the delegates, "Sit down and be quiet."[19] On June 16, William Bell Riley, the Midwest's leading fundamentalist, threw the meeting into an uproar when he moved that the convention formally adopt the New Hampshire Confession of Faith of 1833 as its official creed. The impatient Riley believed the fundamentalists had bungled their chance the year before. At the 1921 Des Moines convention, the Fundamentalist Fellowship had drawn up a seven-point confession that combined elements of the New Hampshire Confession and the Philadelphia Confession, but for reasons unknown decided not to press the issue. Following the 1921 meeting, the *Baptist*, the official newspaper of the NBC, gloated that "fundamentalism is dead." Laws spent the next three weeks editorializing to prove this false and charged that the *Baptist* had made itself a laughingstock by suggesting it.[20] Still, Riley believed that through their own indecision fundamentalists had missed a golden opportunity, and he was not about to let it happen again. This time he decided to press the issue on his own.

But Riley's move played right into the hands of the liberals. Woelfkin proceeded to the podium and submitted a substitute resolution. It read, "That the Northern Baptist Convention affirm that the New Testament is the all-sufficient ground of faith and practice, and that we need no other."[21] As one reporter put it, "From that moment on it was the New Hampshire Confession against the New Testament."[22]

In the debate leading up to the vote, Woelfkin regaled the crowd with stories. He told of his family's persecution for being Baptist and how his mother read to him from the New Testament, not the New Hampshire Confession. "Baptists have never been strong on statements," he said. Massee responded, telling the delegates that Woelfkin's resolution was simply a parliamentary maneuver. Massee charged that Woelfkin and another prominent liberal had just months before signed an interdenominational statement called the "Evangelical Confession of Faith." What does it mean, Massee asked, for these men to sign a confession in the spring, then declare in the summer "that they have no confession but the New Testament"?[23] Massee explained further that the Bible must be interpreted, so it is nonsensical to say we need nothing but the New Testament. Seminaries train preachers to interpret Scripture, while ordination councils and missionary societies examine prospective preachers and missionaries on doctrinal questions that turn on one's interpretation of the New Testament. Moreover, Massee argued, "If you need nothing but the New Testament for a confession of faith, close up the Sunday school classes and stop the teachers . . . shut up the theological seminaries . . . stop every bit of your program of world missions and world service except the circulation of the New Testament."[24]

After due deliberation, someone called the question, and Montgomery led in prayer preceding the vote. She prayed in part that those present "may accept the decision of this body as the decision of the great Head of the Church Himself."[25] Woelfkin's resolution carried. The liberals had clearly outmaneuvered the fundamentalists, who were, in Laws's words, "caught in the trap." What Baptist could vote against the New Testament as the "all-sufficient ground of faith and practice"? Had the Confession been considered on its own merits, Laws believed, the vote in favor of the New Hampshire Confession would have been much higher.[26] The following day fundamentalists attempted to attach doctrinal conditions to the report of the committee on financial contributions. They failed.

On June 18, A. W. Beaven of the Lake Avenue Baptist Church in Rochester, New York, preached the convention sermon. He exhorted liberals not to gloat over their victory. "In God's name," he thundered, "if the only work we can carry back to our churches . . . from this convention is that there has been achieved here the victory of a party, then both factions have lost."[27] Woelfkin's sermon later that day hit on standard progressive themes. He preached an immanent God who was as intimately involved in the flow of history as in the original creation. "He was as much behind the emancipation of slaves as He was the older exodus. He was the inspiration of the Declaration of Independence as he was that of the Decalogue."[28] He then trumpeted progressive ideas such as Prohibition, the abolition of war, labor relations, and general goodwill among nations. "A true modernist," he said, "has the deepest reverence for the Holy Scriptures and believes them inspired. But he cannot believe that God has exhausted himself, but still inspires men to write noble Hymns and other literature."[29] Such a conflation of biblical inspiration with modern literature and social movements was precisely what concerned and enraged fundamentalists.

As if to symbolize the general lack of decorum of the 1922 convention, a circus paraded by the auditorium for a half hour on the second-to-last day. One speaker had to wait for screeching elephants to pass before he could continue his report.[30] But not all was rancor and ruckus. In the spirit of Beaven's advice not to gloat, liberal leaders invited fundamentalists to dinner at the Claypool Hotel, where the liberal steering committee had plotted strategy all week. "We smoked the pipe of peace [and] just told funny stories," Woelfkin said to reporters.[31]

Before leaving Indianapolis, the fundamentalists formed yet another organization, with Massee as the head and a 150-member steering committee. The purpose was to generate support for the conservative cause across the NBC and to reach out to fundamentalists in other Baptist denominations as well as among Presbyterians, Methodists, and Congregationalists.[32] Such efforts symbolized the growth of a transdenominational evangelical movement that had been underway for more than a decade.

WHILE DIVIDED THEOLOGICALLY, liberals and fundamentalists of most Protestant denominations continued in the 1920s to agree on many cultural issues, chief among them Prohibition. At the 1920 meeting of the Northern Baptist Convention, amid rancorous debates over the IWM and the appointment of a committee to sniff out heresy at Baptist schools, delegates voted unanimously to urge the upcoming Democratic National Convention to vote down any attempt to include a "wet" plank in its platform. Many African American Baptists also tended to support Prohibition, warning that intemperate use of alcohol was a debilitating burden for too many blacks. As early as 1877, Richmond's First African Baptist resolved to expel any members who ran a bar. (Most Primitive Baptists, although teetotalers themselves, frowned on prohibition as a worldly distraction.)

In the wake of a report that a Baptist minister had performed the wedding of Mary Pickford and Douglas Fairbanks, Northern Baptists also passed a resolution condemning laxity on the issue of divorce. Pickford had divorced her first husband on March 2, 1920, and married Fairbanks on March 28. The two film stars had been involved in an adulterous affair for more than four years.[33]

Although liberal and fundamentalist Northern Baptists agreed on Prohibition, they did not on evolution. The premillennialist wing of the

fundamentalists fought as fervently for creationism as for orthodox theology. But evolution never became part of the denominational fight as
such. Laws consistently sought to define fundamentalism as including
premillennialists and non-premillennialists, as well as theistic evolution-
ists and antievolutionists. For him, fundamentalism included a broad
array of conservatives who had a shared concern for orthodox theology but
who differed on nonessentials such as end-times prophecy and the proper
stance toward modern science. For this reason, fundamentalists never
attempted to make the issue a creedal matter within the denomination.

Some Baptists, however, became convinced that evolution would ruin
America and therefore moved antievolution to the top of their cultural
agenda. World War I was largely responsible for the turn against evolution.
Fundamentalists drew a connection between liberal theology and evolution, and they noted that such ideas had taken root in Germany—birthplace
of higher criticism—more than anywhere else. If American Protestant
denominations adopted liberal theology, therefore, and American schools
taught evolution, America would end up just like Germany—defeated.
This line of reasoning turned what had been a preachers' fight over theology into a cultural crusade over evolution that culminated in the infamous
Scopes trial of 1925.[34] One might say that the fundamentalist movement
proceeded along two tracks—a theological track within the northern
denominations and an antievolution track in the larger culture.

Concern over evolution caused tension among fundamentalists themselves. Those most inclined to join the battle against evolution pushed
the hardest for interdenominational fundamentalism, often playing down
their Baptist identity in favor of a more generally fundamentalist one.
Denominationally oriented Baptist fundamentalists tended to follow the
moderate lead of Laws, while the more militant, interdenominational, and
increasingly antievolution Baptists followed Riley. Each side blamed the
other for the devastating defeat over the New Hampshire Confession at
the 1922 convention meeting.

Laws and the moderates became ever more committed to working
within the NBC, while Riley and the militants worked increasingly outside it. Riley and the hard-liners left the NBC's Fundamentalist Fellowship
and formed the Baptist Bible Union (BBU). Joining Riley on the executive committee were Canadian T. T. Shields as president, A. C. Dixon,
R. E. Neighbor, and J. Frank Norris. Norris was at the time shopping for
northern allies in his fight over evolution with Baylor University and the
Baptist General Convention of Texas.[35]

The first resolution of the BBU denounced Cornelius Woelfkin by name and characterized his 1922 actions as "a repudiation of these fundamentals of the Baptist position while at the same time professing adherence to the New Testament." Ironically, the resolution also declared "our determination not to withdraw from the various conventions represented by our membership."[36] The fundamentalist strategy resembled the efforts of seventeenth-century Puritan colonists who left England but not the Church of England. Like them, some fundamentalist Baptists hoped to purify their denominations, even if it was necessary to leave them in order to do so. It remains unclear how leaving these denominations would lead to their reform. And what actually happened was predictable in light of similar developments throughout American church history. The BBU began to break apart, then morphed into a new and separate denomination in 1932, the General Association of Regular Baptist Churches (GARBC). Ironically, in all his efforts to promote the BBU, Riley remained technically within the "modernist-tainted" NBC even as his Northwest Bible College in Minneapolis trained preachers to staff churches in the BBU and eventually the GARBC.[37]

MODERNIST NORTHERN BAPTISTS quickly became cultural insiders. Though they were the insurgents, they had the support of the secular organs of opinion, *The New York Times* in particular. In May 1923, the newspaper editorialized against the fundamentalists, writing, "Fundamentalists seem to derive their name from their lack of interest in the fundamentals of Christianity and their passionate addiction to odds and ends of dogma borrowed from other religions." The editorial then summed up Baptist history as "little more than variations on the theme of liberty for the individual conscience and the individual congregation."[38] This view was in keeping with an editorial from the previous June, during the 1922 convention meeting, that claimed, "The Baptist liberals stand only for [the Bible's] interpretation according to the individual conscience, which is about as fundamental a fundamental of their faith as could be imagined."[39] The triumph of 1922, the paper claimed, lived up to the ideals of Roger Williams, the colonial religious liberty firebrand who was a Baptist for roughly four months. The *Times* editorial board commended the Northern Baptists for "setting their faces forward."

Two issues were at play here. First, *The New York Times* too easily reduced Baptist history to freedom of the individual conscience and the autonomy of congregations. In the editors' view, the liberals embodied tolerance, indeed modernity. The editors pointed out correctly that Baptists had practiced congregational autonomy, or at least congregational independence, for the entirety of Baptist history. But they ignored the fact that throughout their history Baptist confessions routinely discussed specific points of "dogma," often in twenty or more carefully enumerated clauses, before mentioning anything remotely resembling individual liberty or congregational autonomy. Historically, Baptists have been obsessed with doctrinal orthodoxy. Leaving that out of the Baptist equation and reducing Baptist identity to instrumentals such as individual liberty and congregational autonomy was in keeping with the growing American emphasis on autonomy, or what today is called freedom of choice. The view that Baptists were in the vanguard of modern individualism ran parallel to Southern Baptist views. George Truett and E. Y. Mullins were more akin to the fundamentalists in the NBC than the modernists on specific theological fundamentals. But like the liberal Baptists, they, too, equated the forward march of democracy with the spread of Baptist ways. Early twentieth-century Baptists had a hard time resisting the temptation to conflate soul freedom with the autonomy of the individual, a secular notion that liberal Protestants and secular liberals alike embraced.

Not all secular opinion makers shared the *Times*'s view that the modernists had the best argument. When the northern Presbyterians experienced the most intense chapter of their own fundamentalist-modernist controversy on the heels of the Baptist fight, secular journalist Walter Lippmann acknowledged that fundamentalist J. Gresham Machen had the better argument. In his book *Christianity and Liberalism* (1923), Machen argued that the modernist version of the faith was not Christianity but a new religion. When the book appeared Lippmann wrote, "It is an admirable book . . . , the best popular argument produced by either side in the current controversy."[40] Meanwhile, the editor of the *Nation* wrote, "Fundamentalism is undoubtedly in the main stream of the Christian tradition while modernism represents a religious revolution as far-reaching as the Protestant Reformation."[41] Absent from both Lippmann and the *Nation* was the assumption that a newer version of Christianity, or a newer version of anything, necessarily trumped the older view.

For today's evangelicals who are not fundamentalists, it might be disconcerting that in both the Northern Baptist Convention and the Presbyterian Church USA, moderate fundamentalists lost their battles. The moderates, who were very much like today's nonfundamentalist evangelicals, or "neo-evangelicals," tried to tolerate liberal theology even while disagreeing with it, only to be steamrolled by the liberals who were often as militant as the more thoroughgoing fundamentalist followers of Riley. There is a plausible explanation for why liberals won, however. In the 1920s, American culture was increasingly embracing science as the arbiter of truth even in matters of theology. At the same time, individual freedom and tolerance were triumphing against Victorian communitarian standards. In other words, the spirit of science, which easily leaves outdated views behind, became the paradigm for all intellectual and spiritual endeavors. New was always better than old. When it became difficult to reconcile Christian supernaturalism with scientific naturalism, liberals divorced the two from each other, reducing religion to subjective experience, safely beyond the reach of scientific inquiry.

Liberal theology was exactly what it purported to be—a revision of Protestantism accommodating the spirit of the modern age. That spirit pushed individual religious experience of a natural yet romantic sort to the forefront of the Christian faith, while the old traditions of orthodoxy receded into the background. Fundamentalists, whether militant or moderate, were clearly out of sync with such a spirit. Fundamentalist Baptists in the North once again became cultural outsiders, like their forebears in the eighteenth century, while liberal Baptists retained their insider status by adjusting their faith to fit the times. Baptists had faced this same choice a number of times in history and would do so once more at the end of the twentieth century. Again, it would produce a bitter fight over Baptist identity.

Insiders and Outsiders at Mid-Twentieth Century

BY THE MID-TWENTIETH century, three large denominations dominated Baptist America—the white Southern and Northern Baptist Conventions, and the black National Baptist Convention USA Inc. In an effort to transcend its regionalism, in 1950 the Northern Baptist Convention changed its name to the American Baptist Convention (then to the American Baptist Churches USA in 1972). Convention delegates passed a motion to invite smaller Baptist groups, ethnic Baptist denominations, black Baptists, and even the SBC to unite under the new umbrella. Such a merger proved unrealistic, however, and the following year American Baptist leaders backed off. The SBC had already scheduled its 1950 and 1951 meetings for Chicago and San Francisco, signaling a new drive toward expansion outside the South. The two denominations had previously observed agreements not to encroach on each other's territory, but clearly those informal arrangements had outlived their usefulness. In response to the ABC name change, the SBC announced that previous understandings had expired.[1]

Besides the three major groups, close to fifty other significant Baptist bodies dotted the landscape by the mid-twentieth century. Many of these smaller groups formed in the nineteenth and twentieth centuries, but some traced their origins back much further. Among the older groups were General Baptists, who had nearly died out by 1800, only to be revived in Indiana in the 1820s. Seventh Day Baptists, who began in the 1650s, came together in 1801 as the General Conference of Seventh Day Baptists, which is still around today. At least four Freewill Baptist denominations existed, including one that is predominantly black and another that is Pentecostal. The largest, the National Association of

Free Will Baptists, formed in Nashville in 1935. The group traces its history through a "Palmer" line in North Carolina and a "Randall" line in New Hampshire, both of which began in the eighteenth century. The Primitive Baptist movement produced five separate denominations, all of which came at least indirectly from the nineteenth-century antimission movement. Finally, there were ethnic Baptists, including Swedish, Russian, German, Polish, French, and Romanian. Among the ethnics, Swedish and German Baptists have constituted significant, if not major, Baptist denominations, while more recent decades have seen the explosive growth of Hispanic and Asian congregations, mostly within the Southern Baptist Convention.[2]

Joining these older groups were twentieth-century Baptist denominations often referred to as fundamentalist. Many of these emerged from the permanent rift created by the fundamentalist-modernist controversy. But some also emerged from the Landmark Baptist movement of the nineteenth century, and thus predate fundamentalism. In addition to the smattering of small Landmark denominations and some independent Landmark congregations, a small minority of Southern Baptist churches still hold Landmark views. It is difficult to say whether Landmark Baptists should be included among fundamentalists. Some Landmarkers prefer a separate identity and at times even see Baptist fundamentalists as their competitors. But when the American Baptist Association formed in Texarkana in 1924, leaders adopted the New Hampshire Confession of Faith and added ten doctrinal points of their own. The additions were nearly identical to the fundamentals of the faith touted by fundamentalists in the Northern Baptist Convention. The ABA statement affirmed the infallibility of the Bible, the creation account in Genesis, the virgin birth of Christ, the bodily resurrection of Christ, the literal second coming of Christ, and so forth—nearly all the doctrines challenged by theological modernists.[3] Some argue that twentieth-century fundamentalist Baptists are the successors to Landmarkers, especially in the South. And many of the so-called independent Baptist congregations and denominations espouse both fundamentalist theology and Landmark ecclesiology.

While some fundamentalist Baptists adhere to Landmarkism, militancy and separatism are more central to the fundamentalist identity. The first refers to the militant defense of orthodox doctrine—that is, the fundamentals of the faith. The second refers to the insistence that true Christians must separate themselves from theological liberals, departing mainline denominations that promulgate what fundamentalists believe to be liberal heresy. Following the fundamentalist-modernist controversy in the northern denominations, Presbyterian as well as Baptist fundamentalists began to separate from the mainline bodies and start new denominations. Chief among the fundamentalist Baptist denominations that emerged was the General Association of Regular Baptist Churches (GARBC). As we saw in the previous chapter, the GARBC evolved from the Baptist Bible Union, which had been formed by T. T. Shields from Canada, Northern Baptists William Bell Riley and A. C. Dixon, and Southern Baptist J. Frank Norris. In 1923, the year after the fundamentalist debacle over the New Hampshire Confession, representatives met in Kansas City to create the BBU. Known as "come-outers," the separatists believed they could no longer fellowship with liberal unbelief. Riley promoted the new denomination while at the same time remaining active in the NBC in an effort to both promote separatism and steer the larger denomination back to orthodoxy. Norris tried to do the same in the SBC. The BBU adopted the New Hampshire Confession and added a premillennial twist to the clause on eschatology. While proclaiming its resistance to denominational power, within a few years the BBU had all the trappings of a denomination—officers, missions programs, a newspaper, Sunday school literature, and a college in Des Moines, Iowa.[4]

A dispute over the college proved to be the denomination's undoing. The BBU took over the bankrupt Northern Baptist college known as Des Moines University in 1927. As president of the BBU, Shields was also the college's chairman of the board. He fired theologically suspect faculty and hired students to monitor the others and report doctrinal deviance. Almost immediately after H. C. Wayman was appointed as president of the school, Shields and Wayman had a falling-out. Among other matters, Shields and those who sided with him charged that Wayman had not earned the academic degrees he claimed. By 1929, the controversy had spread to students, faculty, administration, and denominational officials. In the midst of the controversy, opponents accused Shields of having an affair with the secretary for the denomination and the college. Students who opposed Shields rioted during a board meeting, prompting police intervention. The school collapsed, and the BBU never fully recovered.[5]

The nearly moribund BBU limped along until 1932, when thirty-two delegates formed the General Association of Regular Baptist Churches. The GARBC began as a decentralized body that relied on a variety of independent agencies rather than create its own centralized bureaucracy. This was a return to the society model of the nineteenth century, when Baptists worked through the Triennial Convention, the American Baptist Tract Society, and the American Baptist Home Mission Society. The GARBC remains a vibrant conservative Baptist denomination with roughly fourteen hundred churches comprising 132,000 members.

While promoting the BBU and then the GARBC, Riley kept alive the fundamentalist cause within the Northern Baptist Convention. His Northwestern Bible and Missionary Training School trained many Northern Baptist pastors in Minnesota and across the upper Midwest. In 1936, "Riley's boys" took control of the Minnesota Baptist Convention. Fundamentalist control of a state convention in a largely liberal denomination proved untenable in the long run, as the NBC beefed up its efforts to marginalize fundamentalists. Liberal and conservative factions skirmished over educational requirements for Northern Baptist pastors and missionaries. Like the denomination as a whole, the American Baptist Missions Society of the NBC took an inclusive approach, sending both conservatives and liberals to the mission field. Conservatives protested this policy, believing that liberals diluted the gospel and fostered the decline of world evangelism.

In 1943, the Missions Society appointed Elmer A. Fridell, whom conservatives viewed as a theological liberal and a political leftist. The conservatives rose to battle, with Riley claiming, "The board evidently thinks that it needs no further cover for its unitarian tendencies."[6] As they had done with the New Hampshire Confession in the 1920s, conservatives attempted to persuade the NBC to impose a test of theological orthodoxy on missionary candidates. The denomination refused. In response, conservatives formed their own Conservative Baptist Foreign Missions Society and by the end of the year sent workers into the field.

The Minnesota Baptist Convention, still under the control of Riley's boys, established a mechanism whereby congregations in the state could fund the Conservative Baptist Missions Society rather than the NBC's American Baptist Foreign Missions Society. There was a good deal of fundamentalist support for this plan from individual congregations outside Minnesota as well. Conservatives hoped that the NBC would recognize the new missions society as a legitimate entity to which NBC congregations could send their missions funds if they desired. Many fundamentalist congregations already financed a handful of fundamentalist Bible colleges founded by Riley and others like him.

Not only did the NBC refuse to recognize the Conservative Baptist Foreign Missions Society, but denominational officials also moved to exclude congregations whose financial support for NBC causes slipped below a designated minimum. In response, Riley ran successfully for president of the Minnesota Baptist Convention in 1944 and attempted to allow states to restrict how their funds were used by the national denomination. Then, at the Northern Baptist Convention annual meeting in 1946, Riley and the fundamentalists attempted a nearly exact repeat of 1922. The conservatives once again proposed a litmus test for all denominational officials and missionaries. The test included standard fundamentalist points of doctrine: the virgin birth of Christ, the resurrection of Christ, miracles, and the inspiration of the New Testament "in all its contents." The liberals responded with nearly the same resolution they had pushed through successfully a quarter century earlier. The resolution read in part, "We reaffirm our faith in the New Testament as a divinely inspired record and therefore a trustworthy, authoritative, and all sufficient rule of our faith and practice."[7] In other words, the NBC would not be bound by a creed—New Hampshire, fundamentalist, or otherwise. The resolution passed overwhelmingly.

Compounding the fundamentalist defeat was the passage of a liberal amendment to the NBC constitution that created a new method for apportioning delegates to annual meetings. The number of delegates a congregation could send was tied to the percentage of a church's giving that went to the NBC. This meant that conservative churches that routed their money through alternative agencies such as the Conservative Baptist Foreign Missions Society lost delegates. In response, the Minnesota Baptist Convention withdrew from the NBC, and Riley urged fundamentalist churches outside Minnesota to do the same and affiliate individually with the newly formed Conservative Baptist Association. In May 1947, the eighty-six-year-old Riley wrote a letter to the president of the NBC, finally acknowledging the clear logic of his longtime fundamentalist position: he would separate from the NBC. Riley died later that year.[8]

Like liberal and fundamentalist Baptists in the NBC, Riley's own conservatives soon divided. Some identified with the burgeoning neo-evangelical movement that began in the 1940s. Represented by the National Association of Evangelicals and later identifying with Fuller Theological Seminary and *Christianity Today* magazine, neo-evangelicals held on to conservative theology while moving away from the militant and separatist spirit of fundamentalism. Neo-evangelical leaders such as Baptist theologian Carl F. H. Henry believed that doctrinally conservative Christians should become a more positive, reforming force in the world rather than distinguishing themselves by their attacks on liberals and denunciations of mainstream society. Henry believed conservatives should stop berating each other over differences in interpretation of end-times prophecy and expend more energy presenting a winsome, intellectually respectable witness to the larger culture.

By the 1950s, the key neo-evangelical figure was also America's and the world's most popular Baptist, Billy Graham. On his deathbed, Riley summoned the twenty-eight-year-old Graham to his side, pointed his bony finger at the young preacher, and said, "Billy, you are the man to succeed me. I've known it for a long time. You will be disobeying God if you don't."[9] Unable to say no, Graham served as the often absentee president of Northwestern Bible College until 1952, by which time he was already on the cusp of his career as world-renowned evangelist. Graham tried to move the school toward an evangelical model like that of Wheaton, his alma mater. Separatists resisted the move, then broke away from Northwestern in 1956, forming two schools, Central Baptist Seminary and Pillsbury Baptist Bible College, both of which exist today.[10]

The General Association of Regular Baptist Churches and the Conservative Baptist Association are still thriving. Meanwhile, in the South there emerged an even stronger fundamentalist Baptist denomination, the Baptist Bible Fellowship (BBF). Whereas the Conservative Baptist Association, and to a lesser extent the General Association of Regular Baptist Churches, emerged from Riley's Midwestern fundamentalist empire, the BBF found its origins in the southern fundamentalism of J. Frank Norris.

SOMETIMES CALLED THE Texas Cyclone, Norris pastored First Baptist, Fort Worth from 1909 until his death in 1952. From 1935 until 1950, he simultaneously pastored Temple Baptist in Detroit. Shuttling back and forth between the two churches, Norris was often absent from both as he crisscrossed the country holding revival meetings. Already a rising figure in national fundamentalism, he became infamous in 1926 when he shot and killed an unarmed man in the pastor's office at First Baptist. After a change of venue due to Norris's notoriety in Fort Worth, he went to trial in Austin in January 1927. He pled self-defense, claiming that the deceased businessman, D. E. Chipps, had challenged him to a fight and threatened bodily harm. Chipps had come to Norris's office to defend the Catholic mayor of Fort Worth, whom Norris had accused of misappropriating city funds to benefit a Catholic parish and school. Witnesses testified in the trial that Chipps had been drinking prior to the confrontation and that he had threatened to kill Norris. Norris was acquitted, just as he had been when tried for arson and perjury in conjunction with the burning of First Baptist in 1912.[11]

Norris's ministry hardly missed a beat. First Baptist continued to grow, and with the addition of Temple Baptist in 1935, Norris boasted twenty-five thousand parishioners in two churches. He published a well-circulated weekly newspaper called the *Fundamentalist* and routinely agitated in politics, especially during the presidential election of 1928, when Catholic Al Smith was the Democratic nominee.

After 1924, First Baptist, Fort Worth was essentially barred from participation in the Baptist General Convention of Texas, largely because of Norris's role in the formation of the Baptist Bible Union, which Southern Baptists viewed as a rival denomination siphoning off support from the SBC. The Southern Baptist Convention had no mechanism by which to oust Norris, and his church continued to send in its nominal contribution to the denomination, largely so Norris could attend SBC annual meetings and make trouble. He engaged in relentless attacks on SBC stalwarts such as George Truett, J. M. Dawson of First Baptist, Waco, and to a lesser extent E. Y. Mullins. Norris eventually took to setting up rival meetings, usually adjacent to or just down the street from the meeting hall where the BGCT or SBC held their own gatherings. Norris's anticonvention message often sounded like Landmarkism, but Landmark leader Ben Bogard saw Norris and his brand of Texas Baptist fundamentalism as Landmarkers' chief competitors. While commending fundamentalists for their stand against modernism, Bogard argued that Norris, Riley, and their fundamentalist followers failed to stand militantly enough for the fundamentals. He referred to them as "Funnymentalists." Still, given their common effort to fight Southern Baptists, Bogard eventually made peace with Norris, and the 1935 ABA meeting took place at First Baptist, Fort Worth.[12]

After the collapse of the BBU, Norris formed the Premillennial Baptist Missionary Fellowship in 1933, a fundamentalist denomination that eventually consisted largely of churches staffed by graduates of the Bible Baptist Seminary Norris founded in 1938. This development mirrored Riley's Midwestern fundamentalist empire. Having already undergone a slight name change, Norris's denomination changed its name again in 1950, becoming the World Baptist Fellowship. That same year a split in the denomination and seminary led to the founding of the Baptist Bible Fellowship.

The schism of 1950 centered around G. B. Vick, who for years served as Norris's Sunday school superintendent at Temple Baptist. In 1948, Norris asked Vick to move to Fort Worth to lead the seminary. Vick reluctantly agreed, knowing that it would be difficult for Norris to actually delegate authority at the school. Shortly after Vick moved to Fort Worth, Norris instituted new bylaws for the seminary, consulting neither Vick nor the board of trustees. Vick then discovered that Norris had used money raised for specific projects to fund other endeavors. In one case, Vick concluded that enough money had been raised to build a new dormitory twice over, yet there was no dorm and no money. When Vick and others protested the new bylaws and Norris's heavy-handed leadership, Norris replied that they could vote any way they wanted, but the bylaws would remain in place.

This was the last straw in a long series of frustrations for Vick. He and his supporters moved to Springfield, Missouri, and founded Baptist Bible College and the Baptist Bible Fellowship. By the time of the split, Norris had been looking for a suitable successor for his movement, but each time he proved incapable of giving up the reins of power. In one case, he appointed his son George as the pastor of First Baptist. Predictably, within months the two had a falling-out, and George and his faction moved across town to form Gideon Baptist. Norris had similar experiences with other would-be successors. Just before his death in 1952 he settled on a twenty-six-year-old protégé named Homer Ritchie, who pastored First Baptist for several years. The church coasted along for a while, dwindled, sold its downtown property, and exists today as a moderately sized congregation on the outskirts of Fort Worth. A remnant of the Norris movement persists in the form of the World Baptist Fellowship, headquartered in Arlington, Texas, complete with its own Bible college and a statue of Norris.

While Norris's church, seminary, and fundamentalist denomination declined, the Springfield faction led by G. B. Vick and his successors built the Baptist Bible Fellowship into the largest fundamentalist Baptist denomination in America. The BBF maintains a strong sense of independence and separatism, with Landmark tendencies. Indeed, it is the largest of the groups that go by the name "independent Baptist." Noel Smith, longtime BBF leader and editor of the *Baptist Bible Tribune*, spoke for many independent fundamentalist Baptists when he wrote in 1986, "We have a continuity of doctrines, principles, and practices that go back to the apostolic age. Our continuity is the longest of any Christian group in the world."[13]

As independent Baptists, members of BBF churches do not view their movement as a denomination but rather as a voluntary collection of independent congregations. In Landmark fashion, they recognize no ecclesial entity beyond the local congregation. Technically, only pastors, not congregations, belong to the BBF. The BBF has little in the way of centralized bureaucracy. The missions office, Baptist Bible College, and *Baptist Bible Tribune* exist in Springfield, but even the missionaries are called and commissioned by congregations, not by the BBF.

In 1952, a newly converted roughneck from Virginia named Jerry Falwell enrolled at Baptist Bible College to train for the ministry. Falwell grew up in Lynchburg, Virginia, the son of a pious mother and bootlegger father. His father shot and killed his own brother in a 1931 duel, then died of cirrhosis of the liver in 1948, when Jerry was fifteen. Falwell and his twin brother were baptized at the age of twelve, but the experience proved little more than a cultural formality. "We went in dry sinners and came out wet sinners," Falwell recalled later.[14] After graduating as valedictorian of his high school, Falwell attended Lynchburg College. During his second year there, he was converted at Lynchburg's Park Avenue Baptist Church. The pastor's father taught on the faculty of Baptist Bible College, and he recommended that Falwell transfer to the fledgling school. Falwell graduated in 1956.

Returning to Lynchburg, he rented space in a soft drink bottling plant and with just a handful of members founded Thomas Road Baptist Church. By the 1970s, Thomas Road had developed into a modern fundamentalist megachurch, and Falwell was nationally known largely because of the church's television ministry, the *Old Time Gospel Hour*. He also founded Liberty University in 1971. In 1979, political operatives from the Republican Party approached Falwell about starting an organization that would bring fundamentalists and other conservative evangelicals into politics. As a theological and cultural separatist, Falwell had previously denounced political engagement. But he changed his mind. The result was the Moral Majority, which burst onto the political scene during the 1980 presidential election that brought Ronald Reagan and the conservative wing of the Republican Party to power and launched the New Religious Right, now more commonly known as the Christian Right.

Falwell's fame transcended the BBF, and he was known nationally more as a fundamentalist and Christian Right political leader than as a Baptist. A frequent visitor to the Reagan White House, he served as one of America's leading religious spokespersons for fundamentalists and conservative evangelicals. Ironically, the president he helped Reagan defeat, Jimmy Carter, was a Baptist, and Reagan was not. Falwell and Thomas Road Baptist would eventually join a transformed SBC in the 1980s, but he remained a singular figure. He died a nominal Southern Baptist in 2007.

As Carter and Falwell demonstrate, Baptists could be cultural insiders and political leaders in either party. At one point in the 1990s, with the government divided between the parties, Baptists simultaneously served as US president (Bill Clinton), vice president (Al Gore), Speaker of the House (Newt Gingrich), and Senate majority leader (Trent Lott), showing that they could be as diverse in political views as in theology.

THE POLITICAL DIVERSITY of Baptists often manifested itself in their divergent views of church-state relations and approaches to religious liberty. As we saw earlier, during the American Revolution and its aftermath, Baptists helped lead the fight for religious liberty and clamored incessantly for disestablishment of religion (i.e., an end to tax-supported churches). Baptists united in that fight, but only because the issues were so clear. They accepted nothing less than the end to established churches and the right to worship according to the Bible and their consciences, free from burdens imposed by the state. But following disestablishment and the lifting of discrimination, Baptists exhibited a range of views. How should a free church relate to government, and to what degree should the state accommodate religion while not financially supporting churches? These questions have vexed Baptists no less than Christians from other denominations.

Even Isaac Backus and John Leland differed as to how church and state should relate to each other, once establishment no longer existed. Leland liked to say, "Government has no more to do with the religious opinions of men than it has with the principles of mathematics." Yet he preached to the US Congress with President Thomas Jefferson in attendance. Backus, in contrast, held a position less strict than Leland's. He advocated a voluntary "Christian Commonwealth" where government did not support religion directly but nevertheless sought to promote conditions where religion would flourish. Even while supporting the US Constitution's prohibition against religious tests for office, he praised the broadly Christian oath required of officeholders in his own state of Massachusetts. Moreover, he endorsed a petition calling on the US government to set up a bureau to license Bible publications, an effort to ensure no heretical editions saw the light of day. After his death, his New England Baptist followers even favored government grants to aid frontier missionaries. Leland represented what is today known as the separationist position in church-state matters, while Backus was an accommodationist.[15]

In the second half of the twentieth century, church-state issues emerged as a contentious part of what came to be called America's culture wars. In a Jehovah's Witness case from 1940, the Supreme Court incorporated the First Amendment's free exercise clause—that is, made the clause applicable to state and local governments. Freedom of speech, press, and assembly had already been incorporated in the 1920s and 1930s. In 1947, in the *Everson* bus case, the Supreme Court also incorporated the establishment clause. Fittingly, the majority opinion was written by Baptist Hugo Black, who invoked the "wall of separation" from Jefferson's letter to the Danbury Baptists. From *Everson* forward, the first sixteen words of the First Amendment applied equally to national, state, and local governments: "Congress shall make no law respecting an establishment of religion or prohibiting the free exercise thereof." But what constitutes an establishment of religion, and what qualifies as a violation of free exercise? On these questions Baptists have been divided.

Never was this disagreement clearer than when the court ruled—in *Engel v. Vitale* (1962) and *Abington v. Schempp* (1963)—that prayer and Bible reading in public schools violated the establishment clause. Billy Graham denounced the prayer decisions, as did numerous Southern Baptist members of the US Congress. Meanwhile, on the other side of the debate, Emmanuel Carlson, executive director of the Baptist Joint Committee, remarked that he was not disturbed by the elimination of required prayer in schools because he had never believed such rote recitals of prayer had any religious value.[16] The Baptist Joint Committee represented several Baptist bodies on church-state issues. The SBC was by far the largest and the BJC's chief source of funding. But Carlson and his successors understood that they spoke for the BJC, not all Baptists. Even the Baptists in denominations that funded the BJC were all over the map on church-state issues.

Black Baptists could also be found on both sides of the debate. The same month the Supreme Court issued its *Engel* decision, five out of six black Baptist pastors surveyed in Philadelphia opposed restricting prayer in schools. The pastors expressed concern that a decline in schoolhouse religion would undermine morality among children, and some issued calls for a constitutional amendment overturning *Engel.* Likewise, a council of black Baptists in Philadelphia registered its "profound disagreement" with the high court's decision. A spokesman for the council implored the Court to stay out of "our greatest institutions—homes, churches, and schools."[17]

But America's most famous black Baptist, Martin Luther King Jr., believed the prayer decisions had been decided correctly. The rulings "sought to outlaw neither prayer nor belief in God," he said in 1965. The question in a pluralistic society was "Who is to determine what prayer is spoken, and by whom?" King pointed out that those seeking to overturn the prayer decisions were motivated by a desire to embarrass the Court. Echoing editorials in New York's most influential black newspaper, the *Amsterdam News*, King noted that segregationists like George Wallace usually led resistance to the prayer decisions. As he told an interviewer, "When I saw brother Wallace go up to Washington to testify against the decision at the congressional hearings, it only strengthened my conviction that the decision was right."[18]

For some black Baptists the prayer decisions complicated the quest for full civil rights. On the one hand, civil rights leaders called on the courts to intervene to end segregation in schools, even while the black Baptist preachers of Philadelphia and elsewhere demanded that the courts stay out of the schools when it came to prayer. On the other hand, southern white segregationists issued a unified call for the courts to stay out of schools entirely.[19]

Like the courts, Congress also got involved in the prayer decisions. In September 1963, Congressman Frank Becker (R-N.Y.) offered an amendment to the US Constitution that would have overridden *Engel.* The Becker amendment came before Congress numerous times over the next several years but each time failed to garner the required two-thirds majority. A similar amendment offered in the US Senate by Everett Dirksen (R-Ill.) also failed. In May 1964, Southern Baptists passed a resolution affirming the First Amendment and opposing "the adoption of any further amendment to that Constitution respecting establishment of religion or free exercise thereof." On the same day, the American Baptist Churches USA also passed a resolution rejecting the Becker amendment and affirming the First Amendment.[20] These two major Baptist groups took a vigorous stand for separation of church and state. But just three months before the 1964 SBC meeting, the Conservative Baptist Association of Oregon unanimously passed a resolution of support for the Becker amendment.[21]

Many conservative and fundamentalist Baptist groups have sided with the Oregon Baptists.

Baptist resolutions passed at denominational annual meetings represent the majority sentiment of the delegates (or messengers) present at that time. Whether or not such resolutions represent a majority of the denomination is always questionable. Denominational employees and other elites dominate denominational meetings. These elites tend to be more liberal than rank-and-file Baptists, especially, for example, in the pre-1980 Southern Baptist Convention. The experience of Alabama Southern Baptists is instructive in this regard. Leading Alabama pastors and state Baptist officials came out immediately in favor of the prayer in schools decisions as necessary for upholding the cherished Baptist principle of separation of church and state. At the same time, other pastors saw the decisions as a lurch toward secularism. In the context of the Cold War, some even feared the decisions played into the hands of communists.

Initially, Leon Macon, editor the *Alabama Baptist*, editorialized in favor of the prayer decisions and against the Becker amendment. He received a barrage of criticism from grassroots Alabama Baptists, as did Baptist congressmen from Alabama who opposed the Becker amendment. Macon wavered, then retired, largely because of declining health. He died in 1965. In 1966, his successor, Hudson Baggett, backed away from Macon's opposition to Becker, noting there were plenty of Alabama Baptists on both sides of the prayer debate. By that time the debate had shifted from the Becker to the Dirksen amendment. Baggett said he had no serious objections to the content of Dirksen but remained reticent to amend the Constitution unless absolutely necessary. Within three years, Baggett began editorializing more about the threat of secularism than about the need to defend separation of church and state.[22]

The debate in Alabama was a microcosm of the SBC as a whole. Southern Baptist resolutions notwithstanding, it is doubtful there was ever anything remotely resembling a consensus among Southern Baptists in favor of the Supreme Court's position. Rather, prayer in schools resolutions reflected which group happened to be in charge of the denomination. When moderates controlled the convention, they pushed through resolutions supporting the prayer decisions. Once conservatives took control, convention messengers in 1982 passed a resolution supporting an amendment that would have protected the right to have group prayer in schools and other public institutions as long as no one was required to participate. The amendment maintained that "for 170 years following the writing of the First Amendment, the right of prayer in public schools was a time-honored exercise and a cherished privilege."[23] The SBC resolution supporting the amendment became a contentious issue as moderates and conservatives struggled for control of the SBC. James Dunn, the executive director of the Baptist Joint Committee and the key moderate spokesperson on church-state issues, even alleged that the SBC resolution of 1982 had been composed in the Reagan White House by a Republican operative.[24]

In 1992, with the SBC firmly under conservative control, the annual convention passed another resolution, this time titled "On Free Exercise of Religion in Public Schools." The resolution expressed hope that the Supreme Court was moving toward a more "accommodationist" position and proclaimed, "The free exercise rights of students are not forfeited at the doors of America's schools."[25] As the resolution indicated, conservative Baptists did not view prayer in schools as an establishment clause issue. Rather, they saw the prayer decisions as denying students their free exercise rights.

Diverse Baptist interpretations of church-state separation extended to other issues as well. For much of the twentieth century, most Baptists opposed vouchers for private schools. But that was when most private schools were Catholic. Meanwhile, Catholics claimed that public schools were pervasively Protestant and that as a matter of fairness the state should assist Catholic schools at least indirectly through vouchers or tax credits. In other words, Catholics believed the state discriminated against their schools much as conservative Southern Baptists came to believe the state infringed the right of their children to have group prayer in public schools. The voucher debate broke down largely along Protestant-Catholic lines into the 1970s, with Baptists among the most vocal opponents of vouchers. This all began to change in the 1970s and 1980s as many conservative evangelicals, among them Baptists, came to the conclusion that the public schools were pervasively secular and hostile to religion. Desegregation compounded the problem in the South, as many white Baptist congregations started their own all-white academies rather than send their children to integrated public schools. As this happened, Baptists began to migrate toward a pro-voucher position.

In the American Baptist Churches in the United States, denominational control has remained in the hands of moderates and liberals, and their official positions on church-state issues continue to be separationist. Independent fundamentalist Baptists, while less active politically, usually side with the accommodationists, but some, like the Baptist Bible Fellowship, have no central bureaucracy capable of issuing official statements. Black Baptists, who are often conservative on social issues such as abortion and gay rights, can be either separationist or accommodationist on church-state issues.

AS IS THE case within American religion generally, Baptists do not stand together against other groups on political and cultural issues. Rather, conservative and fundamentalist Baptists find themselves holding church-state positions in common with conservatives in other denominations and even with conservative Catholics. Meanwhile, moderate and liberal Baptists generally hold positions in common with moderates and liberals from non-Baptist denominations. Religion is still one of the strongest predictors of political behavior and attitudes toward the wider culture. But the key variable is not the name of the denomination but whether the group, congregation, or individual identifies as *theologically* conservative, moderate, or liberal within those groups.

12

Baptists and the Civil Rights Movement

IN MARCH 1953, the year before the landmark Supreme Court decision in *Brown v. Board of Education*, Billy Graham personally removed the rope barrier that divided blacks from whites at his Chattanooga crusade. He acted so subtly that local newspapers failed to notice or report the incident, and most black people who attended the crusade avoided the section formerly marked off for whites. Over the previous two years, Graham had maintained that his ministry would honor local custom, sidestepping anything that might cause controversy and thereby limit crowds and potential conversions. With the urging of black Baptist leaders, some of whom organized boycotts of segregated crusades, Graham realized he could not preach against the sin of segregation while participating in it. After the Chattanooga crusade, he backslid briefly by accepting segregated arrangements in Dallas. Ushers at that crusade, however, made no attempt to hinder blacks who chose to cross the color line and sit in the white section. Some have cited the actions of these black attendees as among the earliest acts of civil disobedience in the civil rights movement.[1]

These acts were just a small part of a growing civil rights struggle in the 1950s. And that struggle was born, or at least reborn, in a Baptist church in Montgomery, Alabama. On December 1, 1955, Rosa Parks refused to give up her seat to a white man on a city bus, as custom and law required. She was arrested. While Parks allegedly claimed that she was simply too tired to move that day, she had actually prepared for this act of civil disobedience well in advance. She had served for a decade as the secretary of the Montgomery chapter of the NAACP, and four days before her arrest she attended a meeting where black resisters discussed the case of

Emmett Till, a Chicago teenager brutally lynched in Mississippi for allegedly flirting with a white woman. Along with the *Brown* decision, Till's
murder emboldened Parks and others to resist segregation.

Following Parks's arrest, black leaders met at Martin Luther King Jr.'s
church, Dexter Avenue Baptist. They opened the meeting with prayer
led by H. H. Hubbard, president of the Baptist Ministerial Alliance. At
the time, nothing in King's background suggested he would become the
leader of a mass movement of civil disobedience and nonviolent resistance. King came from a long line of Georgia Baptist preachers. He had
earned his undergraduate degree from Morehouse College, did his seminary training at Crozer Theological Seminary in Chester, Pennsylvania,
and took his doctorate in theology at Boston University. The year of the
Brown school desegregation decision, 1954, he accepted a call to preach
at Dexter Avenue Baptist Church. King married Coretta Scott, who had
a degree from Antioch College in Ohio and had studied voice at the New
England Conservatory of Music. A predictable career path for King would
have been to move from Dexter Avenue to a more prominent church in
Birmingham or Atlanta. Eventually he might have assumed the pulpit
of one of the great black churches of the North or Midwest, perhaps in
Chicago or New York, where he would become a wealthy and powerful
individual. As he put it, "When I went to Montgomery as a pastor, I had
not the slightest idea that I would later become involved in a crisis in
which nonviolent resistance would be applicable. I neither started the protest nor suggested it."[2]

Without realizing it, King had stepped into the heart of black Baptist
activism. Vernon Johns, King's predecessor at Dexter Avenue, preached
on race issues in the mid-1940s. And Johns was hardly the only black
preacher in Alabama to speak out against segregation. In 1948, the black
preachers of Birmingham issued a public statement calling on Christians
to bring an end to the practice. Similar calls came from black Baptists in
other states. Harrison Humes, president of the black Baptist Convention
of Mississippi, used his annual address of 1948 to warn, "We don't want
the white leadership in Mississippi to misrepresent the Negroes' request.
The Negro is requesting free participation in a government that he has
given his blood to defend from the Revolutionary War to the recent World
War II." The president of the Georgia Baptist Missionary and Education
Convention, William Holmes Borders, likewise argued, "The Negro
Preacher must take the lead in fighting for the civic rights of the Southern
Negro and he must not flinch before the Ku Klux Klan."[3]

By the end of January, King faced a decision. Would he become the leader of this burgeoning resistance movement? Late one night, he sat alone at his kitchen table pondering this question. The most recent of many threatening phone calls he had received had warned that his opponents would "blow his brains out" and dynamite his house. He thought of his sleeping infant daughter and of Coretta. Then, in his words, he "experienced the presence of the Divine as I had never experienced Him before." He heard the still small voice of God whisper in his spirit, saying, "'Martin Luther, stand up for righteousness. Stand up for justice. Stand up for truth. And lo I will be with you, even until the end of the world." "My uncertainty disappeared," King recalled. "I was ready to face anything."[4] Three nights later, his home was bombed.

A crowd of his supporters gathered after the bombing, eager for a confrontation. King calmed them, saying there had to be a better way. For a year, blacks in the city walked and carpooled in a successful effort to force integration of the city's public transportation. The Montgomery bus boycott followed a similar one in Baton Rouge in 1953, led by Theodore Jemison, pastor of Mount Zion First Baptist Church. Blacks in Montgomery were harassed and even shot at, but they persisted. Their actions not only ended segregation of public transportation in Montgomery but also led eventually to *Browder v. Gayle* (1956), a case in which the Supreme Court ruled that segregation in all public transportation was unconstitutional. It also sparked similar resistance across the South. Sit-ins at segregated lunch counters began in 1960, often led by young men studying for the ministry and by the sons and daughters of black preachers. By the end of 1962, some two hundred cities had desegregated places of public accommodation.[5]

The civil rights movement took place mostly in the streets, not the churches, but its leaders, marchers, and even singers were more likely to be black Baptists than anything else. Fred Shuttlesworth, for example, worked alongside King while remaining a full-time pastor at Bethel Baptist Church in North Birmingham from 1953 to 1961. During that period he was arrested more than eight hundred times and helped launch scores of criminal proceedings and civil suits. He founded the Alabama Christian Movement for Human Rights (ACMHR) in 1956 and served as the group's president until 1969. The year after the founding of the ACMHR, he served with King and Ralph Abernathy as one of the founders of the Southern Christian Leadership Conference (SCLC) and became the organization's first secretary.

In 1961, Shuttlesworth accepted a call to the Revelation Baptist Church in Cincinnati, Ohio, but he continued to spend a good deal of time in Birmingham as president of the ACMHR. Shuttlesworth persuaded King, Abernathy, and other leaders of the SCLC to come to Birmingham in 1963 to resist the forces of police commissioner Bull Connor. "I think it's time to give Bull hell before he's finished," Shuttlesworth told King, adding, "If segregation is going to fall, we've got to crack Birmingham."[6] Shuttlesworth's ACMHR took the lead in organizing the pivotal Birmingham campaign. The protests and the brutal response doled out by Connor's officers fueled the drive for the Civil Rights Act of 1964. Shuttlesworth stood near the center of all the important civil rights events of the sixties—the March on Washington, Birmingham, Bloody Sunday in Selma, and more. His fiery approach—some called him crazy—counterbalanced the more measured King. And, as Shuttlesworth's biographer writes, he also "differs from King in that his primary identifying role throughout his career remained that of a local pastor."[7]

IN THE WAKE of the Birmingham campaign, as the civil rights movement gained full steam, so did white resistance. That year Sam Bowers organized the new White Knights of the Ku Klux Klan of Mississippi. The White Knights was a splinter group. Its ten thousand members felt the Klan was too mainstream and moderate. The White Knights had no interest in parading in public in their hooded garb; they were a highly secretive terrorist organization. As the organization's leader, Bowers almost certainly masterminded the murders of the three civil rights workers—Mickey Schwerner, James Chaney, and Andy Goodman—in Neshoba County, Mississippi, in June 1964. The Neshoba murders were among the highest-profile acts of anti–civil rights violence in the entire era, rivaled only by the infamous bombing of Birmingham's Sixteenth Street Baptist Church that took the lives of four young girls and, of course, the assassination of King in 1968. Two years after the murders of Schwerner, Chaney, and Goodman, Bowers ordered the killing and burning of Vernon Dahmer, former leader of the Forrest County branch of the NAACP. That same year Bowers joined Hillcrest Baptist Church of Laurel and became a Sunday school teacher.

The murders were part of a widespread campaign of violence designed to appear random in order to terrorize civil rights workers. The White Knights engaged in hundreds of such acts. Bowers was tried four times for Dahmer's murder, but each case resulted in a hung jury or mistrial.

Four other Klansmen were convicted, and three received life sentences. While Bowers was never convicted for the murders of Schwerner, Chaney, and Goodman, in 1967 he was found guilty in a federal trial of conspiring to violate their civil rights. He served just shy of six years in federal prison in the 1970s. Finally, in 1998, Bowers was convicted of Dahmer's murder and sentenced to life in prison. He died in the Mississippi State Penitentiary in 2006.

Bowers rooted his terrorist acts in an elaborate theology. While idiosyncratic and frightening in its conclusions, that theology nevertheless contained elements common to many Protestants in American history. First, he connected the founding of America with the Protestant Reformation, particularly the concept of the priesthood of believers. He then made the typical Protestant argument that the Reformation represented the recovery of the New Testament concept of grace. And grace was the gift of God through Christ's death and resurrection. Bowers presented his twisted theology as "The Five Tiered Crystalized Logos of Western Civilization":

1. The empirical fact of the resurrection of Jesus Christ
2. The Reformation
3. The Declaration of Independence
4. The Constitution
5. The Great Writs of Common Law[8]

Bowers then made his key theological leap. Civil rights workers were communists because they called for the federal government to interfere with the freedom of southern states. Communists were anti-American; to be anti-American was to be anti-Reformation and therefore anti-grace, which meant civil rights workers were heretics who denied the death and resurrection of Christ. Heretics must be exterminated, and as a priest in the priesthood of all believers, Bowers believed God had called him to do it.

Theologian Charles Marsh believes that although Bowers was raised Methodist, he joined First Baptist, Laurel in 1966 in part because Baptists endorsed the priesthood of believers, which allowed him to serve his priestly function without official recognition from a denominational board of bishops. As Marsh writes, "Baptist theology and polity, with its happy distrust of creeds and hierarchy, better fit his anti-clerical bent."[9]

Whether Bowers should be viewed primarily as a Baptist is an open question. Was Bowers a Baptist terrorist, or a terrorist who just happened to become a Baptist? Ironically, his actions and those of others in the

KKK drove many Baptists away from the vigorous defense of segregation, the exact opposite of Bowers's intention. Following the attack on Vernon Dahmer, for example, the mayor of Laurel, a staunch segregationist, spoke out against the "Klan fanatics who talk so much about God." The mayor's denunciation garnered a resolution of support from the Jones County Baptist Association and its forty-six congregations.[10]

A FANATICAL TERRORIST, Bowers was certainly not typical of white Baptists in the South. But just as rare were those white Southern Baptists who worked vigorously for racial equality. In the 1920s, Walter Nathan (Walt) Johnson started a newsletter called *The Next Step in the Churches*. A Southern Baptist pastor, Johnson had served in denominational leadership positions in the North Carolina and Louisiana Baptist State Conventions. Put off by the increasing institutionalization of the SBC, Johnson used his newsletter to advocate for a new and radical approach to Christian life. Influenced by his reading of Walter Rauschenbusch and other Social Gospelers, he advocated that congregations live out a witness for peace, economic justice, and racial equality. As a result of Johnson's work, there developed across the South a loose network of Baptists who were progressive on many issues, including race. Johnson's influence touched Clarence Jordan and Martin England, as well as Foy Valentine and Carlyle Marney, all Southern Baptist activists. This influence has been aptly called a "genealogy of dissent." Unlike the conservative dissent-ers of the 1980s, Southern Baptists on the Left had little desire to take over the Southern Baptist Convention. Rather, they operated as a prophetic conscience of the denomination, constantly pressuring the moderates in power to take more progressive positions on race, poverty, war and peace, and the ordination of women.[11]

Within this genealogy of dissent, Clarence Jordan is perhaps the most famous and revered Baptist. Jordan came from rural Georgia and earned a doctorate in New Testament from Southern Baptist Seminary. He grew increasingly concerned about the economic plight of poor black and white southern farmers. While working at a black community center in Louisville, Kentucky, he envisioned a "witness in the dirt." With the help of his friend Martin England and their wives, Florence Jordan and Mabel England, in the early 1940s Jordan secured farmland in Sumter County, Georgia, and founded Koinonia Farms. Koinonia became an inte-grated farm cooperative and Christian community, just the sort of thing Walt Johnson had envisioned. By the 1950s, the efforts at Koinonia met resistance from local whites. The Jordans and Englands were expelled from Rehoboth Baptist Church in nearby Americus for bringing black people to the services. After Jordan helped two black students enroll in Georgia State University, hostility to Koinonia increased, as did death threats against Jordan. In actions that resembled persecution of Baptists in the eighteenth century, local authorities brought bogus legal charges against the farm, then harassed and arrested Koinonia workers. Ironically, this time many of the persecutors were Baptists too. Locals boycotted Koinonia produce, bombed Koinonia property, and beat Koinonia residents, but Jordan and the others pushed on with their incarnational witness for racial equality.[12]

The Englands left Koinonia in 1944 to serve as foreign missionaries with the American Baptist Foreign Mission Board. In the early 1950s, they moved to New York, where Martin took a position with the northern denomination's Ministers and Missions Benefit Board. In that capacity he spent time in the South encouraging progressive Southern Baptist churches to align with both the SBC and the American Baptist Churches (formerly the Northern Baptist Convention). He also helped Baptist ministers enroll in the American Baptist pension and life insurance programs. Eventually, he established an office in Greenville, South Carolina.

As a social justice troubleshooter, England reached out to black civil rights leaders, including King. They had both attended Crozer Theological Seminary (though not simultaneously), which England used as a point of contact to develop a relationship. Over time, England succeeded in winning King's trust. In 1963, he visited the incarcerated civil rights leader in Birmingham and helped King get his famous "Letter from a Birmingham Jail" published in newspapers.[13]

Renegade Baptist preacher Will Campbell, called by his biographer a "Radical Prophet of the South," provided an even more countercultural civil rights witness.[14] Born in 1924, the same year as Sam Bowers, Campbell grew up in rural and poor Amite County, Mississippi. Baptists so dominated his community that he claimed he knew hardly any Methodists or Presbyterians, let alone Episcopalians or Catholics. He preached his first sermon at the age of sixteen and felt the overflowing support of his congregation. As he remarked later, "I could have denounced Christianity as a capitalistic myth . . . , the youth choir could have sung Ukrainian folk songs, and the Sunday School superintendent could have lectured on 'The Origin of Species,' and all the people would have said 'Amen.'"[15]

East Fork Baptist Church ordained Campbell during his senior year of high school. To train for the ministry, he enrolled at Louisiana College, but the outbreak of World War II interrupted his education. After serving in the South Pacific, Campbell completed college at Wake Forest and then attended Yale Divinity School, graduating in 1952. After a few years as a Baptist pastor in Louisiana and a stint as a campus minister at the University of Mississippi, he took a position as a field director with the Department of Racial and Cultural Relations of the National Council of Churches (NCC). In that capacity he assisted blacks and whites in racial hot spots as an adviser and advocate, much as Martin England did in his position with the Benefit Board of the American Baptist Churches.

Campbell's activism took him to Little Rock, Arkansas, in 1957, where he participated in the integration of Central High School. Under federal order and with the protection of the 101st Airborne Division of the US Army, nine black students enrolled at Central. Campbell served as one of four civilians who, along with the soldiers, escorted the Little Rock Nine as they negotiated their way through a massive and hostile anti-integration demonstration. Campbell made several return trips over the next year and a half as the drama in Little Rock unfolded. The same year as the Little Rock incident, Campbell was the only white person to appear at the inaugural meeting of the Southern Christian Leadership Conference (SCLC). Founded by King and other key black civil rights leaders, the SCLC became one of the most important organizations of the entire era.

In the early 1960s, Campbell's battles against segregation grew into a critique of all sides of the civil rights issue. He became increasingly anti-institutional, and some perceived his transition as going soft on civil rights. Campbell began to argue that black people were not the only victims of segregation; white southerners, especially common people, suffered as well. White folks—even the white supremacists, Campbell claimed—needed a minister. As Campbell would put his case later, "Mr. Jesus died for the bigots as well."[16] Campbell's empathy for white racists became evident first in 1961 and 1962, in the midst of what was called the Albany Movement. In late summer 1962, roughly seventy-five mostly white Protestant, Catholic, and Jewish clergy descended on the town of Albany, Georgia. Sheriff's deputies duly arrested them for violating segregation laws and parade restrictions. Campbell participated in his capacity as field officer for the NCC along with King aide Andrew Young, who was in charge of posting bail to get the protesters out of jail.

After the event Campbell wrote an account for the *Christian Century* in which he empathized with local sheriff Laurie Pritchett. Pritchett was a Southern Baptist in the process of becoming a Roman Catholic. Commenting on Pritchett's pilgrimage, Campbell wrote, "Only a religious man can leap so far. But the chief is a big and a good man, and he has taken big leaps before."[17] In Campbell's view, implicitly at least, Pritchett was caught in the complex web of legal segregation that trapped whites and blacks, and he negotiated his conflicted status by doing his best to treat the civil rights protesters with respect even as he arrested them.[18] Others, however, viewed Pritchett's methods as nothing more than strategy, a deliberate attempt to avoid the negative publicity that violent police attacks on civil rights workers engendered. And he was quite effective in keeping the Albany Movement from producing significant changes.[19]

Campbell's sympathetic account of the enforcers of segregation was not well received, but the article's unpopularity paled compared with a speech he gave just a few months later. In January 1963, major Protestant, Catholic, and Jewish organizations, including the National Council of Churches, convened in Chicago for the National Conference on Religion and Race. Afterward, King called this massive meeting "the most significant and historic [convention] ever held for attacking racial injustice."[20] Invited to speak, Campbell prepared an address that included the following lines: "If I live to be as old as my father I expect to see whites marched into the gas chambers, the little children clutching their toys to their breasts in Auschwitz fashion, at the hands of a black Eichmann."[21] Campbell wanted to make the point that all human beings, white and black, the oppressors and the oppressed, were corrupted by sin. But his off-the-charts hyperbole obliterated whatever good his speech might have accomplished. Having read an advance copy, organizers of the conference required him to omit the passage. The offensive sentences, however, were not edited out of the copy released to the press, and some conference participants also received the unedited version. Campbell followed orders not to recite the lines about Auschwitz and Eichmann. Instead, he paused at that point in the speech and remained silent while those with his original text in their hands had sufficient time to read the offensive words. The rest of his speech was a vigorous call for civil rights and equality in all areas, so much so that Mississippi newspapers reported that he had called for virtually total social integration. As has been said aptly of his performance in Chicago, "In Campbell's attempt to be consistent, he was now consistently offending everyone."[22]

The NCC responded by placing restrictions on Campbell's activities, and by the end of the year he had resigned. Disillusioned with both liberals and conservatives, Campbell developed his own anti-institutional, outsider approach to social activism that he promoted through speaking and writing, the latter done mostly from his farm in Tennessee. Later in life he would occasionally hold visiting lectureships at colleges and universities such as Wake Forest, where some claim he showed up for his first class with a guitar and a bottle of whiskey. He died in 2013, a renegade Baptist to the end.

On the spectrum of white Baptists in the South, Campbell was as radical and unrepresentative on one end as Sam Bowers was on the other. Foy Valentine expressed a racially progressive message similar to that of Jordan and the early Campbell. But he did so while working within the SBC. Having written his doctoral dissertation on Southern Baptist race relations, Valentine made the issue the centerpiece of his activism, first as head of the Texas Baptist Christian Life Commission (1953–1960), then as director of the SBC's Christian Life Commission from 1960 to 1987. Valentine hoped that by working within the system he could more effectively nudge Southern Baptists toward integration and racial justice. When Valentine died in 2006, his conservative rival and successor, Richard Land, remarked, "While Dr. Valentine and I had significant differences of opinion on many issues, all Southern Baptists will be forever in his debt for his courageous and prophetic stance on racial reconciliation and racial equality in the turbulent middle third of the 20th century."[23]

Valentine's moderate pro–civil rights position remained the minority report among white Baptists in the South during the civil rights era. For every preacher who supported the *Brown* decision, there seemed to be at least ten who did not. At a South Carolina evangelism conference in 1956, W. A. Criswell of the mammoth First Baptist, Dallas spoke so vigorously against *Brown* that the state's governor asked him to reprise the performance at a joint session of the state legislature. There, Criswell unleashed perhaps his most infamous rhetorical flourish, saying, "Let them integrate. Let them sit up there in their dirty shirts and make all their fine speeches. But they are all a bunch of infidels, dying from the neck up."[24] The typical white Baptist response fell somewhere between England and Valentine, on one end of the spectrum, and Criswell and Bowers, on the other. Douglas Hudgins personified this moderate position.

On the night of November 21, 1967, two days before Thanksgiving, the Klan bombed the home of rabbi and civil rights advocate Perry Nussbaum of Jackson, Mississippi. His Beth Israel Congregation synogogue had been bombed in September. Standing in his bathrobe next to his wife, Arene, who was picking glass out of her hair, Nussbaum told his neighbor to go call Douglas Hudgins, pastor of First Baptist, Jackson. The next morning, both Hudgins and the governor of Mississippi stood with Nussbaum outside his destroyed home as an NBC TV camera crew filmed the aftermath of the violence. Nussbaum turned to Hudgins, shook his finger in the Baptist pastor's face, and exclaimed, "If you had spoken out from your pulpit after the synagogue was bombed and told your people it was wrong to have done that, this wouldn't have happened."[25] The following Sunday Hudgins made a passing general reference to bombings but did not specifically mention the rabbi's home. Then he moved quickly from these preliminary remarks to his sermon on a scriptural text having nothing to do with racism, saying as he did, "The Lord works in mysterious ways."[26]

Most white Baptists in the South were like Hudgins. Neither a rabid segregationist nor a civil rights supporter, he believed his Baptist faith had nothing to do with civil rights in the political sense. Hudgins began studies at Southern Baptist Seminary in Louisville in 1931, three years after the end of E. Y. Mullins's twenty-eight-year reign as president. Mullins may never have dreamed that his approach to theology would be put into the service of maintaining segregation. But that is exactly the effect Mullins's *Axioms of Religion* had on Hudgins and, by extension, millions of other Southern Baptists.

When Hudgins was a student, Southern Seminary took a moderate stance on race but was home to some progressive professors, such as Charles S. Gardner. Responding to the question of whether black people could go to heaven, Gardner once told a class, "In my judgment the Negroes have a much better chance than a preacher who would raise such a question."[27] In 1940, just a few years after Hudgins's sojourn at Southern, seminary president John R. Sampey tried to integrate the school, only to be advised by the Kentucky attorney general that the action would violate a state law that required segregation of educational institutions. Sampey and the Southern faculty nevertheless instructed a few black students privately in faculty offices, an effort organized by the seminary's newly developed Negro Extension Department. In 1944, Southern graduated its first black master's student in theology. By the early 1950s, about the same time Billy Graham began integrating his crusades, most Southern Baptist seminaries accepted black students. In doing so, Southern Seminary issued a news release making clear this was a practical matter of ministry. "The action of Southern Seminary trustees has in it no radical implications concerning the race issue," the release said.[28]

Isolated efforts to break the color line notwithstanding, the dominant theology of Southern Baptists could all too easily serve to maintain segregation. Hudgins's faith has been called the "piety of the pure soul," and he got it straight from Mullins.[29] Hudgins basically distilled three axioms from Mullins's six: (1) the New Testament as the only rule of faith and practice, (2) religious individualism, and (3) local church autonomy. The first of these served primarily to ensure that the Christian faith not degenerate into mere subjectivity. This reflected one of Mullins's evangelical answers to theological liberals who elevated individual experience to a level of authority equal to or even surpassing Scripture. In the Southern Baptist view, a Christian could not believe anything he or she wanted, or say that an experience with Jesus led one to contradict the Bible. But interpretation of Scripture remained highly individual. Hudgins believed that no external creed or corporate body carried authority over the individual. Even Hudgins's emphasis on point 3, the autonomy of the local church, provided no check on the individual reading his or her Bible. The autonomous congregation of Hudgins's third point was nothing more than a voluntary association of individual souls who had an inward experience with Christ. In other words, the congregation had no authority over an individual believer.

The heart of Hudgins's theology as it pertained to civil rights was point 2, the individuality of the Christian life. This was Mullins's soul competency at work. Each person is competent to stand before God on his or her own; in fact, each soul has the right to do so. No outward authority can stand between the individual and God—no church hierarchy, bishop, priest, creed, or even congregation. The upshot of this moderate Southern Baptist theology was that nothing external to the individual soul had anything to do with the Christian life; rather, Christian faith was almost entirely an interior matter.

Hudgins laid out his theology in a June 1947 sermon entitled "Distinctive Principles of Baptists," in which he quoted extensively from Mullins. "The individual not man en masse, is the primary object of God's love," Hudgins said. He buttressed this point with words from Mullins: "God loves the whole world, but the whole is reached by contacting individuals one by one." Hudgins continued, "Individuals do not respond to God as a part of a group; each acts on his own responsibility. Each must act in his own sovereign power of choice." Then, another quote from Mullins: "The individual not only must act for himself; he is the only one who can. God has made him competent." Hudgins concluded, "A man's relationship to God is his own responsibility."[30] As Southern Baptist theologian Fisher Humphreys put it later, "[Mullins] was intoxicated by personal freedom, even personal rights—a category which owes more to the Enlightenment than to the New Testament—even to the loss of the indispensability of society and social relationships for personal life."[31] The same could be said of Hudgins.

First Baptist, Jackson's most famous parishioner was longtime men's Sunday school teacher Ross Barnett, who was better known as governor of Mississippi from 1960 to 1964. In the fall of 1962, a US federal court ordered the University of Mississippi to integrate by admitting James Meredith. Declaring that "God was the original segregationist," Barnett defied the order. "There is no case in history where the Caucasian race has survived social integration," he said. "We will not drink from the cup of genocide."[32] Citing the pre–Civil War political doctrine of nullification, Barnett called on all state officials to defy the federal government. For this a court cited him personally with contempt, fined him $10,000, and sentenced him to six months in jail.

When three hundred federal deputy marshals escorted Meredith onto campus on October 1, a mob of whites attacked them. Forced to retreat to a university administration building, the marshals remained pinned down for hours, eventually dispersing the rioters with tear gas. Two people were killed in the melee, and six marshals were shot but survived. Roughly twenty-five hundred US Army troops arrived early the next day to reinforce the marshals. President John F. Kennedy then nationalized the Mississippi National Guard and ordered it to protect Meredith. The president also called Barnett on the phone and persuaded him to stand down and let Meredith enroll, which he did. Yet Barnett continued to share the enthusiasm Mississippians had for their all-white university. At halftime of the September 29 football game against Kentucky, Barnett appeared on the field and delivered his brief but nevertheless famous "I Love Mississippi" speech. "I love Mississippi! I love her people! Our customs. I love and I respect our heritage," he thundered while the crowd roared. All charges against Barnett were dropped in 1965.

Besides Barnett, the two most influential members of Hudgins's flock, as well as the church's two largest benefactors, were Thomas and Robert Hederman. They owned one of the largest newspapers in the state, and both supported segregation ardently. While these high-profile elites within Hudgins's church took a clear political stance against civil rights, they did so as a politician and as newspaper owners, not Baptists. Barnett and the Hedermans were members of Hudgins's autonomous congregation merely because as individual, competent souls, they had chosen to join. As Hudgins said to his former seminary friend turned racial progressive H. Hansel Stembridge Jr., "You simply don't understand. You know Baptists have no business tinkering in political matters."[33] And so it was that Hudgins had little to say when his rabbi friend's home was bombed three years after the Meredith incident. One can scarcely imagine a more complete perversion of the Baptist concept of soul competency.

Like Hudgins, typical white Baptists in the South viewed civil rights as at best irrelevant to the Christian faith and at worst a threat to their culture. In an attempt to keep politics out of the churches, some Baptist organizations spoke against explicitly segregationist Baptist enterprises in much the same way they spoke against civil rights agitators. The Alabama Baptist Convention, for example, demanded that the breakaway white supremacist organization called Baptist Laymen of Alabama drop "Baptist" from its name. *Alabama Baptist* editor Leon Macon has been called "probably the most highly placed devotee of segregation in the entire SBC," yet even he and other Alabama Baptist officials avoided politicizing the state convention. Macon attempted to carve out a middle way. He called on fellow Alabama Baptists to support segregation laws but also to resist the temptation of the rabble-rousing segregationists.[34]

Historian David Chappell argues that white resistance to integration was weak and disorganized—in stark contrast to the vigorous theological defense of slavery a century before. And this, he claims, is why the resistance collapsed in the face of King's theology of liberation and his appeal to the rights of all Americans.[35] To be sure, this interpretation is contested. One might say that white resistance was furious, almost desperate and hysterical. But the most vigorous defenses of segregation came from constitutional thinkers, not theologians, and segregation was defended in the streets for the most part by the authorities of the state, not parishioners marching out of their churches. It is plausible that resistance collapsed as quickly as it did precisely because so many Southern Baptists believed that their individual experience as Christians had little to do with politics.

In the face of the incursion of civil rights workers and federal agents into Mississippi, Hudgins washed his hands of responsibility, preaching, "Our greatest enemy is not flesh and blood; it is the intangibles, the rulers of the darkness of this world, the spiritual wickedness in high places."[36]

Still, whatever success Governor Barnett, the Hedermans—or even Bowers, the Klan, and Bull Connor—had in maintaining segregation, their actions were made possible in part by the indifference of Hudgins, who preached weekly sermons that were broadcast across the state via radio.[37] In sum, the Baptist theology of soul competency and individualism kept most white Baptists on the sidelines, neither supporting civil rights nor engaging politically to stop Bowers and the White Knights of the Ku Klux Klan. The Baptist theology articulated by Mullins and mediated through preachers such as Hudgins helped answer the question, "Why were the enemies of the civil rights movement, for one fleeting but decisive moment, so weak?"[38]

WHITE SOUTHERN BAPTISTS spanned the spectrum of racial views, though the majority stood in Hudgins's camp. Black Baptists also exhibited diversity on the issue of civil rights. In the 1950s, the National Baptist Convention USA Inc. and the National Baptist Convention of America Unincorporated, which split off from it in 1915, remained the largest and most influential black Baptist denominations in America. In conjunction with the civil rights movement, the National Baptist Convention USA Inc. experienced another schism. While personal issues surrounding convention president Joseph H. Jackson played a significant role in the split, different approaches to civil rights were also at its heart.

As pastor of the historic Olivet Baptist Church on Chicago's South Side, Jackson was one of the most influential black Baptists in America. By the time of his death in 1990, his church boasted twenty thousand members. Jackson was a gradualist, a "civil rights law and order" man, staunchly opposed to even nonviolent civil disobedience. A permanent rift between King and Jackson developed at a National Baptist symposium on civil rights in 1956, where King denounced gradualism. The two leaders' fractured relationship dovetailed with a dispute over how many terms an individual could serve as president of the NBC. The 1961 convention in Kansas City exploded in controversy, and a Detroit preacher fell to his death from the platform during a violent melee. King, Ralph Abernathy, and others who supported Gardner C. Taylor for the presidency left the National Baptist Convention and formed the Progressive National Baptist

Convention.[39] Black Baptists now had another major denomination, this one firmly behind the civil rights movement.

Still, most black churches, whether Baptist or not, have been aptly characterized as "sympathetic spectators" during the civil rights movement, at least at the institutional level. The churches provided money for civil rights organizations, and most of the marchers in the early years of the movement came from black churches. Institutionally, however, most black denominations and many black preachers kept a safe distance from radicalism. And the National Baptist Convention USA Inc. refused to identify with King, especially after the formation of the Progressive National Baptist Convention.[40] The tension between progressive resistance and accommodation to the realities of a segregated society had been part of the black religious experience since Booker T. Washington and W. E. B. Du Bois squared off in the early twentieth century. The proper response to the realities of segregation and discrimination continued to divide black Baptists during the civil rights movement.[41]

Institutional church support for civil rights finally came, in the mid-sixties, from the predominantly white and northern National Council of Churches. The head of the NCC, Presbyterian Eugene Carson Blake, acknowledged at the March on Washington in 1963 that the churches came late to the struggle. There is no doubt that the prophetic strain of black Christianity, with its strong liberation theme, motivated and fueled the civil rights movement. And individual black Baptists were more often than not at the forefront. Still, even the Baptist dissenting tradition could not sustain much of a corporate movement among black denominations.

While King's faction lost the struggle within the NBC, he emerged from the Montgomery bus boycott as the unparalleled leader of the civil rights movement. But Baptists can claim him exclusively no more than they can Billy Graham. Graham transcended his denomination, becoming an international evangelical figure, and King did the same as a global human rights icon. King counted as his influences Baptist theologian Walter Rauschenbusch and Christian Realist Reinhold Niebuhr, but also Indian leader Mohandas Gandhi and Jewish philosopher Martin Buber. Still, as has been said, King combined these influences "with the folk religion and revival techniques of the black Baptist Preacher."[42]

Ironically, the white Southern Baptist Convention often supported civil rights with official resolutions, even while most Southern Baptists opposed integration. The SBC meeting of 1954 adopted a statement supporting the *Brown* decision, acknowledging that *Brown* was consistent with both "the Constitutional guarantee of equal freedom to all citizens" and "the Christian principles of equal justice and love for all men."[43] Douglas Hudgins opposed it but left the convention before the vote. Meanwhile, two relatively unknown messengers took to the floor to denounce the resolution, one of them saying, "Some of you who sit in this audience today will have grandchildren with mixed blood." After Hudgins's name was linked to the two firebrand racists, he attempted to extricate himself from embarrassment by emphasizing congregational autonomy and Baptists' individual freedom, contending that the Supreme Court decision "was a purely civic matter . . . not appropriate nor necessary before a religious body."[44]

Forty years later, the SBC acknowledged the hollowness of the resolution supporting *Brown*. In May 1995, eight black and eight white Southern Baptists met in Nashville to draft a resolution on race in conjunction with the SBC's sesquicentennial celebration. As one black member of the group commented, "We were the sons of slaves and the sons of slave owners sitting down together."[45] The resulting resolution, adopted by SBC messengers in June, acknowledged the role slavery played in the founding of the SBC, as well as the indifference and opposition to civil rights on the part of white Southern Baptists. The most significant clause of the lengthy resolution read in part: "Be it further resolved that we apologize to all African Americans for condoning and/or perpetuating individual and systemic racism in our lifetime, and we genuinely repent of racism of which we have been guilty, whether consciously (Psalm 19:13) or unconsciously (Leviticus 4:27)." The resolution then "ask[ed] forgiveness from our African American brothers and sisters, acknowledging that our own healing is at stake."[46]

Black and white Baptist responses to civil rights were nearly the opposite of each other. While the SBC institutionally supported the civil rights movement with its 1954 resolution, most Southern Baptist congregations and individuals went the other direction. By contrast, the largest black Baptist denomination refused to become involved institutionally, while individual black Baptists and congregations threw themselves into the fray with great conviction. Soul competency, particularly in its twentieth-century permutation, left even matters of racial justice largely to the individual. The 1995 SBC resolution notwithstanding, Baptists often find themselves trying to unite around the very individualism that creates their disunity.

Schism in Zion

THE SOUTHERN BAPTIST CONTROVERSY

IN 1979, ADRIAN ROGERS became president of the Southern Baptist Convention. Pastor of Bellevue Baptist outside of Memphis, one of the largest churches in the country, with a nationally known television ministry, Rogers was the most visible "fundamentalist" pastor in the SBC.[1] Many observers believed his election amounted to little more than a nod to the conservative wing of the denomination. It had happened before, when W. A. Criswell of First Baptist, Dallas served two terms as convention president (1968–1970). But they were wrong. The election of Rogers set in motion a political and theological battle for control of America's largest Protestant denomination. It would become one of the most significant religious events of the twentieth century.

Paige Patterson and Paul Pressler devised the strategy for the "conservative resurgence." Patterson was a theologian-preacher and dean of the Criswell Institute in Dallas. Pressler served for years as a Texas state appeals court judge and active Baptist layman. Patterson was the unofficial theologian of the conservative movement, Pressler its political strategist, and Rogers the popular preacher.[2]

Conservatives believed that moderates had allowed the denomination to drift too far leftward, and they sought to take the SBC back to its conservative, biblical roots. Pressler studied the SBC's constitution and determined that if he and Patterson engineered the election of conservative SBC presidents like Rogers, and those presidents appointed conservatives to the boards of the denominational agencies and seminaries, the entire apparatus of the SBC would be in conservative hands within ten years.[3]

Rogers's 1979 election was the first step in executing this strategy. It took a few years for moderates to realize what they were up against, largely because they believed in what Southern Baptist historian Bill Leonard called the "Grand Compromise." Because of the theological diversity of the denomination, moderate SBC officials sought to keep theological controversy at bay while uniting all factions around missions and evangelism. Southern Baptists may not be able to agree on a particular view of the inspiration of Scripture, the historicity of Old Testament stories, Calvinist versus Arminian theology, or women in ministry, the reasoning went, but all were united around the need to share Christ with a lost world and to win sinners to the faith.[4] This Grand Compromise had held for so long that moderates did not see the threat coming. They proved slow to organize resistance, and by the time they did, the conservative juggernaut was rolling. For reasons that remain mysterious, Rogers did not run for the perfunctory second one-year term, but conservatives rallied around Bailey Smith of First Baptist, Del City, Oklahoma, who served two terms, as did his successor, Dallas area megachurch pastor James Draper Jr. Conservatives won these elections by rallying their supporters around the inerrancy of Scripture. The term "inerrancy" appeared in the late nineteenth century, and the evangelical debate over inerrancy reached a fever pitch in the 1970s. In 1976, evangelical Baptist scholar and *Christianity Today* editor Harold Lindsell published the book *The Battle for the Bible*, which identified inerrancy as the most important issue of his generation. An entire chapter was devoted to the Southern Baptists. Lindsell argued that the denomination was moving away from the belief that the Bible is inerrant in matters of not only theology and Christian practice but also history and science, and he singled out a handful of SBC moderates for scorn.

Moderates believed the inerrancy debate amounted to a false choice. They emphasized the authority of Scripture once interpreted properly, and they denied that the Bible's authority relied on its historic or scientific accuracy in every detail. Nevertheless, Lindsell's book stunned some SBC conservatives and emboldened others.[5]

Conservatives convinced a growing number of people that the SBC's moderate leaders were out of touch with the denomination's grass roots. Then, through sophisticated campaigning, conservatives got their sympathizers to the SBC annual meetings to vote. Complex issues of inspiration, authority, and interpretation of Scripture fell to the wayside in the political battle over inerrancy. Other theological issues also came to the fore, such as the ordination of women, and cultural and political issues like abortion and separation of church and state became embroiled in the controversy as well. Conservatives charged that moderate leaders were liberals, a charge that was more accurate politically than theologically. But it worked. By 1985, moderates were in trouble. More than halfway into their ten-year plan, conservatives had already started to remake the denomination. As agency and seminary boards fell into the hands of conservative appointees, the moderates desperately needed to break the conservative momentum at the SBC annual convention that summer. The meeting took place at the Dallas Convention Center, where one year earlier Republicans had nominated Ronald Reagan for a second term. Both the Reagan and SBC revolutions were part of a conservative shift taking place in the wider culture.

By the SBC convention in 1985, both factions had developed get-out-the-vote campaigns with unofficial but clearly identifiable candidates for the presidency. Charles Stanley, pastor of First Baptist Church, Atlanta, had been elected president in 1984, the fourth conservative in a row. Like Rogers, Stanley's television ministry made him a virtual household name in both Baptist and wider evangelical circles. In keeping with their central theological concern, all four conservative presidents required members of agency and seminary boards to affirm the inerrancy of Scripture. Conservative-dominated annual convention meetings had also passed resolutions against abortion (1980) and the ordination of women (1984), and in favor of a constitutional amendment allowing prayer in public schools (1982).[6]

The moderates chose Winfred Moore of First Baptist, Amarillo to run against Stanley. With the stakes so high and both sides organized for battle, attendance at the 1985 convention swelled to more than forty-five thousand, double the previous record. The Great Hall and newly added West Room of the Dallas Convention Center had seating and standing room for only thirty thousand, so roughly a third of the messengers were relegated to meeting rooms, where they watched convention business via closed-circuit television. Convention officials worried whether they had enough printed ballots to accommodate voters.[7] The meeting captured the attention of the national news media. More than six hundred writers and broadcasters from newspapers and television stations across the country jammed the press rooms in Dallas. Nearly all the major television networks, many independent stations, most major newspapers, and, of course, all state Baptist newspapers sent representatives.

Moore may have been the moderates' candidate, but he believed in the inerrancy of Scripture and was nearly as conservative as Stanley. What distinguished him was that he supported the Grand Compromise and therefore opposed conservative efforts to drive moderates and liberals out of the seminaries and off the agency boards. He seemed the perfect choice to peel off conservative votes by arguing that Southern Baptists needed to stop fighting about theology and get back to the business of missions and evangelism.

Moderates also touted soul competency as the key to the Grand Compromise. Church historian Walter Shurden told a preconvention audience at a moderate gathering called the Forum that individual soul competency and theological diversity were indispensable Baptist doctrines. "Soul competency asserts the inalienable right and responsibility of every person to interpret God for himself. There must not be a middle person save for Jesus Christ," he said. "Southern Baptists were built on a principle which permits, not prohibits diversity," he continued. "Our denominational identity has been fostered by a unity which comes out of our commitment to diversity, not by a unity squeezed out of some kind of imposed uniformity."[8]

Moderates argued that the conservative activists were an intolerant minority bent on controlling the denomination for political ends. As moderate leader Cecil Sherman—pastor of Broadway Baptist Church, Fort Worth, Texas—characterized the conservative movement, "[They believe that] they're good and we're bad; they're orthodox and we're unorthodox, they believe the Bible and we don't." Speaking at a preconvention meeting at Wilshire Baptist Church in Dallas, he rallied the moderate troops, charging, "There has always been a spirit of live and let live and now [the fundamentalists] are putting us out of policy-making posts as they exercise their political rhetoric."[9]

Conservatives countered with a call for clear theological parameters. On Sunday, from his pulpit at First Baptist, Euless, outside Dallas, former SBC president James Draper countered the moderate line of argument, saying, "There is no such thing as theological diversity. . . . The New Testament never speaks of theological diversity."[10] Ed Young, pastor of Second Baptist Church, Houston, told the conservative-dominated preconvention Pastor's Conference that while most Southern Baptist seminary professors were warmhearted evangelicals, "there are some who have gone too far in offering other explanations for the miracles of the Old Testament and raising questions about the New Testament." Like Draper, Young also critiqued the moderate commitment to theological pluralism.[11]

While differing visions concerning the proper theological parameters for the SBC lay at the heart of the controversy, by 1985 it had become clear that moderates and conservatives differed in other ways as well. Conservatives were fighters, not Grand Compromisers. In this sense they exuded a key trait of fundamentalism, the militant defense of orthodoxy. But they rejected fundamentalist separatism, calling instead for engagement in politics and culture. Conservatives also promoted a robust American civil religion that marked the Reagan era of the 1980s. When pulpiteers regaled the preconvention Pastor's Conference, a giant American flag stretched across the speaker's platform behind them. The conference opened with a written greeting from Republican president Ronald Reagan and his wife, Nancy. Having Republican presidents and vice presidents address the convention became standard procedure once the conservatives gained control. Conservative sermons at the 1985 Pastor's Conference dealt with theological rigor and the importance of inerrancy but also included frequent reference to political and cultural issues. The most important of these were abortion, gay rights, prayer in schools, and evolution, as the leading conservative pastors and televangelists in the country called America back to God. Meanwhile, at the moderate-sponsored Forum, held in an adjacent hall of the Dallas Convention Center, preachers and activists emphasized soul competency, separation of church and state, freedom, cooperation, social justice, and spiritual renewal.[12]

The legendary W. A. Criswell spoke last at the Pastor's Conference. He reminded the audience of the decline of mainline denominations in both the United States and Great Britain. That decline began, he argued, when evangelical denominations endorsed higher criticism of Scripture. This, he said, is precisely what happened in nineteenth-century Great Britain, where only the legendary Charles Spurgeon held out for inerrancy. Rejecting the idea that the Grand Compromise could be held together by missions and evangelism, Criswell argued, "My brother, if the higher critical approach to scriptures dominates our institutions and our denomination, there will be no missionaries to hurt. They will cease. . . . As with the Baptists of Great Britain, whether we continue to live or ultimately die lies in our dedication to the infallible Word of God."[13] As future SBC president

Jerry Vines put it in 1986, "The view that the Bible contains error is worth fighting against. That's the first domino to fall."[14]

Conservatives such as Criswell believed that the vast majority of Southern Baptists ascribed to biblical inerrancy. Pressler routinely put the percentage at 90 percent. A study by Baptist sociologist Nancy Ammerman in 1985 found that 85 percent of Southern Baptist pastors and lay leaders affirmed the view that "the scriptures are the inerrant Word of God, accurate in every detail." Conservatives such as Pressler, Patterson, and Criswell routinely interpreted inerrancy to mean an affirmation of a literal view of biblical stories such as the Genesis creation accounts. They argued that the Bible was inerrant historically and scientifically, which meant that an allegorical reading of creation would not do. If Genesis spoke of Adam and Eve as two individual human beings, then it was unacceptable to view them as mere representations of humanity.

Ammerman discovered, however, that fewer than half of SBC pastors and lay leaders interpreted inerrancy this way. "Whatever Southern Baptists mean by inerrancy," she concluded from her surveys and interviews at the 1985 convention, "not all of them mean that Genesis is to be read as history or science. The number of Southern Baptists who insist on such a reading of the creation stories is well under half."[15] On the other hand, 59 percent of Ammerman's respondents were willing to, in her words, "claim not only that the Bible is inerrant, but that it speaks clearly and precisely about the history of the world from creation to the end of time." Moreover, she declared to the delight of conservatives, "That is certainly the position of the denomination's fundamentalist leaders, and it has been the position of most fundamentalists since the movement began."[16] During the controversy, the only safe position was a clear and consistent affirmation of inerrancy, whatever one meant by the term. Quibbling about what inerrancy actually was, or doubts concerning the term's importance, would not suffice. As Pressler liked to put it, "Once you have crossed the theological Rubicon of saying that the Bible is sufficiently man's work so that it can be in error and make mistakes, then you have opened the floodgates for the individual to determine the categories which are truth, and that is [an] extremely presumptuous thing for a man to do."[17]

On inerrancy and most other issues, conservatives believed that Ammerman's study confirmed that moderate elites in the denominational agencies and on the seminary faculties were more liberal than rank-and-file Southern Baptists in the pews. In short, moderates were out of step with the people who paid their salaries. As the leading conservative periodical, the *Southern Baptist Advocate*, editorialized, "Two messages need to be sent in Dallas. One is a reaffirmation of our absolute commitment to the Bible as the inerrant and infallible Word of God. Secondly, a message needs to be sent to the bureaucracy, whose salaries we pay, whose budgets are supported by us." That message, the editor continued, is that "we, the people of the Southern Baptist Convention, committed to the Word of God and to our world missions programs, will determine the course and the direction our Convention will take."[18]

TWO DAYS BEFORE the presidential vote, conservatives divulged a June 5 telegram from an associate of Billy Graham to Charles Stanley saying, "Billy Graham called me from Europe and said, 'Do me a favor. I want you to call Dr. Charles Stanley and tell him that I will be praying for him during the Southern Baptist Convention in Dallas. Tell him that if I could be there I would vote for him.'"[19] Moderates howled, some in disbelief, as a pall fell over the Forum meeting when word of the endorsement circulated. How could it be that the usually nonpartisan Graham would endorse Stanley? One moderate, a former Graham associate, said he had been with Graham two weeks earlier when the world-renowned evangelist claimed he was not going to get involved in the fight over the SBC presidency.[20] Several days later Graham apologized, saying he did not intend for his endorsement to be made public. Moreover, he claimed, he supported Stanley because it was customary for a president to serve two years and because he thought Stanley's ouster after one year would split the denomination.[21]

With more than forty-four thousand messengers casting votes in the presidential race, Stanley emerged victorious with 55.3 percent of the vote. After the ballots were counted, Stanley summoned his opponent, Winfred Moore, to the platform and asked, "Would you accept the nomination for first vice president?" "Are you asking me?" Moore joked, to the roar of the crowd. Actually, a messenger from Virginia had nominated Moore, and the Amarillo pastor easily ousted first vice president Zig Ziglar, the famous motivational speaker from Dallas's First Baptist Church. When asked if he thought Graham's leaked endorsement of Stanley made a difference in the presidential election, Moore responded, "Sure it had an impact. . . . Mr. Graham is a highly respected man." Stanley, however, argued that 95 percent of messengers came to the convention with their minds made up.[22]

With the defeat of Moore for the presidency and Stanley's solid re-election, the conservatives turned a corner. They had withstood their most serious challenge. Moderates continued to fight for several more years, but they never won the presidency. Eventually, they simply quit contesting presidential elections, and many stopped going to annual convention meetings. Two years after the record attendance at the Dallas convention, only 25,000 showed up in St. Louis. After 1995, attendance averaged just over 10,000, and by 2011 was under 5,000.[23]

IN ADDITION TO Stanley's re-election, the most significant action taken at the 1985 convention was the creation of a Peace Committee to study the reasons for the controversy and to suggest ways to reconcile the two factions. The resolution put before messengers would have created an all-male, eighteen-member committee, with the SBC president as an ex officio member. Amendments from the floor resulted in the addition of two women as well as first vice president Winfred Moore, who would serve ex officio along with Stanley. Pressler opposed the idea of a Peace Committee, believing nothing substantive would come of it and that it might even prove to be a whitewash, obscuring or downplaying conservative charges of moderate heresy.

The Peace Committee met off and on for two years and sent subcommittees to various SBC agencies and to the seminaries to query denominational employees about the controversy. The committee targeted seminary faculty in particular, sending many of them questionnaires intended to gauge what sort of teaching occurred at SBC schools. In October 1986, the Peace Committee held a retreat at the Glorieta Baptist Conference Center near Santa Fe, New Mexico. Joining members of the Peace Committee were heads of SBC agencies and the presidents of the six Southern Baptist seminaries. Moderates still controlled the seminaries, and at the meeting the presidents heard the concerns of the Peace Committee, particularly the belief that the seminaries did not adequately represent the view of Scripture held by the vast majority of Southern Baptists.

The presidents submitted what came to be called the Glorieta Statement, which among other things affirmed, "The sixty-six books of the Bible are not errant in any area of reality."[24] The presidents then committed themselves to enforcing among faculty the seminaries' own confessional statements, which were often more explicit than the denomination's confession, the Baptist Faith and Message. The presidents also agreed to hire faculty who represented the spectrum of views within the denomination. Because the Peace Committee had already determined that seminaries such as Southern and Southeastern tilted toward the liberal side, the Glorieta Statement essentially meant those schools would hire more conservatives. Moreover, the statement's acknowledgment that "the sixty-six books of the Bible are not errant in any area of reality" meant, in the words of moderate historian Bill Leonard, "that fundamentalists had won and the seminary presidents knew it."[25]

The Peace Committee Report filed at the 1987 SBC convention in St. Louis cited significant diversity within SBC seminaries: some faculty members believed Adam and Eve were literal individuals, others believed they were figurative representations of humankind; some believed that all events in the Bible were historically accurate, while others did not; some believed that each book in the Bible was authored exclusively by the stated author, while others accepted higher critical interpretations that questioned traditional authorship and dating of biblical books; and some believed every miracle recorded in Scripture literally took place, while others held that some miracles, especially some in the Old Testament, were parables meant to illustrate a point.

By contrast, the Peace Committee reported, most rank-and-file Southern Baptists agreed with conservatives on all these questions. The report added, "We call upon Southern Baptist institutions to recognize the number of Southern Baptists who believe this interpretation of our confessional statement and, in the future, to build their professional staffs and faculties from those who clearly reflect such dominant convictions and beliefs held by Southern Baptists at large."[26]

Conservatives rejoiced at the Peace Committee's findings because they believed the report documented widespread heresy in the denomination.[27] They inferred, reasonably, from the Peace Committee Report that the seminaries were out of step with the people who paid their salaries. The report implied strongly that the seminaries should hire more conservatives. While some moderates hoped the Peace Committee might actually bring peace, others believed conservatives had used the body to further their agenda. As one member said, "The Peace Committee is just another place for the fundamentalists to win. Our meetings are war, not peace."[28]

Conservatives on the Peace Committee believed that inerrancy lacked adequate representation on the seminary faculties. As the Peace Committee Report said, "[We] found there was not a theological balance represented in the faculties at Southern Baptist Theological Seminary or Southeastern Baptist Theological Seminary." The Peace Committee also deemed Midwestern problematic but cleared Southwestern, Golden Gate, and New Orleans Seminaries.[29] While parts of the Peace Committee Report seemed to indicate a need for greater representation of inerrantist views in denominational institutions, the "Findings" section actually put the case more strongly. The report said that the cause of peace in the denomination would be "enhanced by the affirmation of the whole Bible as being 'not errant in any area of reality.'" Moderates interpreted this to mean that peace would come when the conservatives had won. Cecil Sherman saw where the process was heading and resigned his seat on the Peace Committee in protest midway through the body's deliberations.

The pledge of the seminary presidents to seek greater balance in hiring proved insufficient. The Peace Committee suggested that because peace would be enhanced by an acceptance of inerrancy, "Therefore, we exhort the trustees and administrators of our seminaries and other agencies to . . . only employ professional staff who believe in the divine inspiration of the whole Bible and that the Bible is 'truth without any mixture of error.'" (The latter phrase was an affirmation from the 1833 New Hampshire Confession of Faith, as well as SBC's Baptist Faith and Message Statement.)[30] Henceforth, "Truth without any mixture of error" meant "inerrancy," according to the Peace Committee Report. From 1987 onward, conservatives cited the Peace Committee Report as justification for hiring only inerrantists to the seminary faculties and to positions in all other denominational agencies. The result was the near-complete personnel turnover at some of the schools and almost all of the agencies. Particularly wrenching was the experience of Southern Baptist Seminary in Louisville in the mid-1990s.

IN THE EARLY 1990s, Southern Seminary became a microcosm of the entire SBC controversy. By 1992, conservatives held the majority of seats on the Southern Seminary board. Moderate Roy Honeycutt remained as president and worked to bring more inerrantist conservatives onto the faculty. His effort coincided not only with the Glorieta Statement but also with the seminary's own Covenant Renewal document. The latter came into existence in 1991 as part of an agreement between Southern's pervasively moderate and non-inerrantist faculty and the conservative board. The seminary administration promised to hire more "conservative evangelical scholars" in order to achieve better balance, a kind of affirmative action for conservatives who were underrepresented on the faculty. The seminary administration could say that the vast majority of the Southern faculty held to fundamental truths such as the Trinity, the incarnation, the resurrection of Christ, salvation by faith, and the need for conversion. But such issues were often open for discussion in ways that, from a conservative point of view, seemed to undercut the very foundations of those beliefs. Moreover, many Southern faculty did not believe in a literal interpretation of the Genesis creation stories, the historicity of Adam and Eve, the historical accuracy of every Old Testament event, or that all supernatural events in the Bible should be taken literally. And nearly every faculty member at Southern affirmed the ordination of women for pastoral ministry. These views rankled conservatives on the board.[31]

David Dockery served as provost under Honeycutt and began recruiting evangelical Baptists, all of whom affirmed their commitment to the inerrancy of Scripture. Still, most of the new faculty Dockery recruited tended to be mainstream evangelical scholars. This all changed in 1993 when R. Albert Mohler became president. Mohler had been a Honeycutt protégé, serving as his chief assistant while completing doctoral studies in the 1980s. But Mohler had moved into the conservative inerrantist camp, largely as a result of the influence of Carl F. H. Henry. The first editor of *Christianity Today* magazine and a founding faculty member at Fuller Theological Seminary, Henry was, like Billy Graham, a highly visible leader whose profile as an evangelical outshone his Baptist identity. Having spent his entire career outside the Southern Baptist orbit, Henry was nevertheless technically a Southern Baptist by virtue of membership in a dually aligned (American and Southern) Baptist church in Washington, DC. Conservative Southern Baptist leaders regarded Henry as the most important theologian of the twentieth century, and in the 1980s Henry threw his considerable weight behind the SBC conservative movement. During his doctoral studies, Mohler succeeded in getting Henry to the Southern Seminary campus for lectures, and the two became friends, with Henry taking on the role of mentor for the young Mohler.

Mohler came to the presidency believing that he had a mandate to hire only inerrantist faculty. More radically, he believed that mandate extended to hiring only those who believed that Scripture forbade the ordination of women. Nearly all the longtime moderate faculty at Southern affirmed the ordination of women, as did most of the new "conservative evangelical scholars" who had been brought on by Dockery. Church historian Timothy Weber was one of the first faculty hired at Southern Seminary under the Covenant Renewal agreement. He affirmed both the inerrancy of Scripture and the ordination of women, a stance that befuddled the conservatives on the board and many moderates on the faculty. When Mohler arrived as president the next year, he developed a four-pronged test for all new faculty: the inerrancy of Scripture, opposition to women's ordination, a pro-life position on abortion (the seminary was pervasively pro-choice when the moderates were in charge), and opposition to homosexuality. Moreover, he set out to hire predominantly Reformed Calvinist faculty, in keeping with the seminary's nineteenth-century founders and the doctrinal statement (the Abstract of Principles) they adopted.

All this came to a head when the seminary's Carver School of Social Work wanted to hire a Reformed inerrantist faculty member who nevertheless affirmed the ordination of women. Carver School dean Diana Garland took a public stand against Mohler and was essentially fired. The seminary exploded in public controversy, with Weber and some of the other evangelical faculty brought in by Dockery taking a stand against Mohler. Mohler survived the uproar, and over the course of the next few years the seminary experienced a massive turnover in faculty, with nearly all moderates and recently appointed evangelicals exiting. Eventually even Dockery himself left Southern, albeit for the presidency of Union University, a Baptist school in Jackson, Tennessee. The departures cleared the decks for Mohler to completely remold the seminary into a conservative, evangelical, and Reformed institution.

The controversy at Southern Seminary signaled that Southern Baptist conservatives sought to create an identity that would be thoroughly evangelical, and planted firmly on the conservative side of the evangelical spectrum. Moderates had often looked askance at alliances with evangelicals, even evangelical leaders such as Henry who were also Baptist. When *Newsweek* proclaimed 1976 "The Year of the Evangelical," director of the SBC's Christian Life Commission (CLC) Foy Valentine spoke for many moderates when he said: "Southern Baptists are not evangelicals. That's a Yankee word. . . . We don't share their politics or their fussy fundamentalism, and we don't want to get involved in their theological witch-hunts."[32] By contrast, Southern Baptist conservatives embraced the term "evangelical" and sought alliances with conservative evangelicals outside the South. Mohler, Richard Land (director of the Ethics and Religious Liberty Commission), and some other key leaders in the movement claimed not only Henry but also the non-Baptist popular evangelical leader Francis Schaeffer as important influences.

The new dual identity of Southern Baptists—both Baptist and evangelical—mirrored the experience of white Baptists outside the South.

Within the American Baptist Churches, for example, conservative congregations often identify with the broader American evangelical subculture against the liberal leaders of their own denomination. Likewise, in
conservative Baptist denominations such as the General Association of
Regular Baptists and the Conservative Baptist Association, congregations
and individuals routinely identify as evangelical. Like other Christian
groups in America, many Baptists by the end of the twentieth century
downplayed Baptist particularity in favor of evangelicalism. This was not
true in all quarters, but many Baptists felt more kinship with evangelicals in non-Baptist denominations than with liberals in their own. This
"restructuring of American religion" had both theological and cultural
components.[33]

OUTSIDE THE SOUTH, white Baptists in the twentieth century had never
been a dominant force, religiously or culturally. While they did not often
experience the kind of discrimination they had suffered during earlier
periods, they nevertheless learned to live in tension with an increasingly
secular culture. No longer could they take for granted that businesses
would close on Sunday, that Christmas decorations would adorn their
towns in December, or that their children would begin their public school
day with classroom prayer. All of these persisted longer in the South,
where Baptists remained insiders and the culture stayed religiously intact.
But by the end of the century these sorts of changes began to come to the
South as well, and Southern Baptists had to deal with them.

As they did, key Southern Baptist conservatives began to see themselves not so much as the dominant religion of the South but rather as
part of an evangelical resistance to a national culture that is secular and
hostile to traditional Christian morality. This was a lesson they learned in
part from the Baptist Carl F. H. Henry and Presbyterian Francis Schaeffer.
Henry had argued since the 1940s that evangelicals should shrug off fundamentalist separatism and re-engage the culture as nineteenth-century
Protestants had. Schaeffer taught that secular humanism had replaced
America's Christian base as society's dominant worldview. Believing they
could no longer take for granted a Judeo-Christian cultural foundation,
SBC conservatives set out to fashion a countercultural witness, seeking to
remake American society in exactly the same ways as Mohler had remade
Southern Seminary. Believing in the separation of church and state, conservatives saw no role for the state in purely doctrinal matters such as
inerrancy or the ordination of women. But on abortion, homosexuality,

and the role of women within families they sought to move the denomination to the forefront of the conservative side of America's culture wars. Abortion proved the first and easiest issue on which to form a Southern Baptist consensus.

Throughout the 1970s, largely as a result of the leadership of Foy Valentine and the CLC, the moderate SBC passed a series of resolutions that rejected abortion on demand while advocating that abortion remain an option wherever continuation of pregnancy might result in the "likelihood of damage to the emotional, mental, and physical health of the mother."[34] Conservatives viewed the reference to the mental health of the mother as a cop-out, an exception so broad that it nearly amounted to a pro-choice position. As Southern Baptist abortion awareness grew in the wake of *Roe v. Wade*, subsequent resolutions moved gradually toward the pro-life position. Moderate resolutions emphasized the grave moral nature of abortion, the need to protect life, and a rejection of abortion for casual and selfish reasons. At the same time, however, the resolutions retained the broad "physical and mental health" exception, stressed the "limited role of government," and supported "the right of expectant mothers to the full range of medical services," which presumably included abortion. Such phrases could be interpreted to support at least a soft pro-choice position. In 1979, the same year conservatives engineered the election of Adrian Rogers, convention messengers rejected a resolution of support for a constitutional amendment overturning *Roe*.

The next year everything changed. Conservatives pushed through a resolution opposing abortion on demand and the use of taxpayer funds to finance abortions. The 1980 resolution also included a ringing endorsement of a pro-life amendment to the constitution. Schaeffer's pro-life film *Whatever Happened to the Human Race?*, which appeared in 1979, played a significant role, as Southern Baptist churches began using it as a teaching tool. All ambiguity concerning the SBC's official position disappeared, and Southern Baptists embarked on a quest to become the most pro-life denomination in America. In 1986, fresh off their defeat of moderates the year before in Dallas, Paige Patterson allegedly remarked, "We want an open and pro-life position in all our institutions and agencies, dealing with abortion and euthanasia."[35] A decade later Mohler explained that while it was sometimes difficult for rank-and-file Baptists to discern just when inerrancy was being denied, they understood clearly what it meant when they heard that a professor at one of their seminaries was pro-choice. As he put it, "I think moderates, to their dying day, are going to underestimate that issue. They just don't get it."[36]

This is not to say that abortion was merely a cultural or political issue for conservatives. Theologian Timothy George spoke for all Southern Baptist conservatives and nearly all evangelicals when he argued that because persons are created in God's image, any attack on human life, especially in embryonic form, "is nothing less than an attack on the Creator of life itself."[37] After becoming director of the Christian Life Commission, Richard Land made abortion one of his key concerns. With Land and the CLC in charge of abortion advocacy, the SBC subsequently defunded the Baptist Joint Committee, whose director James Dunn refused to take a position on abortion. Dunn's predecessor at the BJC had been Baptist church-state scholar James Wood, who argued that the right to abortion was protected by the free exercise clause of the First Amendment. Dunn never took that view, but he did not repudiate it either. Land immediately put the CLC (later renamed the Ethics and Religious Liberty Commission) on record as pro-life, then took to the airwaves and to the halls of Congress to push the new agenda.

As on abortion, SBC conservatives also took a countercultural, outsider position on the role of women in marriage and in churches. When the SBC adopted its resolution "On Racial Reconciliation" in 1995, it was major news across America. Still, such a stance in favor of racial equality was little more than an affirmation of what had already become the cultural mainstream. To hold out for different roles for men and women, by contrast, put the conservatives squarely in opposition to the cultural mandate for full equality of women in all spheres of life.

Before the controversy, Southern Baptists were as divided as the larger evangelical subculture on issues of women in ministry. Their views ranged from allowing women carefully circumscribed roles to full ordination and everything in between. The seminaries stood as bastions of the progressive view, which is why opposition to the ordination of women became one of Mohler's four hiring criteria at Southern Seminary.

A few Baptist groups began ordaining small numbers of women pastors in the 1880s. But the practice remained controversial throughout the twentieth century. The American Baptist Churches (formerly the Northern Baptist Convention) firmed up its support for women's ordination in a 1989 statement, even as the Southern Baptist debate over the issue began to turn the other way. Ordained by the Watts Street Baptist Church in Durham, North Carolina, Addie Davis is generally regarded as the first woman ordained in the SBC. From 1974 to 1983, the number of ordained women in the denomination grew from under ten to roughly two hundred, then rose to more than three hundred by the mid-1990s.[38]

In the 1980s, moderate SBC biblical scholars such as Charles Talbert at Wake Forest University (and later at Baylor) and Jan Aldredge Clanton, at the time serving as a minister to family life in a Methodist church in Waco, Texas, laid out careful arguments for ordination of women. Both argued that the apparent prohibitions against women in ministry found in 1 Timothy and 1 Corinthians were meant to be local and temporary prohibitions, not universal teaching on female submission. Moreover, moderate Baptist Bible scholars suggested there was tension between Jesus and Paul on this question and concluded that the Bible left the matter open.

Conservatives, by contrast, argued in favor of a straightforward reading of 1 Timothy 2:8–15 and I Corinthians 14:33–35, in which Paul spoke of women remaining silent in church and not exercising authority over men. In 1984, with the SBC controversy still very much alive, they pushed through a resolution encouraging "the service of women in all aspects of church life and work other than pastoral functions and leadership roles entailing ordination." The statement was premised in part on the apostle Paul's teaching that "man was first in creation and the woman first in the Edenic fall (I Tim 2:13ff)."[39]

Fifteen years later, firmly ensconced in power, the conservatives went further, addressing the role of women in marriage, but not by resolution. Rather, they revised the Baptist Faith and Message Statement (BFMS), the denomination's basic confession of faith. Their statement read in part, "A wife is to submit herself graciously to the servant leadership of her husband even as the church willingly submits to the headship of Christ."[40] Crafted by a study committee that included Dorothy Patterson and Mary Mohler, as well as Richard Land, the change in the confession brought conservatives directly into conflict with the secular culture, which was part of its purpose. As Al Mohler, Land, and Dorothy Patterson all explained later, it is appropriate for Baptist confessions to respond to cultural crises in which theological issues are at play.

The media howled, and conservatives seemed to relish the opportunity to take a stand against the secular mainstream. The report on the "submission statement" appeared above the fold on the front page of *The New York Times*. Journalist-scholar Gustav Niebuhr pointed out that the statement put the SBC to the right of the American Catholic bishops, who four years earlier had issued a statement in support of "mutual submission" of husbands and wives. Three days later another *Times* writer outlined Pope John Paul II's 1988 apostolic letter *Mulieris Dignitatum (On the Dignity of Women)*, which also laid out mutual submission as the proper understanding of Ephesians 5.[41] Al Mohler appeared on *Larry King Live*, the popular prime-time interview show on CNN. There, he sat in a roundtable discussion with Christian Right leader Jerry Falwell, Patricia Ireland of the National Organization of Women, and well-known television preacher Robert Schuller of Southern California's Crystal Cathedral. King asked Mohler why Southern Baptists wanted to make such a statement at this time in history. Mohler responded, "No one really thought it needed to be said until recently. . . . Southern Baptists are responding to what we see as a real crisis in the culture over the family."[42]

The next day, Mohler squared off with Molly Marshall on CBS's *Saturday Morning*. Marshall, who later became president of the American Baptist–affiliated Central Baptist Theological Seminary in Kansas, had been driven from Southern Seminary shortly after Mohler arrived, in part because of her insistence on gender-inclusive language in Scripture. Mohler reiterated the cultural consensus that Southern Baptists felt called to repudiate. Wifely submission had been the norm for two thousand years, he argued, but now came under attack. Similarly, Land said in an interview, "This is not issued in a vacuum. This is issued in a situation where people are trying to define homosexuals as a family, lesbians as a family, people living [together] out of wedlock as a family. . . . We reject this."[43] Dorothy Patterson likewise endorsed this interpretation.

In 2000, the SBC revised the BFMS again, retaining the 1998 submission statement and adding a clause stipulating that only men should serve as pastors. This move raised the 1984 resolution against ordination of women to the level of confessional doctrine. The prohibition on women pastors was so uncontroversial that no one challenged it during the floor debate.[44]

The submission statement symbolized the larger SBC conservative view that Christians today live in a hostile culture, a Babylon, where they must actively dissent from the mainstream. As such, Southern Baptists seek to recapture the outsider status of their forebears in the seventeenth and eighteenth centuries. Back then Baptists played the role of free-church dissenters in a culture dominated by other Protestants. Today, SBC conservatives position themselves as dissenters against a secular culture.

Nowhere has this transition to an intentional outsider status appeared more conspicuously than in the 2013 appointment of Russell Moore to replace Richard Land as the head of the SBC's Ethics and Religious Liberty Commission. Moore represents a generation of Southern Baptists who came of age after the advent of the Moral Majority and who are sensitive to perceived political compromises of an earlier generation. Moore had served as dean of the School of Theology at Albert Mohler's Southern Seminary, and though he was always complimentary of his predecessor at the Ethics and Religious Liberty Commission, Land, he also signaled that Baptists had become too comfortable with their access to political power, especially the religious Right and the Republican Party.

"We can no longer pretend that we are a moral majority in this country," Moore said in his inaugural speech at the Ethics and Religious Liberty Commission. "We are a prophetic minority." He acknowledged that America was important to American Christians, but said that "the end goal of the gospel is not a Christian America. The end goal of the gospel is redeemed from every tribe and tongue and nation and language in a New Jerusalem." He called on Baptists to self-consciously return to the mode of their colonial forebears, prophetically witnessing to gospel truth, and not expecting support or applause from the surrounding culture. But, of course, Moore remains one of the most high-profile, media-savvy representatives of the largest Protestant denomination in America, placing limits on the extent of his, or the SBC's, standing as outsiders.[45]

IN CONTRAST TO their stance on gender, on the issue of race, Southern Baptists are happy to join a cultural mainstream that touts diversity. Of all Baptist groups, the Southern Baptist Convention most closely approximates an integrated denomination, albeit with very few integrated congregations. In 1986, church growth scholar C. Peter Wagner called the SBC America's "most ethnically diverse denomination."[46] Wagner referred primarily to Southern Baptist mission congregations among ethnic groups in large urban centers. On a given Sunday, he pointed out, SBC worship services were conducted in eighty-seven different languages in forty-six hundred "language-culture congregations." SBC missions to immigrant communities in urban centers and to Hispanics in the Southwest have gone hand in hand with outreach to African Americans. Building on the resolution "On Racial Reconciliation" (1995), the SBC's North American Mission Board has engaged in a concerted effort to recruit black preachers and plant SBC churches in urban areas with large African American populations. Franklin Avenue Baptist Church in New Orleans is perhaps the most significant example of this effort.

Franklin Avenue Baptist thrived as an all-white downtown church until white flight to the suburbs began in the 1970s. As the last of the white members left the church, they donated the buildings to the Baptist Association of Greater New Orleans. The church subsequently became a mission of the Gentilly Baptist Church with aid from the SBC Home Mission Board (now called the North American Mission Board). In 1986, the congrega- tion of roughly sixty members called Fred Luter as its pastor. Luter started his career in 1977 as a street preacher in the city's Lower Ninth Ward. He eventually moved onto the staff of the Greater Liberty Baptist Church, a congregation affiliated with the National Baptist Convention USA, Inc. He had virtually no experience with Southern Baptists before being called to Franklin Avenue. Under Luter's leadership, by 2005 Franklin Avenue Baptist had become the largest Southern Baptist church in Louisiana, with more than seven thousand members. That year, Hurricane Katrina flooded the church and dispersed many of its members to other cities. Luter relo- cated temporarily in Birmingham, Alabama, and for the next three years traveled to Franklin Avenue diaspora congregations in New Orleans, Baton Rouge, and Houston. The congregation moved back into its renovated Franklin Avenue home in 2008 but views itself today as one church in three cities. Luter mans the pulpit in New Orleans, Sam Young in Houston, and Manuel Pigee in Baton Rouge. In 2013, Luter became the first black president of the Southern Baptist Convention, an event that Danny Akin, the president of Southeastern Baptist Theological Seminary, called "the most significant event to happen in our history."[47] The growth of black and ethnic churches notwithstanding, the Southern Baptist Convention remains overwhelmingly white, as do its positions of greatest institutional power (the SBC president is highly visible but lacks much actual authority). Moreover, as is the case in most denominations, there are few integrated congregations—that is, congregations where the largest racial or ethnic group constitutes less than 80 percent of the membership.[48]

The Southern Baptist Convention remains America's largest Protestant denomination. Even as the denomination's leaders position themselves as dissenters, the SBC in some ways still represents the dominant ethos of large portions of the American South and Midwest. Ironically, they often voice their dissent as invited guests in the halls of Congress, on network television programs, or in op-eds in major newspapers and magazines. They drift from the center to the margins and back again, depending on the issue.

14

Conclusion

BEING BOTH INSIDERS and outsiders makes Baptists much like other religious denominations in America. Some scholars and cultural commentators have argued that by the end of the twentieth century nearly all groups in America experience minority status some of the time and therefore fear discrimination. In America's so-called culture wars, religious and secular liberals fear a Christian Right takeover, while conservative Christians claim discrimination at the hands of an elite dominated by secular humanists. Most Americans reside in between the warring factions and often feel their voices are crowded out of the discussion by the culture warriors.[1] Baptists are no less ambivalent than others about their position in the culture. But in early America there was no doubt where Baptists stood. They were the outlaws, double outsiders to the established and dominant churches: (1) they did not baptize infants, and (2) they took no money from the state. Their outsider status provided Baptists a common identity they would never have again.

Baptists caught the revivalist fervor of the First Great Awakening and were well positioned to move aggressively into the religious free market created by the American Revolution and the First Amendment. As the churches that formerly enjoyed state support struggled to adjust, Baptists thrived. They joined Methodists, Presbyterians, and other smaller denominations in evangelizing the frontier and converting the South. By the 1840s, near the end of the Second Great Awakening, Baptists were a major Protestant force. But attempts to unify around evangelism and missions faltered. No longer held together by their outsider status, Baptists found it much more difficult to paper over social and theological differences. Moreover, as is usually the case, the more dominant

Baptists became, the more pressure they experienced to conform to the larger culture. Most white Baptists dropped antislavery impulses, adopted the racial norms of the day, and then internalized the national debate over slavery. The disagreement over slavery led to division, producing the two major white Baptist denominations, which after the Civil War gave rise to the need for black Baptist denominations. Baptists entered the twentieth century completely segregated by race, much like the larger American culture and nearly every other Protestant denomination. Like other Protestants, white Baptists experienced major theological schism in the fundamentalist-modernist controversy of the Northern Baptist Convention in the 1920s and the Southern Baptist Controversy of 1980s. Meanwhile, black Baptists unified—then fractured—over a variety of issues. But amid all the fractious infighting, Baptists continued to grow.

Baptists entered the twenty-first century with almost 34 million self-identified adherents. A decade later, that number had grown to more than 36 million, 17.2 percent of the US population. Only the Catholic Church, with roughly 57 million members, is larger.[2]

But what makes a Baptist a Baptist? As we have seen in this book, Baptists have been unified on very little throughout their history. In the colonial period, when they shared a common experience as dissenting outsiders, Baptists still divided along Calvinist and Arminian lines. As Baptists grew in numbers in the nineteenth century, they experienced increased diversity not only in theology but also in positions on slavery and approaches to missions. By the twentieth century, they ranged across the theological and social spectrum from fundamentalist to liberal, sectarian to denominational, insider to outsider, and everything in between. Baptists fought against each other in denominational civil wars and in the real Civil War. They divided racially and apologized for it. They responded to the civil rights movement by becoming Ku Klux Klan terrorists and by becoming advocates for racial justice and equality. Today they appear on all sides and no side of America's ferocious culture wars. As historian Mark Noll has said, Baptists offer attitudes and dispositions but not much in the way of distinctive theological, intellectual, or academic positions.[3] One might add, not much in the way of social or cultural positions either. There is no Baptist social thought that rivals that of Catholics or Baptist political theory that rivals Reformed philosophy. Catholic and Reformed thinkers each have reasonably coherent bases of authority and tradition for thinking about politics, social theory, and philosophy. Baptists do not. As is often said, there is no Baptist Church, only Baptist churches. Similarly, there is no Baptist theology, only Baptist theologies. The liberal theology of Harry Emerson Fosdick, the moderate theology of Augustus H. Strong, the womanist theology of Nannie Helen Burroughs, the experiential theology of E. Y. Mullins, the social theology of Helen Montgomery, the evangelical theology of Carl F. H. Henry, the fundamentalist theology of William Bell Riley, and the Calvinist theology of John Piper all count as Baptist.

For this reason, Baptists rarely agree among themselves about what makes them distinct. Some point to a doctrine of soul freedom that has led to an emphasis on religious liberty. And Baptists have indeed championed religious liberty, always for themselves and often for everyone else. But they cannot always agree on what religious liberty is. Baptists have also championed separation of church and state, but in diverse ways. Nearly all Baptists in the colonial and early national periods of American history advocated the disestablishment of religion—that is, an end to tax support for churches. Once disestablishment occurred, however, Baptists could be found on all sides of nearly every church-state debate in history.

Using issues such as soul freedom, soul competency, religious liberty, and separation of church and state as distinctive markers for Baptists leads to another problem: such matters have never been near the top of the Baptist agenda. In denominational confessions, individual freedom is hardly mentioned. To take the three most prominent Baptist confessions in American history as examples, in the Philadelphia Confession of 1742 the statement "Of Christian Liberty and Liberty of Conscience" appears as chapter 21; in the New Hampshire Confession of 1833, "Of Civil Government" appears as section 16; while in the SBC's Baptist Faith and Message Statement—first written in 1925 and revised in 1963, 1998, and 2000—the "Religious Liberty" section is seventeenth. All three of these historic Baptist confessions begin with statements on Scripture followed by sections on God, the Trinity, the Holy Spirit, man, creation, and other doctrinal issues. Given that baptism is paired with the Lord's Supper in all three confessions and listed twenty-ninth in the Philadelphia Confession, fourteenth in the New Hampshire, and seventh in the Baptist Faith and Message, one may not want to put too much emphasis on the order in which doctrinal issues appear. Still, if one were to look at these confessions to discover what is important to Baptists, it would be easy to conclude that they are first and foremost obsessed with orthodoxy. Generally, in their confessions, Baptists have not attempted to clarify what makes them distinct among Christians. Rather, their confessions trumpet to the world that Baptists are orthodox Christians.[4] But there are exceptions even to this doctrinal emphasis. Northern Baptist liberals and Southern Baptist moderates have resisted fiercely efforts to define doctrine for their respective conventions.

Historically, the Bible has been supremely important for Baptists. Ironically, those Northern Baptist liberals who resisted the New Hampshire Confession in the 1920s used the Bible to do so, even though their ultimate aim was to leave doctrine undefined. Moreover, the major Baptist confessions all start with sections on the Bible, as does the London Confession that predated them. The Bible is discussed even ahead of the doctrine of God, the Trinity, or salvation. Most Baptists in history believe that because the Bible is the sole authority on theological matters, they must get straight what they believe about the Bible before proceeding to its interpretation. Once the interpretation process begins, all bets are off. Baptists fight about the Bible more than anything else. They disagree over interpretations of the Bible and also divide over its inerrancy. Some argue that the Bible is inerrant in all matters including history and science, others say just in theology and Christian practice, while others charge that inerrancy statements are creeds. And everyone knows Baptists are averse to creeds, except when they are not.

To argue that Baptists are noncreedal, one must make a distinction between a creed and a confession, because the theological landscape is littered with Baptist confessions. In addition to the three major confessions cited earlier, there are a myriad of associational confessions, denominational confessions, and even congregational confessions. Baptist historian William Lumpkin's classic *Baptist Confessions of Faith* lists more than thirty confessions worldwide. In his 1959 foreword, he acknowledged there were many other confessions not in his volume that were "intended for local use [and] are interesting but are not of major significance."[5] Noncreedal Baptists hold that a creed imposes orthodoxy, while a confession is a voluntary agreement about what a congregation or denomination believes. Such a distinction breaks down outside of Baptist circles, of course. The Westminster Confession of Faith, for example, was for a short time imposed by the English Parliament and has been used to enforce orthodoxy in a handful of Reformed denominations, even though it is by name a "confession." Others maintain that any distinction between a creed and a confession exists purely in the eye of the beholder. Meanwhile, a few Baptist congregations accept confessions and creeds, occasionally reciting the Nicene Creed or the Apostles' Creed at baptisms. Even the

Baptist World Alliance has from time to time included recitation of the Apostles' Creed in worship.

In all of this, Baptists are notorious for two things—evangelism and schism. White Baptists usually divide over theology, black Baptists over social issues, and both over missions strategy and control of publishing houses, denominational machinery, and schools. Nearly all agree they should take the gospel to a lost world, but they have disagreed on what that gospel should look like. The vast majority of Baptists have emphasized individual soul winning, but beginning in the early twentieth century, liberal Baptists stressed the Social Gospel instead. Moreover, in the anti-mission controversy of the nineteenth century, Primitive Baptists rejected any institution beyond the local congregation as the proper vehicle for spreading the message of individual salvation.

It seems the time is long past when we can make broad claims about what makes Baptists distinct. Perhaps a good rule of thumb is that we place the modifiers "most" or "some" before "Baptist" anytime we want to make a general claim. So we might say, most Baptists are Bible-only, some are anticreedal, most are inerrantists, some are Calvinist, most tout religious liberty, some espouse strict separation of church and state, most support missions and evangelism, some are liberal, most are evangelical, and so forth.

In the end, there still may be three features that mark all Baptists throughout history. First, baptism. By definition, Baptists advocate baptism for believers and deny that any sort of baptism of infants would ever suffice. Second, almost all Baptists advocate the independence of the local congregation to one degree or another. Whether completely independent and unaffiliated with other congregations, voluntarily associated with other Baptists in a society, or bound together in a relatively centralized convention, Baptists claim that their congregations are independent. If they disagree with the body they are affiliated with, Baptist congregations can walk away and in most cases take their property with them.[6] There are other groups in the free church tradition that hold those two distinctives as fiercely as Baptists—to cite but one example, the Churches of Christ, with whom frontier Baptists battled like rival cousins. Some Anabaptist Mennonite groups also fight as fiercely for baptism and congregational independence as do Baptists. And so there needs to be a third marker that makes Baptists unique, and that is simply the willingness to call oneself a Baptist. Historically, a Baptist church is a local body of baptized believers who come together and call themselves Baptists. Beyond that, they can be

Calvinist or Arminian, fundamentalist or liberal, liturgical or nonliturgical, premillennial or postmillennial, church-state separationist or accommodationist, individualist or communitarian, and a million other things. As we have seen in this book, they can also be insiders or outsiders in American culture, and often both simultaneously. If we had to pick one characteristic attitude, we might say that "Baptists have a record of not kowtowing to authority," even when they are the authority.[7]

In the midst of America's churning culture wars, such an attitude comes in handy. Baptist culture warriors operate as outsider/dissenters who refuse to submit to a dominant secular culture. Other Baptists refuse to be co-opted into culture wars that might divert their attention from meeting together in Christian community, raising their children in the ways of God, and evangelizing their neighbors.

To return to where we started, today almost every group in America can claim outsider, minority status on some issue. Baptists were merely the first Americans to experience this. In an increasingly pluralistic nation, no group, secular or religious, constitutes the center. All groups exist on the periphery of culture and gravitate toward the center only temporarily as they align and realign with others on certain issues. Even when they become insiders, Baptists still carry in their spiritual DNA a fierce outsider resistance. With this insider-outsider history, they are well positioned to thrive in the future. For almost any cultural encounter or theological controversy, Baptist history provides good examples for how to proceed—and how not to.

Notes

PREFACE

1. Christian Smith, *American Evangelicalism: Embattled and Thriving* (Chicago: University of Chicago Press, 1998), 121.

CHAPTER 1

1. John Clarke, *Ill Newes from New England* (London, 1652), in John Clarke, *Colonial Baptists: Massachusetts and Rhode Island* (New York: Arno Press, 1980), 50–51.
2. Everett Ferguson, *Baptism in the Early Church: History, Theology, and Liturgy in the First Five Centuries* (Grand Rapids, Mich.: Eerdmans, 2009), 198. Thanks to Brian Brewer of Truett Theological Seminary for his help on baptism in the early church.
3. Ferguson, *Baptism in the Early Church*, 363–366.
4. Ferguson, *Baptism in the Early Church*, 378–379.
5. Ferguson, *Baptism in the Early Church*, 807, 857.
6. Norman Cohn, *The Pursuit of the Millennium: Revolutionary Millenarians and Mystical Anarchists of the Middle Ages*, rev. ed. (New York: Oxford University Press, 1970), 255–280.
7. Samuel Fisher, *Christianismus redivivus* (London, 1655), 568.
8. Menno Simons, *Reply to Gellius Faber* (1554), in J. C. Wenger, ed., *The Complete Writings of Menno Simons* (Scottdale, Pa.: Herald Press, 1986), 668; William R. Estep, *The Anabaptist Story*, rev. ed. (Grand Rapids, Mich.: Eerdmans, 1975), 116.
9. David Bebbington, *Baptists Through the Centuries: A History of a Global People* (Waco, Texas: Baylor University Press, 2010), 36.

10. Stephen Wright, *The Early English Baptists, 1603–1649* (Rochester, N.Y.: Boydell Press, 2006), 13.

11. James Robert Coggins, *John Smyth's Congregation: English Separatism, Mennonite Influence, and the Elect Nation* (Scottdale, Pa.: Herald Press 1991), 56–60.

12. John Smyth, *The Character of the Beast* (1609), in W. T. Whitley, ed., *The Works of John Smyth* (Cambridge: Cambridge University Press, 1915), 2:567.

13. Thomas Helwys, *A Short Declaration of the Mystery of Iniquity* (London, 1612), inscription from scanned copy in Bodleian Library, Early English Books online.

14. Nathaniel Morton, *New England's Memorial* (Boston: Congregational Board of Publication, 1855), 102.

15. Roger Williams, *Mr. Cotton's Letter Lately Printed, Examined, and Answered* (London, 1644), 5.

16. *The Charter Granted by His Majesty King Charles the Second, to the Colony of Rhode-Island* (Boston: John Allen, 1719), 2; Edmund S. Morgan, *Roger Williams: The Church and the State* (New York: Harcourt, Brace and World, 1967), 88–90, 102–103.

17. James Kendall Hosmer, ed., *Winthrop's Journal* (New York: C. Scribner's Sons, 1908), 1:286.

18. Hosmer, *Winthrop's Journal*, 1:297.

19. Hosmer, *Winthrop's Journal*, 1:309; Roger Williams to John Winthrop, Jr., December 10, 1649, in Roger Williams, *The Complete Writings of Roger Williams* (New York: Russell and Russell, 1963), 6:188.

20. Clarke, *Ill Newes*, 23–24; Sydney V. James, *John Clarke and His Legacies: Religion and Law in Colonial Rhode Island, 1638–1750*, ed. Theodore Dwight Bozeman (University Park, Pa.: Pennsylvania State University Press, 1999), 21.

21. Clarke, *Ill Newes*, 81; James, *John Clarke*, 30–31.

22. Clarke, *Ill Newes*, 96; James, *John Clarke*, 37.

23. Hosmer, *Winthrop's Journal*, 2:177; Edwin S. Gaustad, *Baptist Piety: The Last Will and Testament of Obadiah Holmes* (Grand Rapids, Mich.: Christian University Press, 1978), 16.

24. Thomas Shepard, "To the Reader," in George Phillips, *A Reply to a Confutation of Some Grounds for Infant Baptisme* (London, 1645), iii, viii–ix.

25. Alonzo Lewis and James R. Newhall, *History of Lynn, Essex County, Massachusetts* (Boston: John L. Shorey, 1865), 209, 219; William G. McLoughlin, *New England Dissent, 1630–1833: The Baptists and the Separation of Church and State* (Cambridge, Mass.: Harvard University Press, 1971), 1:18–19.

26. Williams to Winthrop, Jr., December 10, 1649, in Williams, *Complete Writings*, 6:188.

27. Clarke, *Ill Newes*, 46; Gaustad, *Baptist Piety*, 17–21.

28. Clarke, *Ill Newes*, 28–30.

29. Clarke, *Ill Newes*, 31–32.

30. Clarke, *Ill Newes*, 32–33; James, *John Clarke*, 47.

31. Roger Williams to John Endicott, August 1651, in Williams, *Complete Writings*, 6:225; Gaustad, *Baptist Piety*, 33.

32. Jeremiah Chaplin, *Life of Henry Dunster, First President of Boston College* (Boston: J. R. Osgood, 1872), 122; McLoughlin, *New England Dissent*, 1:21–22.

33. McLoughlin, *New England Dissent*, 1:22.

34. Nathan E. Wood, *The History of the First Baptist Church of Boston* (Boston: American Baptist Publication Society, 1899), 42–43; McLoughlin, *New England Dissent*, 1:51–55.

35. William G. McLoughlin and Martha Whiting Davidson, eds., "The Baptist Debate of April 14–15, 1668," in *Colonial Baptists*, 117; McLoughlin, *New England Dissent*, 1:55–56 n. 13.

36. Wood, *First Baptist Church*, 56.

37. Wood, *First Baptist Church*, 65–66.

38. Wood, *First Baptist Church*, 67; Carla Gardina Pestana, *Quakers and Baptists in Colonial Massachusetts* (New York: Cambridge University Press, 1991), 54–55.

39. Isaac Backus, *A History of New England with Particular Reference to the Denomination of Christians Called Baptists*, ed. David Weston, 2nd ed. (Newton, Mass.: Backus Historical Society, 1871), 1:300.

40. McLoughlin and Davidson, "Baptist Debate," 98–100, 116.

41. Wood, *First Baptist Church*, 85–86; Pestana, *Quakers and Baptists*, 57–58.

42. Pestana, *Quakers and Baptists*, 58–59; McLoughlin, *New England Dissent*, 1:73–74.

43. McLoughlin, *New England Dissent*, 1:74–75.

CHAPTER 2

1. Isaac Backus, *A History of New England with Particular Reference to the Denomination of Christians Called Baptists* ed. David Weston, 2nd ed. (Newton, Mass.: Backus Historical Society, 1871), 2:421; Carla Gardina Pestana, *Quakers and Baptists in Colonial Massachusetts* (New York: Cambridge University Press, 1991), 167–171.

2. Backus, *History of New England*, 1: 404.

3. Morgan Edwards, *Materials towards a History of the American Baptists* (Philadelphia, 1770), 9–10; David Spencer, *The Early Baptists of Philadelphia* (Philadelphia: W. Syckelmoore, 1877), 22–25.

4. Jon Butler, *Awash in a Sea of Faith: Christianizing the American People* (Cambridge, Mass.: Harvard University Press, 1990), 121.

5. Butler, *Awash in a Sea of Faith*, 122.

6. Nathaniel Jenkins to John Drake, December 26, 1730, in C. Edwin Barrows, ed., *The Diary of John Comer* (Philadelphia, 1892), 117–118; David Benedict, *A General History of the Baptist Denomination in America* (Boston: Lincoln and Edmands, 1813), 1: 566.

7. Thomas S. Kidd, *The Protestant Interest: New England after Puritanism* (New Haven, Conn.: Yale University Press, 2004), 2–12.

8. Barrows, *Diary of John Comer*, 27, 32.

9. Barrows, *Diary of John Comer*, 34.

10. Barrows, *Diary of John Comer*, 8, 57.

11. Barrows, *Diary of John Comer*, 57.

12. *George Whitefield's Journals* (Carlisle, Pa.: Banner of Truth Trust, 1960), 419.

13. Norman H. Maring, *Baptists in New Jersey: A Study in Transition* (Valley Forge, Pa.: Judson Press, 1964), 51–52.

14. George Whitefield, *A Continuation of the Reverend Mr. Whitefield's Journal* (Philadelphia: B. Franklin, 1740), 59–60; Janet Moore Lindman, *Bodies of Belief: Baptist Community in Early America* (Philadelphia: University of Pennsylvania Press, 2008), 27.

15. *Pennsylvania Gazette*, postscript, July 24, 1740.

16. *Pennsylvania Gazette*, postscript, July 24, 1740, August 14, 1740; A. D. Gillette, ed., *Minutes of the Philadelphia Baptist Association, 1707 to 1807* (1851; reprint, Springfield, Mo.: Particular Baptist Press, 2002), 42.

17. *George Whitefield's Journals*, 440–441; Leah Townsend, *South Carolina Baptists, 1670–1805* (Florence, S.C.: Florence Print. Co.., 1935), 18.

18. *George Whitefield's Journals*, 450.

19. Morgan Edwards, *Materials towards a History of the Baptists*, ed. Eve B. Weeks and Mary B. Warren (Danielsville, Ga.: Heritage Papers, 1984), 2:127–128.

20. Richard Furman, *Rewards of Grace Conferred on Christ's Faithful People* (Charleston, S.C.: J. M'Iver, 1796), 21; Oliver Hart, "Extracts from the Diary of Oliver Hart," *Charleston Year Book* (1896), 378.

21. Furman, *Rewards of Grace*, 22.

22. Hart, "Diary," 379.

23. Oliver Hart, diary, August 4, 1754, South Carolina Baptist Historical Society, Furman University.

24. Hart, diary (Furman), August 26, 1754.

25. *Boston Weekly Post-Boy*, February 21, 1743; C. C. Goen, *Revivalism and Separatism in New England, 1740–1800: Strict Congregationalists and Separate Baptists in the Great Awakening*, rev. ed. (Middletown, Conn.: Wesleyan University Press, 1987), 212.

26. William G. McLoughlin, ed., *The Diary of Isaac Backus* (Providence, R.I.: Brown University Press, 1979), 3:1523–1524.

27. McLoughlin, *Diary of Isaac Backus*, 3:1525–1526.

28. J. M. Bumsted, "Revivalism and Separatism in New England: The First Society of Norwich, Connecticut, as a Case Study," *William and Mary Quarterly*, 3rd ser., 24 (October 1967): 600–601.

29. Frederic Denison, *Notes of the Baptists, and Their Principles, in Norwich, Conn.* (Norwich, Conn.: Manning, Printer., 1857), 21.

30. McLoughlin, *Diary of Isaac Backus*, 3:1528.

31. McLoughlin, *Diary of Isaac Backus*, 1:12.

32. McLoughlin, *Diary of Isaac Backus*, 3:1530.

33. McLoughlin, *Diary of Isaac Backus*, 1:68.

34. McLoughlin, *Diary of Isaac Backus*, 1:71–72, 75.

35. McLoughlin, *Diary of Isaac Backus*, 1:148.

36. Goen, *Revivalism and Separatism*, 262–264.

37. McLoughlin, *Diary of Isaac Backus*, 1:399, 3:1593–1594.

38. Goen, *Revivalism and Separatism*, 224–225.

39. Elizabeth Backus to Isaac Backus, November 4, 1752, in Backus, *History of New England*, 2:98–99.

40. Backus, *History of New England*, 2:94–95.

41. Frederic Denison, *Westerly (Rhode Island) and Its Witnesses* (Providence, R.I.: J. A. and R. A. Reid, 1878), 90; Goen, *Revivalism and Separatism*, 226–227.

42. Richard J. Hooker, ed., *The Carolina Backcountry on the Eve of the Revolution: The Journal and Other Writings of Charles Woodmason, Anglican Itinerant* (Chapel Hill, N.C.: University of North Carolina Press, 1953), 103.

43. Hooker, *Charles Woodmason*, 45.

44. Elder John Sparks, *The Roots of Appalachian Christianity: The Life and Legacy of Elder Shubal Stearns* (Lexington, Ky.: University Press of Kentucky, 2001), 29–30.

45. Robert Baylor Semple, *A History of the Rise and Progress of the Baptists in Virginia* (Richmond, Va., 1894), 13; Sparks, *Shubal Stearns*, 48–55.

46. Benedict, *General History*, 2: 49. Some of these new congregations were probably more like branch meetings or house churches than fully independent congregations.

47. Morgan Edwards, *Materials towards a History of the Baptists* (reprint, Danielsville, Ga., 1984), 93.

48. Benedict, *General History*, 2: 106-108.

49. Thomas S. Kidd, "'Do the Holy Scriptures Countenance Such Wild Disorder?': Baptist Growth in the Eighteenth-Century American South," in Ian M. Randall and Anthony R. Cross, eds., *Baptists and Mission: Papers from the Fourth International Conference on Baptist Studies* (Milton Keynes, England: Paternoster, 2007), 124; John Asplund, *The Universal Register of the Baptist Denomination in North America* (Boston: John W. Folsom, 1794), 6.

50. George W. Paschal, *History of North Carolina Baptists* (Raleigh, N.C.: North Carolina Baptist State Convention, 1930), 1:297.

CHAPTER 3

1. James Manning to John Ryland, November 13, 1776, in Reuben Aldridge Guild, *Life, Times, and Correspondence of James Manning* (Boston: Gould and Lincoln, 1864), 244.

2. *Minutes of the Proceedings of the Warren Association* (Boston, 1776), 7.

3. John David Broome, ed., *The Life, Ministry, and Journals of Hezekiah Smith* (Springfield, Mo.: Particular Baptist Press, 2004), 439–440.

4. Samuel Stillman, *Good News from a Far Country* (Boston, 1766), 7, 31–34.

5. "I cannot see" quote in Thomas Green to Ebenezer Hinds, September 1, 1766, quoted in C. C. Goen, *Revivalism and Separatism in New England, 1740–1800: Strict Congregationalists and Separate Baptists in the Great Awakening*, rev. ed. (Middletown, Conn.: Wesleyan University Press, 1987), 276; Backus quoted in Thomas S. Kidd, "Becoming Important in the Eye of Civil Powers": New Light Baptists, Cultural Respectability, and the Founding of the College of Rhode Island," in *The Scholarly Vocation and the Baptist Academy : Essays on the Future of Baptist Higher Education*, Roger Ward and David P. Gushee, eds. (Macon, Ga., Mercer University Press, 2008), 59.

6. Warren Association, *The Sentiments and Plan of the Warren Association* (Germantown, Pa., 1769), 3.

7. *Newport Mercury*, October 1, 1764; Ann Fairfax Withington, *Toward a More Perfect Union: Virtue and the Formation of American Republics* (New York: Oxford University Press, 1991), 98.

8. Town of Ashfield quoted in William G. McLoughlin, *New England Dissent, 1630–1833: The Baptists and the Separation of Church and State* (Cambridge, Mass.: Harvard University Press, 1971), 1:539; Isaac Backus, *A History of New England with Particular Reference to the Denomination of Christians Called Baptists*, ed. David Weston, 2nd ed. (Newton, Mass.: Backus Historical Society, 1871), 2:153–159; Ashfield pastor quoted in Preserved Smith, "Chronicles of a New England Family," *New England Quarterly* 9 (September 1936): 424.

9. David Benedict, *A General History of the Baptist Denomination* (Boston: Lincoln and Edmands, 1813): 2:332, 336–337.

10. Thomas S. Kidd, *The Great Awakening: The Roots of Evangelical Christianity in Colonial America* (New Haven, Conn.: Yale University Press, 2007), 248.

11. John Taylor, "Extracts from the History of Ten Baptist Churches," in William Warren Sweet, ed., *Religion on the American Frontier: The Baptists, 1783–1830* (New York: Henry Holt, 1931), 115.

12. [Isaac Backus], *An Account of the Remarkable Recovery of Mrs. Mary Read* (Providence, R.I., 1769?), 1; Thomas S. Kidd, "The Healing of Mercy Wheeler: Illness and Miracles among Early American Evangelicals," *William and Mary Quarterly*, 3rd ser., 63 (January 2006): 168.

13. John Rippon, "An Account of the Life of Mr. David George," in *Baptist Annual Register for 1790, 1791, 1792, and Part of 1793* (London, 1793), 473–476.

14. Terry Wolever, ed., *The Life, Journal and Works of David Jones, 1736–1820* (Springfield, Mo.: Particular Baptist Press, 2007), 212, 236.

15. Wolever, *David Jones*, 236–238.

16. John M. Bumsted and Charles E. Clark, "New England's Tom Paine: John Allen and the Spirit of Liberty," *William and Mary Quarterly*, 3rd ser., 21 (October 1964): 562–565.

17. John Allen, *An Oration upon the Beauties of Liberty* (New London, 1773), in Ellis Sandoz, ed., *Political Sermons of the American Founding Era, 1730–1805*, 2nd ed. (Indianapolis, Ind.: Liberty Fund, 1998), 1:307.

18. Isaac Backus, *An Appeal to the Public for Religious Liberty* (Boston, 1773), in Sandoz, *Political Sermons*, 1:362.

19. William G. McLoughlin, ed., *The Diary of Isaac Backus* (Providence, R.I.: Brown University Press, 1979), 2:916–917.

20. Franklin Bowditch Dexter, ed., *The Literary Diary of Ezra Stiles* (New York: C. Scribner's Sons, 1901), 1:491.

21. Dexter, *Ezra Stiles*, 2:23.

22. Oliver Hart, diary transcription, August 10–11, 1775, South Caroliniana Library, University of South Carolina, Columbia, South Carolina; Kidd, *Great Awakening*, 292–293.

23. Dexter, *Ezra Stiles*, 2:29.

24. Miles quoted in Marjoleine Kars, *Breaking Loose Together: The Regulator Rebellion in Pre-Revolutionary North Carolina* (Chapel Hill, N.C.: University of North Carolina Press, 2002), 213–214.

25. Richard Furman, "An Address to the Residents between the Broad and Saluda Rivers Concerning the American War for Independence, November, 1775," in James A. Rogers, *Richard Furman: Life and Legacy* (Macon, Ga.: Mercer University Press, 2001), 271; also 30.

26. Rogers, *Richard Furman*, 40–42.

27. "Journal of Convention, August 16, 1775," in Charles F. James, ed., *Documentary History of the Struggle for Religious Liberty in Virginia* (Lynchburg, Va.: J. P. Bell, 1900), 52; "Minutes of the Philadelphia Baptist Association" (1776), in A. D. Gillette, ed., *Minutes of the Philadelphia Baptist Association, 1707 to 1807* (1851; reprint, Springfield, Mo.: Particular Baptist Press, 2002), 155.

28. Leah Townsend, *South Carolina Baptists, 1670–1805* (Florence, S.C.: Florence Print. Co.., 1935), 27; on the Shrewsbury church, S. Scott Rohrer, *Wandering Souls: Protestant Migrations in America, 1630–1865* (Chapel Hill, N.C.: University of North Carolina Press, 2010), 179–180.

29. Benedict, *General History*, 1:551–552.

30. Biel Ledoyt to Isaac Backus, June 13, 1780, in Leigh Johnsen, ed. *The Papers of Isaac Backus* (Ann Arbor, Mich.: UMI, 2003); Backus, *History of New England*, 2:272 n. 1.

31. Alfred F. Young, *Masquerade: The Life and Times of Deborah Sampson, Continental Soldier* (New York: Alfred A. Knopf, 2004), 72–80.

32. Young, *Masquerade*, 86–87.

33. Kidd, *Great Awakening*, 315.

34. John Buzzell, *The Life of Elder Benjamin Randal* (Limerick, Maine: Hobbs, Woodman, 1827), 87–89.

35. Backus, *History of New England*, 264–265.

36. Broome, *Hezekiah Smith*, 452–454.

37. Reuben A. Guild, *Chaplain Smith and the Baptists* (Philadelphia: American Baptist Publication Society, 1885), 226–230.

38. Frederick Cook, ed., *Journals of the Military Expedition of Major General John Sullivan* (Auburn, N.Y.: Knapp, Peck and Thomson, 1887), 250, 252.

39. Warren Association, *Minutes of the Warren Association* (Boston[?], 1784), 6–7.

CHAPTER 4

1. *The Minutes of the Baptist Association. Held at Danbury September 1790* (New York, 1790), 8.

2. "Letter from Danbury Baptist Association to Thomas Jefferson (October 7, 1801)," in Daniel L. Dreisbach and Mark David Hall, eds., *The Sacred Rights of Conscience: Selected Readings on Religious Liberty and Church-State Relations in the American Founding* (Indianapolis, Ind.: Liberty Fund, 2009), 526.

3. "Letter from Thomas Jefferson to Attorney General Levi Lincoln (January 1, 1802)," in Dreisbach and Hall, *Sacred Rights of Conscience*, 527.

4. "Letter from Thomas Jefferson to Messrs. Nehemiah Dodge, Ephraim Robbins, and Stephen S. Nelson (January 1, 1802)," in Dreisbach and Hall, *Sacred Rights of Conscience*, 528.

5. Thomas S. Kidd, *God of Liberty: A Religious History of the American Revolution* (New York: Basic Books, 2010), 4–5; Justice Hugo Black, opinion of the court, *Everson v. Board of Education* (1947), http://www.law.cornell.edu/supct/html/historics/USSC_CR_0330_0001_ZO.html.

6. Steven K. Green, *The Second Disestablishment: Church and State in Nineteenth-Century America* (New York: Oxford University Press, 2010), 83–84.

7. Charles F. James, ed., *Documentary History of the Struggle for Religious Liberty in Virginia* (Lynchburg, Va.: J. P. Bell, 1900), 32.

8. James Madison to William Bradford, January 24, 1774, and James Madison to William Bradford, April 1, 1774, in William T. Hutchinson and William M. E. Rachal, eds., *The Papers of James Madison* (Chicago: University of Chicago Press, 1962), 1: 106, 112.

9. "To the Honourable Peyton Randolph, Esq.," August 14, 1775, in James, *Documentary History*, 218, also 53.

10. "Petition of Baptists of Prince William County," May 19, 1776, in Brent Tarter and Robert L. Scribner, eds., *Revolutionary Virginia: The Road to Independence*, vol. 7, part 1 (Charlottesville, Va.: University Press of Virginia, 1973), 188–189.

11. Article XVI of the Virginia Declaration of Rights, George Mason's Draft, and Final Version, in Dreisbach and Hall, *Sacred Rights of Conscience*, 241.

12. *Virginia Gazette* (Purdie), August 23, 1776; John A. Ragosta, *Wellspring of Liberty: How Virginia's Religious Dissenters Helped Win the American Revolution and Secured Religious Liberty* (New York: Oxford University Press, 2010), 56.

13. "Ten Thousand Name" Petition, October 16, 1776, Early Virginia Religious Petitions, American Memory, Library of Congress, http://memory.loc.gov/cgi-bin/query/P?relpet:2:./temp/~ammem_X6Uc.

14. Kidd, *God of Liberty*, 54; Ragosta, *Wellspring of Liberty*, 56.

15. Ragosta, *Wellspring of Liberty*, 60.

16. "An Observer," *Massachusetts Spy*, May 24, 1776.

17. Isaac Backus, *Government and Liberty Described* (Boston: Powars and Willis, 1778), 16.

18. Backus, *Government and Liberty Described*, 17.

19. *Founders' Constitution*, http://press-pubs.uchicago.edu/founders/print_documents/v1ch156.html.

20. Isaac Backus, *Independent Chronicle*, December 2, 1779, in William G. McLoughlin, ed., *The Diary of Isaac Backus* (Providence, R.I.: Brown University Press, 1979), 3:1612.

21. William G. McLoughlin, *New England Dissent, 1630–1833: The Baptists and the Separation of Church and State* (Cambridge, Mass.: Harvard University Press, 1971), 1:607, 627, 631; John Witte Jr., "'A Most Mild and Equitable Establishment of Religion': John Adams and the Massachusetts Experiment," in James H. Hutson, ed., *Religion and the New Republic: Faith in the Founding of America* (Lanham, Md.: Rowman and Littlefield, 2000), 15.

22. John Leland, "The Virginia Chronicle," in L. F. Greene, ed., *The Writings of the Late Elder John Leland* (New York: G. W. Wood, 1845), 115.

23. William S. Simpson Jr., ed., "The Journal of Henry Toler, Part II: 1783–1786," *Virginia Baptist Register* 32 (1993): 1639, 1643.

24. Simpson, "Henry Toler," 1648–1649.

25. Robert B. Semple, *A History of the Rise and Progress of the Baptists in Virginia* (Richmond, Va.: Published by the author, 1810), 131–132.

26. Semple, *Rise and Progress*, 172.

27. James B. Taylor, *Lives of Virginia Baptist Ministers* (Richmond, Va.: Yale and Wyatt, 1838), 85.

28. George Washington Ranck, *"The Travelling Church": An Account of the Baptist Exodus from Virginia to Kentucky in 1781* (Louisville, Ky., 1910), 8, 11.

29. Ranck, "The Travelling Church," 22; *Minutes of the South Kentucky Baptist Association* (Lexington, Ky., 1801), 2.

30. Semple, *Rise and Progress*, 79; John R. McKivigan and Mitchell Snay, eds., *Religion and the Antebellum Debate over Slavery* (Athens, Ga.: University of Georgia Press, 1998), 39; Lacy K. Ford, *Deliver Us from Evil: The Slavery Question in the Old South* (New York: Oxford University Press, 2009), 151–152.

31. "Minutes of the Elkhorn Baptist Association, Kentucky, 1785–1805," in William Warren Sweet, ed., *Religion on the American Frontier: The Baptists, 1783–1830* (New York: Henry Holt, 1931), 417–418; Philadelphia Baptist Association, *A Confession of Faith*, 6th ed. (Philadelphia: B. Franklin, 1743), 21–22, 101–102; Keith Harper, "'And All the Baptists in Kentucky Took the Name *United Baptists*': The Union of the Separate and Regular Baptists of Kentucky," *Register of the Kentucky Historical Society* 110 (Winter 2012): 18–19.

32. Sweet, *Religion on the American Frontier*, 421, 423, 437.

33. Sweet, *Religion on the American Frontier*, 444, 447, 508; Ford, *Deliver Us from Evil*, 44.

34. John Taylor, *Baptists on the American Frontier: A History of Ten Baptist Churches*, Chester Raymond Young, ed. (Macon, Ga.: Mercer University Press, 1995), 195, 201.

35. Semple, *Rise and Progress*, 70; James Madison to James Monroe, November 27, 1784, in J. C. A. Stagg, ed., *The Papers of James Madison Digital Edition*, http://rotunda.upress.virginia.edu/founders/JSMN.html.

36. James, *Documentary History*, 138; James Madison, *A Memorial and Remonstrance*, *Founders' Constitution*, http://press-pubs.uchicago.edu/founders/documents/amendI_religions43.html; Kidd, *God of Liberty*, 184.

37. Thomas Jefferson, "Bill for Establishing Religious Freedom," at *Founders' Constitution*, http://press-pubs.uchicago.edu/founders/documents/amendI_religions37.html; Semple, *Rise and Progress*, 65.

38. Joseph Spencer to James Madison, February 28, 1788, in *Papers of James Madison Digital Edition*.

39. John Leland, "Objections to the Federal Constitution," in Lyman H. Butterfield, "Elder John Leland, Jeffersonian Itinerant," *Proceedings of the American Antiquarian Society* 62, no. 2 (October 1952): 188; Semple, *Rise and Progress*, 77.

40. *New York Packet*, October 12, 1787, in John P. Kaminski et al., eds., *The Documentary History of the Ratification of the Constitution Digital Edition*, vol. 13, *Commentaries on the Constitution*, no. 1 (Charlottesville, Va.: University of Virginia Press, 2009); McLoughlin, *Diary of Isaac Backus*, February 6, 1788, 3:1221.

41. Joseph Spencer to James Madison, February 28, 1788, in *Papers of James Madison*; Kidd, *God of Liberty*, 223.

42. James Madison to George Eve, January 2, 1789, in *Papers of James Madison*.

43. Kentucky Constitution of 1792, Article 12, sec. 3, http://courts.ky.gov/NR/rdonlyres/7471028C-8BCC-41A2-BA80-02013D4FA550/0/1stKYConstitution.pdf.

CHAPTER 5

1. "Autobiography of Jacob Bower," in William Warren Sweet, ed., *Religion on the American Frontier: The Baptists, 1783–1830* (New York: Henry Holt, 1931), 190.

2. "Jacob Bower," 191.

3. "Jacob Bower," 193–194.

4. "Jacob Bower," 197–198; Frank M. Masters, *A History of Baptists in Kentucky* (Louisville, Ky.: Baptist Historical Society, 1953), 88.

5. "Jacob Bower," 200; Stephen Aron, *How the West Was Lost: The Transformation of Kentucky from Daniel Boone to Henry Clay* (Baltimore, Md.: Johns Hopkins University Press, 1996), 184–186; Walter B. Posey, *The Baptist Church in the Lower Mississippi Valley, 1776–1845* (Lexington, Ky.: University Press of Kentucky, 1957), 155; Mark A. Noll, *America's God: From Jonathan Edwards to Abraham Lincoln* (New York: Oxford University Press, 2002), 181; David W. Bebbington, *Baptists through the Centuries: A History of a Global People* (Waco, Texas: Baylor University Press, 2010), 83–84. Estimates of the number of Baptists are necessarily rough, due to inconsistent or nonexistent records, and due to the fact that in the eighteenth and nineteenth centuries, many more people often attended Baptist churches than necessarily joined them. (In recent decades, the opposite is often true—far more people are listed as members of Baptist churches than regularly attend them.)

6. *Minutes of the Shaftsbury Association* (Bennington, Vt., 1790), 6; Stephen Wright, *History of the Shaftsbury Baptist Association* (Troy, N.Y.: A. G. Johnson, 1853), 3; *Minutes of the Charleston Association* (Charleston, S.C., 1795), 2; *Minutes of the Woodstock Association* (Norwich, Conn., 1796), 8.

7. John Asplund, *Universal Register of the Baptist Denomination* (Boston: John W. Folsom, 1794), 91; Jonathan M. Brewster, *The Centennial Record of Freewill Baptists, 1780–1880* (Dover, N.H., 1881), 16. Asplund separately counted five "Negro" churches, and three Native American, and did not note their theology. Robert Gardner says that Particular or Regular churches constituted 82 percent of all Baptist churches in America in 1790; Gardner, *Baptists of Early America: A Statistical History, 1639–1790* (Atlanta: Georgia Baptist Historical Society, 1983), 61.

8. "Job Seamans," in William B. Sprague, ed., *Annals of the American Pulpit* (New York: R. Carter and Brothers, 1865), 6:149–150; Elder John Peak, *Memoir of Mrs. Esther Peak* (Boston, 1840), in Terry Wolever, ed., *An Anthology of Early Baptists in New Hampshire* (Springfield, Mo.: Particular Baptist Press, 2001), 502–503.

9. "Job Seamans," 6:149–150; Isaac Backus, *A History of New England with Particular Reference to the Denomination of Christians Called Baptists*, ed. David Weston, 2nd ed. (Newton, Mass.: Backus Historical Society, 1871), 2:538; William McLoughlin, "Isaac Backus and the Separation of Church and State in America," *American Historical Review* 73 (June 1968): 1409.

10. Justin A. Smith, *A History of the Baptists in the Western States East of the Mississippi* (Philadelphia: American Baptist Publication Society, 1896), 26–27; Jim Duvall, ed., "Columbia Baptist Church Declaration of Faith

(1790)," accessed June 17, 2013, http://baptisthistoryhomepage.com/columbia-hist.html.

11. Posey, *Lower Mississippi Valley*, 5–7; Jesse L. Boyd, *A Popular History of the Baptists in Mississippi* (Jackson, Miss.: Baptist Press, 1930), 18–27; John G. Jones, *A Concise History of the Introduction of Protestantism into Mississippi and the Southwest* (St. Louis, Mo.: P. M. Pinckard, 1866), 30–48; Randy J. Sparks, *On Jordan's Stormy Banks: Evangelicalism in Mississippi, 1773–1876* (Athens, Ga.: University of Georgia Press, 1994), 8–10.

12. *Biographical and Historical Memoirs of Louisiana* (Chicago: Goodspeed, 1892), 2:144–145; Walter H. Brooks, "The Evolution of the Negro Baptist Church," *Journal of Negro History* 7 (January 1922): 13; Patricia Waak, *My Bones Are Red: A Spiritual Journey with a Triracial People in the Americas* (Macon, Ga.: Mercer University Press, 2005), 55–59. Starting in the 1930s, there was a concerted but ultimately inconclusive effort by some of Willis's descendants to demonstrate that "there was not a drop of Negro blood in [Willis's] veins." Waak, *My Bones Are Red*, 59–67.

13. Eleven years earlier, Valentine Rathbun had briefly converted to the messianic movement of Shakerism, led by Mother Ann Lee, but subsequently became one of the sect's fiercest critics, publishing an anti-Shaker tract that went through seven editions by 1783. "As [Satan] at first deceived the woman," Rathbun observed, "and made use of her to delude the man; so he is playing his old prank over again" through Lee. *Minutes of the Stonington Baptist Association* (New London, Conn., 1791), 5; Valentine Rathbun, *Some Brief Hints, of a Religious Scheme* (Norwich, Conn.: John Trumbull, 1781), 21. See also Erik Seeman, "Sarah Prentice and the Immortalists: Sexuality, Piety, and the Body in Eighteenth-Century New England," in *Sex and Sexuality in Early America*, ed. Merril D. Smith (New York: New York University Press, 1998), 126; *Minutes of the Shaftsbury Association* (Bennington, Vt., 1791), 5; *Minutes of the Charleston Association* (Charleston, S.C., 1791), 1.

14. *Minutes of the Neuse Baptist Association* (Wilmington, N.C., 1794), 3; these rules were a version of ones adopted widely by other Baptist associations, Asplund, *Universal Register of the Baptist Denomination*, 86.

15. *Minutes of the Groton Union Conference* (Norwich, Conn., 1800), 7; *Minutes of the Rensselaerville Conference* (Albany, N.Y., 1799), 2–3.

16. *Minutes of the Danbury Association* (Danbury, Conn., 1791), 4; *Minutes of the North Carolina Neuse Baptist Association* (New Bern, N.C., 1797), 4.

17. Jarrett Burch, *Adiel Sherwood: Baptist Antebellum Pioneer in Georgia* (Macon, Ga.: Mercer University Press, 2003), 243; *Minutes of the Danbury Baptist Association* (Newfield, Conn., 1795), 4; Gregory A. Wills, *Democratic Religion: Freedom, Authority, and Church Discipline in the Baptist South, 1785–1900* (New York: Oxford University Press, 1997), 86–87.

18. John Buzzell, "A Short History of the Church of Christ, Gathered at New Durham, N.H., 1780," *A Religious Magazine, Containing a Short History of the Church of Christ, Gathered at New Durham, N.H. in the Year 1780,* (Portland, Maine: Arthur Shirley, 1812), 1; Scott Bryant, *The Awakening of the Freewill Baptists: Benjamin Randall and the Founding of an American Religious Tradition* (Macon, Ga.: Mercer University Press, 2011), 95; Thomas S. Kidd, *The Great Awakening: The Roots of Evangelical Christianity in Colonial America* (New Haven, Conn.: Yale University Press, 2007), 314–316.

19. Wills, *Democratic Religion,* 22, 51; Monica Najar, *Evangelizing the South: A Social History of Church and State in Early America* (New York: Oxford University Press, 2008), 60, 110, 172; Sparks, *On Jordan's Stormy Banks,* 154; Charles F. Irons, *The Origins of Proslavery Christianity: White and Black Evangelicals in Colonial and Antebellum Virginia* (Chapel Hill, N.C.: University of North Carolina Press, 2008), 83–84.

20. Janet Moore Lindman, *Bodies of Belief: Baptist Community in Early America* (Philadelphia: University of Pennsylvania Press, 2008), 103–111; Najar, *Evangelizing the South,* 173; Wills, *Democratic Religion,* 54–56, 59–60; Susan Juster, *Disorderly Women: Sexual Politics and Evangelicalism in Revolutionary New England* (Ithaca, N.Y.: Cornell University Press, 1994), 106; Wayne Flynt, *Alabama Baptists: Southern Baptists in the Heart of Dixie* (Tuscaloosa, Ala.: University of Alabama Press, 1998), 40.

21. *Minutes of the Bethel Association* (Charleston, S.C., 1794), 2; Lindman, *Bodies of Belief,* 102–103; Irons, *Origins of Proslavery Christianity,* 84–86.

22. *Minutes of the Bethel Association,* 2; Mechal Sobel, *The World They Made Together: Black and White Values in Eighteenth-Century Virginia* (Princeton, N.J.: Princeton University Press, 1987), 194.

23. Furman quoted in John Boles, *The Great Revival: Beginnings of the Bible Belt,* 2nd ed. (Lexington, Ky.: University Press of Kentucky, 1996), 33; *Minutes of the Charleston Association* (Charleston, S.C., 1793), 2.

24. J. H. N., "Hardware Dwight," *Circular,* August 8, 1870, 162–163; J. N. Murdock, "Revivals and Missions," *Baptist Missionary Magazine,* September 1876, 327; George Punchard, *History of Congregationalism from about A.D. 250 to the Present* (Boston: Congregational Publishing House, 1881), 5:502; Leonard W. Bacon, *A History of American Christianity* (New York: Scribner, 1901), 230; David Benedict, *A General History of the Baptist Denomination in America* (Boston: Lincoln and Edmands, 1813), 2:164; Theodore Roosevelt, *The Winning of the West* (New York: Putnam's, 1896), 4:247.

25. James D. Bratt, "The Reorientation of American Protestantism, 1835–1845," *Church History* 67 (March 1998): 57–58; John Wolffe, *The Expansion of Evangelicalism: The Age of Wilberforce, More, Chalmers, and Finney* (Downers Grove, Ill.: InterVarsity Press, 2007), 46–48.

26. Semple quoted in Donald G. Mathews, "The Second Great Awakening as an Organizing Process, 1780–1830: An Hypothesis," *American Quarterly* 21 (Spring 1969): 37; David Hempton, *Methodism: Empire of the Spirit* (New Haven, Conn.: Yale University Press, 2005), 13; Ellen Eslinger, *Citizens of Zion: The Social Origins of Camp Meeting Revivalism* (Knoxville, Tenn.: University of Tennessee Press, 1999), 166–168; Roger Finke and Rodney Stark, *The Churching of America, 1776–2005: Winners and Losers in Our Religious Economy* (New Brunswick, N.J.: Rutgers University Press, 1992), 76.

27. Wright, *History of the Shaftsbury Baptist Association*, 59, 64, 67–68.

28. *Minutes of the Groton Union Conference* (Norwich, Conn., 1801), 5; "Extract of a Letter from a Gentleman to His Sister in Philadelphia, Dated Lexington, Kentucky, Aug. 10, 1801," in Sweet, *Religion on the American Frontier*, 610; Boles, *Great Revival*, 65, 72; Eslinger, *Citizens of Zion*, 201.

29. "Extract of a Letter from a Gentleman to His Friend at the City of Washington, Dated Lexington, Kentucky, Mar. 8, 1801," in Sweet, *Religion on the American Frontier*, 609; John Taylor, *Baptists on the American Frontier: A History of Ten Baptist Churches*, ed. Chester Raymond Young (Macon, Ga.: Mercer University Press, 1995), 268, 272.

30. *Minutes of the Elkhorn Association of Baptists* (Lexington, Ky., 1800), 1; Sweet, *Religion on the American Frontier*, 484–488; *Minutes of the Salem Association* (Frankfort, Ky., 1802), 1; "A Peculiar Work in America," January 7, 1802, in Sweet, *Religion on the American Frontier*, 614; *Minutes of the Elkhorn Association of Baptists* (Lexington, Ky., 1804), 1; Eslinger, *Citizens of Zion*, 197–201.

31. "A Peculiar Work in America," 614–615.

32. *Minutes of the North-District Association of Baptists* (Lexington, Ky. 1802), 4; *Minutes of the Elkhorn Association of Baptists* (Lexington, Ky., [1804]), 2; *Minutes of the Bracken Association of Baptists* (Lexington, Ky., 1803), 4.

33. *Minutes of the Bowdoinham Association* (Portland, Me., 1808), 7–8; Wills, *Democratic Religion*, 103; E. Brooks Holifield, *Theology in America: Christian Thought from the Age of the Puritans to the Civil War* (New Haven, Conn.: Yale University Press, 2003), 278–290.

34. Lemuel Burkitt and Jesse Read, *A Concise History of the Kehukee Baptist Association* (Philadelphia: Lippincott, Grambo, 1850), 144–145, 148–149.

35. Burkitt and Read, *Kehukee Baptist Association*, 149–152; Boles, *Great Revival*, 76.

36. Burkitt and Read, *Kehukee Baptist Association*, 158; *Minutes of the Charleston Baptist Association* ([Charleston, S.C., 1803]), 8–9.

37. "Kentucky Stile" quote from Boles, *Great Revival*, 77; Richard Furman to John Rippon, August 11, 1802, in Benedict, *General History*, 2:167–171.

38. Charles Roy Keller, *The Second Great Awakening in Connecticut* (New Haven, Conn.: Yale University Press, 1942), 195.

39. Smith, *Western States East of the Mississippi*, 44–45, 54; Flynt, *Alabama Baptists*, 6; Isaac Case to the Secretary of the Society, June 29, 1804, in *Massachusetts Baptist Missionary Magazine*, September 1804, 86–87.

40. *Massachusetts Baptist Missionary Magazine*, September 1810, 342–343.

41. *Massachusetts Baptist Missionary Magazine*, September 1805, 158–159; compare *Massachusetts Baptist Missionary Magazine*, September 1807, 348–351.

42. "Extract of a Letter from Elder Thomas," *The Vehicle, or New York Northwestern Christian Magazine*, February 1, 1816, 308–309; Joshua Bradley, *Accounts of Religious Revivals in Many Parts of the United States from 1815* (Albany, N.Y.: G. J. Loomis, 1819), 216–217; Lewis Halsey, *History of the Seneca Baptist Association* (Ithaca, N.Y.: Journal Association Book and Job Printing House, 1879), 256.

43. Andrew Porter, *Religion versus Empire? British Protestant Missionaries and Overseas Expansion, 1700–1914* (New York: Manchester University Press, 2004), 15.

44. "Address of the Tuscarora Chiefs," October 6, 1800, Elkanah Holmes to Secretary Mason, October 29, 1800, in Frank H. Severance, ed., "Letters of the Reverend Elkanah Holmes," *Publications of the Buffalo Historical Society* 6 (1903): 192, 195–197; *Gospel News, or, A Brief Account of the Revival of Religion in Kentucky* (Baltimore, 1801), 9.

45. Lisa Joy Pruitt, *A Looking-Glass for Ladies: American Protestant Women and the Orient in the Nineteenth Century* (Macon, Ga.: Mercer University Press, 2005), 13–14.

46. Jacob Ide, ed., *Works of Nathanael Emmons* (Boston, 1861), 1:188; Robert Caldwell, "New England's New Divinity and the Age of Judson's Preparation," in Jason G. Duesing, ed., *Adoniram Judson: A Bicentennial Appreciation of the Pioneer American Missionary* (Nashville, Tenn.: B & H Academic, 2012), 50–51.

47. Gregory A. Wills, "From Congregationalist to Baptist: Judson and Baptism," in Duesing, *Adoniram Judson*, 153–154.

48. Francis Wayland, *A Memoir of the Life and Labors of the Rev. Adoniram Judson* (Boston: Phillips, Sampson, 1853), 1:106; Wills, "From Congregationalist to Baptist," 157–158.

49. *Proceedings of the Baptist Convention for Missionary Purposes* (Philadelphia, 1814), 3, 24; Robert G. Torbet, *A History of the Baptists*, rev. ed. (Valley Forge, Pa.: Judson Press, 1963), 249–250.

50. R. S. Duncan, *A History of the Baptists in Missouri* (St. Louis, Mo.: Scammell, 1882), 38–40; *Minutes of the Appomattox Association* (Lynchburg, Va., 1819), 11–12; Sweet, *Religion on the American Frontier*, 59–61; Rufus Babcock, ed., *Forty Years of Pioneer Life: Memoir of John Mason Peck* (Carbondale, Ill.: Southern Illinois University Press, 1965), 159.

51. Miles Mark Fisher, "Lott Cary, the Colonizing Missionary," *Journal of Negro History* 7 (October 1922): 383–386; *Proceedings of the General Convention of the Baptist Denomination in the United States* (Philadelphia, 1817), 180. Although

later admirers would spell his name "Carey," "Cary" was the most common spelling during his lifetime.

52. *Minutes of the Elkhorn Baptist Association* ([Lexington, Ky., 1819]), 7; Wood Creek Church minutes quotes in Sweet, *Religion on the American Frontier*, 270; "antimission" quote from John G. Crowley, *Primitive Baptists of the Wiregrass South, 1815 to the Present* (Gainesville, Fla.: University of Florida Press, 1998), 58.

CHAPTER 6

1. William Warren Sweet, *Religion on the American Frontier: The Baptists, 1783–1830* (New York: Henry Holt, 1931), 316, 335.

2. Sweet, *Religion on the American Frontier*, 323–325; *Minutes of the Elkhorn Association* (Lexington, Ky., 1805), 4; Monica Najar, "'Meddling with Emancipation': Baptists, Authority, and the Rift over Slavery in the Upper South," *Journal of the Early Republic* 25 (Summer 2005): 157–186.

3. Sweet, *Religion on the American Frontier*, 328–330.

4. Paul Harvey, "'Yankee Faith' and Southern Redemption: White Southern Baptist Ministers, 1850-1890," in Randall M. Miller, Harry S. Stout, and Charles R. Wilson, eds., *Religion and the American Civil War* (New York: Oxford University Press, 1998), 168–171.

5. *Minutes of the Elkhorn Association of Baptists* (Lexington, Ky., 1805), 3; Jonathan Maxcy, *An Oration, Delivered in the Baptist Meeting-House in Providence* (Providence, R.I.: Carter and Wilkinson, 1795), 5–6; Ricardo Howell, "Slavery, the Brown Family of Providence and Brown University," *Brown University News Service*, July 2001, accessed July 9, 2013, http://web.archive. org/web/20080409001105/; http://www.brown.edu/Administration/News_ Bureau/Info/Slavery.html; Jay Spears, "Slave Quarters on the Campus of South Carolina College, 1801 to 2010," research paper, accessed July 9, 2013, http:// tundra.csd.sc.edu/slaveryorigin/docs/hist%20497f%20final%20draft.pdf.

6. John H. Spencer, *A History of Kentucky Baptists* (Cincinnati, Ohio: J. R. Baumes, 1885), 1: 183–184; Sweet, *Religion on the American Frontier*, 79; Leah Townsend, *South Carolina Baptists, 1670–1805* (Florence, S.C.: Florence Print. Co., 1935), 241–242, 281; Charles F. Irons, *The Origins of Proslavery Christianity: White and Black Evangelicals in Colonial and Antebellum Virginia* (Chapel Hill, N.C.: University of North Carolina Press, 2008), 72.

7. *Minutes of the Shaftsbury Association* (Bennington, Vt., 1792), 11.

8. *Minutes of the Georgia Baptist Association* (Augusta, Ga., 1794), 8; *Minutes of the Ketocton Baptist Association* ([Dumfries, Va., 1796]), 4; *Minutes of the Ketocton Baptist Association* [1797?], 4, 6; *Minutes of the Ketocton Baptist Association* (Winchester, Va., 1801), 7; Janet Moore Lindman, *Bodies of Belief: Baptist Community in Early America* (Philadelphia: University of Pennsylvania Press, 2008), 143–144.

9. *Minutes of the Ketocton Baptist Association* (Alexandria, Va., 1810), 4; church history of Alfred Street Baptist Church, Alexandria, Virginia, accessed July 9, 2013, http://www.alfredstreet.org/asbc-history.htm.

10. *Minutes of the Ketocton Baptist Association* (Alexandria, Va., 1810), 4; *Minutes of the Ketocton Baptist Association* (Winchester, Va., 1811), 6; Irons, *Origins of Proslavery Christianity*, 48, 84–85.

11. Patrick H. Breen, "Contested Communion: The Limits of White Solidarity in Nat Turner's Virginia," *Journal of the Early Republic* 27 (Winter 2007): 688–689; Carlos R. Allen, Jr., "David Barrow's Circular Letter of 1798," *William and Mary Quarterly*, 3d. ser., 20, no. 3 (July 1963): 445–447, 450–451.

12. *Minutes of the North District Association of Baptists* ([1806]), 3; Sweet, *Religion on the American Frontier*, 82–83, 354, 566–567; Jacob Grigg, *Remarks and Selections on Some of the Most Important Subjects Lately in Dispute* (Lebanon, Ohio: John M'Clean, 1807), 66–67; H. Shelton Smith, *In His Image, But . . . Racism in Southern Religion, 1780–1910* (Durham, N.C.: Duke University Press, 1972), 50–52.

13. Lacy K. Ford, *Deliver Us from Evil: The Slavery Question in the Old South* (New York: Oxford University Press, 2009), 94–95.

14. Ford, *Deliver Us from Evil*, 143–150.

15. Ford, *Deliver Us from Evil*, 243–244.

16. Richard Furman, "Exposition of the Views of the Baptists Relative to the Colored Population" (1822), in James A. Rogers, *Richard Furman: Life and Legacy* (Macon, Ga.: Mercer University Press, 2001), 277–279, 283–284; Ford, *Deliver Us from Evil*, 258–261; John Patrick Daly, *When Slavery Was Called Freedom: Evangelicalism, Proslavery, and the Causes of the Civil War* (Lexington, Ky.: University Press of Kentucky, 2002), 39–44.

17. John Taylor, *Baptists on the American Frontier: A History of Ten Baptist Churches*, ed. Chester Raymond Young (Macon, Ga.: Mercer University Press, 1995), 296–298.

18. Eddie S. Glaude, *Exodus! Religion, Race, and Nation in Early Nineteenth-Century Black America* (Chicago: University of Chicago Press, 2000), 25–26.

19. David Benedict, *A General History of the Baptist Denomination* (Boston: Lincoln and Edmands, 1813), 2: 190–191; W. W. Woodward, *Increase of Piety, or, The Revival of Religion in the United States* (Newburyport, Mass., 1802), 77–78; "Of the Colored Baptists in Savannah," *Georgia Analytical Repository*, November/December 1802, 185–188; Albert J. Raboteau, *Slave Religion: The "Invisible Institution" in the Antebellum South*, updated ed. (New York: Oxford University Press, 2004), 141.

20. John Dowling, "Rev. Thomas Paul and the Colored Baptist Churches," *Baptist Memorial and Monthly Record* 8 (1849): 295–299; Elias Smith, *Five Letters, with Remarks* (Boston: J. Ball, 1804), 18; Glaude, *Exodus!*, 25–26; John Ernest, *A Nation within a Nation: Organizing African-American Communities before the Civil War* (Lanham, Md.: Rowman and Littlefield, 2011), 58; Lindman, *Bodies of Belief*, 151.

21. Terry Wolever, ed., *The Autobiography of Isaac McCoy* (Springfield, Mo.: Particular Baptist Press, 2011), 8–9, 37; George A. Schultz, *An Indian Canaan: Isaac McCoy and the Vision of an Indian State* (Norman, Okla.: University of Oklahoma Press, 1972), 14–15.

22. Isaac McCoy, *History of Baptist Indian Missions* (New York: H. and S. Raynor, 1840), 250–251.

23. McCoy, *History*, 302–303.

24. McCoy, *History*, 265.

25. McCoy, *History*, 252–255.

26. McCoy, *History*, 451–453; Isaac McCoy letter in *American Baptist Magazine* 12 (1832): 396–397; I. M. Allen, *The Triennial Baptist Register* (Philadelphia: Baptist General Tract Society, 1836), 30; Gary Zellar, *African Creeks: Estelvste and the Creek Nation* (Norman, Okla.: University of Oklahoma Press, 2007), 26–27; Henry Burrage, *Baptist Hymn Writers and Their Hymns* (Portland, Maine: Brown Thursten, 1888), 68–69.

27. Thomas Armitage, *History of the Baptists* (New York: Bryan, Taylor, 1890), 840.

28. *Latter Day Luminary* 3 (1822): 91; George W. Paschal, *History of North Carolina Baptists* (Raleigh, N.C.: North Carolina Baptist State Convention, 1955), 2:538–545.

29. William G. McLoughlin, *Champions of the Cherokees: Evan and John B. Jones* (Princeton, N.J.: Princeton University Press, 1990), 91–93.

30. Evan Jones letters of June 12, June 27, 1831, in *Christian Secretary*, September 10, 1831; McLoughlin, *Champions*, 93–95.

31. McLoughlin, *Champions*, 171–178, 184.

32. S. C. Gwynne, *Empire of the Summer Moon: Quanah Parker and the Rise and Fall of the Comanches* (New York: Scribner, 2010), 12–20.

33. James R. Mathis, *The Making of the Primitive Baptists: A Cultural and Intellectual History of the Antimission Movement* (New York: Routledge, 2004), 66.

34. Byron C. Lambert, *The Rise of the Anti-Mission Baptists* (1957; reprint, New York: Arno Press, 1980), 254, 261.

35. Daniel Parker, *A Public Address*, (reprint, Carthage, Ill.: Primitive Baptist Library, 1988), 2–3, 26–27, 39; Mathis, *Primitive Baptists*, 77.

36. Parker, *Public Address*, 51–52.

37. John G. Crowley, *Primitive Baptists of the Wiregrass South: 1815 to the Present* (Gainesville, Fla.: University of Florida Press, 1998), 58.

38. Mathis, *Primitive Baptists*, 135–136; Joshua Aaron Guthman, "'What I Am 'Tis Hard to Know': Primitive Baptists, the Protestant Self, and the American Religious Imagination" (PhD diss., University of North Carolina at Chapel Hill, 2008), 121–122.

39. Joshua Lawrence, *The American Telescope* (Philadelphia, 1825), 8, 10, accessed July 18, 2013, http://docsouth.unc.edu/nc/lawrence/lawrence.html; Mathis, *Primitive Baptists*, 87–88.

40. "Declaration of the Reformed Baptist Churches in the State of North Carolina," *New York Telescope*, October 28, 1826, 85.

41. "The Dark Ages Returning," *Christian Watchman*, February 1, 1828, 18; Crowley, *Primitive Baptists*, 59.

42. W. J. Berry, ed. *Kehukee Declaration and Black Rock Address* (Elon College, N.C.: Primitive Publications, 1974), 24, 33, 36–37.

43. *Christian Secretary*, March 1, 1839, 3; *Christian Secretary*, October 29, 1836, 166; Betram Wyatt-Brown, "The Antimission Movement in the Jacksonian South: A Study in Regional Folk Culture," *Journal of Southern History* 36 (November 1970): 527.

44. William T. Stott, *Indiana Baptist History: 1798–1908* (Franklin, Ind., 1908), 202; Robert G. Torbet, *A History of the Baptists*, rev. ed. (Valley Forge, Pa.: Judson Press, 1963), 270–275.

45. James Leo Garrett, *Baptist Theology: A Four-Century Study* (Macon, Ga.: Mercer University Press, 2009), 128–132; Gregory A. Wills, *Democratic Religion: Freedom, Authority, and Church Discipline in the Baptist South, 1785–1900* (New York: Oxford University Press, 1997), 110.

46. Garrett, *Baptist Theology*, 130; Spencer, *History of Kentucky Baptists*, 1:485; Henry Clay Vedder, *A History of the Baptists in the Middle States* (Philadelphia: American Baptist Publication Society, 1898), 61–62 n. 2. On the elders debate, see, for example, "Ruling Elders among the Baptists," *New York Evangelist*, April 26, 1860, 6; "Elders in the Baptist Church," *New York Evangelist*, April 17, 1862, 8.

47. James Robinson Graves, *Old Landmarkism: What Is It?* (Memphis, Tenn.: Baptist Book House, 1880), ix.

48. Graves, *Old Landmarkism*, 25; E. Brooks Holifield, *Theology in America: Christian Thought from the Age of the Puritans to the Civil War* (New Haven, Conn.: Yale University Press, 2003), 277–278; Bill Leonard, *Baptists in America* (New York: Columbia University Press, 2005), 25–26; James A. Patterson, *James Robinson Graves: Staking the Boundaries of Baptist Identity* (Nashville, Tenn.: B & H Academic, 2012), 70, 118.

CHAPTER 7

1. Thomas Gray, *The Confessions of Nat Turner*, in Milton C. Sernett, ed., *African American Religious History: A Documentary Witness*, 2nd ed. (Durham, N.C., 1999), 92–93.

2. Gray, *Confessions*, 93–95; Stephen B. Oates, *The Fires of Jubilee: Nat Turner's Fierce Rebellion* (New York: Harper and Row, 1975), 125.

3. Deacon John R. Logan, *Sketches, Historical and Biographical, of the Broad River and King's Mountain Baptist Associations* (Shelby, N.C.: Babington, Roberts, 1887), 451; Bobby Gilmer Moss, *A Voice in the Wilderness: A History of Buffalo Baptist Church* (Gaffney, S.C.: Gaffney Printing Company, 1972), 10.

4. W. B. Johnson, "Animating Scenes in Zion," *Christian Index*, September 3, 1831; Stephanie McCurry, *Masters of Small Worlds: Yeoman Households, Gender Relations, and the Political Culture of the Antebellum South Carolina Low Country* (New York: Oxford University Press, 1995), 150–170; Kimberly R. Kellison, "South Carolina Baptists, the Primitive-Missionary Schism, and the Revival of the Early 1830s," *South Carolina Historical Magazine* 110 (July–October 2009): 154–179.

5. "Better Than Our Fears," *Columbian Star*, December 18, 1830; "Pleasing Revival in the Kehukee Association, N.C.," *American Baptist Magazine*, April 1831.

6. William Henry Brisbane, "Revival Meeting," *Christian Index*, August 23, 1832; Anne C. Loveland, *Southern Evangelicals and the Social Order, 1800–1860* (Baton Rouge, La.: Louisiana State University Press, 1980), 130–131.

7. David W. Bebbington, *Victorian Religious Revivals: Culture and Piety in Local and Global Contexts* (Oxford: Oxford University Press, 2012), 53–59.

8. Bebbington, *Victorian Religious Revivals*, 61–74.

9. Robert E. Johnson, *A Global Introduction to Baptist Churches* (New York: Cambridge University Press, 2010), 97–98; C. A. Wooddy, "Baptists of the Pacific Slope," in A. H. Newman, ed., *A Century of Baptist Achievement* (Philadelphia: American Baptist Publication Society, 1901), 100, 108, 111.

10. Johnson, *Global Introduction*, 170.

11. Johnson, *Global Introduction*, 166–167; Juan Francisco Martínez, *Sea la Luz: The Making of Mexican Protestantism in the American Southwest, 1829–1900* (Denton, Texas: University of North Texas Press, 2006), 53–55.

12. Adolf Olson, *A Centenary History as Related to the Baptist General Conference of America* (Chicago: Baptist Conference Press, 1952), 34–36, 79–80; Converge Worldwide, "About Converge Worldwide," accessed August 14, 2013, http://www.convergeworldwide.org/about.

13. William G. McLoughlin, ed., *The American Evangelicals, 1800–1900: An Anthology* (New York: Harper and Row, 1968), 101–102; George Marsden, *Understanding Evangelicalism and Fundamentalism* (Grand Rapids, Mich.: Eerdmans, 1991), 132–133.

14. Durwood Dunn, *Cades Cove: The Life and Death of a Southern Appalachian Community, 1818–1937* (Knoxville, Tenn.: University of Tennessee Press, 1988), 102–115.

15. David Benedict, *A General History of the Baptist Denomination in America* (Boston: Lincoln and Edmands, 1813), 2:207; "Missouri and Illinois," *Zion's Herald*, November 16, 1825; *Minutes of the New York Baptist Association* (New York, 1809), 5; *Minutes of the Scioto Baptist Association* (Chillicothe, Ohio, 1816), 6.

16. Randolph Ferguson Scully, *Religion and the Making of Nat Turner's Virginia: Baptist Community and Conflict, 1740–1840* (Charlottesville, Va.: University of Virginia Press, 2008), 217; Charles F. Irons, *The Origins of Proslavery*

Christianity: White and Black Evangelicals in Colonial and Antebellum Virginia (Chapel Hill, N.C.: University of North Carolina Press, 2008), 138–139, 149.

17. Scully, *Nat Turner's Virginia*, 223–224, 226; Irons, *Origins of Proslavery Christianity*, 152, 158.

18. Andrew T. Foss and Edward Mathews, eds., *Facts for Baptist Churches* (Utica, N.Y.: American Baptist Free Mission Society, 1850), 19

19. Foss and Mathews, *Facts for Baptist Churches*, 15, 23.

20. Foss and Mathews, *Facts for Baptist Churches*, 26; *Christian Secretary*, December 5, 1835.

21. Mary Burnham Putnam, *The Baptists and Slavery, 1840–1845* (Ann Arbor, Mich.: George Wahr, 1913), 16; Stephen Wright, *History of the Shaftsbury Baptist Association* (Troy, N.Y.: A. G. Johnson, 1853), 217; H. Shelton Smith, *In His Image, But. . . Racism in Southern Religion, 1780–1910* (Durham, N.C.: Duke University Press, 1972), 114–115; Mechal Sobel, *Trabelin' On: The Slave Journey to an Afro-Baptist Faith* (Westport, Conn.: Greenwood Press, 1979), 156.

22. Foss and Mathews, *Facts for Baptist Churches*, 46, 48.

23. Foss and Mathews, *Facts for Baptist Churches*, 46–47; Molly Oshatz, *Slavery and Sin: The Fight against Slavery and the Rise of Liberal Protestantism* (New York: Oxford University Press, 2012), 4.

24. Foss and Mathews, *Facts for Baptist Churches*, 50.

25. Foss and Mathews, *Facts for Baptist Churches*, 125.

26. Putnam, *Baptists and Slavery*, 46.

27. Foss and Mathews, *Facts for Baptist Churches*, 136.

28. H. Leon McBeth, *The Baptist Heritage* (Nashville, Tenn.: Broadman Press, 1987), 389; C. C. Goen, *Broken Churches, Broken Nation: Denominational Schism and the Coming of the Civil War* (Macon, Ga.: Mercer University Press, 1985), 97.

29. *Christian Reflector*, June 12, 1845; "Resolution on Racial Reconciliation on the 150th Anniversary of the Southern Baptist Convention," accessed August 7, 2013, http://www.sbc.net/resolutions/amresolution.asp?id=899.

30. John Peacock, *A Sketch of the Christian Experience* (Concord, N.H.: Tripp and Osgood, 1851), 105–107; John Peacock, "Revival Intelligence," *Christian Reflector*, December 17, 1846.

31. George W. Paschal, *History of North Carolina Baptists* (Raleigh, N.C.: North Carolina Baptist State Convention, 1955), 2:397.

32. Albert J. Raboteau, *Slave Religion: The "Invisible Institution" in the Antebellum South*, updated ed. (New York: Oxford University Press, 2004), 176; Irons, *Origins of Proslavery Christianity*, 202.

33. "Religious, Moral, and Intellectual Improvement of Negroes in Slavery," *Christian Inquirer*, July 2, 1853; Sobel, *Trabelin' On*, 140–144.

34. Israel Campbell, *Bond and Free* (Philadelphia, 1861), 288.

35. Putnam, *Baptists and Slavery*, 83–85; John R. McKivigan, *The War against Proslavery Religion: Abolitionism and the Northern Churches, 1830–1865*

(Ithaca, N.Y.: Cornell University Press, 1984), 88–89; John R. McKivigan, "Antislavery 'Comeouter' Sects: A Neglected Dimension of the Abolitionist Movement," in John R. McKivigan, ed., *Abolitionism and American Religion* (New York: Garland, 1999), 245–247.

36. Nathan A. Finn and Keith Harper, eds., *Domestic Slavery Considered as a Scriptural Institution* (Macon, Ga.: Mercer University Press, 2008), 8–9; Mark A. Noll, *The Civil War as a Theological Crisis* (Chapel Hill, N.C.: University of North Carolina Press, 2006), 36–37.

37. Finn and Harper, *Domestic Slavery*, 12, 34–35; Elizabeth Fox-Genovese and Eugene Genovese, *The Mind of the Master Class: History and Faith in the Southern Slaveholder's Worldview* (New York: Cambridge University Press, 2005), 478; Deborah Bingham Van Broekhoven, "Suffering with Slaveholders: The Limits of Francis Wayland's Antislavery Witness," in John R. McKivigan and Mitchell Snay, eds., *Religion and the Antebellum Debate over Slavery* (Athens, Ga.: University of Georgia Press, 1998), 201.

38. Oshatz, *Slavery and Sin*, 66–68; Luke E. Harlow, "Neither Slavery nor Abolitionism: James M. Pendleton and the Problem of Christian Conservative Antislavery in 1840s Kentucky," *Slavery and Abolition* 27 3 (December 2006): 369, 374.

39. Jeremiah Bell Jeter, *The Recollections of a Long Life* (Richmond, Va.: Religious Herald, 1891), 69–70; Loveland, *Southern Evangelicals and the Social Order*, 186–188.

40. Jeter, *Recollections*, 70; Thornton Stringfellow, *A Brief Examination of Scripture Testimony on the Institution of Slavery* (1841), in Drew Gilpin Faust, ed., *The Ideology of Slavery: Proslavery Thought in the Antebellum South, 1830–1860* (Baton Rouge, La.: Louisiana State University Press, 1981), 166; Mark Noll, *America's God: From Jonathan Edwards to Abraham Lincoln* (New York: Oxford University Press, 2002), 388–389.

41. Steven A. Channing, *Crisis of Fear: Secession in South Carolina* (New York: Norton, 1974), 69.

42. "Refuge of Oppression," *Liberator*, November 30, 1860; A. James Fuller, *Chaplain to the Confederacy: Basil Manly and Baptist Life in the Old South* (Baton Rouge: Louisiana State University Press, 2000), 293–295.

43. Samuel Boykin, *History of the Baptist Denomination in Georgia* (reprint, Paris, Ark.: Baptist Standard Bearer, 2001), 1:226–227.

44. Frank Moore, ed., *The Rebellion Record* (New York: D. Van Nostrand, 1862), 2:151–152; George C. Rable, *God's Almost Chosen Peoples: A Religious History of the American Civil War* (Chapel Hill, N.C.: University of North Carolina Press, 2010), 67.

45. Van Broekhoven, "Suffering with Slaveholders," 210–213; Francis Wayland and H. L. Wayland, *A Memoir of the Life and Labors of Francis Wayland* (New York: Sheldon, 1867), 2:262–263.

46. John A. Broadus, *Memoir of James Petigru Boyce* (New York: A. C. Armstrong and Son, 1893), 185; Gregory Wills, *Southern Baptist Theological Seminary, 1859–2009* (New York: Oxford University Press, 2009), 55–61; Thomas J. Nettles, *James Petigru Boyce: A Southern Baptist Statesman* (Phillipsburg, N.J.: P and R, 2009), 186–187; Wayne Flynt, *Alabama Baptists: Southern Baptists in the Heart of Dixie* (Tuscaloosa, Ala.: University of Alabama Press, 1998), 116.

47. Flynt, *Alabama Baptists*, 116.

48. Lewis Halsey, *History of the Seneca Baptist Association* (Ithaca, N.Y.: Journal Association Book and Job Printing House, 1879), 252; "The West's Most Western Town," accessed August 13, 2013, http://www.scottsdaleaz.gov/about/history.

49. John H. Spencer, *A History of Kentucky Baptists* (Cincinnati, Ohio: J. R. Baumes, 1885), 1:741; Sean A. Scott, *A Visitation of God: Northern Civilians Interpret the Civil War* (New York: Oxford University Press, 2011), 187; Rable, *God's Almost Chosen Peoples*, 354.

50. Bruce T. Gourley, *Diverging Loyalties: Baptists in Middle Georgia during the Civil War* (Macon, Ga.: Mercer University Press, 2011), 137–145.

51. Ervin L. Jordan, *Black Confederates and Afro-Yankees in Civil War Virginia* (Charlottesville: University Press of Virginia, 1995), 109; "Beulah Baptist Church," African American Historic Sites Database, accessed August 13, 2103, http://www.aaheritageva.org/search/sites.php?site_id=464.

52. Marion B. Lucas, *A History of Blacks in Kentucky: From Slavery to Segregation, 1760–1891* (Frankfort, Ky.: Kentucky Historical Society, 2003), 221.

53. Kathryn Carlisle Schwartz, ed., *Baptist Faith in Action: The Private Writings of Maria Baker Taylor, 1813–1895* (Columbia, S.C.: University of South Carolina Press, 2003), 128–129, 187; Rable, *God's Almost Chosen Peoples*, 347.

54. Daniel W. Stowell, "Stonewall Jackson and the Providence of God," in Randall M. Miller, Harry S. Stout, and Charles R. Wilson, eds., *Religion and the American Civil War* (New York: Oxford University Press, 1998), 199; William T. Stott, *Indiana Baptist History, 1798–1908* (Franklin, Ind., 1908), 117, 137; Allen C. Guelzo, *Abraham Lincoln: Redeemer President* (Grand Rapids, Mich.: Eerdmans, 1999), 440–441.

55. George Whitfield Pepper, *Personal Recollections of Sherman's Campaigns* (Zanesville, Ohio: H. Dunne, 1866), 290.

56. Jacqueline Jones, *Saving Savannah: The City and the Civil War* (New York: Alfred A. Knopf, 2008), 213.

CHAPTER 8

1. Andrew Billingsley, *Mighty Like a River: The Black Church and Social Reform* (New York: Oxford University Press, 1999), 65–66.

2. Quoted in Andrew Billingsley, *Mighty Like a River*, 68.

3. Philip S. Foner, ed., *W. E. B. Du Bois Speaks: Speeches and Addresses*, vol. 2, *1920–1963* (New York: Pathfinder Press, 1970), 97; Philip S. Foner, ed., *W. E. B. Du Bois Speaks: Speeches and Addresses*, vol. 1, *1890–1919* (New York: Pathfinder Press, 1970), 97. Oddly, both quotes in the two volumes are on page 97.

4. Evelyn Brooks Higginbotham, *Righteous Discontent: The Women's Movement in the Black Baptist Church, 1880–1920* (Cambridge, Mass.: Harvard University Press, 1993), 2–3.

5. Juan Williams and Quinton Dixie, *This Far by Faith: Stories from the African American Religious Experience* (New York: William Morrow/Harper Collins, 2003), 127.

6. Paul Harvey, *Redeeming the South: Religious Cultures and Racial Identities among Southern Baptists, 1865–1925* (Chapel Hill, N.C.: University of North Carolina Press, 1997), 46.

7. Williams and Dixie, *This Far by Faith*, 128.

8. Harvey, *Redeeming the South*, 50.

9. Quoted in Harvey, *Redeeming the South*, 53.

10. Quoted in Harvey, *Redeeming the South*, 54.

11. Quoted in Harvey, *Redeeming the South*, 59.

12. Leroy Fitts, *A History of Black Baptists* (Nashville, Tenn.: Broadman Press, 1985), 233.

13. Fitts, *History of Black Baptists*, 64–67; Harvey, *Redeeming the South*, 62.

14. *Proceedings of the Twenty First Session of the Southern Baptist Convention* (Richmond, Va.: Dispatch Steam Printing House, 1876), 36.

15. Williams and Dixie, *This Far by Faith*, 136.

16. Williams and Dixie, *This Far by Faith*, 138.

17. Fitts, *History of Black Baptists*, 76–77.

18. Fitts, *History of Black Baptists*, 80.

19. Quoted in Williams and Dixie, *This Far by Faith*, 138–139.

20. Fitts, *History of Black Baptists*, 81; Martha Simmons and Frank A. Thomas, eds., *Preaching with Sacred Fire: An Anthology of African American Sermons, 1750–Present* (New York: Norton, 2010), 313–315.

21. Fitts, *History of Black Baptists*, 89–91. See also Bobby L. Lovett, *A Black Man's Dream: The First 100 Years: Richard Henry Boyd and the National Baptist Publishing Board* (Jacksonville, Fla.: Mega Corp., 1993).

22. Quoted in Harvey, *Redeeming the South*, 248.

23. Quoted in Harvey, *Redeeming the South*, 248.

24. Quoted in Harvey, *Redeeming the South*, 249.

25. Harvey, *Redeeming the South*, 244.

26. Williams and Dixie, *This Far by Faith*, 142–146; Harvey, *Redeeming the South*, 249; *Tennessee Encyclopedia of History and Culture*, http://tennesseeencyclopedia.net/imagegallery.php?EntryID=N010.

27. Robert Darden, *People Get Ready: A New History of Black Gospel Music* (New York: Continuum, 2004), 160; Clarence Boyer, *How Sweet the Sound: The Golden Age of Gospel* (Washington, D.C.: Elliott and Clark, 1995), 26–27.

28. Darden, *People Get Ready*, 164; Boyer, *How Sweet the Sound*, 42–43.

29. Quoted in Michael W. Harris, "Conflict and Resolution in the Life of Thomas Andrew Dorsey," in *We'll Understand It Better By and By*, ed. Bernice Johnson Reagon (Washington, D.C.: Smithsonian Institution Press, 1992), 173; Darden, *People Get Ready*, 166–167.

30. Michael W. Harris, *The Rise of the Gospel Blues: The Music of Thomas Andrew Dorsey in the Urban Church* (New York: Oxford University Press, 1992), 75. See Darden, *People Get Ready*, 164–180.

31. Quoted in Darden, *People Get Ready*, 211.

32. Laurraine Goreau, *Just Mahalia, Baby* (Waco, Texas: Word Books, 1975), 286.

33. Quoted in Darden, *People Get Ready*, 220.

34. Higginbotham, *Righteous Discontent*, 66.

35. Quoted in Higginbotham, *Righteous Discontent*, 67.

36. V. W. Broughton, *Twenty Years' Experience of a Missionary* (Chicago: Pony Press, 1907), 16.

37. Broughton, *Twenty Years' Experience of a Missionary*, 60; quoted in Higginbotham, *Righteous Discontent*, 71.

38. Quoted in Williams and Dixie, *This Far by Faith*, 147.

39. Williams and Dixie, *This Far by Faith*, 147.

40. Higginbotham devotes an entire chapter to cooperation between white and black Baptist women. See chapter 4, "Unlikely Sisterhood," 88–119.

41. Higginbotham, *Righteous Discontent*, 155.

42. Quoted in Higginbotham, *Righteous Discontent*, 157.

43. Higginbotham, *Righteous Discontent*, 160–162.

44. Higginbotham, *Righteous Discontent*, 151.

45. Tomeiko Ashford Carter, ed., *Virginia Broughton: The Life and Writings of a National Baptist Missionary* (Knoxville, Tenn.: University of Tennessee Press, 2010), 5.

46. "Baptist Women Encouraged," *National Baptist Union* 3, no. 35 (May 3, 1902), in Carter, *Virginia Broughton*, 58.

47. Elias Camp Morris, "Presidential Address to the National Baptist Convention, 1899," in Simmons and Thomas, eds., *Preaching with Sacred Fire*, 316.

48. Harvey, *Redeeming the South*, 245–248.

49. Hans A. Baer and Merrill Singer, *African American Religion: Varieties of Protest and Accommodation*, 2nd ed. (Knoxville, Tenn.: University of Tennessee Press, 2002), 62–65; Fitts, *History of Black Baptists*, 95–98.

50. Fitts, *History of Black Baptists*, 106.

CHAPTER 9

1. Quoted in Rufus Spain, *At Ease in Zion: A Social History of Southern Baptists, 1865–1900* (Tuscaloosa, Ala.: University of Alabama Press, 2003), 18.

2. Charles Reagan Wilson, *Baptized in Blood: The Religion of the Lost Cause, 1865–1920* (Athens, Ga.: University of Georgia Press, 1980), 1.

3. H. Leon McBeth, *The Baptist Heritage* (Nashville, Tenn.: Broadman Press, 1987), 391–392.

4. Martin Marty, "The Protestant Experience and Perspective," in Rodger Van Allen, ed., *American Religious Values and the Future of America* (Philadelphia: Fortress Press, 1978), 46.

5. Spain, *At Ease in Zion.*

6. Quoted in Spain, *At Ease in Zion,* 51–52,

7. Quoted in Spain, *At Ease in Zion,* 52.

8. William H. Whitsitt, *A Question of Baptist History* (1896; reprint, New York: Arno Press, 1980).

9. Gregory A. Wills, *Southern Baptist Theological Seminary, 1859–2009* (New York: Oxford University Press, 2009), 189–229; quote on 214.

10. J. Kristian Pratt, *The Father of Modern Landmarkism: The Life of Ben M. Bogard* (Macon, Ga.: Mercer University Press, 2013). For Hayden, see McBeth, *Baptist Heritage,* 750–751. Denominational figures come from the Association of Religious Data Archives, www.thearda.com.

11. Quoted in Wayne Flynt, *Alabama Baptists: Southern Baptists in the Heart of Dixie* (Tuscaloosa, Ala.: University of Alabama Press, 1998), 339.

12. Quoted in Eldon G. Ernst, *Moment of Truth for Protestant America: Interchurch Campaigns Following World War I,* Dissertation Series no. 3 (Missoula, Mont., Scholar's Press and American Academy of Religion, 1974), 51.

13. Quoted in Ernst, *Moment of Truth for Protestant America,* 54.

14. Curtis Lee Laws, "The Interchurch World Movement: The World Survey Conference (Editorial Correspondence)," *Watchman Examiner,* January 15, 1920, 73.

15. Curtis Lee Laws, "Convention Side Lights," *Watchman Examiner,* May 20, 1920, 652.

16. "Dr. Straton Against Interchurch Move," *New York Times,* March 17, 1920, 10.

17. "Assails Interchurch Drive," *New York Times,* May 3, 1920, 12.

18. "Answers Attack on Church Drive," *New York Times,* May 4, 1920, 10.

19. Quoted in "Threatens Dr. Haldeman," *New York Times,* May 10, 1920, 13.

20. Quoted in "Threatens Dr. Haldeman," 13.

21. Curtis Lee Laws, "Baptists and the Interchurch Movement," *Watchman Examiner,* June 10, 1920, 751.

22. Laws, "Baptists and the Interchurch Movement," 752.

23. "Baptists Withdraw from Interchurch," *New York Times,* June 25, 1920, 10.

24. "Baptists Attack Infidel Teaching," *New York Times,* June 24, 1920, 16.

25. "Many Hurt in Crash at Baptist Meeting," *New York Times,* June 26, 1920, 6.

26. Quoted in William Vance Trollinger Jr., *God's Empire: William Bell Riley and Midwestern Fundamentalism* (Madison, Wis.: University of Wisconsin Press, 1990), 53.

27. Quoted in "Interchurch Plan Comes Up Again," *New York Times,* October 31, 1920, 15.

28. Quoted in James A. Thompson, *Tried as by Fire* (Macon, Ga.: Mercer University Press, 1982), 11.

29. Quoted in Thompson, *Tried as by Fire*, 11. From Victor I. Masters, "Baptists and the Christianizing of America in the New Order," *Review and Expositor* 17 (July 1920): 297.

30. McBeth, *Baptist Heritage*, 618–621.

31. George Truett, *God's Call to America* (New York: George H. Doran, 1923), 19. The argument of this section on Truett and Mullins is based largely on Christopher Canipe, *A Baptist Democracy: Separating God from Caesar in the Land of the Free* (Macon, Ga.: Mercer University Press, 2011).

32. Truett, *God's Call to America*, 22.

33. George Truett, "The Prayer Jesus Refused to Pray," in *Follow Me* (Nashville, Tenn.: Sunday School Board of the Southern Baptist Convention, 1932), 43.

34. Quoted in Canipe, *Baptist Democracy*, 140.

35. The story and setting of Truett's famous sermon are told well in Canipe, *Baptist Democracy*, 127–152.

36. J. B. Gambrell, foreword to "Baptists and Religious Liberty," Sunday School Board of the Southern Baptist Convention, Nashville, Tennessee. The Sunday School Board is known today as Lifeway Christian Resources. Truett's address can be downloaded from the Baptist Joint Committee's website: http://www.bjconline.org/index.php?option=com_content&task=view&id=4454&Itemid=.

37. See Conrad Henry Moehlman, "The Baptists Revise John Locke," *Journal of Religion* 18 (April 1938): 174–182. Moehlman makes a compelling argument that in a preface to his *Letter Concerning Toleration* (1689), Locke lamented the lack of "absolute liberty, just and true liberty, equal and impartial liberty," and castigated both the English government and the religious sects for failing to promote such. In 1847, Baptist historian Edward Bean Underhill lifted Locke's phrase "absolute liberty, just and true liberty, equal and impartial liberty" and claimed (contra Locke) that Baptists had promoted such. Underhill wrote, "*Thus the Baptists became the first and only propounders of* 'absolute liberty, just and true liberty, equal and impartial liberty.'" Moehlman italicized the first half of the sentence, which comes from Underhill, while only the second comes from Locke. By using quotation marks as Underhill did (notice the interior quotation marks for Locke's words), and considering that Underhill cited Locke in a footnote, it appears that Underhill did not intend to deceive. Nevertheless, future Baptist scholars, including August H. Strong in his *Systematic Theology*, misread Underhill, omitted his interior quotation marks, and made the quote look as if it was entirely from Locke. Strong and others may have honestly misread Underhill and unintentionally fostered an erroneous quote that was too good to pass up.

    As a side note, on two occasions fifteen years apart, a colleague (Barry Hankins) and I assigned graduate students the task of tracking down the Locke quote. Neither search proved fruitful, but the second resulted in finding the Moehlman article, leaving serious doubt about the authenticity of the quote.

38. Quoted in Canipe, *Baptist Democracy*, 147.
39. Edgar Young Mullins, *Faith in the Modern World* (Nashville, Tenn.: Sunday School Board of the Southern Baptist Convention, 1930), 31.
40. Edgar Young Mullins, *The Christian Religion in Its Doctrinal Expression* (Philadelphia: Roger Williams Press, 1917), 68. For a longer discussion of Mullins's theology see Gregory A. Wills, *Southern Baptist Theological Seminary, 1859–2009* (New York: Oxford University Press, 2009).
41. Mullins, *Christian Religion*, 68.
42. Grant Wacker, *Augustus H. Strong and the Dilemma of Historical Consciousness* (Macon, Ga.: Mercer University Press, 1985), 108.
43. Edgar Young Mullins, "Baptists in the Modern World," *Review and Expositor* 8 (July 1911): 348.
44. Edgar Young Mullins, *The Axioms of Religion* (Philadelphia: Judson Press, 1908), 185.
45. Mullins, *Axioms of Religion*, 207.
46. Mullins, *Axioms of Religion*, 255.
47. Canipe, *Baptist Democracy*, 152.
48. Walter Rauschenbusch, *A Theology for the Social Gospel* (New York: Abingdon Press, 1917), 175, 279; quote on 279.

CHAPTER 10

1. Quoted in Robert Moats Miller, *Harry Emerson Fosdick: Preacher, Pastor, Prophet* (New York: Oxford University Press, 1985), 41.
2. Harry Emerson Fosdick, "Shall the Fundamentalists Win?," in Barry Hankins, ed., *Evangelicalism and Fundamentalism: A Documentary Reader* (New York: New York University Press, 2008), 52–58.
3. Fosdick, "Shall the Fundamentalists Win?," 52.
4. Fosdick, "Shall the Fundamentalists Win?," 52–58.
5. Curtis Lee Laws, "Intolerant Liberalism," *Watchman Examiner*, June 15, 1922, 741.
6. Quoted in Miller, *Harry Emerson Fosdick*, 116.
7. Quoted in "War on Modernism in Baptist Church," *New York Times*, June 4, 1922, 32.
8. Quoted in "War on Modernism in Baptist Church," 32.
9. Quoted in "War on Modernism in Baptist Church," 32.
10. Quoted in "Row in Prospect as Baptists Meet," *New York Times*, June 13, 1922, 16.
11. Quoted in "War on Modernism in Baptist Church," 32.
12. Curtis Lee Laws, "Fundamentalism in the Northern Baptist Convention," *Watchman Examiner*, June 15, 1922, 745.

13. Quoted in "Baptist Professor Accused of Heresy," *New York Times*, June 8, 1922, 29.

14. Quoted in "Baptists to Hear Plea to Heal Divisions," *New York Times*, June 15, 1922, 26.

15. "Editorial," *Watchman Examiner*, June 9, 1921, 710.

16. "Editorial," 710.

17. Quoted in "Baptists to Hear Plea to Heal Divisions," 26.

18. "The 'Fundamentalists,'" *New York Times*, June 15, 1922, 15.

19. Quoted in "Baptists Reject a Formal Creed," *New York Times*, June 17, 1922, 9.

20. "'The Baptist' on a Rampage," *Watchman Examiner*, August 14, 1921, 973.

21. Quoted in "Baptists Reject a Formal Creed," 9.

22. "Baptists Reject a Formal Creed," 9.

23. Quoted in Homer De Wilton Brookins, "The Northern Baptist Convention," *Watchman Examiner*, June 29, 1922, 815.

24. Quoted in Brookins, "The Northern Baptist Convention," 815.

25. Quoted in "Baptists Reject a Formal Creed," 9.

26. Curtis Lee Laws, "Convention Side Lights," *Watchman Examiner*, June 29, 1922, 802.

27. Quoted in "Dr. Beaven Rebukes 'Gloating' Baptists," *New York Times*, June 19, 1922, 11.

28. Quoted in "Dr. Beaven Rebukes 'Gloating' Baptists," 11.

29. Quoted in "Dr. Beaven Rebukes 'Gloating' Baptists," 11.

30. "Baptist Factions Agree on Pastors," *New York Times*, June 20, 1922, 9.

31. Quoted in "Dr. Beaven Rebukes 'Gloating' Baptists," 11.

32. "Form New Body," *New York Times*, June 22, 1922, 11.

33. "Demand Democrats Uphold 'Dry' Laws," *New York Times*, June 27, 1920, 16.

34. George Marsden, *Fundamentalism and American Culture: The Shaping of Twentieth Century Evangelicalism, 1870–1925* (New York: Oxford University Press, 1980), 141–153, 169–170.

35. Marsden, *Fundamentalism and American Culture*, 172; William Vance Trollinger Jr., *God's Empire: William Bell Riley and Midwestern Fundamentalism* (Madison, Wis.: University of Wisconsin Press, 1990), 57. See also Barry Hankins, *God's Rascal: J. Frank Norris and the Beginnings of Southern Fundamentalism* (Lexington, Ky.: University Press of Kentucky, 1996), 28–29.

36. Quoted in Trollinger, *God's Empire*, 57.

37. Trollinger, *God's Empire*, 60.

38. "Baptist Fundamentals," *New York Times*, May 30, 1923, 14.

39. "A 'Radical' Triumph," *New York Times*, June 19, 1922, 10.

40. Walter Lippmann, *A Preface to Morals* (New York: Macmillan, 1929; reprint, New York: Time Inc., 1964), 30.

41. Quoted in D. G. Hart, *Defending the Faith: J. Gresham Machen and the Crisis of Conservative Protestantism in Modern America* (Baltimore, Md.: Johns Hopkins University Press, 1994), 79.

CHAPTER 11

1. H. Leon McBeth, *The Baptist Heritage* (Nashville, Tenn.: Broadman Press, 1987), 580.

2. McBeth, *Baptist Heritage*, 702–749; William Davidson, *The Free Will Baptists in History* (Nashville, Tenn.: Randall House Publications, 2001).

3. J. Kristian Pratt, *The Father of Modern Landmarkism: The Life of Ben M. Bogard* (Macon, Ga.: Mercer University Press, 2013), 92.

4. McBeth, *Baptist Heritage*, 757.

5. William Vance Trollinger Jr., *God's Empire: William Bell Riley and Midwestern Fundamentalism* (Madison, Wis.: University of Wisconsin Press, 1990), 60; George Marsden, *Fundamentalism and American Culture* (New York: Oxford University Press, 1980), 190–191.

6. Quoted in Trollinger, *God's Empire*, 142.

7. Quoted in Trollinger, *God's Empire*, 147.

8. Trollinger, *God's Empire*, 148.

9. Quoted in Trollinger, *God's Empire*, 152.

10. Quoted in Trollinger, *God's Empire*, 153–155.

11. For more on Norris, see Barry Hankins, *God's Rascal: J. Frank Norris and the Beginnings of Southern Fundamentalism* (Lexington, Ky.: University Press of Kentucky, 1996).

12. Pratt, *Father of Modern Landmarkism*, 128–129.

13. Quoted in Bill Leonard, "Independent Baptists from Sectarian Minority to 'Moral Majority,'" *Church History* 56 (December 1987): 511.

14. Quoted in Dinesh D'Souza, *Falwell: Before the Millennium: A Critical Biography* (Chicago: Regnery Gateway, 1984), 42.

15. William McLoughlin, ed., *Isaac Backus on Church, State, and Calvinism: Pamphlets 1754–1789* (Cambridge, Mass.: Belknap Press of Harvard University Press, 1968), 50–51.

16. Anthony Lewis, "Both Houses Get Bills to Lift Ban on School Prayer," *New York Times*, June 27, 1962, 20.

17. Quoted in Jonathan Zimmerman, *Whose America? Culture Wars in the Public Schools* (Cambridge, Mass.: Harvard University Press, 2002), 169.

18. "Martin Luther King, Jr.: An Interview with Playboy," *Playboy*, January 1965.

19. Zimmerman, *Whose America?*, 168.

20. "Resolution No. 2—Religious Liberty," *Annual of the Southern Baptist Convention* (Nashville, Tenn.: Southern Baptist Convention, 1964), 80; Paul L. Montgomery, "Baptists Oppose School Prayers," *New York Times*, May 23, 1964, 12.

21. *Eugene Register Guard*, February 22, 1964, 3A.

22. Wayne Flynt, *Alabama Baptists: Southern Baptists in the Heart of Dixie* (Tuscaloosa, Ala.: University of Alabama Press, 1998), 490–491.

23. "Resolution No. 9—On Prayer in Schools," *Annual of the Southern Baptist Convention* (Nashville, Tenn.: Southern Baptist Convention, 1982), 58.

24. Bill Moyers, *God and Politics: The Battle for the Bible* (Princeton, N.J.: Films for the Humanities, 1994), videocassette.

25. See Barry Hankins, *Uneasy in Babylon: Southern Baptist Conservatives and American Culture* (Tuscaloosa, Ala.: University of Alabama Press, 2002), 147; "Resolution No. 5—On Free Exercise in Public Schools," *Annual of the Southern Baptist Convention* (Nashville, Tenn.: Southern Baptist Convention, 1992), 88.

CHAPTER 12

1. William Martin, *A Prophet with Honor: The Billy Graham Story* (New York: Morrow, 1991), 168–172.

2. Gayraud Wilmore, *Black Religion and Black Radicalism: An Interpretation of the Religious History of African Americans*, 3rd ed. (Maryknoll, N.Y.: Orbis Books, 1998), 204–206; quote on 206.

3. Quoted in Andrew Manis, *Southern Civil Religions in Conflict: Black and White Baptists and Civil Rights, 1947–1957* (Athens, Ga.: University of Georgia Press, 1987), 22.

4. Quoted in Paul Harvey, *Freedom's Coming: Religious Culture and the Shaping of the South from the Civil War Through the Civil Rights Era* (Chapel Hill, N.C.: University of North Carolina Press, 2005), 182; Charles Marsh, *The Beloved Community: How Faith Shapes Social Justice, from the Civil Rights Movement to Today* (New York: Basic Books, 2005), 32.

5. Manis, *Southern Civil Religions in Conflict*, 20.

6. Quoted in Andrew M. Manis, *A Fire You Can't Put Out: The Civil Rights Life of Birmingham's Reverend Fred Shuttlesworth* (Tuscaloosa, Ala.: University of Alabama Press, 1999), 331–332.

7. Manis, *Fire You Can't Put Out*, 2–3.

8. Charles Marsh, *God's Long Summer: Stories of Faith and Civil Rights* (Princeton, N.J.: Princeton University Press, 1997), 75.

9. Marsh, *God's Long Summer*, 62.

10. Quoted in Marsh, *God's Long Summer*, 71.

11. David Stricklin, *A Genealogy of Dissent: Southern Baptist Protest in the Twentieth Century* (Lexington, Ky.: University Press of Kentucky, 1999).

12. Stricklin, *Genealogy of Dissent*, 61–62.

13. Stricklin, *Genealogy of Dissent*, 63–65.

14. Merrill M. Hawkins Jr., *Will Campbell: Radical Prophet of the South* (Macon, Ga.: Mercer University Press, 1997).

15. Quoted in Hawkins, *Will Campbell*, 9.

16. Quoted in Frye Galliard, *Race, Rock, and Religion: Profiles from a Southern Journalist* (Charlotte, N.C.: East Woods Press, 1982), 46.

17. Will D. Campbell, "Perhaps and Maybe," *Christian Century*, September 19, 1962, 1133.

18. Hawkins, *Will Campbell*, 44–45. Campbell tells the story of the Albany campaign briefly in his autobiography *Brother to a Dragonfly* (New York: Continuum, 1977), 164–168.

19. See http://mlk-kpp01.stanford.edu/kingweb/about_king/encyclopedia/pritchett_laurie.htm The author of this entry concludes: "In August 1962, King left Albany with no tangible civil rights gains achieved."

20. Quoted in "National Conference on Religion and Race," *Martin Luther King and the Global Freedom Struggle Encyclopedia*, http://mlkkpp01.stanford.edu/index.php/encyclopedia/encyclopedia/enc_national_conference_on_religion_and_race/.

21. Quoted in Hawkins, *Will Campbell*, 45. Also quoted in Campbell, *Brother to a Dragonfly*, 230.

22. Hawkins, *Will Campbell*, 46.

23. Stricklin, *Genealogy of Dissent*, 101–102; Mark Newman, *Getting Right with God: Southern Baptists and Desegregation, 1945–1995* (Tuscaloosa, Ala.: University of Alabama Press, 2001), 29–30, 143; Land quote in Dwayne Hastings, "Foy Valentine, Dead at 82, Led SBC Moral Concerns Arm 27 Years," *Baptist Press*, January 9, 2006, www.bpnews.net.

24. Quoted in Manis, *Southern Civil Religions in Conflict*, 65.

25. Quoted in Jack Nelson, *Terror in the Night: The Klan's Campaign against the Jews* (New York: Simon and Schuster, 1993), 71–72. Marsh covers this story in *God's Long Summer*, 104–106.

26. Quoted in Nelson, *Terror in the Night*, 76.

27. Quoted in Marsh, *God's Long Summer*, 95.

28. Quoted in Newman, *Getting Right with God*, 23; Gregory Wills, *Southern Baptist Theological Seminary, 1859–2009* (New York: Oxford University Press, 2009), 414.

29. Marsh, *God's Long Summer*, 106.

30. Quoted in Marsh, *God's Long Summer*, 108–109.

31. Fisher Humphreys, "E. Y. Mullins," in Timothy George and David S. Dockery, eds., *Theologians of the Baptist Tradition* (Nashville, Tenn.: Broadman and Holman, 2001), 199.

32. Quoted in "Ross Barnett, Segregationist, Dies, Governor of Mississippi in 1960s," *New York Times*, November 7, 1987.

33. Quoted in Marsh, *God's Long Summer*, 104.

34. David Chappell, *A Stone of Hope: Prophetic Religion and the Death of Jim Crow* (Chapel Hill, N.C.: University of North Carolina Press, 2004), 247; Wayne Flynt, *Alabama Baptists: Southern Baptists in the Heart of Dixie* (Tuscaloosa, Ala.: University of Alabama Press, 1998), 460–462.

35. Chappell, *Stone of Hope*.

36. Quoted in Marsh, *God's Long Summer*, 112.

37. Marsh, *God's Long Summer*, 115.

38. Chappell, *Stone of Hope*, 2.

39. "Chicagoan Elected at Baptist Parley," *New York Times*, September 9, 1961, 17; "Dr. King Is Accused in Baptist Dispute," *New York Times*, September 10, 1961, 35; Hans A. Baer and Merrill Singer, *African American Religion: Varieties of Protest and Accommodation*, 2nd ed. (Knoxville, Tenn.: University of Tennessee Press, 2002), 65–67.

40. Wilmore, *Black Religion and Black Radicalism*, 209.

41. Chappell, *Stone of Hope*, 314.

42. Wilmore, *Black Religion and Black Radicalism*, 207–208; quote on 207.

43. Recommendation 3—"Concerning the Supreme Court Decision on Public Education," *Annual of the Southern Baptist Convention* (1954), 56.

44. Quoted in Marsh, *God's Long Summer*, 100.

45. Quoted in Jim Jones, "Baptists Take First Steps," *Fort Worth Star Telegram*, June 25, 1995. See also Barry Hankins, *Uneasy in Babylon: Southern Baptist Conservatives and American Culture* (Tuscaloosa, Ala.: University of Alabama Press, 2002), 240–271.

46. "Resolution No. 1—On Racial Reconciliation on the 150th Anniversary of the Southern Baptist Convention," *Annual of the Southern Baptist Convention* (1995), 80.

CHAPTER 13

1. Conservatives in the SBC controversy were usually referred to in the press as "fundamentalists," and this is what their moderate opponents called them. Because the term is so often used pejoratively and is widely rejected by the conservatives themselves, as a matter of fairness the authors here prefer to use the term "conservative."

2. Walter B. Shurden and Randy Shepley, eds., *Going for the Jugular: A Documentary History of the SBC Holy War* (Macon, Ga.: Mercer University Press, 1996), xii.

3. For Pressler's account, see Paul Pressler, *A Hill on Which to Die: One Southern Baptist's Journey* (Nashville, Tenn.: Broadman and Holman, 1999).

4. Bill Leonard, *God's Last and Only Hope: The Fragmentation of the Southern Baptist Convention* (Grand Rapids, Mich.: Eerdmans, 1990), 29–31, 65–67.

5. Harold Lindsell, *The Battle for the Bible* (Grand Rapids, Mich.: Zondervan, 1976).

6. The "be it resolved" section of the resolution on women read in part, "We encourage the service of women in all aspects of church life and work other than pastoral functions and leadership roles entailing ordination." It was widely interpreted to be a statement against the ordination of women.

7. Helen Parmley, "Baptists Contend with Logistical Problems," *Dallas Morning News*, June 11, 1985. The archived, electronic copies of *Morning News* articles have no page numbers.

8. Quoted in Parmley, "Baptists Contend with Logistical Problems."

9. Quoted in James C. Hefley, *The Truth in Crisis: The Controversy in the Southern Baptist Convention* (Dallas: Criterion, 1986), 120.

10. Quoted in Parmley, "Baptists Contend with Logistical Problems."
11. Quoted in Parmley, "Baptists Contend with Logistical Problems."
12. Nancy Ammerman, *Baptist Battles: Social Change and Religious Conflict in the Southern Baptist Convention* (New Brunswick, N.J.: Rutgers University Press, 1990), 5.
13. Quoted in Ammerman, *Baptist Battles*, 81.
14. Quoted in Ammerman, *Baptist Battles*, 80.
15. Ammerman, *Baptist Battles*, 74–75.
16. Ammerman, *Baptist Battles*, 75. When Paige Patterson reviewed Ammerman's book, he wrote that the only unhappy thing about the book was that it would not make its author a millionaire.
17. Quoted in David Morgan, *The New Crusades, the New Holy Land: Conflict in the Southern Baptist Convention* (Tuscaloosa, Ala.: University of Alabama Press, 1996), 43–44.
18. Quoted in Hefley, *Truth in Crisis*, 123.
19. Quoted in Parmley, "Baptists Contend with Logistical Problems."
20. Parmley, "Baptists Contend with Logistical Problems."
21. Hefley, *Truth in Crisis*, 127.
22. Quoted in Helen Parmley, "Baptists Reelect Fundamentalist," *Dallas Morning News*, June 12, 1985. See also Hefley, *Truth in Crisis*, 127.
23. *Annuals of the Southern Baptist Convention* (reports of the yearly convention meetings) can be accessed at http://digitalcollections.baylor.edu/cdm/landingpage/collection/ml-sbcann.
24. "Report of the Southern Baptist Convention Peace Committee," *Annual of the Southern Baptist Convention*, St. Louis, Missouri, June 16, 1987. The report can be found printed as Report of the Southern Baptist Convention Peace Committee, Item 153, Proceedings of the Southern Baptist Convention, 56, 232–242. The report can be found online at www.baptist2baptist.net.
25. Leonard, *God's Last and Only Hope*, 145.
26. "Report of the Southern Baptist Convention Peace Committee."
27. Leonard, *God's Last and Only Hope*, 144–145.
28. Quoted in Ammerman, *Baptist Battles*, 120–121.
29. "Report of the Southern Baptist Convention Peace Committee."
30. "Report of the Southern Baptist Convention Peace Committee." The entire paragraph reads: "Therefore, we exhort the trustees and administrators of our seminaries and other agencies affiliated with or supported by the Southern Baptist Convention to faithfully discharge their responsibility to carefully preserve the doctrinal integrity of our institutions receiving our support, and only employ professional staff who believe in the divine inspiration of the whole Bible and that the Bible is 'truth without any mixture of error.' "
31. For an overview of the Covenant Renewal document, see Gregory Wills, *Southern Baptist Theological Seminary, 1859–2009* (New York: Oxford University

Press, 2009), 490–501. The characterization of Southern Seminary here is based on the authors' interviews, conversations, and e-mails with Southern Seminary faculty, students, and administrators both moderate and conservative who were at Southern between 1982 and 1995. For an argument that at least four of the Southern Seminary faculty were liberals or neoliberals, see Wills, *Southern Baptist Theological Seminary*, 454–461.

32. Kenneth L. Woodward et al., "Born Again! The Year of the Evangelicals," *Newsweek*, October 25, 1976, 76.

33. Robert Wuthnow, *The Restructuring of American Religion: Society and Faith since World War II* (Princeton, N.J.: Princeton University Press, 1988).

34. "Resolution No. 4—On Abortion," *SBC Annual* 1971, 72.

35. Press release, Baptists Committed to the SBC, 1986, Southern Baptist Archives, Nashville. The quote was also widely reported in state Baptist newspapers. While moderates believed this evidence of the sort of litmus test Mohler would apply years later at Southern Seminary, Patterson claimed he was merely articulating his hope for the convention. See Toby Druin, "Patterson, Reporter Differ on Hiring Story," *Texas Baptist Standard*, July 9, 1986, 5.

36. Quoted in Barry Hankins, *Uneasy in Babylon: Southern Baptist Conservatives and American Culture* (Tuscaloosa, Ala.: University of Alabama Press, 2002), 192; Al Mohler, interview by Barry Hankins, August 5, 1997.

37. Timothy George, "Southern Baptist Heritage of Life," in Richard D. Land and Louis A. Moore, eds., *Life at Risk: The Crisis in Medical Ethics* (Nashville, Tenn.: Broadman and Holman, 1995), 89.

38. See American Baptist Policy Statement on Ordination, Policy 7041, September 1989, http://www.abc-usa.org/wp-content/uploads/2012/06/ordain.pdf. For the best estimates of ordained Southern Baptist women, see Sarah Francis Anders, "Women in Ministry: The Distaff of the Church in Action," *Review and Expositor* 80 (Summer 1983): 30. A sociologist, Anders continued to track the growth into the 1990s and beyond.

39. "Resolution No. 3—On Ordination and the Role of Women in Ministry," *Annual of the Southern Baptist Convention*, 1984, 65.

40. The whole article reads: "A wife is to submit herself graciously to the servant leadership of her husband even as the church willingly submits to the headship of Christ. She, being in the image of God as is her husband and thus equal to him, has the God-given responsibility to respect her husband and to serve as his helper in managing the household and nurturing the next generation."

41. Peter Steinfels, "Beliefs: The Southern Baptists' Declaration That Wives Should 'Submit' Touches Off Debate among Christians on How the Relevant Scripture Evolved," *New York Times*, June 13, 1998, A11.

42. Quoted in Hankins, *Uneasy in Babylon*, 229.

43. Quoted in Hankins, *Uneasy in Babylon*, 229.

44. The 1963 BFMS included the following line on the Bible: "The criterion by which the Bible is to be interpreted is Jesus Christ." The 2000 BFMS changed this to: "All Scripture is a testimony to Christ, who is Himself the focus of divine revelation."

45. Russell Moore, "A Prophetic Minority: Kingdom, Culture, and Mission in a New Era," September 19, 2013, http://www.russellmoore.com/2013/09/19/a-prophetic-minority-kingdom-culture-and-mission-in-a-new-era/.

46. C. Peter Wagner, "A Vision for Evangelizing the Real America," *International Bulletin of Missionary Research*, April 1986, 62.

47. Quoted in Rick Jervis, "Pastor to Become First Black Leader of Southern Baptist Convention," *USA Today*, June 17, 2013, http://usatoday30.usatoday.com/news/religion/story/2012-06-11/fred-luter-to-lead-baptist-convention/55623616/1.

48. This measure of what constitutes an integrated church is used routinely by sociologists. See Michael Emerson and Christian Smith, Divided by Faith: *Evangelical Religion and the Problem of Race in America* (New York: Oxford University Press, 2000).

CHAPTER 14

1. As an example, see Douglas Laycock, "Continuity and Change in the Threat to Religious Liberty: The Reformation Era and the Late Twentieth Century," *Minnesota Law Review* 80 (May 1996): 1085; James Davison Hunter, *Culture Wars: The Struggle to Define America* (New York: Basic Books, 1991).

2. US Census, 2012 Statistical Abstract, http://www.census.gov/compendia/statab/cats/population/religion.html. Also "About One-in-Six Americans Are Baptist," Pew Research: Religion and Public Life Project, June 18, 2009, http://www.pewforum.org/2009/06/18/about-one-in-six-americans-are-baptist/.

3. Mark Noll, "The Bible, Baptists, and the Challenge of Christian Higher Education," in Elizabeth Davis, ed., *A Higher Education: Baylor and the Vocation of a Christian University* (Waco, Texas: Baylor University Press, 2012), 107.

4. L. Russ Bush and Tom J. Nettles, *Baptists and the Bible* (Chicago: Moody Press, 1980), 372.

5. William L. Lumpkin, *Baptist Confessions of Faith*, 2nd rev. ed. (Valley Forge, Pa.: Judson Press, 2011), vii.

6. An exception here would be when a Baptist denomination has funded the building of a mission church or when a congregation has entered into an agreement with the denomination to finance the construction of a church building.

7. Noll, "The Bible, Baptists, and the Challenge of Christian Higher Education," 111.

Bibliography

DENOMINATIONAL PROCEEDINGS

Annual of the Southern Baptist Convention
Minutes of the Appomattox Association (Virginia)
Minutes of the Bethel Association (South Carolina)
Minutes of the Bowdoinham Association (Maine)
Minutes of the Bracken Association of Baptists (Kentucky)
Minutes of the Charleston Baptist Association (South Carolina)
Minutes of the Danbury Association (Connecticut)
Minutes of the Elkhorn Association of Baptists (Kentucky)
Minutes of the Georgia Baptist Association
Minutes of the Groton Union Conference (Connecticut)
Minutes of the Ketocton Baptist Association (Virginia)
Minutes of the Neuse Baptist Association (North Carolina)
Minutes of the New York Baptist Association
Minutes of the North District Association of Baptists (Kentucky)
Minutes of the Proceedings of the Warren Association (Massachusetts)
Minutes of the Rensselaerville Conference (New York)
Minutes of the Salem Association (Kentucky)
Minutes of the Scioto Baptist Association (Ohio)
Minutes of the Shaftsbury Baptist Association (New York/Vermont)
Minutes of the South Kentucky Baptist Association
Minutes of the Stonington Baptist Association (Connecticut)
Minutes of the Warren Association (New England)
Minutes of the Woodstock Association (Connecticut)
Proceedings of the Baptist Convention for Missionary Purposes
Proceedings of the General Convention of the Baptist Denomination in the United States
Proceedings of the Twenty First Session of the Southern Baptist Convention

NEWSPAPERS AND PERIODICALS

American Baptist Magazine
Baptist Memorial and Monthly Record
Baptist Missionary Magazine
Baptist Press
Boston Weekly Post-Boy
Christian Century
Christian Index
Christian Inquirer
Christian Reflector
Christian Secretary
Christian Watchman
Circular
Columbian Star
Dallas Morning News
Eugene Register Guard
Fort Worth Star Telegram
International Bulletin of Missionary Research
Latter Day Luminary
Liberator
Massachusetts Baptist Missionary Magazine
Massachusetts Spy
Newport Mercury
Newsweek
New York Evangelist
New York Telescope
The New York Times
Pennsylvania Gazette
Playboy
Review and Expositor
Texas Baptist Standard
USA Today
The Vehicle, or New York Northwestern Christian Magazine
Virginia Gazette
Watchman Examiner
Zion's Herald

OTHER PRIMARY SOURCES

Allen, I. M. *The Triennial Baptist Register*. Philadelphia: Baptist General Tract Society, 1836.
American Baptist Policy Statement on Ordination, Policy 7041. September 1989. http://www.abc-usa.org/wp-content/uploads/2012/06/ordain.pdf.

Asplund, John. *The Universal Register of the Baptist Denomination.* Boston: John W. Folsom, 1794.

Babcock, Rufus, ed. *Forty Years of Pioneer Life: Memoir of John Mason Peck.* Carbondale, Ill.: Southern Illinois University Press, 1965.

[Backus, Isaac]. *An Account of the Remarkable Recovery of Mrs. Mary Read.* Providence, R.I., 1769?.

Backus, Isaac. *Government and Liberty Described.* Boston: Powars and Willis, 1778.

Backus, Isaac. *A History of New England with Particular Reference to the Denomination of Christians Called Baptists.* 2 vols. 2nd ed. Edited by David Weston. Newton, Mass.: Backus Historical Society, 1871.

Baptist Joint Committee. http://www.bjconline.org/index.php?option=com_content&task=view&id=4454&Itemid.

Barrows, C. Edwin, ed. *The Diary of John Comer.* Philadelphia, 1892.

Berry, W. J., ed. *Kehukee Declaration and Black Rock Address.* Elon College, N.C.: Primitive Publications, 1974.

Bradley, Joshua, ed. *Accounts of Religious Revivals in Many Parts of the United States from 1815.* Albany, N.Y.: G. J. Loomis, 1819.

Brewster, Jonathan M. *The Centennial Record of Freewill Baptists, 1780–1880.* Dover, N.H., 1881.

Broadus, John Albert. *Memoir of James Petrigu Boyce.* New York: A. C. Armstrong and Son, 1893.

Broome, John David, ed. *The Life, Ministry, and Journals of Hezekiah Smith.* Springfield, Mo.: Particular Baptist Press, 2004.

Broughton, V. W. *Twenty Years' Experience of a Missionary.* Chicago: Pony Press, 1907.

Buzzell, John. *A Religious Magazine, Containing a Short History of the Church of Christ, Gathered at New Durham, N.H. in the Year 1780.* Portland, Maine: Arthur Shirley, 1812.

Buzzell, John. *The Life of Elder Benjamin Randal.* Limerick, Maine: Hobbs, Woodman, 1827.

Campbell, Israel. *Bond and Free.* Philadelphia, 1861.

Campbell, Will D. *Brother to a Dragonfly.* New York: Continuum, 1977.

Carter, Tomeiko Ashford, ed. *Virginia Broughton: The Life and Writings of a National Baptist Missionary.* Knoxville, Tenn.: University of Tennessee Press, 2010.

The Charter Granted by His Majesty King Charles the Second, to the Colony of Rhode-Island. Boston: John Allen, 1719.

Clarke, John. *Colonial Baptists: Massachusetts and Rhode Island.* New York: Arno Press, 1980.

Cook, Frederick, ed. *Journals of the Military Expedition of Major General John Sullivan.* Auburn, N.Y.: Knapp, Peck and Thomson, 1887.

"David Barrow's Circular Letter of 1798." *William and Mary Quarterly* 3d ser., 20:3 (1963): 440–451.

Dexter, Franklin Bowditch, ed. *The Literary Diary of Ezra Stiles*. 3 vols. New York: C. Scribner's Sons, 1901.

Dreisbach, Daniel L., and Mark David Hall, eds. *The Sacred Rights of Conscience: Selected Readings on Religious Liberty and Church-State Relations in the American Founding*. Indianapolis, Ind.: Liberty Fund, 2009.

Duvall, Jim, ed. "Columbia Baptist Church Declaration of Faith (1790)." http://baptisthistoryhomepage.com/columbia-hist.html.

Early Virginia Religious Petitions, American Memory, Library of Congress. http://memory.loc.gov/cgi-bin/query/P?relpet:2:./temp/~ammem_X6Uc.

Edwards, Morgan. *Materials towards a History of the American Baptists*. 2 vols. Edited by Eve B. Weeks and Mary B. Warren. Danielsville, Ga.: Heritage Papers, 1984.

Ide, Jacob, ed., *Works of Nathanael Emmons* 6 vols. Boston: Congregational Board of Publication, 1860–1863.

Everson v. Board of Education (1947). http://www.law.cornell.edu/supct/html/historics/USSC_CR_0330_0001_ZO.html.

Faust, Drew Gilpin, ed. *The Ideology of Slavery: Proslavery Thought in the Antebellum South, 1830–1860*. Baton Rouge, La.: Louisiana State University Press, 1981.

Finn, Nathan A., and Keith Harper, eds. *Domestic Slavery Considered as a Scriptural Institution*. Macon, Ga.: Mercer University Press, 2008.

Fisher, Samuel. *Christianismus Redivivus*. London, 1655.

Follow Me. Nashville, Tenn.: Sunday School Board of the Southern Baptist Convention, 1932.

Foner, Philip S., ed. *W. E. B. Du Bois Speaks: Speeches and Addresses*. 2 vols. New York: Pathfinder Press, 1970.

Foss, Andrew T., and Edward Mathews, eds. *Facts for Baptist Churches*. Utica, N.Y.: American Baptist Free Mission Society, 1850.

Founders' Constitution. http://press-pubs.uchicago.edu/founders/print_documents/v1ch1s6.html.

Furman, Richard. *Rewards of Grace Conferred on Christ's Faithful People*. Charleston, S.C.: J. M'Iver, 1796.

Gaustad, Edwin S., ed. *Baptist Piety: The Last Will and Testament of Obadiah Holmes*. Grand Rapids, Mich.: Christian University Press, 1978.

George Whitefield's Journals. Carlisle, Pa.: Banner of Truth Trust, 1960.

Gillette, A. D., ed. *Minutes of the Philadelphia Baptist Association, 1707 to 1807*. 1851. Reprint, Springfield, Mo.: Particular Baptist Press, 2002.

Gospel News, or, A Brief Account of the Revival of Religion in Kentucky. Baltimore, 1801.

Graves, James Robinson. *Old Landmarkism: What Is It?* Memphis, Tenn.: Baptist Book House, 1880.

Greene, L. F. ed. *The Writings of the Late Elder John Leland*. New York: G. W. Wood, 1845.

Grigg, Jacob. *Remarks and Selections on Some of the Most Important Subjects Lately in Dispute*. Lebanon, Ohio: John M'Clean, 1807.

Hankins, Barry, ed. *Evangelicalism and Fundamentalism: A Documentary Reader*. New York: New York University Press, 2008.

Hart, Oliver. "Extracts from the Diary of Oliver Hart." *Charleston Year Book* (1896).

Hart, Oliver. Diary. South Carolina Baptist Historical Society, Furman University, Greenville, South Carolina. Hart, Oliver. Diary transcription. South Caroliniana Library, University of South Carolina, Columbia, South Carolina.

Helwys, Thomas. *A Short Declaration of the Mystery of Iniquity*. London, 1612.

Hooker, Richard J., ed. *The Carolina Backcountry on the Eve of the Revolution: The Journal and Other Writings of Charles Woodmason, Anglican Itinerant*. Chapel Hill, N.C.: University of North Carolina Press, 1953.

Hosmer, James Kendall, ed. *Winthrop's Journal*. 2 vols. New York: C. Scribner's Sons, 1908.

Hutchinson, William T., and William M. E. Rachal, eds. *The Papers of James Madison*. 17 vols. Chicago: University of Chicago Press, 1962–1991.

James, Charles F., ed. *Documentary History of the Struggle for Religious Liberty in Virginia*. Lynchburg, Va.: J. P. Bell, 1900.

Jeter, Jeremiah Bell. *The Recollections of a Long Life*. Richmond, Va.: Religious Herald, 1891.

Johnsen, Leigh, ed., *The Papers of Isaac Backus*. Ann Arbor, Mich.: UMI, 2003.

Kaminski, John P., Gaspare J. Saladino, Richard Leffler, Charles H. Schoenleber, and Margaret A. Hogan, eds. *The Documentary History of the Ratification of the Constitution Digital Edition*. Vol. 13, *Commentaries on the Constitution*. Charlottesville, Va.: University of Virginia Press, 2009.

Kentucky Constitution of 1792, Article 12, sec. 3. http://courts.ky.gov/NR/rdonlyres/7471028C-8BCC-41A2-BA80-02013D4FA550/0/1stKYConstitution.pdf.

Land, Richard D., and Louis A Moore, eds. *Life at Risk: The Crisis in Medical Ethics*. Nashville, Tenn.: Broadman and Holman, 1995.

Lawrence, Joshua. *The American Telescope*. Philadelphia, 1825. http://docsouth.unc.edu/nc/lawrence/lawrence.html.

Lewis, Alonzo, and Newhall, James R. *History of Lynn, Essex County, Massachusetts*. Boston: John L. Shorey, 1865.

Lindsell, Harold. *The Battle for the Bible*. Grand Rapids, Mich.: Zondervan, 1976.

Lippmann, Walter. *A Preface to Morals*. New York: Macmillan, 1929, reprint, New York: Time Inc., 1964.

Logan, Deacon John R. *Sketches, Historical and Biographical, of the Broad River and King's Mountain Baptist Associations*. Shelby, N.C.: Babington, Roberts, 1887.

Maxcy, Jonathan. *An Oration, Delivered in the Baptist Meeting-House in Providence.* Providence, R.I.: Carter and Wilkinson, 1795.

McCoy, Isaac. *History of Baptist Indian Missions.* New York: H. and S. Raynor, 1840.

McLoughlin, William G., ed. *The Diary of Isaac Backus.* 3 vols. Providence, R.I.: Brown University Press, 1979.

McLoughlin, William G., ed. *Isaac Backus on Church, State, and Calvinism: Pamphlets 1754–1789.* Cambridge, Mass.: Belknap Press of Harvard University Press, 1968.

Moore, Frank, ed. *The Rebellion Record.* 2 vols. New York: D. Van Nostrand, 1862.

Moore, Russell. "A Prophetic Minority: Kingdom, Culture, and Mission in a New Era." http://www.russellmoore.com/2013/09/19/a-prophetic-minority-kingdom-culture-and-mission-in-a-new-era/.

Morton, Nathaniel. *New England's Memorial.* Boston: Congregational Board of Publication, 1855.

Mullins, Edgar Young. *The Axioms of Religion.* Philadelphia: Judson Press, 1908.

Mullins, Edgar Young. *The Christian Religion in Its Doctrinal Expression.* Philadelphia: Roger Williams Press, 1917.

Mullins, Edgar Young. *Faith in the Modern World.* Nashville, Tenn.: Sunday School Board of the Southern Baptist Convention, 1930.

Parker, Daniel. *A Public Address.* 1820. Reprint, Carthage, Ill.: Primitive Baptist Library, 1988.

Peacock, John. *A Sketch of the Christian Experience.* Concord, N.H.: Tripp and Osgood, 1851.

Pepper, George Whitfield. *Personal Recollections of Sherman's Campaigns.* Zanesville, Ohio: H. Dunne, 1866.

Philadelphia Baptist Association. *A Confession of Faith.* 6th ed. Philadelphia: B. Franklin, 1743.

Phillips, George. *A Reply to a Confutation of Some Grounds for Infant Baptisme.* London, 1645.

Rathbun, Valentine. *Some Brief Hints, of a Religious Scheme.* Norwich, Conn.: John Trumbull, 1781.

Rauschenbusch, Walter. *A Theology for the Social Gospel.* New York: Abingdon Press, 1917.

Resolution on Racial Reconciliation on the 150th Anniversary of the Southern Baptist Convention. http://www.sbc.net/resolutions/amresolution.asp?id=899.

Rippon, John. "An Account of the Life of Mr. David George." In *Baptist Annual Register for 1790, 1791, 1792, and Part of 1793.* London, 1793.

Sandoz, Ellis, ed. *Political Sermons of the American Founding Era, 1730–1805.* 2nd ed. Indianapolis, Ind.: Liberty Fund, 1998.

Schwartz, Kathryn Carlisle, ed. *Baptist Faith in Action: The Private Writings of Maria Baker Taylor, 1813–1895.* Columbia, S.C.: University of South Carolina Press, 2003.

Semple, Robert B. *A History of the Rise and Progress of the Baptists in Virginia.* Richmond, Va.: Published by the author, 1810.

Sernett, Milton C., ed. *African American Religious History: A Documentary Witness.* 2nd ed. Durham, N.C.: Duke University Press, 1999.

Severance, Frank H., ed. "Letters of the Reverend Elkanah Holmes." *Publications of the Buffalo Historical Society* 6 (1903): 187–206.

Shurden, Walter B., and Randy Shepley, eds. *Going for the Jugular: A Documentary History of the SBC Holy War.* Macon, Ga.: Mercer University Press, 1996.

Simmons, Martha, and Frank A. Thomas, eds. *Preaching with Sacred Fire: An Anthology of African American Sermons, 1750–Present.* New York: Norton, 2010.

Simpson, William S., Jr., ed. "The Journal of Henry Toler, Part II: 1783–1786." *Virginia Baptist Register* 32 (1993): 1629–1649.

Smith, Elias. *Five Letters, with Remarks.* Boston: J. Ball, 1804.

Sprague, William B., ed. *Annals of the American Pulpit.* 9 vols. New York: R. Carter and Brothers, 1865.

Stagg, J. C. A., ed. *The Papers of James Madison Digital Edition.* http://rotunda. upress.virginia.edu/founders/JSMN.html.

Stillman, Samuel. *Good News from a Far Country.* Boston, 1766.

Sweet, William Warren, ed. *Religion on the American Frontier: The Baptists, 1783–1830.* New York: Henry Holt, 1931.

Tarter, Brent, and Robert L. Scribner, eds. *Revolutionary Virginia: The Road to Independence.* 7 vols. Charlottesville, Va.: University Press of Virginia, 1973.

Taylor, John. *Baptists on the American Frontier: A History of Ten Baptist Churches.* Edited by Chester Raymond Young. Macon, Ga.: Mercer University Press, 1995.

Truett, George. *God's Call to America.* New York: George H. Doran, 1923.

Warren Association. *The Sentiments and Plan of the Warren Association.* Germantown, Pa., 1769.

Wayland, Francis. *A Memoir of the Life and Labors of the Rev. Adoniram Judson.* Boston: Phillips, Sampson, 1853.

Wayland, Francis, and H. L. Wayland. *A Memoir of the Life and Labors of Francis Wayland.* 2 vols. New York: Sheldon, 1867.

Wenger, J. C., ed. *The Complete Writings of Menno Simons.* Scottdale, Pa.: Herald Press, 1986.

Whitefield, George. *A Continuation of the Reverend Mr. Whitefield's Journal.* Philadelphia: B. Franklin, 1740.

Whitley, W. T., ed. *The Works of John Smyth.* 2 vols. Cambridge: Cambridge University Press, 1915.

Whitsitt, William H. *A Question of Baptist History.* 1896. Reprint, New York: Arno Press, 1980.

Williams, Roger. *Mr. Cotton's Letter Lately Printed, Examined, and Answered.* London, 1644.

Williams, Roger. *The Complete Writings of Roger Williams.* 7 vols. New York: Russell and Russell, 1963.

Wolever, Terry, ed. *An Anthology of Early Baptists in New Hampshire.* Springfield, Mo.: Particular Baptist Press, 2001.

Wolever, Terry, ed. *The Life, Journal and Works of David Jones, 1736–1820.* Springfield, Mo.: Particular Baptist Press, 2007.

Wolever, Terry, ed. *The Autobiography of Isaac McCoy.* Springfield, Mo.: Particular Baptist Press, 2011.

Woodward, W. W. *Increase of Piety, or, The Revival of Religion in the United States.* Newburyport, Mass., 1802.

SECONDARY SOURCES

African American Historic Sites Database. http://www.aaheritageva.org.

Alfred Street Baptist Church, Alexandria, Virginia. http://www.alfredstreet.org.

Ammerman, Nancy. *Baptist Battles: Social Change and Religious Conflict in the Southern Baptist Convention.* New Brunswick, N.J.: Rutgers University Press, 1990.

Armitage, Thomas. *History of the Baptists.* New York: Bryan, Taylor, 1890.

Aron, Stephen. *How the West Was Lost: The Transformation of Kentucky from Daniel Boone to Henry Clay.* Baltimore: Johns Hopkins University Press, 1996.

Association of Religious Data Archives. www.thearda.com.

Bacon, Leonard W. *A History of American Christianity.* New York: Scribner, 1901.

Baer, Hans A., and Merrill Singer. *African American Religion: Varieties of Protest and Accommodation.* 2nd ed. Knoxville: University of Tennessee Press, 2002.

Bebbington, David W. *Baptists through the Centuries: A History of a Global People.* Waco, Texas: Baylor University Press, 2010.

Bebbington, David W. *Victorian Religious Revivals: Culture and Piety in Local and Global Contexts.* Oxford: Oxford University Press, 2012.

Benedict, David. *A General History of the Baptist Denomination.* 2 vols. Boston: Lincoln and Edmands, 1813.

Billingsley, Andrew. *Mighty Like a River: The Black Church and Social Reform.* New York: Oxford University Press, 1999.

Biographical and Historical Memoirs of Louisiana. 2 vols. Chicago: Goodspeed, 1892.

Boles, John. *The Great Revival: Beginnings of the Bible Belt.* 2nd ed. Lexington: University Press of Kentucky, 1996.

Bowman, Matthew. *The Urban Pulpit: New York City and the Fate of Liberal Evangelicalism.* New York: Oxford University Press, 2014.

Boyd, Jesse L. *A Popular History of the Baptists in Mississippi.* Jackson, Miss.: Baptist Press, 1930.

Boyer, Clarence. *How Sweet the Sound: The Golden Age of Gospel.* Washington, D.C.: Elliott and Clark, 1995.

Boykin, Samuel. *History of the Baptist Denomination in Georgia.* 2 vols. Reprint, Paris, Ark.: Baptist Standard Bearer, 2001.

Brackney, William H. *The Baptists*. Denominations in America no. 2. New York: Greenwood Press, 1988.

Brackney, William H. *Baptists in North America: An Historical Perspective*. Malden, Mass.: Blackwell, 2006.

Bratt, James D. "The Reorientation of American Protestantism, 1835–1845." *Church History* 67 (March 1998): 52–82.

Breen, Patrick H. "Contested Communion: The Limits of White Solidarity in Nat Turner's Virginia." *Journal of the Early Republic* 27 (Winter 2007): 685–703.

Brooks, Walter H. "The Evolution of the Negro Baptist Church." *Journal of Negro History* 7 (January 1922): 11–22.

Bryant, Scott. *The Awakening of the Freewill Baptists: Benjamin Randall and the Founding of an American Religious Tradition*. Macon, Ga.: Mercer University Press, 2011.

Bumsted, J. M. "Revivalism and Separatism in New England: The First Society of Norwich, Connecticut, as a Case Study." *William and Mary Quarterly*, 3rd ser., 24 (October 1967): 588–612.

Bumsted, John M., and Charles E. Clark. "New England's Tom Paine: John Allen and the Spirit of Liberty." *William and Mary Quarterly*, 3rd ser., 21 (October 1964): 561–570.

Burch, Jarrett. *Adiel Sherwood: Baptist Antebellum Pioneer in Georgia*. Macon, Ga.: Mercer University Press, 2003.

Burkitt, Lemuel, and Jesse Read. *A Concise History of the Kehukee Baptist Association*. Philadelphia: Lippincott, Grambo, 1850.

Burrage, Henry. *Baptist Hymn Writers and Their Hymns*. Portland, Maine: Brown Thursten, 1888.

Bush, L. Russ, and Tom J. Nettles. *Baptists and the Bible*. Chicago: Moody Press, 1980.

Butler, Jon. *Awash in a Sea of Faith: Christianizing the American People*. Cambridge, Mass.: Harvard University Press, 1990.

Butterfield, Lyman H. "Elder John Leland, Jeffersonian Itinerant." *Proceedings of the American Antiquarian Society* 62, no. 2 (October 1952): 155–242.

Canipe, Christopher. *A Baptist Democracy: Separating God from Caesar in the Land of the Free*. Macon, Ga.: Mercer University Press, 2011.

Channing, Steven A. *Crisis of Fear: Secession in South Carolina*. New York: Norton, 1974.

Chaplin, Jeremiah. *Life of Henry Dunster, First President of Harvard College*. Boston: J. R. Osgood, 1872.

Chappell, David. *A Stone of Hope: Prophetic Religion and the Death of Jim Crow*. Chapel Hill, N.C.: University of North Carolina Press, 2004.

Coggins, James Robert. *John Smyth's Congregation: English Separatism, Mennonite Influence, and the Elect Nation*. Scottdale, Pa.: Herald Press, 1991.

Cohn, Norman. *The Pursuit of the Millennium: Revolutionary Millenarians and Mystical Anarchists of the Middle Ages*. Rev. ed. New York: Oxford University Press, 1970.

Coker, Joe L. *Liquor in the Land of the Lost Cause: Southern White Evangelicals and the Prohibition Movement.* Lexington, Ky.: University Press of Kentucky, 2007.

Coker, Joe L. "Isaac Backus and John Leland: Baptist Contributions to Religious Liberty in the Founding Era." In *Faith and the Founders of the American Republic,* edited by Daniel L. Dreisbach and Mark David Hall, 305–338. New York: Oxford University Press, 2014.

Converge Worldwide. http://www.convergeworldwide.org.

Crowley, John G. *Primitive Baptists of the Wiregrass South, 1815 to the Present.* Gainesville, Fla.: University of Florida Press, 1998.

Daly, John Patrick. *When Slavery Was Called Freedom: Evangelicalism, Proslavery, and the Causes of the Civil War.* Lexington, Ky.: University Press of Kentucky, 2002.

Darden, Robert. *People Get Ready: A New History of Black Gospel Music.* New York: Continuum, 2004.

Davidson, William. *The Free Will Baptists in History.* Nashville, Tenn.: Randall House, 2001.

Davis, Elizabeth, ed. *A Higher Education: Baylor and the Vocation of a Christian University.* Waco, Texas: Baylor University Press, 2012.

Denison, Frederic. *Notes of the Baptists, and Their Principles, in Norwich, Conn.* Norwich, Conn.: Manning, printer, 1857.

Denison, Frederic. *Westerly (Rhode Island) and Its Witnesses.* Providence, R.I.: J. A. and R. A. Reid, 1878.

Deweese, Charles W., and Pamela R. Durso, eds. *No Longer Ignored: A Collection of Articles on Baptist Women.* Atlanta, Ga.: Baptist History and Heritage Society, 2007.

D'Souza, Dinesh. *Falwell: Before the Millennium: A Critical Biography.* Chicago: Regnery Gateway, 1984.

Duesing, Jason G., ed. *Adoniram Judson: A Bicentennial Appreciation of the Pioneer American Missionary.* Nashville, Tenn.: B & H Academic, 2012.

Duncan, R. S. *A History of the Baptists in Missouri.* St. Louis, Mo.: Scammell, 1882.

Dunn, Durwood. *Cades Cove: The Life and Death of a Southern Appalachian Community, 1818–1937.* Knoxville, Tenn.: University of Tennessee Press, 1988.

Dupont, Carolyn Renée. *Mississippi Praying: Southern White Evangelicals and the Civil Rights Movement, 1945–1975.* New York: New York University Press, 2013.

Durso, Keith E. *Thy Will Be Done: A Biography of George Truett.* Macon, Ga.: Mercer University Press, 2009.

Emerson, Michael, and Christian Smith. *Divided by Faith: Evangelical Religion and the Problem of Race in America.* New York: Oxford University Press, 2000.

Ernest, John. *A Nation within a Nation: Organizing African-American Communities before the Civil War.* Lanham, Md.: Rowman and Littlefield, 2011.

Ernst, Eldon G. *Moment of Truth for Protestant America: Interchurch Campaigns Following World War I.* Dissertation Series no. 3. Missoula, Mont.: Scholar's Press and American Academy of Religion, 1974.

Estep, William R. *The Anabaptist Story,* rev. ed. Grand Rapids, Mich.: Eerdmans, 1975.

Eslinger, Ellen. *Citizens of Zion: The Social Origins of Camp Meeting Revivalism.* Knoxville, Tenn.: University of Tennessee Press, 1999.

Evans, Christopher Hodge. *The Kingdom Is Always But Coming: A Life of Walter Rauschenbusch.* Grand Rapids, Mich.: Eerdmans, 2004.

Ferguson, Everett. *Baptism in the Early Church: History, Theology, and Liturgy in the First Five Centuries.* Grand Rapids, Mich.: Eerdmans, 2009.

Finke, Roger, and Rodney Stark, *The Churching of America, 1776–2005: Winners and Losers in Our Religious Economy.* New Brunswick, N.J.: Rutgers University Press, 1992.

Fisher, Miles Mark. "Lott Cary, the Colonizing Missionary." *Journal of Negro History* 7 (October 1922): 380–418.

Fitts, Leroy. *A History of Black Baptists.* Nashville, Tenn.: Broadman Press, 1985.

Flowers, Elizabeth Hill. *Into the Pulpit: Southern Baptist Women and Power since World War II.* Chapel Hill, N.C.: University of North Carolina Press, 2012.

Flynt, Wayne. *Alabama Baptists: Southern Baptists in the Heart of Dixie.* Tuscaloosa, Ala.: University of Alabama Press, 1998.

Ford, Lacy K. *Deliver Us from Evil: The Slavery Question in the Old South.* New York: Oxford University Press, 2009.

Fox-Genovese, Elizabeth, and Eugene Genovese. *The Mind of the Master Class: History and Faith in the Southern Slaveholder's Worldview.* New York: Cambridge University Press, 2005.

Fuller, A. James. *Chaplain to the Confederacy: Basil Manly and Baptist Life in the Old South.* Baton Rouge, La.: Louisiana State University Press, 2000.

Galliard, Frye. *Race, Rock, and Religion: Profiles from a Southern Journalist.* Charlotte, N.C.: East Woods Press, 1982.

Gardner, Robert G. *Baptists of Early America: A Statistical History, 1639–1790.* Atlanta: Georgia Baptist Historical Society, 1983.

Garrett, James Leo. *Baptist Theology: A Four-Century Study.* Macon, Ga.: Mercer University Press, 2009.

Gaustad, Edwin. *Liberty of Conscience: Roger Williams in America.* Grand Rapids, Mich.: Eerdmans, 1991.

Gaustad, Edwin. *Roger Williams.* New York: Oxford University Press, 2005.

George, Timothy, and David S. Dockery, eds. *Theologians of the Baptist Tradition.* Nashville, Tenn.: Broadman and Holman, 2001.

Glaude, Eddie S. *Exodus! Religion, Race, and Nation in Early Nineteenth-Century Black America.* Chicago: University of Chicago Press, 2000.

Goen, C. C. *Broken Churches, Broken Nation: Denominational Schism and the Coming of the Civil War.* Macon, Ga.: Mercer University Press, 1985.

Goen, C. C. *Revivalism and Separatism in New England, 1740–1800: Strict Congregationalists and Separate Baptists in the Great Awakening.* Rev. ed. Middletown, Conn.: Wesleyan University Press, 1987.

Goreau, Laurraine. *Just Mahalia, Baby.* Waco, Texas: Word Books, 1975.

Gourley, Bruce T. *Diverging Loyalties: Baptists in Middle Georgia during the Civil War*. Macon, Ga.: Mercer University Press, 2011.

Green, Steven K. *The Second Disestablishment: Church and State in Nineteenth-Century America*. New York: Oxford University Press, 2010.

Guelzo, Allen C. *Abraham Lincoln: Redeemer President*. Grand Rapids, Mich.: Eerdmans, 1999.

Guild, Reuben Aldridge. *Life, Times, and Correspondence of James Manning*. Boston: Gould and Lincoln, 1864.

Guild, Reuben A. *Chaplain Smith and the Baptists*. Philadelphia: American Baptist Publication Society, 1885.

Guthman, Joshua Aaron. "'What I Am 'Tis Hard to Know': Primitive Baptists, the Protestant Self, and the American Religious Imagination." PhD diss., University of North Carolina at Chapel Hill, 2008.

Gwynne, S. C. *Empire of the Summer Moon: Quanah Parker and the Rise and Fall of the Comanches*. New York: Scribner, 2010.

Halsey, Lewis. *History of the Seneca Baptist Association*. Ithaca, N.Y.: Journal Association Book and Job Printing House, 1879.

Hankins, Barry. *God's Rascal: J. Frank Norris and the Beginnings of Southern Fundamentalism*. Lexington, Ky.: University Press of Kentucky, 1996.

Hankins, Barry. *Uneasy in Babylon: Southern Baptist Conservatives and American Culture*. Tuscaloosa, Ala.: University of Alabama Press, 2002.

Harlow, Luke E. "Neither Slavery nor Abolitionism: James M. Pendleton and the Problem of Christian Conservative Antislavery in 1840s Kentucky." *Slavery and Abolition* 27 (December 2006): 367–389.

Harlow, Luke E. *Religion, Race, and the Making of Confederate Kentucky, 1830–1880*. New York: Cambridge University Press, 2014.

Harper, Keith. *The Quality of Mercy: Southern Baptists and Social Christianity, 1890–1920*. Tuscaloosa, Ala.: University of Alabama Press, 1996.

Harper, Keith. "'And All the Baptists in Kentucky Took the Name United Baptists': The Union of the Separate and Regular Baptists of Kentucky." *Register of the Kentucky Historical Society* 110 (Winter 2012): 3–31.

Harris, Michael W. "Conflict and Resolution in the Life of Thomas Andrew Dorsey." In *We'll Understand It Better By and By*, by Bernice Johnson Reagon, 165–184. Washington, D.C.: Smithsonian Institution Press, 1992.

Harris, Michael W. *The Rise of the Gospel Blues: The Music of Thomas Andrew Dorsey in the Urban Church*. New York: Oxford University Press, 1992.

Hart, D. G. *Defending the Faith: J. Gresham Machen and the Crisis of Conservative Protestantism in Modern America*. Baltimore, Md.: Johns Hopkins University Press, 1994.

Harvey, Paul. *Redeeming the South: Religious Cultures and Racial Identities among Southern Baptists, 1865–1925*. Chapel Hill, N.C.: University of North Carolina Press, 1997.

Harvey, Paul. *Freedoms Coming: Religious Culture and the Shaping of the South from the Civil War to the Civil Rights Era*. Chapel Hill: University of North Carolina Press, 2005.

Hawkins, Merrill M., Jr. *Will Campbell: Radical Prophet of the South*. Macon, Ga.: Mercer University Press, 1997.

Hefley, James C. *The Truth in Crisis: The Controversy in the Southern Baptist Convention*. Dallas: Criterion, 1986.

Hempton, David. *Methodism: Empire of the Spirit*. New Haven, Conn.: Yale University Press, 2005.

Heyrman, Christine. *Southern Cross: The Beginnings of the Bible Belt*. New York: Alfred A. Knopf, 1997.

Higginbotham, Evelyn Brooks. *Righteous Discontent: The Women's Movement in the Black Baptist Church, 1880–1920*. Cambridge, Mass.: Harvard University Press, 1993.

Holifield, E. Brooks. *Theology in America: Christian Thought from the Age of the Puritans to the Civil War*. New Haven, Conn.: Yale University Press, 2003.

Hudson, Winthrop. *Baptist Concepts of the Church*. Chicago: Judson Press, 1959.

Hunter, James Davison. *Culture Wars: The Struggle to Define America*. New York: Basic Books, 1991.

Hutson, James H., ed. *Religion and the New Republic: Faith in the Founding of America*. Lanham, Md.: Rowman and Littlefield, 2000.

Irons, Charles F. *The Origins of Proslavery Christianity: White and Black Evangelicals in Colonial and Antebellum Virginia*. Chapel Hill, N.C.: University of North Carolina Press, 2008.

Isaac, Rhys. *The Transformation of Virginia, 1740–1790*. Chapel Hill, N.C.: University of North Carolina Press, 1982.

James, Sydney V. *John Clarke and His Legacies: Religion and Law in Colonial Rhode Island, 1638–1750*. Edited by Theodore Dwight Bozeman. University Park, Pa.: Pennsylvania State University Press, 1999.

Johnson, Robert E. *A Global Introduction to Baptist Churches*. New York: Cambridge University Press, 2010.

Jones, Jacqueline. *Saving Savannah: The City and the Civil War*. New York: Alfred A. Knopf, 2008.

Jones, John G. *A Concise History of the Introduction of Protestantism into Mississippi and the Southwest*. St. Louis, Mo.: P. M. Pinckard, 1866.

Jordan, Ervin L. *Black Confederates and Afro-Yankees in Civil War Virginia*. Charlottesville, Va.: University Press of Virginia, 1995.

Juster, Susan. *Disorderly Women: Sexual Politics and Evangelicalism in Revolutionary New England*. Ithaca, N.Y.: Cornell University Press, 1994.

Kars, Marjoleine. *Breaking Loose Together: The Regulator Rebellion in Pre-Revolutionary North Carolina*. Chapel Hill, N.C.: University of North Carolina Press, 2002.

Kell, Carl L. *Against the Wind: The Moderate Voice in Baptist Life*. Knoxville, Tenn.: University of Tennessee Press, 2009.

Keller, Charles Roy. *The Second Great Awakening in Connecticut.* New Haven, Conn.: Yale University Press, 1942.

Kellison, Kimberly R. "South Carolina Baptists, the Primitive-Missionary Schism, and the Revival of the Early 1830s." *South Carolina Historical Magazine* 110 (July–October 2009): 154–179.

Kidd, Thomas S., "Becoming Important in the Eye of Civil Powers": New Light Baptists, Cultural Respectability, and the Founding of the College of Rhode Island." In *The Scholarly Vocation and the Baptist Academy : Essays on the Future of Baptist Higher Education*, edited by Roger Ward and David P. Gushee, 50–67. Macon, Ga.: Mercer University Press, 2008.

Kidd, Thomas S. *The Protestant Interest: New England after Puritanism.* New Haven, Conn.: Yale University Press, 2004.

Kidd, Thomas S. "The Healing of Mercy Wheeler: Illness and Miracles among Early American Evangelicals." *William and Mary Quarterly*, 3rd ser., 63 (January 2006): 149–170.

Kidd, Thomas S. *The Great Awakening: The Roots of Evangelical Christianity in Colonial America.* New Haven, Conn.: Yale University Press, 2007.

Kidd, Thomas S. *God of Liberty: A Religious History of the American Revolution.* New York: Basic Books, 2010.

Lambert, Byron C. *The Rise of the Anti-Mission Baptists.* 1957. Reprint, New York: Arno Press, 1980.

Laycock, Douglas. "Continuity and Change in the Threat to Religious Liberty: The Reformation Era and the Late Twentieth Century." *Minnesota Law Review* 80 (May 1996): 1047–1102.

Leonard, Bill. "Independent Baptists from Sectarian Minority to 'Moral Majority.'" *Church History* 56 (December 1987): 504–517.

Leonard, Bill. *God's Last and Only Hope: The Fragmentation of the Southern Baptist Convention.* Grand Rapids, Mich.: Eerdmans, 1990.

Leonard, Bill. *Baptist Ways: A History.* Valley Forge, Pa.: Judson Press, 2003.

Leonard, Bill. *Baptists in America.* New York: Columbia University Press, 2005.

Lovett, Bobby L. *A Black Man's Dream: The First 100 Years: Richard Henry Boyd and the National Baptist Publishing Board.* Jacksonville, Fla.: Mega Corp., 1993.

Lindman, Janet Moore. *Bodies of Belief: Baptist Community in Early America.* Philadelphia: University of Pennsylvania Press, 2008.

Loveland, Anne C. *Southern Evangelicals and the Social Order, 1800–1860.* Baton Rouge, La.: Louisiana State University Press, 1980.

Lucas, Marion B. *A History of Blacks in Kentucky: From Slavery to Segregation, 1760–1891.* Frankfort, Ky.: Kentucky Historical Society, 2003.

Lumpkin, William L. *Baptist Confessions of Faith.* 2nd rev. ed. Valley Forge, Pa.: Judson Press, 2011.

Manis, Andrew M. *Southern Civil Religions in Conflict: Black and White Baptists and Civil Rights, 1947–1957.* Athens, Ga.: University of Georgia Press, 1987.

Manis, Andrew M. *A Fire You Can't Put Out: The Civil Rights Life of Birmingham's Reverend Fred Shuttlesworth.* Tuscaloosa, Ala.: University of Alabama Press, 1999.

Maring, Norman H. *Baptists in New Jersey: A Study in Transition.* Valley Forge, Pa.: Judson Press, 1964.

Marsden, George. *Fundamentalism and American Culture: The Shaping of Twentieth Century Evangelicalism, 1870–1925.* New York: Oxford University Press, 1980.

Marsden, George. *Understanding Evangelicalism and Fundamentalism.* Grand Rapids, Mich.: Eerdmans, 1991.

Marsh, Charles. *God's Long Summer: Stories of Faith and Civil Rights.* Princeton, N.J.: Princeton University Press, 1997.

Marsh, Charles. *The Beloved Community: How Faith Shapes Social Justice, from the Civil Rights Movement to Today.* New York: Basic Books, 2005.

Martin, William. *A Prophet with Honor: The Billy Graham Story.* New York: Morrow, 1991.

Martínez, Juan Francisco. *Sea la Luz: The Making of Mexican Protestantism in the American Southwest, 1829–1900.* Denton, Texas: University of North Texas Press, 2006.

Martin Luther King and the Global Freedom Struggle Encyclopedia. http://mlk-kpp01.stanford.edu/index.php/encyclopedia/encyclopedia_contents.

Marty, Martin, "The Protestant Experience and Perspective." In *American Religious Values and the Future of America*, edited by Rodger Van Allen, 130–151. Philadelphia: Fortress Press, 1978.

Masters, Frank M. *A History of Baptists in Kentucky.* Louisville, Ky.: Baptist Historical Society, 1953.

Mathews, Donald G. "The Second Great Awakening as an Organizing Process, 1780–1830: An Hypothesis." *American Quarterly* 21 (Spring 1969): 23–43.

Mathews, Donald G. *Religion in the Old South.* Chicago: University of Chicago Press, 1977.

Mathis, James R. *The Making of the Primitive Baptists: A Cultural and Intellectual History of the Antimission Movement.* New York: Routledge, 2004.

McBeth, H. Leon. *The Baptist Heritage.* Nashville, Tenn.: Broadman Press, 1987.

McCurry, Stephanie. *Masters of Small Worlds: Yeoman Households, Gender Relations, and the Political Culture of the Antebellum South Carolina Low Country.* New York: Oxford University Press, 1995.

McKivigan, John R. *The War against Proslavery Religion: Abolitionism and the Northern Churches, 1830–1865.* Ithaca, N.Y.: Cornell University Press, 1984.

McKivigan, John R., ed. *Abolitionism and American Religion.* New York: Garland 1999.

McKivigan, John R., and Mitchell Snay, eds. *Religion and the Antebellum Debate over Slavery.* Athens, Ga.: University of Georgia Press, 1998.

McLoughlin, William G., ed. *The American Evangelicals, 1800–1900: An Anthology.* New York: Harper and Row, 1968.

McLoughlin, William G. "Isaac Backus and the Separation of Church and State in America." *American Historical Review* 73 (June 1968): 1392–1413.

McLoughlin, William G. *New England Dissent, 1630–1833: The Baptists and the Separation of Church and State.* 2 vols. Cambridge, Mass.: Harvard University Press, 1971.

McLoughlin, William G. *Champions of the Cherokees: Evan and John B. Jones.* Princeton, N.J.: Princeton University Press, 1990.

Miller, Randall M., Harry S. Stout, and Charles R. Wilson, eds. *Religion and the American Civil War.* New York: Oxford University Press, 1998.

Miller, Robert Moats. *Harry Emerson Fosdick: Preacher, Pastor, Prophet.* New York: Oxford University Press, 1985.

Moehlman, Conrad Henry. "The Baptists Revise John Locke." *Journal of Religion* 18 (April 1938): 174–182.

Morgan, David. *The New Crusades, the New Holy Land: Conflict in the Southern Baptist Convention.* Tuscaloosa, Ala.: University of Alabama Press, 1996.

Morgan, Edmund S. *Roger Williams: The Church and the State.* New York: Harcourt, Brace and World, 1967.

Moss, Bobby Gilmer. *A Voice in the Wilderness: A History of Buffalo Baptist Church.* Gaffney, S.C.: Gaffney Printing Company, 1972.

Moyers, Bill. *God and Politics: The Battle for the Bible.* Princeton, N.J.: Films for the Humanities, 1994. Videocassette.

Najar, Monica. "'Meddling with Emancipation': Baptists, Authority, and the Rift over Slavery in the Upper South." *Journal of the Early Republic* 25 (Summer 2005): 157–186.

Najar, Monica. *Evangelizing the South: A Social History of Church and State in Early America.* New York: Oxford University Press, 2008.

Nelson, Jack. *Terror in the Night: The Klan's Campaign against the Jews.* New York: Simon and Schuster, 1993.

Nettles, Thomas J. *James Petigru Boyce: A Southern Baptist Statesman.* Phillipsburg, N.J.: P & R Publishing, 2009.

Newman, A. H., ed. *A Century of Baptist Achievement.* Philadelphia: American Baptist Publication Society, 1901.

Newman, Mark. *Getting Right with God: Southern Baptists and Desegregation, 1945–1995.* Tuscaloosa, Ala.: University of Alabama Press, 2001.

Noll, Mark A. *America's God: From Jonathan Edwards to Abraham Lincoln.* New York: Oxford University Press, 2002.

Noll, Mark A. *The Civil War as a Theological Crisis.* Chapel Hill, N.C.: University of North Carolina Press, 2006.

Oates, Stephen B. *The Fires of Jubilee: Nat Turner's Fierce Rebellion.* New York: Harper and Row, 1975.

Olson, Adolf. *A Centenary History as Related to the Baptist General Conference of America.* Chicago: Baptist Conference Press, 1952.

Oshatz, Molly. *Slavery and Sin: The Fight against Slavery and the Rise of Liberal Protestantism.* New York: Oxford University Press, 2012.

Paschal, George W. *History of North Carolina Baptists.* 2 vols. Raleigh, N.C.: North Carolina Baptist State Convention, 1930–1955.

Patterson, James A. *James Robinson Graves: Staking the Boundaries of Baptist Identity.* Nashville, Tenn.: B & H Academic, 2012.

Pestana, Carla Gardina. *Quakers and Baptists in Colonial Massachusetts.* New York: Cambridge University Press, 1991.

Pew Research: Religion and Public Life Project. http://www.pewforum.org.

Porter, Andrew. *Religion versus Empire? British Protestant Missionaries and Overseas Expansion, 1700–1914.* New York: Manchester University Press, 2004.

Posey, Walter B. *The Baptist Church in the Lower Mississippi Valley, 1776–1845.* Lexington, Ky.: University Press of Kentucky, 1957.

Pratt, J. Kristian. *The Father of Modern Landmarkism: The Life of Ben M. Bogard.* Macon, Ga.: Mercer University Press, 2013.

Pressler, Paul. *A Hill on Which to Die: One Southern Baptist's Journey.* Nashville, Tenn.: Broadman and Holman, 1999.

Pruitt, Lisa Joy. *A Looking-Glass for Ladies: American Protestant Women and the Orient in the Nineteenth Century.* Macon, Ga.: Mercer University Press, 2005.

Punchard, George. *History of Congregationalism from about A.D. 250 to the Present.* 5 vols. Boston: Congregational Publishing House, 1881.

Putnam, Mary Burnham. *The Baptists and Slavery, 1840–1845.* Ann Arbor, Mich.: George Wahr, 1913.

Rable, George C. *God's Almost Chosen Peoples: A Religious History of the American Civil War.* Chapel Hill, N.C.: University of North Carolina Press, 2010.

Raboteau, Albert J. *Slave Religion: The "Invisible Institution" in the Antebellum South.* Updated ed. New York: Oxford University Press, 2004.

Ragosta, John A. *Wellspring of Liberty: How Virginia's Religious Dissenters Helped Win the American Revolution and Secured Religious Liberty.* New York: Oxford University Press, 2010.

Ranck, George Washington. *"The Travelling Church": An Account of the Baptist Exodus from Virginia to Kentucky in 1781.* Louisville, Ky., 1910.

Randall, Ian M., and Anthony R. Cross, eds. *Baptists and Mission: Papers from the Fourth International Conference on Baptist Studies.* Milton Keynes, England: Paternoster, 2007.

Rogers, James A. *Richard Furman: Life and Legacy.* Macon, Ga.: Mercer University Press, 2001.

Rohrer, S. Scott. *Wandering Souls: Protestant Migrations in America, 1630–1865.* Chapel Hill, N.C.: University of North Carolina Press, 2010.

Roosevelt, Theodore. *The Winning of the West.* 4 vols. New York: Putnam's, 1889–1899.

Schultz, George A. *An Indian Canaan: Isaac McCoy and the Vision of an Indian State.* Norman, Okla.: University of Oklahoma Press, 1972.

Scott, Sean A. *A Visitation of God: Northern Civilians Interpret the Civil War.* New York: Oxford University Press, 2011.

Scully, Randolph Ferguson. *Religion and the Making of Nat Turner's Virginia: Baptist Community and Conflict, 1740–1840.* Charlottesville, Va.: University of Virginia Press, 2008.

Seeman, Erik. "Sarah Prentice and the Immortalists: Sexuality, Piety, and the Body in Eighteenth-Century New England." In *Sex and Sexuality in Early America,* edited by Merril D. Smith, 116–132. New York: New York University Press, 1998.

Smith, Christian. *American Evangelicalism: Embattled and Thriving.* Chicago: University of Chicago Press, 1998.

Smith, H. Shelton. *In His Image, But . . . Racism in Southern Religion, 1780–1910.* Durham, N.C.: Duke University Press, 1972.

Smith, Justin A. *A History of the Baptists in the Western States East of the Mississippi.* Philadelphia: American Baptist Publication Society, 1896.

Smith, Preserved. "Chronicles of a New England Family." *New England Quarterly* 9 (September 1936): 417–446.

Sobel, Mechal. *Trabelin' On: The Slave Journey to an Afro-Baptist Faith.* Westport, Conn.: Greenwood Press, 1979.

Sobel, Mechal. *The World They Made Together: Black and White Values in Eighteenth-Century Virginia.* Princeton, N.J.: Princeton University Press, 1987.

Spain, Rufus. *At Ease in Zion: A Social History of Southern Baptists, 1865–1900.* Nashville, Ala.: Vanderbilt University Press, 1967.

Spangler, Jewel L. *Virginians Reborn: Anglican Monopoly, Evangelical Dissent, and the Rise of the Baptists in the Late Eighteenth Century.* Charlottesville, Va.: University of Virginia Press, 2008.

Sparks, Elder John. *The Roots of Appalachian Christianity: The Life and Legacy of Elder Shubal Stearns.* Lexington, Ky.: University Press of Kentucky, 2001.

Sparks, Randy J. *On Jordan's Stormy Banks: Evangelicalism in Mississippi, 1773–1876.* Athens, Ga.: University of Georgia Press, 1994.

Spears, Jay. "Slave Quarters on the Campus of South Carolina College, 1801 to 2010." Research paper. http://tundra.csd.sc.edu/slaveryorigin/docs/hist%20 497f%20final%20draft.pdf.

Spencer, David. *The Early Baptists of Philadelphia.* Philadelphia: W. Syckelmoore, 1877.

Spencer, John H. *A History of Kentucky Baptists.* 2 vols. Cincinnati, Ohio: J. R. Baumes, 1885.

Stott, William T. *Indiana Baptist History: 1798–1908.* Franklin, Ind., 1908.

Stricklin, David. *A Genealogy of Dissent: Southern Baptist Protest in the Twentieth Century.* Lexington, Ky.: University Press of Kentucky, 1999.

Sullivan, Regina D. *Lottie Moon: A Southern Baptist Missionary to China in History and Legend.* Baton Rouge, La.: Louisiana State University Press, 2011.

Taylor, James B. *Lives of Virginia Baptist Ministers.* Richmond, Va.: Yale and Wyatt, 1838.

The Tennessee Encyclopedia of History and Culture. http://tennesseeencyclopedia.net.

Thompson, James J. *Tried as by Fire: Southern Baptists and the Religious Controversies of the 1920s*. Macon, Ga.: Mercer University Press, 1982.

Torbet, Robert G. *A History of the Baptists*. Rev. ed. Valley Forge, Pa. Judson Press, 1963.

Townsend, Leah. *South Carolina Baptists, 1670–1805*. Florence, S.C.: Florence Print. Co., 1935.

Trollinger, William Vance, Jr. *God's Empire: William Bell Riley and Midwestern Fundamentalism*. Madison: University of Wisconsin Press, 1990.

US Census. 2012 Statistical Abstract. http://www.census.gov/compendia/statab/cats/population/religion.html.

Vedder, Henry Clay. *A History of the Baptists in the Middle States*. Philadelphia: American Baptist Publication Society, 1898.

Waak, Patricia. *My Bones Are Red: A Spiritual Journey with a Triracial People in the Americas*. Macon, Ga.: Mercer University Press, 2005.

Wacker, Grant. *Augustus H. Strong and the Dilemma of Historical Consciousness*. Macon, Ga.: Mercer University Press, 1985.

Wardin, Albert W., Jr. *The Twelve Baptist Tribes in the United States: A Historical and Statistical Analysis*. Atlanta, Ga.: Baptist History and Heritage Society, 2007.

Weaver, C. Douglas. *In Search of the New Testament Church: The Baptist Story*. Macon, Ga.: Mercer University Press, 2008.

"The West's Most Western Town." http://www.scottsdaleaz.gov/about/history.

Williams, Juan, and Quinton Dixie. *This Far by Faith: Stories from the African American Religious Experience*. New York: William Morrow/Harper Collins, 2003.

Williams, Michael E. *Isaac Taylor Tichenor: The Creation of the Baptist New South*. Tuscaloosa, Ala.: University of Alabama Press, 2005.

Williams, Michael E., and Walter B. Shurden, eds. *Turning Points in Baptist History: A Festschrift in Honor of Harry Leon McBeth*. Macon, Ga.: Mercer University Press, 2008.

Willis, Alan Scot. *All According to God's Plan: Southern Baptist Missions and Race, 1945–1970*. Lexington, Ky.: University Press of Kentucky, 2005.

Wills, Gregory A. *Democratic Religion: Freedom, Authority, and Church Discipline in the Baptist South, 1785–1900*. New York: Oxford University Press, 1997.

Wills, Gregory A. *Southern Baptist Theological Seminary, 1859–2009*. New York: Oxford University Press, 2009.

Wilmore, Gayraud. *Black Religion and Black Radicalism: An Interpretation of the Religious History of African Americans*. 3rd ed. Maryknoll, N.Y.: Orbis Books, 1998.

Wilson, Charles Reagan. *Baptized in Blood: The Religion of the Lost Cause, 1865–1920*. Athens, Ga.: University of Georgia Press, 1980.

Wilson, Mark R. *William Owen Carver's Controversies in the Baptist South*. Macon, Ga.: Mercer University Press, 2010.

Withington, Ann Fairfax. *Toward a More Perfect Union: Virtue and the Formation of American Republics.* New York: Oxford University Press, 1991.

Wolffe, John. *The Expansion of Evangelicalism: The Age of Wilberforce, More, Chalmers, and Finney.* Downers Grove, Ill.: InterVarsity Press, 2007.

Wood, Nathan E. *The History of the First Baptist Church of Boston.* Boston: American Baptist Publication Society, 1899.

Wright, Stephen. *History of the Shaftsbury Baptist Association.* Troy, N.Y.: A. G. Johnson, 1853.

Wright, Stephen I. *The Early English Baptists, 1603–1649.* Rochester, N.Y.: Boydell Press, 2006.

Wuthnow, Robert. *The Restructuring of American Religion: Society and Faith since World War II.* Princeton, N.J.: Princeton University Press, 1988.

Wyatt-Brown, Betram. "The Antimission Movement in the Jacksonian South: A Study in Regional Folk Culture." *Journal of Southern History* 36 (November 1970): 501–529.

Young, Alfred F. *Masquerade: The Life and Times of Deborah Sampson, Continental Soldier.* New York: Alfred A. Knopf, 2004.

Zellar, Gary. *African Creeks: Estelvste and the Creek Nation.* Norman, Okla.: University of Oklahoma Press, 2007.

Zimmerman, Jonathan. *Whose America? Culture Wars in the Public Schools.* Cambridge, Mass.: Harvard University Press, 2002.

Index

$75 Million Campaign, 175, 177–178

Abernathy, Ralph, 213–214, 225

Abington v. Schempp (1963), 205

Abortion, 210, 230, 232, 239–242

Abyssinian Baptist Church (New York), 106

Act of Toleration (1689), 22

Adams, John, 49–50, 60, 66

Adams, Samuel, 49–50

Adult baptism. *See* Believer's baptism

Affusion, 6, 115, 168

African American Baptists
  and the American Revolution, 46–47
  and church discipline cases, 83, 98–99
  and the Civil Rights movement, 211–214, 225–227
  and the Civil War, 137–139
  in colonial America, 24–25, 45–47
  conversion testimony of, 67, 104
  growth of, 95, 118, 129
  and independent churches in the antebellum era, 47, 69, 104–106, 124, 130
  and missions, 47, 80, 95–96, 152, 160–164
  music of, 156–160
  and participation in white churches, 84, 100–101, 124
  and Prohibition, 191
  schism among, 164–165, 248
  and separatism after the Civil War, 149–156, 160–164, 248
  and slavery, 123, 126, 130
  and social issues, 206–207, 210, 251
  in the Southern Baptist Convention, 245–246
  and women's roles, 160–164
  See also specific organizations and people

African Methodist Episcopal Church, 103, 163

Aitchison, John Y., 174

Akin, Danny, 246

Alabama, Baptists in
  and the Civil War, 133, 135
  and church-state issues, 208
  growth of, 85, 90, 111, 151–152
  and segregation, 224
  and slavery, 128
  Social Gospel in, 171–172
  See also specific cities and organizations

Alabama Christian Movement for Human Rights (ACMHR), 213–214

Alaska, first Baptists in, 121

Albany Movement, 218–219

Alcohol. *See* Prohibition; and Temperance

Alexandria, Virginia, 100–101, 105, 137

Allen, John, 48–49

Allensworth, Allen, 137

American Baptist Anti-Slavery
  Convention, 126
American Baptist Association (ABA),
  169–170, 197, 202
American Baptist Churches USA
  (ABC), 196, 207, 209, 217–218,
  240, 242, 244. *See also* Northern
  Baptist Convention
American Baptist Convention. *See*
  American Baptist Churches USA
American Baptist Foreign Missions
  Society, 199, 217
American Baptist Free Mission Society,
  131
American Baptist Home Mission
  Society (ABHMS), 120–122, 127,
  155, 161, 199
American Baptist Missionary Union,
  130
American Baptist Publication Society,
  128, 160, 162, 198–199
American Bible Society, 96
American Board of Commissioners for
  Foreign Missions, 94–95, 109
American Indian Mission Association,
  107
American National Baptist Convention,
  153–154
American Revolution
  Baptists' ambivalence about,
    39–40, 49–51
  Baptists' growing enthusiasm for,
    56–58, 99
  Events leading up to, 40–44, 48–49
  Revivals during, 53–55
  See also Chaplains, in the American
    Revolution; Loyalists; Patriots; and
    Religious Liberty
Ammerman, Nancy, 233
Amsterdam, 6, 8
Anabaptists, 3–5, 8, 10, 13, 15, 179, 251
Andover Theological Seminary, 94

Anglicans
  Baptists converting from, 5, 51
  and conflict with Baptists, 6, 50,
    62, 113
  and establishment in Southern
    colonies/states, 7, 35, 46, 62–64, 71
  and the Great Awakening, 24, 26–27
  and infant baptism, 5, 29
  and Puritans, 5, 8, 193
  See also Episcopalians
Anointing the sick, 37
Anti-Catholicism, 6, 35, 52, 113,
  174, 179
Anti-Federalists, 73–74
Antimission Baptists. *See* Primitive
  Baptists
Antinomianism, 9–10, 113–114
Antioch College (Ohio), 212
Anxious seat, 89, 109, 114
Apostolic authority, 9, 44, 80, 89–90,
  116, 168, 203
Appomattox Court House, 136, 138
Arkansas, Baptists in, 108, 152, 154, 163,
  169–170, 218
Arkansas Baptist College, 154
Arminianism, 19, 23, 81–82, 88, 115,
  229, 248, 252. *See also* Freewill
  Baptists
Armstrong, Annie, 164
Asian American Baptists, 121, 197
Atlanta, 136, 138, 153, 155, 158, 177,
  212, 230
Atonement. *See* Fuller, Andrew;
  General atonement; and Limited
  atonement
Auburn University, 135
Augustine of Hippo, 2
Auschwitz, 219
Austin, Junius C., 159
Awakenings. *See* Revivals
The Axioms of Religion (1908), 181,
  221–222

Backus, Isaac, 30–34, 36, 42, 45–46,
    49–50, 55–57, 66, 73, 79, 205–206
Bacon, Leonard Woolsey, 84
Baggett, Hudson, 208
Baker, Desolate. *See* Loveall, Henry
Baldwin, Thomas, 106
Baptism. *See* Affusion; Believer's
    baptism; Devoting children;
    Halfway Covenant; Immersion;
    Infant baptism; Laying on
    of Hands; Rebaptism; and
    Self-baptism
The Baptist, 189
Baptist Bible College (Springfield,
    Missouri), 203–204
Baptist Bible Fellowship (BBF),
    201–204, 210
Baptist Bible Union (BBU), 192–193,
    198–199, 202
Baptist Faith and Message
    Statement (BFMS), 115, 235, 237,
    243–244, 249
Baptist Foreign Mission Convention,
    153
Baptist General Committee (Virginia),
    72–73
Baptist General Conference. *See*
    Converge Worldwide
Baptist General Convention of Texas
    (BGCT), 170, 192, 202
Baptist Joint Committee (BJC), 206,
    209, 242
Baptist Ministerial Alliance, 212
Baptist Missionary Alliance (BMA),
    169–170
Baptist World Alliance (BWA), 178,
    180, 251
Baptist Young People's Union
    Congress, 157
Baptized Licking-Locust Association,
    Friends of Humanity, 102
Barnett, Ross, 223–225

Barrow, David, 101–102
Baton Rouge, Louisiana, 102, 213, 246
Baylor, Robert Emmett Bledsoe, 120
Baylor University, x, 43, 120, 123,
    192, 243
Beaven, A. W., 190–191
Bebbington, David, 120
Becker, Frank, 207–208
Bellamy, Joseph, 94
Believer's baptism
    African Americans' supposed
        preference for, 130
    Anabaptists and, 3–4, 251
    Baptist arguments for, 1, 9,
        14–16, 30, 94
    Baptists persecuted because of, 12–13
    conversion and, 5, 20, 30, 41, 51, 55,
        68, 77, 79, 86–87, 89. 92–93, 104,
        106, 112, 114, 119
    as defining practice of Baptists, 1, 7,
        18, 251
    as difficult choice, 22, 33–34
Benedict, David, 123
Bethel Association (South Carolina),
    83, 100
Bible
    authority of, xi, 2, 16, 173, 179, 182,
        184, 189, 197, 222, 229, 250–251
    Baptists' devotion to, x, 10, 32–33, 36,
        45, 55, 89, 102, 113, 249–250
    inspiration of, x, 190–191, 200,
        229, 237
    interpretation of, 122, 190, 193, 222,
        229, 243
    See also Biblicism; Higher Criticism;
        Inerrancy; and Slavery, the Bible
Bible Bands, 161–162
Bible Baptist Seminary, 202
Biblicism, x, 7, 14, 29, 37, 110–111,
    114–115, 228, 251
Bill for Establishing Religious Freedom
    in Virginia (1786), 60, 72

Bill of Rights. *See* First Amendment

Birmingham, Alabama, 159, 171,
    212–214, 217, 246

Black, Hugo, 61, 206

Blake, Eugene Carson, 226

Blood, Caleb, 85–86

Board of Foreign Missions (Triennial
    Convention), 106, 108, 111, 125–127

Bockelson, Jan, 3–4

Bogard, Ben M., 169–170, 202

Borders, William Holmes, 212

Boston. *See* Massachusetts

Boston Personalism, 180

Boston University, 212

Bowie, Alice, 163

Boyce, James P., 135

Bowdoinham Association (Maine), 88

Bower, Jacob, 76–77, 97

Bowers, Sam, 214–217, 220–221, 225

Boyd, Richard Henry, 154–157, 160, 162,
    164–165

Bracken Association (Kentucky), 88

Brantley, Etheldred, 117

Brisbane, William Henry, 119

Broad River Association (North
    Carolina), 129

Brookes, Iveson, 133

Broonzy, Big Bill, 158

Broughton, Virginia, 161–164

Browder v. Gayle (1956), 213

Brown University, 42–43, 57, 94,
    99, 122

Brown v. Board of Education (1954),
    211–212, 220, 227

Bryan, Andrew, 105, 139

Bryan, Jonathan, 105

Bryan, William Jennings, 186

Buber, Martin, 226

Burgoyne, John, 56

Burkitt, Lemuel, 88–89

Burroughs, Nannie Helen,
    162–163, 249

Bushyhead, Jesse, 109–110

California, first Baptists in, 121

Callender, Elisha, 22–23, 43

Callender, Ellis, 43–44

Calvin, John, 82, 94, 179

Calvinism
    and African American Baptists, 165
    in Baptist confessions, 70, 88, 115
    Baptist debates over, ix, 23, 54,
        82, 86
    decline of, 88
    and infant baptism, 30, 32
    and modern conservative Baptists,
        239, 249, 251
    See also Arminianism; Limited
        atonement; New Divinity theology;
        Original sin; Particular Baptists;
        and Predestination

Cambridge Platform (1648), 10

Campbell, Alexander, 114

Campbell, Israel, 130

Campbell, Lucie, 157, 159

Campbell, Will, 217–220

Campbellites. *See* Disciples of Christ

Canadian Baptists, 78, 188, 192, 198.
    See also Nova Scotia, Baptists in

Cane Ridge revival, 78, 85–86

Canipe, Christopher, 182

Carey, William, 92, 94, 108

Carlson, Emmanuel, 206

Carter, Jimmy, 205

Carver School of Social Work
    (Southern Baptist Theological
    Seminary), 239

Cary, Lott, 95–96, 105. *See also*
    Lott Carey Foreign Mission
    Convention

Catholics
    and American politics, 174,
        201–202, 209
    Baptists' common cause with,
        209–210
    Baptists compared with, 166,
        243, 248

in the Civil Rights movement, 218–219

in colonial America, 52, 80, 107, 121

and infant baptism, 5

as minority in the South, 217

in the Reformation Era, 2–4

See also Anti-Catholicism

Central Baptist Seminary (Minnesota), 201

Central Baptist Theological Seminary (Kansas), 244

Cessationism. *See* Miracles

Chaney, James, 214–215

Chanler, Isaac, 26–28

Chaplains

in the American Revolution, 40, 56–57, 62–63

in the Civil War, 133, 135, 137

Chappell, David, 224

Charles I (king of England), 48

Charleston Baptist Association, 28, 81, 84, 89, 125–126

Charleston, South Carolina, 20, 26–28, 41, 50–53, 103, 133

Chattanooga, Tennessee, 80, 211

Cherokees, 80, 108–110, 119, 121

Chicago, Illinois, 158–160, 196, 212, 219–220, 225

Chipps, D. E., 201

Christian Index, 156, 166

Christian Life Commission (CLC), 220, 239, 241–242. *See also* Ethics and Religious Liberty Commission

Christian Century, 219

Christianity Today, 200, 229, 238

Church discipline, 26, 51, 81–84, 98, 123

Church of England. *See* Anglicans

Church-state issues. *See* Abortion; Prayer in public schools; and Religious liberty

Churches of Christ. *See* Disciples of Christ

Cincinnati, 79, 137, 171, 214

Civil rights movement. *See* African American Baptists; King, Martin Luther, Jr.; Segregation

Civil Rights Act (1964), 214

Civil War

Baptist participation in, 133–139, 248

denominational schism presaging, 128

and effect on missions, 121

in Southern memory, 166, 177

Clanton, Jan Aldredge, 243

Clarke, John, 9–14, 23

Clarke, William Newton, 183

Clinton, Bill, 205

Coercive Acts (1774), 49

Colby College (Maine), 43

Cold War, 208

Colgate University (New York), 43, 183

College of New Jersey. *See* Princeton University

College of Rhode Island. *See* Brown University

Colley, W. W., 152–153

Comanches, 110

Comer, John, 22–23

Communion. *See* Lord's Supper

Condy, Jeremiah, 19, 22

Confessions. *See* Creedalism; and specific confessions

Congregational autonomy, 21, 116, 188, 193–194, 222, 227, 251, 253

Congregationalists

Baptists converting from, 22, 30, 36, 42, 50, 94

and cooperation with Baptists, 42, 123, 170, 191

and conflict with Baptists, 42, 50, 65

declining size of, 77, 122

and establishment in New England colonies/states, 22, 30, 44, 49–50, 60–61, 65

Congregationalists (Cont.).
  and the Great Awakening, 26, 30, 78
  and infant baptism, 29
  and missions, 93–94, 109, 151
  See also Separate Congregationalists
Connecticut
  Baptists and religious liberty in,
    36, 59–61
  revivals in, 30–31, 53, 90, 129
  Separate Baptists in, 32–36
Connor, Bull, 214, 225
Conservative Baptist Association,
  200–201, 240
Conservative Baptist Association of
  Oregon, 207
Conservative Baptist Foreign Missions
  Society, 199–200
Consolidated American Baptist
  Convention (CABC), 152
Constantine, 39
Constitution of the United States, 205,
  215. *See also* First Amendment
Converge Worldwide, 122
Conversion, 5, 19, 26, 29–31, 76–77, 91,
    104, 112
  doctrine of, 19, 26, 29–30, 171, 238
  experiences of, x, 4–5, 25, 29–31,
    35–36, 55, 67, 71, 78–79, 91, 97,
    104, 109, 122
  testimonies of, 15, 31, 33, 37, 54, 67,
    77, 86, 91, 114, 119
  See also Believer's baptism,
    conversion and; Revivals;
Cook, Charles, 84
Cotton, John, 10
Covenant Renewal document, 237–238
Craig, Lewis, 68–69
Crandall, John, 12–13
Crane, William, 95–96
Creationism. *See* Evolution
Creedalism, 70, 187–189, 200, 215, 222,
  250–251

Creeks, 46, 108
Criswell, W. A., 220–221, 228, 232–233
Crosby, Fanny, 157
Crozer Theological Seminary, 173, 187,
  212, 217
  respectability of, 22, 42–44
Curtis, Richard, 80

Dahmer, Vernon, 214–216
Dallas, 177–178, 211, 220, 228–232,
  234–235, 241
Danbury Baptist Association
  (Connecticut), 59–61, 82, 206
Dark Day. *See* New Light Stir
Davenport, James, 30
David, William J., 153
Davis, Addie, 242
Davis, Jefferson, 133
Davis, John, 108
Dawson, J. M., 202
Deacon and deaconess, office of,
  3, 37, 46
Declaration of Independence, 40, 65,
  190, 215
Deists, 59, 76, 78, 86, 120
Delaney, Emma, 163
Democracy, 167, 178–182, 188, 194
Democrats, 136, 174, 191, 202, 205
Denison University (Ohio), 43
Des Moines University (Iowa), 198
Desiring God Ministries, 122
Detroit. *See* Michigan, Baptist growth
  in; and Temple Baptist Church
Devoting children, 37
Dexter Avenue Baptist Church
  (Montgomery, Alabama), 212
Dirksen, Everett, 207–208
Disciples of Christ, 85, 114, 178, 251
Disestablishment. *See also* Religious
  liberty
Dixon, A. C., 192, 198
Dockery, David, 238–239

Dodd, M. E., 177
*Domestic Slavery Considered as a
    Scriptural Institution* (1846), 131
Dorsey, Thomas Andrew, 158–160
Dover Association (Richmond,
    Virginia), 129
Draper, James, Jr., 229, 231–232
Dreams. *See* Visions
Dsulawee (Andrew Fuller), 109
Du Bois, W. E. B., 150, 155–156, 226
Dunkards. *See* German Baptists
Dunn, James, 209, 242
Dunster, Henry, 14
Durrett, Peter, 69, 106

Ecumenism. *See* Congregationalist,
    and cooperation with; Interchurch
    World Fellowship (IWM);
    Methodists, and cooperation with
    Baptists; and Presbyterians, and
    cooperation with Baptists
Education. *See* specific institutions and
    organizations
Edwards, Jonathan, 78, 94
Edwards, Morgan, 27–28
Egalitarianism, 83, 102, 118
Eichmann, Adolf, 219
Elder and eldress, office of, 8, 23, 37,
    46, 85, 91, 115
Ellington, Duke, 160
Election. *See* Predestination
Elkhorn Baptist Association
    (Kentucky), 69–71, 87–88, 96,
    98–99, 102, 116
Emmons, Nathaniel, 93–94
Endicott, John, 13–14
Engel v. Vitale (1962), 206–207
England, Mabel, 216–217
England, Martin, 216–218, 220
English Baptists
    beginnings of, 4–7, 29, 58, 168
    and correspondence with American
    Baptists, 39, 87, 125
    growth of, 77
    immigrating to America, 12, 15, 17,
        20, 26, 48
    and missions, 92–94
    writings of, 6–7, 11, 70, 82, 92
Enlightenment, 184, 223
Enthusiasm, 25, 62, 67, 71, 89–90, 92
Episcopalians, 71, 77, 122, 217
Ethics and Religious Liberty
    Commission, 239, 242, 244–245
Evangelical Confession of Faith, 190
Evangelicalism
    and Baptist identity, ix-x, 77,
        239–240, 251
    Baptists against, 115, 239
    definition of, x
    and fundamentalism, 184, 194
    See also Conversion; and Revivals
Evans, Milton G., 187
Eve, George, 74
Everson v. Board of Education (1947),
    61, 206
Evolution, 173, 175, 184–186, 191–192,
    197, 232–233, 238
Excell, E. O., 158
Excommunication. *See* Church
    discipline

Fairbanks, Douglas, 191
Falwell, Jerry, 204–205, 244
Federal Council of Churches (FCC),
    172, 176
Federalists, 60
Fellowship, 33–34, 37, 54, 70, 113, 116,
    119, 123–124, 126, 131, 198
Female Society for Missionary
    Purposes, 93–94
Finney, Charles, 119
First Amendment, 59–61, 73–74, 181,
    206–207, 209, 242, 247
First Great Awakening
    effects on American Baptists, 18–20,
        24–31, 34–35, 38, 91, 247

First Great Awakening (Cont.).
  effect on the South, 35
  hymnody of, 45
  and relationship to the Second Great
    Awakening, 78, 84–85
Fisk University, 153
Fitzgerald, Ella, 160
Flat Rock Association (Indiana), 138
Florida, Baptists in, 111, 115, 137, 170
Foot washing, 37
Foreign missions
  in Africa, 47, 92, 96, 102, 152, 162
  in Asia, 92, 94–95, 108
Fort Worth, Texas. *See* Norris, J. Frank;
    and Sherman, Cecil
Fosdick, Henry Emerson, 183–186,
    188, 249
Foster, Lafayette, 134
Franklin, Aretha, 160
Franklin, Benjamin, 25, 47
Franklin, C. L., 160
Franklin Avenue Baptist Church (New
    Orleans), 245–246
Freemasons, 81
Freewill Baptists, 54–55, 78, 82, 114,
    129, 196–197
French American Baptists, 197
French Revolution, 85
Fridell, Elmer A., 199
Frontier. *See* West, The
Frye, Theodore, 159
Fuller, Andrew, 82, 88
Fuller, Richard, 127, 131, 134
Fuller Theological Seminary, 200, 238
Fundamentalist Fellowship, 186,
    189, 192
Fundamentalist-modernist controversy,
    180–181, 183–195, 197, 248
Fundamentalism
  and the Interchurch World
    Movement (IWM), 173–176
  and Landmarkism, 197

  in the Midwest, 176, 189, 199,
    201–202
  origins of, 173
  and politics, 209–210
  and separatism, 197–198, 200,
    232, 240
  in the South, 201–204
  See also Fundamentalist-modernist
    controversy; Inerrancy; Southern
    Baptist Convention, conservative
    resurgence; and specific
    organizations and people
Furman, James C., 135
Furman, Richard, 51–53, 81, 84, 90, 95,
    103–104, 137
Furman University, 43, 135

Gainsborough, England, 5–6
Galusha, Elon, 126–127
Gambrell, James E., 177
Gandhi, Mohandes, 226
Gano, Stephen, 79, 81, 86
Garden, Alexander, 26
Gardner, Charles S., 221
Garland, Diana, 239
Garvey, Marcus, 156
Gay rights. *See* Homosexuality
Gender. *See* Women
General Association of Baptist
    Churches of the United States of
    America (GABCUSA), 169–170
General Association of Regular Baptist
    Churches (GARBC), 193, 198–199,
    201, 240
General atonement, 5–6, 55, 82, 88
General Baptists, 5, 196
General Missionary Convention of the
    Baptist Denomination in the United
    States of America, for Foreign
    Missions. *See* Triennial Convention
George III (king of England), 41,
    44, 48–49

George, David, 46, 92, 102, 105
George, Timothy, 242
Georgia, Baptists in
    and the Civil War, 136, 138, 166
    and race, 151, 156, 216–219
    and slavery, 100, 127–128, 134
    and theological controversy, 82, 96,
        111–112
    See also specific cities and
        organizations
Georgia Baptist Missionary and
    Education Convention, 212
Georgia State University, 217
German American Baptists, 76–77,
    170, 197
Gingrich, Newt, 205
Gladden, Washington, 170–171
Glorieta Statement (1986), 235–237
Glorious Revolution, 21
Golden Gate Baptist Theological
    Seminary, 237
Goodchild, Frank, 188
Goodman, Andy, 214–215
Goold, Thomas, 14–18
Gore, Al, 205
Gospel Pearls (GP), 157–159
Graham, Billy, ix, 160, 201, 206, 211,
    222, 226, 234, 238
"Grand Compromise," 229, 231–232
Graves, James R. (Robinson), 115–116,
    168–169
Great Awakening. *See* First Great
    Awakening
Great Migration, 159
Greater Salem Baptist Church, 159–160
    (Chicago), 159–160
Groton Union Conference
    (Connecticut), 81, 86
Gwaltney, L. L., 171

Haldeman, I. M., 174–176
Halfway Covenant, 15–17, 32

Hamilton Seminary, 183
Hampton, Lionel, 158
Hancock Baptist Association (Maine),
    126
Handy, W. C., 158
Harding, Warren, 123
Harp of Zion, 157
Harris, Samuel, 44
Hart, Oliver, 28–29, 41, 50–52
Harvey, Paul, 156
Hasseltine, Ann, 94–95
Harvard College, 14, 19, 22, 42
Hayden, Samuel A, 169–170
Hayes, Rutherford B., 150
Healings. *See* Miracles
Hederman, Thomas and Robert,
    224–225
Hell's Kitchen, 170–171
Helwys, Thomas, 6–7
Henry, Carl F. H., 200–201,
    238–240, 249
Henry, Patrick, 52, 62–64, 71–72
Hephzibah Association (Georgia),
    96, 112
Higginbotham, Evelyn Brooks, 164
Higher criticism, 173, 181, 184, 192,
    232, 236
Hispanic American Baptists, 121,
    197, 245
Hokum Boys, 158
Holiness churches, 157–159
Holliman, Ezekiel, 9
Holmes, Elkanah, 93
Holmes, James R., 149
Holmes, Obadiah, 1, 12–13
Holy Spirit. *See* Antinomianism;
    Conversion; Enthusiasm;
    Miracles; Revivals; and Visions
Homosexuality, 210, 232,
    239–240, 244
Honeycutt, Roy, 237–238
Hopewell Academy (New Jersey), 42

Hovey, Alva, 149

Howard College. *See* Samford
    University

Hubbard, H. H., 212

Huckins, James, 120, 123

Hudgins, Douglas, 221–225, 227

Hudson River Baptist Association
    (New York), 134

Humes, Harrison, 212

Humphreys, Fisher, 223

Hunt, Asa, 53–54

Hutchinson, Anne, 9–10

Illinois, Baptists in
    growth of, 90, 121–122, 124, 152
    and theological controversy, 96
    See also Chicago

Immersion, 1–2, 9, 12, 15, 33, 35,
    45, 55, 70, 77, 94, 109, 115, 120,
    168

Independent Baptists, 197,
    203–204, 209

Indian Removal Act (1830), 108–109

Indiana, Baptists in,
    and the Civil War, 136, 138
    growth of, 90, 106, 196
    and theological controversy, 114
    See also Northern Baptist
        Convention (NBC), Indianapolis
        convention (1922)

Indianapolis Association, 138

Indians. (46–47, 93, 106–108) *See*
    Native Americans

Individualism. *See* Soul competency

Inerrancy, xi, 229–241, 250–251

Infant baptism
    Baptist arguments against, 5–6, 11,
        13–16, 29–30, 32–34, 70
    in the early church, 2
    and established churches in colonial
        America, 7, 17, 22, 20
    in the Reformation era, 2–5

Insiders, Baptists as, ix, 165–167,
    180, 182, 193, 195, 205, 240,
    247–248, 252

"Institutional churches," 171

Interchurch World Movement (IWM),
    172–177, 185, 191

Integration. *See* Segregation

Ireland, James, 44–45

Ireland, Patricia, 244

Irish Baptists, 20

Iroquois, 57

Isaac, Edward W. D., 156

Italian American Baptists, 172

Jackson, Andrew, 109

Jackson, Joseph H., 225

Jackson, Mahalia, 159–160

Jackson, Mississippi. *See* Barnett, Ross;
    and Hudgins, Douglas

Jacksonian democracy, 110–111

James I (king of England), 7

James II (king of England), 22

James, Philip, 27–28

Jefferson, Thomas, 59–61, 64, 72, 74,
    133, 180, 205–206

Jehovah's Witnesses, 206

Jemison, Theodore, 213

Jenkins, Nathaniel, 21

Jeter, Jeremiah, 131–132

Jews, 218–219, 221, 226

Jim Crow laws. *See* Segregation

John Paul II, 243

John the Baptist, 1

Johns, Vernon, 212

Johnson, Amelia, 160–162, 164

Johnson, Harvey, 160

Johnson, Robert, 120

Johnson, Walter Nathan, 216

Johnson, William B., 128

Johnson Singers, 159

Jones County Baptist Association
    (Mississippi), 216

Jones, Evan, 108–110
Jones, David, 47
Jones, J. A., 156
Jones, Jenkin, 24–26, 28–29
Jordan, Clarence, 216–217, 220
Jordan, Florence, 216–217
Jordan, Lewis G., 163
Judson, Adoniram, 94–95, 102
Judson, Ann. *See* Hasseltine, Ann.
Judson College (Alabama), 43

Kaneeda (John Wickliffe), 109
Kansas City, 198, 225
Kansas-Nebraska Act (1854), 134
Keach, Elias, 20–21
Kehukee Baptist Association (North
    Carolina), 81, 88, 112–113, 119
Kelly, Erasmus, 51
Kennedy, John F., 160, 223
Kentucky
    and the Civil War, 136
    controversy over slavery in, 101–102,
        124, 134
    religious liberty in, 74–75
    theological controversy in, 114
    See also the West, the Great
        Revival in, 84–92; and specific
        organizations and places
Ketocton Association (Virginia), 100–101
King, Coretta Scott, 160, 212–213
King, Larry, 244
King, Martin Luther, Jr., 156, 160, 207,
    212–214, 217–219, 224–226
Kinnersly, Ebenezer, 25–26
Kiss of charity, 37
Koinonia Farms, 216–217
Ku Klux Klan (KKK), 152, 212, 214–216,
    221, 225, 248

Land, Richard, 220, 239, 242–244
Landmark Baptists, 115–116, 168–170,
    197, 202–204

Lane, Tiden, 37
Laurel, Mississippi. *See* Bowers, Sam
Lawrence, Joshua, 112–113
Laws, Curtis Lee, 172–176, 184–186,
    188–190, 192
Laying on of hands, 21, 23, 37
Lee, Mother Ann, 54
Leland, John, 61, 67, 69, 71, 73–74, 86,
    111, 205–206
Leonard, Bill, 229, 236
Letty (slave in Kentucky), 104
Lexington, Kentucky. *See*
    Durrett, Peter
Lexington and Concord, battles of, 39–40
Leyden, John of. *See* Bockelson, Jan
Liberal Protestants. *See* Modernism
Liberty University, 204
Liele, George, 46, 105
Limited atonement, 5, 82, 88, 101, 115
Lincoln, Abraham, 123, 133, 138
Lindsell, Harold, 229
Lippmann, Walter, 194
Little Rock, Arkansas, 218
Locke, John, 179
London Baptist Confession of Faith
    (1689), 70, 250
Long, Patty, 91
Lothrop, Nathaniel, 31
Lord, Benjamin, 31
Lord's Supper, 4, 15, 27, 33–34, 37, 86,
    105, 107, 109, 249
Lost Cause mythology. *See* Civil War, in
    Southern memory
Lott Carey Foreign Mission
    Convention, 162, 165
Lott, Trent, 205
Louisiana, Baptist growth in, 80, 170.
    See also Franklin Avenue Baptist
    Church, New Orleans
Louisiana College, 218
Louisville, Kentucky, 107, 137, 216
Love feasts, 37

Loveall, Henry, 21
Loyalists, 50–52, 57, 180
Lucar, Mark, 12
Lumpkin, William, 250
Luter, Fred, 246
Luther, Martin, 2–3, 94
Lutherans, 3, 179

Macartney, Clarence, 184
Machen, J. Gresham, 194
Macon, Leon, 208, 224
Madden, Samuel, 137
Madison, James, 59, 62–64, 72–74, 180
Maine
    Baptist growth in 20, 55,
    Baptist revivals in, 90–91, 129
Manly, Basil, 43, 123, 133
Manning, James, 39, 42–43, 49–50, 57,
    66, 79, 99
March on Washington, 160, 214, 226
Marney, Carlyle, 216
Marsden, George, 122
Marsh, Charles, 215
Marshall, Daniel, 36, 44
Marshall, John, 109
Marshall, Martha, 36
Marshall, Molly, 244
Maryland, 21, 113
Mason, George, 63
Massachusetts
    American Revolution in, 41, 49–50
    founding of, 7
    disestablishment in, 49–50, 66, 73–74
    persecution of Baptists in, ix, 1, 11–14,
        16–17, 44, 49, 65–66
    respectability of Baptists in, 19,
        21–22, 43–44
    revivals in, 24, 53–54, 86, 129
    toleration of Baptists in, 18, 21–22
    See also Puritans
Massachusetts Baptist Missionary
    Society, 106

Massee, J. C., 176, 185–186, 189–191
Mather, Increase and Cotton, 22
Maxcy, Jonathan, 99, 123
McCoy, Isaac, 106–109, 111
Mennonites, 4–6, 251
Mercer, Silas, 82
Mercer University, 174
Meredith, James, 223–224
Methodists, 215, 217, 243
    Baptist criticism of, 114, 116
    and cooperation with Baptists, 86,
        90, 116, 170
    and fundamentalism, 173, 191
    growth of, 77, 85–86, 247
    and missions, 109, 178
    and revivalism, 84, 86, 90, 116
    and sectionalism, 128, 166
    See also African Methodist
        Episcopal Church
Michigan, Baptist growth in, 90, 96,
    106–107, 201
Midwestern Baptist Theological
    Seminary, 237
Miles, James, 51
Millennialism 99, 184–185, 191–192,
    198, 201–202, 252
Minneapolis. See Piper, John; and
    Riley, William Bell
Minnesota Baptist Convention,
    199–200
Miracles, 46, 90
Missions. See Foreign missions; Native
    American Baptists; and specific
    organizations
Mississippi
    Baptist growth in, 80, 85, 96, 151–152
    and the Civil Rights movement, 212,
        214–221, 223, 225
Missouri, Baptist growth in, 95, 106,
    124, 161, 203. See also Southern
    Baptist Convention, St. Louis
    convention (1987)

Modernism
  definition of, 173
  and the Interchurch World
    Movement, 173–176
  See also Fundamentalist-modernist
    controversy; Higher criticism; and
    specific people
Mohler, Mary, 243
Mohler, R. Albert, 238–245
Montgomery, Alabama, 133, 135, 151, 153,
    156, 211–213, 226
Montgomery, Helen Barrett,
    187–190, 249
Moore, Joanna, 161, 164
Moore, Russell, 244–245
Moore, Winfred, 230–231, 234–235
Moral Majority, 204, 244
Morehouse College (Atlanta, Georgia), 212
Morgan, Abel, Jr., 24–25, 28
Morris, Elias Camp, 154–155, 160, 162,
    164–165
Morse, Joshua, 34, 36
Moses (biblical prophet), 56
Moulton, Ebenezer, 34
Mulkey, Philip, 50–51
Mullins, Edgar Young (E. Y.), 178,
    180–183, 194, 202, 221–223,
    225, 249
Münster, 3–4
Mysticism. *See* Visions

Nam, Fung Seung, 121
Napoleonic Wars, 95
Nashville, Tennessee, 115, 155–156,
    197, 227
National Association for the
    Advancement of Colored People
    (NAACP), 163, 211, 214
National Association of Colored
    Women, 163
National Association of Evangelicals,
    200

National Baptist Convention of
    America, 165, 225
National Baptist Convention USA Inc.
    (NBC), 155, 246
  and black separatism, 154, 156
  and the Civil Rights movement,
    225–226
  formation of, 151–154
  and music, 157–158
  schism in, 164–165, 225–226
  size of, ix, 151, 153, 196, 225
  women's roles in, 162–164
National Baptist Educational
    Convention, 153
National Baptist Publishing Board
    (NBPB), 155–157, 162, 164–165
National Conference on Religion and
    Race, 219
National Council of Churches (NCC),
    218–220, 226
National Missionary Baptist
    Convention of America, 165
National Negro Doll Company, 156
National Organization for Women, 244
Native American Baptists, 36, 47–48,
    93, 104, 106–110, 118–119. *See also*
    specific people
Neighbor, R. E., 192
Neo-evangelicalism, 194, 200–201
Neuse Baptist Association (North
    Carolina), 81–82
New birth. *See* Conversion, doctrine of
New Divinity theology, 94
New England. *See* Connecticut;
    Massachusetts; and Rhode Island
New England Conservatory of Music, 212
New Hampshire Baptist Association,
    115
New Hampshire Confession of Faith
    (1833), 115, 189–190, 192, 197–200,
    237, 249–250
New Light Stir, 53–55, 77

New Mexico, first Baptists in, 121. *See also* Glorieta Statement
New Orleans Baptist Theological Seminary, 237
New Testament. *See* Bible
New York, 119, 126, 135, 190, 207, 217
  and the American Revolution, 40, 53–54, 56–57
  Baptist growth in, 78
  revivals in, 91–92, 119
  and slavery, 100
  See also New York City and specific organizations
New York Baptist Association, 93, 124
New York City, 40, 106, 170–174, 183, 188, 212
New York Missionary Society, 93
New York Times, 189, 193–194, 243
New World Movement, 175, 177
Newport, Rhode Island, 9–10, 12, 23, 42, 50–51, 160
Niebuhr, Gustav, 243
Niebuhr, Reinhold, 226
Nix, W. M., 157–159
Nixon, Richard, 160
Noll, Mark, 131, 248
Nomini Baptist Church (Virginia), 67–68
Norris, J. Frank, 192, 198, 201–203
Norris, George, 203
Northern Baptist Convention (NBC)
  and the Southern Baptist Convention, 167, 170, 196
  and cultural issues, 191
  and ecumenism, 172–176, 185
  and fundamentalism, 173–175, 180–194, 198
  and modernism, 181–182, 193
  moderates within, 181, 184, 192, 194
  Indianapolis convention (1922), 186–191
  See also American Baptist Churches USA

North Carolina
  African American Baptists in, 152
  revivals in, 36–37, 90, 108, 129
  See also specific organizations
North District Association (Kentucky), 102
Northwest Territory, 79
Northwestern Bible College (Minnesota), 193, 199, 201
Nova Scotia, Baptists in, 46, 92
Nullification controversy, 118, 223
Nussbaum, Perry, 221, 224

Ohio, Baptist expansion into, 79, 85, 152. *See also* Cincinnati
Okazaki, Fukumatsu, 121
Oklahoma, Baptists in, 108, 170, 229
Old Time Gospel Hour, 204
Oliver, Andrew, 41
Oregon, Baptists in, 120–121, 207–208
Original sin, 2, 88, 171
Osborne, Thomas, 16
Ottawas, 106–107
Outsiders, Baptists as, ix, 123, 165, 182, 195, 220, 242, 244–245, 247–248, 252

Pacifism, 11, 50–51
Paedobaptism. *See* Infant baptism
Paine, Thomas, 49, 85
Palmer, Wait, 36, 46
Palmquist, Gustaf, 121–122
Park Avenue Baptist Church (New York), 188
Parker, Cynthia Ann, 110
Parker, Daniel, 110–113, 120, 170
Parker, John, 110
Parker, Quanah, 110
Parks, Rosa, 211–212
Parrish, Charles H., 163
Particular Baptists, 5, 23, 26–29, 38, 70, 78, 81, 110, 112–113, 129. *See also* General Association of Regular Baptist Churches (GARBC)

Paternalism, 69, 102–105, 152, 156, 160–161.

Patriots, 39, 48–52, 56–57, 62–64, 66

Patterson, Dorothy, 243–244

Patterson, Paige, 228, 233, 241

Paul (biblical apostle), 26, 88, 99, 102, 164, 179, 243

Paul, Thomas, 106

Peace Committee (Southern Baptist Convention), 235–237

Peacock, John, 129

Peak, Esther, 79

Peck, John M., 95

Pendleton, James, 132

Pennsylvania, Baptists in
    beginnings of, 20–21
    connection with South Carolina, 27–28
    See also Philadelphia

Pentecostals, 157–159, 196

Pepper, George Whitfield, 138

Persecution
    in the American Revolution, 49–50, 62, 65
    in Baptist memory, 180, 189
    in colonial America, x, 1, 8, 11–14, 16–18, 20–22, 34–35, 43–45, 217
    and disestablishment, 62, 65–68, 72, 74
    in the Early Republic, 80, 105
    in Europe, 3–7, 179
    of Baptists, x, 1, 7, 11, 13–14, 21, 34–35, 44, 62, 65, 67–68

Philadelphia, 49, 57, 81, 95, 113, 171, 178, 184, 206–207

Philadelphia Association of Baptists, 19, 21, 24–29, 42–43, 52, 73, 115

Philadelphia Baptist Confession (1742), 70, 88, 115, 189, 249

Philip (biblical disciple), 1–2

Pickford, Mary, 191

Pigee, Manuel, 246

Pillsbury Baptist Bible College, 201

Piper, John, 122, 249

Plymouth Colony, 6, 8, 12, 14

Polish American Baptists, 197

Polygamy, 3, 21

Portsmouth Association (Virginia), 124–125

Prayer in public schools, debates over, 206–209

Predestination, 5, 19, 55, 78–80, 82, 88, 101, 110, 115. *See also* Particular Baptists

Premillennial Baptist Missionary Fellowship, 202

Premillennialism. *See* Millennialism

Presbyterians
    and cooperation with Baptists, 25, 27, 29, 50, 86, 90, 93, 116, 170, 183, 185, 191
    cultural influence of, 42, 122, 217, 226
    and fundamentalism, 173, 183–184, 186–187, 191, 194, 198, 240
    growth of, 85–86, 247
    and the Interchurch World Movement (IWM), 172, 175–176
    and missions, 93, 116, 172, 178
    and revivalism, 25, 29, 84, 86, 90, 116, 119
    and schism, 128, 166, 173

Pressler, Paul, 228, 233, 235

Primera Iglesia Bautista Mexicana (San Antonio), 121

Primitive Baptists, 96, 110–115, 119–120, 123, 125, 170, 191, 197, 251

Princeton University, 40, 42

Pritchett, Laurie, 219

Progressive National Baptist Convention, 225–226

Prohibition, 190–191

Prophesying, 10–11, 16–17, 90

Protestant Reformation. *See* Reformation

Providence, Rhode Island, 8–9, 12, 39, 43, 113

Puritans, ix, 5, 7–17, 22, 29, 65, 193

Quakers, 14, 16, 20, 50

Quebec Act (1774), 51–52

Race. *See* African American Baptists; Paternalism; Segregation; and Slavery

Rainey, Ma, 158

Randel, Benjamin, 54–55, 82

Randolph, Thomas Jefferson, 124

Rappahannock Baptist Association (Virginia), 138

Rathbun, Valentine, 81

Rauschenbusch, Walter, 170–171, 181–182, 216, 226

Read, Mary, 45–46

Read, Jesse, 88–89

Reagan, Nancy, 232

Reagan, Ronald, 204–205, 209, 230, 232

Rebaptism, 3–4, 12–14, 22

Reconstruction era, 149–152, 155, 167

Reformation, 2–3, 84, 165, 194, 215

Reformed Baptists. *See* Particular Baptists

Reformed Protestants. *See* Calvinism

Regular Baptists. *See* Particular Baptists

Religious liberty
  Baptist disagreements about, 205–210, 249, 251–252
  as Baptist principle, x, 7, 74–75, 99, 171, 178–182, 189, 193, 232, 249
  in colonial America, 5, 7–8, 17, 20, 22, 36
  and disestablishment in the Revolutionary era, 41–44, 49–50, 52, 58–66, 69, 71–75
  See also First Amendment; Soul competency;

Rensselaerville Conference (New York), 81

Republicans, 133, 136, 150, 167, 204–205, 209, 230, 232, 245

Revivals
  See also Cane Ridge revival; First Great Awakening; New Light Stir; Second Great Awakening; Sun Spot Revival; Visions; the West, the Great Revival in; and specific places

Revolutionary War. *See* American Revolution

Rhode Island
  founding of, 8
  as haven for religious dissenters, 9–10
  revivals in, 129
  See also Brown University; Newport; Providence; and Warren Association

Rice, Luther, 95

Richardson, Richard, 52

Richmond African Baptist Missionary Society, 95

Richmond, Virginia, 64, 95, 105, 124, 129, 131, 149–151, 162, 191

Riis, Jacob, 170

Riley, William Bell, 176, 189, 192–193, 195, 198–202, 249

Rippon, John, 87

Ritchie, Homer, 203

Robinson, Mrs. C. J., 163

Robinson, Clement, 137

Robinson, John, 6

Rochester Theological Seminary, 170–171, 181

Rockefeller, John D., 188

Roe v. Wade (1973), 241

Rogers, Adrian, 228–230, 241

Rogers, William, 57

Roman Catholic Church. *See* Catholicism

Romanian American Baptists, 197
Roosevelt, Theodore, 85, 154
Rowland, John, 25–26
Russell, Sr., John, 18
Russian American Baptists, 197
Ryland, John, 39
Ryland, Robert, 149

Saddleback Community Church
    (California), ix
Salem Association (Kentucky), 99
Saluda Baptist Association (South
    Carolina), 118
Samford University, 171
Sampey, John R., 221
Sampson, Deborah, 54
Sandy Creek Association (North
    Carolina), 36–37, 44, 51
Saratoga, Battle of, 56
Savannah, Georgia, 29, 105, 138–139
Scarborough, Lee R., 177
Schaeffer, Francis, 239–241
Schleiermacher, Friedrich, 180
Schuller, Robert, 244
Schwerner, Mickey, 214–215
Scioto Baptist Association (Ohio), 124
Scopes trial (1925), 192
Scott, Catherine, 9
Scott, Winfield, 135–136
Scottsdale, Arizona, 136
Screven, William, 20
Scripture. *See* Bible
Seamans, Job, 78–79
Second Great Awakening, 61, 77–78,
    84–85, 90, 247
Segregation
    black responses to, 149–150, 153–157,
        160–163, 207, 211–214, 225–227
    in churches, 124–125, 149–151,
        167–168, 245–246, 248
    white attitudes toward, 124–125, 150,
        167–168, 209, 211, 214–227

Self-baptism, 6, 8
Selma, Alabama, 214
Semple, Robert Baylor, 36, 68, 85
Separate Baptists, 20, 29–30, 33–37,
    42–43, 46, 51–52, 54, 70, 81, 85,
    92, 111, 115
Separate Congregationalists, 30–34
Separation of Church and State. *See*
    Religious liberty
Separatists, 4–6, 8–9, 17, 29
Servetus, Michael, 179
Seventh-Day Baptists, 53, 196
Shakers, 54, 77, 81
Shaftsbury Baptist Association
    (New York/Vermont), 78, 81,
    100, 126
Shays's Rebellion, 73
Shepard, Thomas, 11
Sherman, Cecil, 231, 237
Sherman, William Tecumseh, 138–139
Sherwood, William H., 157
Shields, T. T., 192, 198
Shiloh, Battle of, 135
Shurden, Walter, 231
Shuttlesworth, Fred, 213–214
Silver Bluff Church (South Carolina),
    46–47, 105
Simmons, Thomas, 27–28
Simons, Menno, 4
Slavery
    and the American Revolution,
        49, 69, 99
    and Baptist schism, 127–131, 167, 248
    Baptists' acceptance of, 99–100, 102,
        124, 248
    Baptists' criticism of, 46, 69, 71,
        99–102, 111–113, 123–127, 130–133
    Baptists' defense of, 103–104, 123,
        127, 131–133, 224
    the Bible and, 69, 100, 102–103, 113,
        126–127, 131–133
    in colonial America, 9, 25

Slavery (Cont.).
    and effects on Baptist congregations,
        70–71, 83–84, 101, 105, 118
    and evangelization, 46, 69, 96,
        103–104, 126, 158
    legacy of, 129, 164–165, 227
    Native Americans and, 80, 108
    spread of, 85, 99, 103, 134
    See also Civil War; Paternalism
Slavery Abolition Act (1833), 125
Smith, Al, 174, 202
Smith, Bailey, 229
Smith, Christian, x
Smith, Hezekiah, 40, 56–57
Smith, J. H. L., 159
Smith, Josiah, 26
Smith, Noel, 203
Smyth, John, 5–9
Social Gospel, 170–172, 175–176, 182,
    186, 216, 251
Sons of Liberty, 44, 48
Soul competency, 179, 188, 193–194,
    222–225, 227, 231–232, 249, 251
South, The
    Baptist growth in, 35–36, 46, 99, 129
    as culturally distinctive, 166–167, 181,
        240, 246
    nationalization of, 177–178
    theological controversy in, 96, 112
    See also Southern Baptist Convention
South Carolina
    and the American Revolution, 50–52
    Baptist growth in, 29, 36–37
    and the Civil War, 133, 135
    revivals in 26, 90, 118–119, 129
    and slavery, 100, 102–103, 119, 127
    See also specific organizations
        and places
South Carolina Baptist Convention,
    103, 128
South Carolina College, 99, 123
South Kentucky Association, 69–70

Southeastern Baptist Theological
    Seminary, 236, 246
Southern Baptist Advocate, 234
Southern Baptist Convention (SBC)
    African Americans and, 129, 151–152,
        156, 227, 245–246
    and church-state issues, 206–209
    conservative resurgence, 228–245
    cultural prominence of, 166–167
    formation of, 128–129, 131, 151, 166
    and fundamentalism, 180, 189, 198,
        202, 205
    Landmarkism in, 116, 168–169
    as largest Protestant denomination
        in America, ix, 129, 166, 228,
        245–246
    and missions, 128–130, 152, 175, 177–178
    and race, 167–168, 197, 216–217,
        220–224, 226–227, 245–246
    and relationship with Northern
        Baptists, 167, 196
    St. Louis convention (1987), 235–236
    and slavery, 128–130, 134
    and triumphalism, 178, 182
    See also Inerrancy; Southern Baptist
        Theological Seminary; Women,
        ordination of; and specific people
        and institutions
Southern Baptist Theological
    Seminary, 135, 168–169, 174, 176,
    180, 216, 221–222, 231, 236–240,
    242, 244–245
Southern Christian Leadership
    Conference (SCLC), 213–214, 218
Southern Seminary. See Southern
    Baptist Theological Seminary
Southwestern Baptist Theological
    Seminary, 177, 237
Spain, Rufus, 166
Speer, Robert, 172
Spotsylvania, Virginia, 68–69, 135
Spurgeon, Charles, 232

Stamp Act (1765), 40–41

Stanley, Charles, 230–231, 234–235

Stearns, Shubal, 35–37

Stembridge, H. Hansel, Jr., 224

Stiles, Ezra, 42, 50

Stillman, Samuel, 41, 106

Stonington Baptist Association, 81

Strange, Mary, 172

Straton, John Roach, 173–176, 184–186

Stringfellow, Thornton, 132–133

Strong, Augustus H., 181, 249

Sugar Act (1764), 43

Sun Spot Revival, 118

Supreme Court, 61, 109, 179, 206,
    208–209, 211, 213, 227

Swedish American Baptists, 121–122,
    197. *See also* Converge Worldwide

Talbert, Charles, 243

Tastheghetehee. *See* Bushyhead, Jesse

Taylor, Gardiner C., 225

Taylor, John, 45, 71, 86–87, 104

Taylor, Maria Baker, 137–138

Temperance, 119

Temple Baptist Church (Detroit),
    201–203

Tennent, William, III, 50–51

Tennessee, Baptists in, 114, 123, 161–163,
    169, 220. *See also* Chattanooga;
    and Nashville

Tertullian, 2

Texas, Baptists in, 110, 120, 154,
    169–170, 220, 231. *See also* Baptist
    General Convention of Texas; and
    specific places

Thomas, Minor, 91–92

Thomas Road Baptist Church
    (Lynchburg, Virginia), 204–205

Thrumble, John, 15

Tichenor, I. T., 135–136

Till, Emmett, 212

Toler, Henry, 67–68

Tories. *See* Loyalists

Total depravity. *See* Original sin

Townsend, Willa A., 157

Trail of Tears, 110

"The Traveling Church." *See*
    Spotsylvania, Virginia

Treaty of Paris (1783), 57

Triennial Convention, 95–96, 108,
    125, 127–128, 130–131, 198. *See
    also* Board of Foreign Missions
    (Triennial Convention)

Trinity, 16, 88, 238, 249–250

Truett, George, 177–180, 182, 194, 202

Tryon, William, 120

Turner, Nat, 117–118, 124, 129–130, 132,
    139, 150–151

Turner, William, 17

Union Theological Seminary, 183

Union University (Tennessee), 239

United Association of Virginia, 81

United Negro Improvement
    Association, 156

United Society for the Spread of the
    Gospel, 95, 111

Universal atonement. *See* General
    atonement

Universalists, 76, 81, 86

University of Alabama, 43, 123

University of Berlin, 168, 170

University of Michigan, 123

University of Mississippi, 218, 223

University of South Carolina. *See* South
    Carolina College

University of Virginia, 168

Upper Spotsylvania Baptist Church.
    See Spotsylvania, Virginia

Valentine, Foy, 216, 220, 239, 241

Vance, James I., 172

Vedder, Henry Clay, 187

Vesey, Denmark, 103–104

Vick, G. B., 203

Vines, Jerry, 233

Virginia, 84, 100, 124, 152
    Baptist growth in, 36–37, 152
    Baptist persecution in, 44–45, 62, 68
    and migration to Kentucky,
        68–70, 101
    religious liberty in, 60, 62–65, 71–75
    revivals in, 67–68
    slavery in, 70, 84, 96, 100–101,
        124, 132
    See also specific organizations
        and places

Virginia Baptist Missionary Society,
    128

Virginia Declaration of Rights, 63, 72

Virginia Union University, 149

Visions, 3, 24–25, 27, 36–37, 45–46,
    67, 71, 78–79, 86, 89, 91–92, 112,
    117–118, 133

Wabash Baptist Association (Indiana),
    111

Wagner, C. Peter, 245

Wake Forest University, 43, 218,
    220, 243

"Wall of separation" letter. *See*
    Jefferson, Thomas

Wallace, George, 207

War of 1812, 95, 107

Warren Association (New England),
    43–44, 49, 57

Warren, Rick, ix

Washington, Booker T., 153, 155–157,
    163–164, 226

Washington, George, 40, 50, 57, 65, 73,
    99, 180

Washington Association (Maine), 126

Washington-on-the-Brazos, Texas,
    119–120

Watchman Examiner, 173, 175–176

Watts, Isaac, 45–46, 91, 157

Wayland, Francis, 122, 130–132,
    134–135

Wayman, H. C., 198

Webb, Mary, 93–94

Weber, Timothy, 238–239

Welsh Baptists, 20, 26

Welsh Neck Church (South Carolina),
    27–28

Wesley, Charles, 157

West, The
    Baptist expansion into, 47, 66, 68,
        71, 77–80, 85, 95–96, 106, 119–121,
        136, 154, 247
    the Great Revival in, 84–92
    Indian colonization in, 107–108
    theological controversy in, 112,
        114, 251

Westminster Confession of Faith
    (1646), 187, 250

Wheaton College, 201

White Knights. *See* Ku Klux Klan

Whitefield, George, 19, 24–28, 34, 36,
    54, 105

Whitney, Eli, 102

Whitsitt, William H., 168–169, 180

Whittaker, Tampa Red, 158

William and Mary (king and queen of
    England), 22

Williams, Roger, ix, 7–9, 11–14, 193

Wilson, Woodrow, 179

Williams, Roger, ix, 7–10, 12–13

Willis, Joseph, 80

Winney (slave in Kentucky),
    98–99, 116

Winthrop, John, 7, 9–10

Winthrop, Jr., John, 9

Witter, William, 11–12

Woelfkin, Cornelius, 188–191, 193

Woman's Convention Auxiliary,
    163–164

Woman's Missionary Union (WMU),
    164, 172

Women, 25, 29, 31, 36–37, 83, 86–87, 91, 93–94, 104, 137–138, 157, 160–164, 229
    and role in early Baptist churches, 37, 67–68, 83
    ordination of, 162, 216, 230, 238–240, 242–244
    See also African American Baptists, women's roles in; and specific organizations and people
Women's Baptist Home Mission Society, 161
Wood, James, 242
Woodmason, Charles, 35
World Baptist Fellowship, 202–203

World War I, 172, 177, 179, 192
World War II, 212, 218
Worcester v. Georgia, 109
Worrell, W. B., 119

Yale College, 22, 42
Yale Divinity School, 218
Yorktown, Battle of, 57, 66, 68
Young, Andrew, 218
Young, Ed, 231–232
Young, Sam, 246

Ziglar, Zig, 234
Zubly, John, 29
Zwingli, Ulrich, 179

DATE DUE

DEC 1 1 2017		
APR 1 7 2024		

GAYLORD   #3523PI   Printed in USA